Women and Social Change in North Africa

Women's voices are brought to the fore in this comprehensive analysis of women and social change in North Africa. Focusing on grass-roots perspectives, readers will gain a rare glimpse into how both the intentional and unintentional actions of men and women contribute to societal transformation. Most chapters are based on extensive field work that illuminates the real-life experiences, advocacy, and agency of women in the region. The book considers frequently less studied issues including migration, legal changes, oral and written law, Islamic feminism, and grass-roots activism. It also looks at the effectiveness of shelters for abused women and the changes that occurred in the wake of the 2011 Arab uprisings, as well as challenging conventional notions of feminist agency by examining Salafi women's life choices. Recommended for students and scholars, as well as international development professionals with an interest in the MENA region.

DORIS H. GRAY is Associate Professor of Gender Studies at Al Akhawayn University in Ifrane, Morocco, and Director of the Hillary Clinton Center for Women's Empowerment. Her work focuses on contemporary gender issues in North Africa, Islamic Feminisms and Transitional Justice. She is author of: *Beyond Feminism and Islamism – Gender and Equality in North Africa* (2012 and revised edition 2014) and *Muslim Women on the Move – Moroccan Women and French Women of Moroccan Origin Speak Out* (2007) and numerous book chapters and articles in academic journals.

NADIA SONNEVELD is a researcher in the Centre for Migration Law at Radboud University in Nijmegen, the Netherlands. Her research focuses on gender and law in the Muslim world, Egypt and Morocco in particular. She is the author of *Women Judges in the Muslim World: A Comparative Study of Discourse and Practice*, co-authored with Monika Lindbekk (2017), and *Khul' Divorce in Egypt: Public Debates, Judicial Practices, and Everyday Life* (2012).

Women and Social Change in North Africa

What Counts as Revolutionary?

Edited by

DORIS H. GRAY
Al Akhawayn University, Morocco

NADIA SONNEVELD
Radboud University, the Netherlands

CAMBRIDGE
UNIVERSITY PRESS

CAMBRIDGE
UNIVERSITY PRESS

University Printing House, Cambridge CB2 8BS, United Kingdom

One Liberty Plaza, 20th Floor, New York, NY 10006, USA

477 Williamstown Road, Port Melbourne, VIC 3207, Australia

314–321, 3rd Floor, Plot 3, Splendor Forum, Jasola District Centre,
New Delhi – 110025, India

79 Anson Road, #06–04/06, Singapore 079906

Cambridge University Press is part of the University of Cambridge.

It furthers the University's mission by disseminating knowledge in the pursuit of
education, learning, and research at the highest international levels of excellence.

www.cambridge.org
Information on this title: www.cambridge.org/9781108419505
DOI: 10.1017/9781108303415

First published 2018

Printed in the United Kingdom by Clays, St Ives plc

A catalogue record for this publication is available from the British Library.

Library of Congress Cataloging-in-Publication Data
Names: Gray, Doris H., 1955- editor. | Sonneveld, Nadia, editor.
Title: Women and social change in North Africa : what counts as revolutionary? /
edited by Doris Gray, Nadia Sonneveld.
Description: New York : Cambridge University Press, 2018. | "This volume was first
conceived at a workshop entitled "Gender, Law and Social Change in North Africa,"
jointly organized by the Hillary Clinton Center for Women's Empowerment (HCC)
at Al Akhawayn University in Ifrane (AUI), Morocco, and the Middle East Center
at the University of Oxford, UK, in the spring of 2015." | Includes bibliographical
references and index.
Identifiers: LCCN 2017051610 | ISBN 9781108419505 (hardback : alk. paper)
Subjects: LCSH: Women–Africa, North–Social conditions. | Women's rights–Africa,
North. | Women–Legal status, laws, etc.–Africa, North. | Social change–Africa, North.
Classification: LCC HQ1790.5 .W65 2018 | DDC 305.420961–dc23
LC record available at https://lccn.loc.gov/2017051610

ISBN 978-1-108-41950-5 Hardback

"The main thing for the powerless is to have a dream ... a true one – a dream alone, without the bargaining power to go with it, does not transform the world or make the walls vanish. But it does help you keep ahold of dignity."

Fatima Mernissi (1940–2015)

"Either you shut up and you are humiliated or you do what I'm doing. You scream."

Fatema Mernissi in 1994

Contents

List of Figures   *page* x

List of Tables   xi

List of Contributors   xii

Acknowledgments   xvii

Notes on Transliteration   xviii

Introduction   1
Doris H. Gray and Nadia Sonneveld

Part I   What Is Social Change?   19

1   Capturing Change in Legal Empowerment Programs
    in Morocco and Tunisia: Shared Challenges and
    Future Directions   21
    Stephanie Willman Bordat and Saida Kouzzi

2   Safe Havens and Social Embeddedness: An Examination
    of Domestic Violence Shelters in Morocco   45
    Megan O'Donnell

3   Reforming Gendered Property Rights: The Case of
    Collective Land in Morocco   69
    Yasmine Berriane

4   Micro-Credit, Gender, and Corruption: Are Women
    the Future of Development?   91
    *Nicolas Hamelin, Mehdi el Boukhari, and
    Sonny Nwankwo*

Part II   Religion and Social Change   117

5   Morocco's Islamic Feminism: The Contours of a
    New Theology?   119
    Doris H. Gray and Habiba Boumlik

6   Moroccan Mothers' Religiosity: Impact on Daughters'
     Education   143
     Imane Chaara

7   Pious and Engaged: The Religious and Political
     Involvement of Egyptian Salafi Women after the
     2011 Revolution   166
     Laurence Deschamps-Laporte

     Part III   Migration and Social Change   187

8   Morocco at the Crossroads: The Intersection of Race,
     Gender, and Refugee Status   189
     Karla McKanders

9   Speaking of the Dead: Changing Funeral Practices
     among Moroccan Migrants in the Netherlands
     and Belgium   215
     Khadija Kadrouch-Outmany

10   Dying with a Clear Mind: Pain and Symptom Control
     in Palliative Care for Dutch Moroccan Patients in
     the Netherlands   237
     Roukayya Oueslati

     Part IV   What Is Law? Oral and Codified Law   261

11   *Kol B'Isha Erva*: The Silencing of Jewish Women's
     Oral Traditions in Morocco   263
     Vanessa Paloma Elbaz

12   Customary Law and Women's Rights among the
     Imazighen of the Middle Atlas and Southeast Morocco   289
     Michael Peyron

13   Family Law Reform in Algeria: National Politics,
     Key Actors, and Transnational Factors   308
     Dörthe Engelcke

14   The Case of Women's Unilateral Divorce Rights
     in Egypt: Revolution and Counterrevolution?   331
     Nadia Sonneveld

15 Emerging Norms: Writing Gender in the Post-Revolution
     Tunisian State   353
     Zoe Petkanas

Bibliography   378
Index   394

Figures

2.1 Domestic violence shelter constraints.   *page* 59
11.1 Maurice Bengio and his Choir at Temple Beth El in
the 1960s, Casablanca.   270
11.2 Celebrating the bride during the weeklong festivities
in Tangier. After a drawing by Beauclerk during his
voyage in 1826.   276
11.3 Zahra Mechaly, Jauk Amram Elmaleh's mother,
singing a song she wrote for the occasion at his bar
mitzvah in Casablanca in 1957.   277
11.4 Sultana Azeroual singing Judeo-Sahraoui women's
songs, October 20, 2015, Casablanca.   283
12.1 A French officer presiding over Customary Law
Tribunal, Ayt Hadiddou.   294
12.2 Marriage certificate delivered in 1935 by Customary
Law Tribunal at Agoudim, Ayt Yahya area.   296
12.3 Traditional home in Anefgou. "The Shangri-La effect
had seemingly worn off."   298
12.4 Ayt Hadiddou women listening to a lecture on birth
control, near Imilshil.   303

Tables

2.1 Dahlia residents integrated into professions annually,
2006–2013   *page* 52
2.2 Postshelter residence of women exiting Dahlia, 2014   52
4.1 Corruption intention by gender   105
4.2 Corruption intention by sociodemographic factor   105
4.3 Factors associated with corruption intention for
females   106

Contributors

YASMINE BERRIANE is Senior Researcher and Lecturer at the University of Zurich in Switzerland and Associate Researcher at the Center for Research in Economy, Society, and Culture (Polytechnic University) in Rabat, Morocco. She specializes in the fields of Political Sociology and Middle Eastern Studies and her research focuses on political and social transformations in North Africa and the Middle East, particularly in contexts where neoliberal reforms and norms are introduced. She is the author of *Femmes, Associations et Politique à Casablanca* (2013) and of several articles on women's political participation and the negotiation of land rights in Morocco.

STEPHANIE WILLMAN BORDAT is a founding partner at Mobilising for Rights Associates (MRA), an international nonprofit women's rights organization based in Rabat and currently working in Morocco, Algeria, Tunisia, and Libya. She has worked as a human rights lawyer and grassroots activist for over seventeen years in collaboration with local women's rights NGOs, development associations, and lawyers across the Maghreb. Her work involves human rights education, legal accompaniment, strategic litigation, monitoring and documentation, and national and international advocacy. She has both civil and common law degrees from Columbia University and Paris I-Sorbonne and was a Fulbright Scholar at the Mohammed V University Law School in Rabat, Morocco.

MEHDI EL BOUKHARI is a product manager in the pharmaceutical industry. He graduated with honors from Al Akhawayn University in Ifrane, Morocco, with a dual degree in Marketing and International Business.

HABIBA BOUMLIK is Associate Professor in the Department of Education and Language Acquisition at the City University of New York.

She teaches Arabic and French language and literature, linguistics, and Women Across Cultures. Her research interests encompass francophone literature, feminism, North African immigration to France, Moroccan Judaism, and Berber identity. Her most recent article is entitled "Conscientization and Third Space: A Case Study of Tunisian Activism."

IMANE CHAARA is Research Associate at the Oxford Department of International Development at the University of Oxford, United Kingdom, where she was Departmental Lecturer in Development Economics between October 2012 and September 2017. Her research focuses on institutional transformations in developing countries, legal reforms and the change of social norms, access to justice and rule of law, gender issues, and women's rights, as well as intra-household decision-making. Her work is both theoretical and empirical, mostly using first-hand original data.

LAURENCE DESCHAMPS-LAPORTE is a doctoral candidate at the University of Oxford, United Kingdom, in the Faculty of Oriental Studies. She is researching Salafism in Egypt and has a background in international development and Islamic studies. Her areas of expertise include contemporary Islamism and Salafi movements (especially in Egypt, but also in the Levant and West Africa), marginalization and poverty, and women's relations to religious leaders.

VANESSA PALOMA ELBAZ is Director of KHOYA, a sound archive based in Casablanca. Paloma Elbaz is a doctoral candidate at the Center for Middle Eastern and Mediterranean Research of the Sorbonne's National Institute of Eastern Languages and Civilizations (INALCO) and Research Associate of the Hadassah-Brandeis Institute in Massachusetts, United States, which focuses on Jews and gender at Brandeis University. She is Fellow of the Tangier American Legation Institute for Moroccan Studies. She is a specialist on Sephardic and Maghrebi women's music and its function in Jewish life. Her work has been featured in the international press such as *The New York Times, France24, PBS, Jerusalem Post,* and *Al Jazeera.*

DÖRTHE ENGELCKE is a senior research fellow at the Max Planck Institute for Comparative and International Private Law. She received her PhD from St Antony's College, University of Oxford, in 2015. She is the co-winner of the 2016 BRISMES Leigh Douglas Memorial Prize for the best PhD dissertation on a Middle Eastern topic in the Social Sciences or Humanities awarded by a British University. Prior to coming to Oxford she completed an MA in Near and Middle Eastern Studies at the School of Oriental and African Studies in London (SOAS). She has held fellowships at the Islamic Legal Studies Program at Harvard Law School and the Lichtenberg-Kolleg, the Göttingen Institute of Advanced Study. Her research focuses on the interaction of law and society in the MENA region as well as questions of legal pluralism, Islamic law, and legal politics. She is a contributor to the *Brill Encyclopedia of Law and Religion*. Her work has appeared in *Law & Social Inquiry* and is forthcoming in *Islamic Law and Society*.

DORIS H. GRAY is Associate Professor of Gender Studies at Al Akhawayn University in Ifrane, Morocco, and Director of the Hillary Clinton Center for Women's Empowerment. Her work focuses on contemporary gender issues in North Africa, Islamic Feminisms and Transitional Justice. She is author of: *Beyond Feminism and Islamism – Gender and Equality in North Africa* (2012 and revised edition 2014) and *Muslim Women on the Move – Moroccan Women and French Women of Moroccan Origin Speak Out* (2007) and numerous book chapters and articles in academic journals.

NICOLAS HAMELIN is Associate Professor of Marketing at Franklin University, Switzerland, and neuroscience lab director at the S.P. Jain School of Global Management, Sydney, Australia. Previously, he served as Assistant Professor in the School of Business at Al Akhawayn University in Ifrane, Morocco. He serves as an analyst for Euromonitor International, a London-based global marketing research agency. His main research interests are in the fields of Consumer Behavior, Neuro-Marketing, Social Marketing, and Environmental Management.

KHADIJA KADROUCH-OUTMANY is an anthropologist and a scholar in law and religious studies at the University of Groningen, Netherlands. She focuses on funeral rituals of Muslim migrant communities in the Netherlands and Belgium. She is currently working as a postdoctoral researcher in a project on Hajj and transnational belonging of Moroccan-Dutch Muslims.

SAIDA KOUZZI is a founding partner at Mobilising for Rights Associates (MRA), an international nonprofit women's rights organization based in Rabat and currently working in Morocco, Algeria, Tunisia, and Libya. She has worked as a grassroots activist for over seventeen years in collaboration with diverse local women's rights NGOs, development associations, and lawyers across the Maghreb. Her work involves human rights education, legal accompaniment, strategic litigation, monitoring and documentation, and national and international advocacy. She worked at a leading human rights law firm in Rabat, Morocco, and was a long-time active member of the *Association Marocaine des Droits de l'Homme*. She has a law degree from Mohammed V University in Rabat.

KARLA MCKANDERS is Clinical Professor of Law at Vanderbilt University School of Law, United States, where she directs the School's Immigration Clinic dedicated to educating law students to practice immigration and refugee law. In addition to teaching in the Immigration Clinic, she teaches Refugee Law and Policy and Immigration Law. Her work has taken her around the United States and internationally, researching the efficacy of legal institutions charged with processing migrants and refugees. She has also been cited as an authority on immigration and refugee law in *Reuters, ABC News*, and *Al-Jazeera*. McKanders received her JD from Duke University in North Carolina, United States.

SONNY NWANKWO is Professor of Marketing and Entrepreneurship at the University of East London and currently Provost of the Nigerian Defence Academy. Previously, he was Director of Research and Enterprise, Director of the Noon Centre for Equality and Diversity in Business, Director of the Petchey Centre for Entrepreneurship at the University of East London (United Kingdom), and inaugural President of the International Academy of African Business and Development (IAABD).

MEGAN O'DONNELL is Policy Manager for Gender Issues at the ONE Campaign, where her work focuses on the intersection of gender and international development issues including health, nutrition, education, and economic empowerment. Previously, she was Gender and Development Program Coordinator at the Center for Global Development, a think tank in Washington, DC. She has conducted research in Morocco on women's rights, constitutional reform, and civil society. She earned a Master of Philosophy in Modern Middle Eastern Studies at the University of Oxford, United Kingdom.

ROUKAYYA OUESLATI is a Health Scientist, Arabist, and scholar in Religious Studies. She currently works as a lecturer and researcher at the Leiden Islam Academy (Leiden University) and the Leiden University Medical Center, the Netherlands. Her expertise is on the intersection between religion, medical sciences, and migration. Outside academia, she convenes workshops in medical institutions on Islam, medical ethics and minorities promoting cultural-sensitive care.

ZOE PETKANAS is a doctoral candidate at the Department of Politics and International Studies at the University of Cambridge, United Kingdom. Her research analyzes the writing of gender into the Tunisian Second Republic, the development of gender parity laws since 2011, and the (re)making of the female citizen. Her previous research includes gender and elections in Tunisia, gendered discourses in Tunisian media, and microcredit and women's empowerment in Palestinian refugee camps in Jordan. She also has a background in international development and political communications in American politics.

MICHAEL PEYRON spent more than forty years researching Tamazight culture, poetry in particular, while serving as a professor at Mohammed V University in Rabat, Morocco and also in Grenoble Alpes University. He has been a visiting professor at the King Fahd School of Translation, Tangier, Lecturer in English and Amazigh History & Culture at Al Akhawayn University in Ifrane, and Lecturer in Amazigh History & Culture at AMIDEAST, Rabat, Morocco. He has authored numerous books and articles on Berber cultures and customs.

NADIA SONNEVELD is a researcher in the Centre for Migration Law at Radboud University in Nijmegen, the Netherlands. Her research focuses on gender and law in the Muslim world, Egypt and Morocco in particular. She is the author of *Women Judges in the Muslim World: A Comparative Study of Discourse and Practice*, co-authored with Monika Lindbekk (2017), and *Khul' Divorce in Egypt: Public Debates, Judicial Practices, and Everyday Life* (2012).

Acknowledgments

This volume was first conceived at a workshop entitled "Gender, Law, and Social Change in North Africa," jointly organized by the Hillary Clinton Center for Women's Empowerment (HCC) at Al Akhawayn University in Ifrane (AUI), Morocco, and the Middle East Center at the University of Oxford, United Kingdom, in the spring of 2015. The workshop was sponsored by the British Council and the National Center for Scientific and Technical Research (Centre National pour la Recherche Scientifique et Technique, CNRST) in Morocco. Later, the Heinrich Böll Foundation in Rabat supported additional work for the chapters on migration.

We are indebted to friends and colleagues who have provided valuable insights along the way. The anonymous reviewers at Cambridge University Press provided detailed suggestions for revisions of all chapters. At Cambridge University Press, Maria Marsh is a most helpful and always cheerful editor. We owe much gratitude to Jayme Harpring, who was initially solicited as a language editor since several authors are not native English speakers. Jayme went out of her way to do additional fact checks, suggested a more coherent structure, and made suggestions that rendered the chapters more readable for a non–North African expert readership. Alison Elder, an intern at HCC, spent countless hours verifying and formatting endnotes, the index, and the bibliography.

While we started out as professional colleagues, in the process of working on this volume, we came to appreciate the authors as friends with whom we share a common vision and passion to give meaning to our work for the improvement of the lives of men and women in North Africa and beyond.

Most of all, we wish to thank our partners, Mike Painter and Tom Thomas, for their patience and endless support. We dedicate this book to our children, Lancy, Tunuka and Khadijah; Daniel, David, Alexander, and Elias.

Notes on Transliteration

A simplified system of transliteration is used to make the book accessible to nonspecialists. Regarding Arabic, we use just two diacritical marks: the single closing apostrophe (') to represent the hamza and a single opening apostrophe (') to represent the 'ayn. Vowels are not marked. In the case of Morocco, Algeria, and Tunisia, we use the French transliteration of common words such as "moudawana" (Family Law) and Nahda instead of Al Nahda (political party in Tunisia) as this is how these terms are customarily used.

Introduction

DORIS H. GRAY AND NADIA SONNEVELD

On Tuesday, December 1, 2015, a large crowd followed the casket carrying Fatima Mernissi to her last resting place at the Sidi Messaoud cemetery in Rabat. It was an unusual crowd burying an unusual person. Two advisors of Moroccan King Mohamed VI were present, as well as several ministers, writers, and poets. Even Abderrahim Chikhi, president of the Islamist movement *Mouvement Unicité et Réforme* (Movement for Unity and Reform, MUR) came to bid a final farewell to Morocco's pioneer feminist.[1] Yet, apart from the presence of certain public figures something else made this funeral procession unusual – the large number of women in attendance.[2]

Instead of the usual gender-segregated event where only men walk the coffin to the graveyard and bury the deceased, women honored Mernissi's last wish by attending her burial. Mernissi's passing and burial generated national and international headlines.[3] Yet, this was not merely the last "scream" of an exceptional Moroccan woman. As one of the chapters in this book shows, ordinary Moroccan migrant women living in Western Europe have been challenging gender segregation in Muslim funeral and burial rituals both before and since Fatema Mernissi, who, from the hereafter, ostentatiously tipped another sacred cow.

The primary purpose of this book is to present scholarship that sheds light on particular experiences and perspectives of ordinary women in Morocco, and to a lesser extent, Algeria, Tunisia, and Egypt, as they relate to social change in four broad fields of inquiry: women's rights, religion, migration, and law. The main question connecting each of the chapters is a deceptively simple one: What is social change and how does it happen – or not?

We believe that looking at social change at the grassroots level rather than from top-down reveals a dimension of real life transformation that is often missed when discussing legal and policy changes. With or without a revolution, social change happens on many levels – the

1

intrapersonal and interpersonal, as well as within and among communities. This book, then, lends legitimacy to alternative methods for understanding social changes that defy standardized assessments, particularly with regard to populations beyond urban centers. These alternative methods also make it possible to focus on themes that traditionally have been overlooked. Land ownership rights of rural women, for example, may not appear as a major national or international issue despite its paramount importance to the women and communities concerned. Similarly, the impact of mothers' religiosity on their daughters' education has rarely been studied, yet, as one author found, this factor is significant.

We argue that detailed ethnographic and micro-level analyses of the aspirations and everyday realities of women in these Muslim majority countries are critical in unearthing four categories of social change: (1) social change generated by social nonmovements, (2) nonchanges, (3) noncontentious social change, and (4) contentious social action. Though these categories have been studied before, the collection in this volume brings them together for the first time, presenting macro-, meso-, and micro-level analyses that reveal the depth and breadth of social changes affecting women in North Africa.

Certainly, social change is a moving target. Hence, each chapter focuses on one or more categories of social change at a particular moment in time. Some authors in this volume document and analyze particular social changes resulting, for example, from specific legal reforms or the application of less studied oral legal traditions within minority populations, such as Berbers and Jews in Morocco. Others address the impact of major forces like migration, corruption, and new interpretations of Islam on the social realities of individuals on a micro-level. Thus, this volume contributes to the existing body of literature on women and North Africa by focusing on a wide variety of issues that influence women's lives and, by extension, society in general. Though some chapters, such as those on Jews and Berbers, address historical factors that have shaped challenges within these communities, most chapters zero in on contemporary themes. Further, while most authors focus on Morocco, others shed light on changes in the larger North African region that are symptomatic of transformations in this part of the world.

Social change does not occur in a linear fashion. A variety of push-and-pull factors propel countries forward, sideways, and occasionally backward again. Some authors in this volume analyze legal changes, expanding on theory and documenting impacts on women, while others pioneer areas of inquiry that have not been studied in this manner to date, such as controversies around pain control, end of life care, funeral rites, and women's shelters.

In section one of this introduction we ask what is social change – in women's rights, religion, migration, and law – and when it counts as revolutionary. In section two we describe our focus on North Africa and Morocco in particular, and in section three, we explain our emphasis on women. In the last section of this introduction we explain the organization of the volume and present its 15 chapters.

Social Change: What Counts as Revolutionary?

In asking what social change is and when it counts as revolutionary, we argue for the importance and sensitivity of context. In other words, what are the circumstances that surround a particular transformation? Hence, we include a chapter on Moroccan women who have success-fully fought for their right to communal land as well as one on Salafi women in postrevolutionary Egypt who advocated for upholding strict gender-segregation. In both of these cases, social change is embodied in women's agency, but in achieving their goals they may deviate from conventional academic and societal understandings of "progress."

Generally speaking, social change refers to changes or variations in the structure of social relationships and organization of a society that leads to social transformations; a definition that includes such varied large-scale transformations as colonization, industrialization, and urbanization. Social transformations may be seen as positive and/or negative depending on the viewpoint of stakeholders. In this volume, our main aim is to offer a window into changes that contribute to human development, based in part on the capabilities approach developed by Martha Nussbaum in *Women and Human Development*.[4] Instead of assessing development by standardized measures, such as per capita gross national product or literacy levels, we argue that development should be conceptualized in terms of people's cap-abilities. Human development, Nussbaum insists, must include the promotion of individual capabilities, which, by consequence change the larger community. Capabilities include such behaviors or assets as the opportunity to work, to educate one's children, and to have access to justice. Certainly, Nussbaum's approach belongs to the secular-liberal tradition and has been criticized for its concentration on the rational individual making free and autonomous choices, with less weight accorded to the influence of factors like religion or the economy on the lives of individuals. Nussbaum considers the capabilities approach to be a feminist philosophical project that is both "strongly universalist" and "sensitive to local particularity" and to the many ways in which circumstances shape not only options but also beliefs and preferences."[5] In fact, in her *Women and Human Development* Nussbaum does address the effects of religion on the lives of individuals.

In this volume, we present practices that embody "good" human development from a liberal perspective (the rational individual who makes autonomous choices leading to a better life) *as well as* practices that might be labeled "bad" or irrational from a liberal perspective, such as gender-segregation. Based on our observations, some "bad" practices actually represent desired change to those involved. Yet, we do not adhere to culturalist assumptions or justify "illiberal" practices such as, for example, forced gender segregation.

In fact, we believe that cultural relativism often fails to see diversity and change within the full context of a tradition/ideology and it is precisely these *arguments from culture*[6] that we wish to capture in this volume. We aim to present a picture of social change in its entirety, a picture that often gets lost in cultural relativist analyses. For example, in her influential *Politics of Piety*,[7] Saba Mahmood depicts the Cairo-based Salafi women of her study as rather homogeneous in their wish to live pious lives. By contrast, Laurence Deschamps-Laporte (Chapter 7) offers a much less homogenous view of the Salafi community she studied in Alexandria, Egypt. Deschamps-Laporte found that while women upheld strict gender-segregation, they engaged in internal competition to attract male attention. Just as importantly, her work revealed that Salafi men did not form a homogeneous group either. She documents the diversity within groups previously seen as homogenous.

In our endeavor to present a comprehensive picture of social change based on human development, we go beyond Nussbaum in arguing for an even more contextual approach. Our rationale for doing so is based on a desire to understand how a particular set of "capabilities" leads to certain "functionings," that is, certain achievements, such as having a job, educating one's children, and having access to justice. Similar to Crocker,[8] we argue for extending the capabilities approach by shifting to a more agency-focused approach to see whether a certain achievement or social change is indeed the result of an intentional activity or rather a coincidence. Moreover, we consider that what may appear good on its surface – from the perspective of liberal-secular development – such as building domestic shelters for battered women or introducing women-friendly legislation, might actually be a form of nonchange – for example, when such legislation is not implemented in practice.

We embed our discussions according to the four categories of social change mentioned above: social change generated by social nonmovements, nonchanges, noncontentious social changes, and contentious social action. While presented separately here, the reader should note that such categories almost always overlap in people's everyday lives, as is evident in the chapters in this volume.

Social Change Generated by Social Nonmovements

Revolutionary social change does not conjure images of the often subtle but significant changes that take place at local levels, that is, within households, neighborhoods, or communities. Sociologist Asef Bayat contends that these changes are generated by *social nonmovements*, that is, "the collective actions of non-collective actors; they embody shared practices of large numbers of ordinary people whose fragmented but similar activities trigger much social change."[9] Such actions are contentious, for example, when women insist on choosing their marriage partners, women file for divorce, or street vendors spread out their merchandise on urban sidewalks.[10] Other actions may be illegal, such as the urban poor building houses on land that does not belong to them, or migrants crossing borders. Those who perform these actions usually know they are contentious because they are performed at the expense or in defiance of the state, the rich, or the powerful.[11] For these actors the goal is not to initiate revolutionary change but to use the limited "capabilities" at their disposal to change the few aspects of their life over which they do have some control. Thus, there is a close connection between social non-movements and everyday practices. Karla McKanders' chapter (Chapter 8) on undocumented African migrants in Morocco is an example of how the accumulated and contentious actions of social nonmovements lead to social change such as legislation pertaining to migrants. Chapter 10 by Roukayya Oueslati also exemplifies such a type of social change, albeit more subtly; it deals with the difficult process of negotiating differences in "good care" between medical doctors, terminally ill migrant patients and their families.

Nonchanges

A micro-level analysis of men and women's experiences and perspectives is equally important in detecting achievements and positive changes that may go unnoticed in traditional evaluation processes. The chapter by Stephanie Bordat and Saida Kouzzi on legal empowerment programs in Morocco and Tunisia (Chapter 1) directs our attention to significant changes that remain invisible to donors and other international actors, such as shifts from hierarchical to more egalitarian relationships within local NGOs as well as between local NGOs and their beneficiaries. The authors also highlight "changes" that are applauded by international and national actors but which in fact are nonchanges, such as long-announced but not enacted laws related to women's rights. Similarly, in her work on the women's rights movement in Algeria, Dörthe Engelcke (Chapter 13) shows that exploiting a certain set of "capabilities" (such as having the cultural and economic capital to advocate for legal change) does not necessarily result in a "functioning," in this case new legislation aimed at improving the rights of women.

Megan O'Donnell's contribution on domestic shelters in Morocco (Chapter 2) is another example of a situation that appears "good" on the surface but that, on closer inspection, represents a nonchange. The establishment of a small number of domestic shelters in different parts of Morocco seems to be an act of Bayat's "contentious social nonmovement" because their mere establishment violates Moroccan law. Yet, as O'Donnell discovered, the purpose of these shelters – namely to protect battered women and empower them – is rarely achieved because a stay in the shelter actually enforces women's dependence, in this case, on the women in charge of these establishments. Her examination uncovered the reproduction of hierarchical power relationships by the very actors who were supposed to be changing these power relationships.

Alternative approaches to gauging social change is not unique to Morocco but applies to the whole of North Africa[12] and beyond.[13] If we want to obtain a meaningful understanding of social change in a given society we must go beyond conventional ideas about prescribed interventions. Ethnographic research is necessary to uncover the extent to which expected changes have actually occurred. Scholars must also be vigilant about observing changes that might not be significant from the point of view of donors or policy makers but that are meaningful to the intended beneficiaries of development policies. In fact, what seems like a non-change might well reveal unconventional and novel conceptions of agency, an issue to which we will turn next.

Noncontentious Social Changes

In this volume, then, we present the reader with a spectrum of specific social changes, initiated by ordinary people, sometimes deliberately and sometimes not. In addition to focusing on contentious social changes brought about by practices of nonmovements, we also focus on those initiated by ordinary men and women whose activities are usually *not* contentious, both on the grassroots level and on the state and international level. For example, Imane Chaara (Chapter 6) documents that religiosity of mothers can result in better educational opportunities for their daughters, a much appreciated – albeit not always uncontroversial – social change. In the long run education results in far-reaching changes, not all of them good for the individual woman.[14] In all, social change is a complex issue and difficult to define as it is subject to the viewpoint of concerned stakeholders.

Contentious Social Action

In an era when the populations of different North African countries have challenged and continue to challenge their political leaders, we also focus on contentious collective action representing an "organized, sustained, self-conscious challenge to existing authorities."[15] Doris Gray and Habiba Boumlik (Chapter 5), for example, analyze organized challenges to religious authority and show how a rereading of sacred texts by women led to a rethinking of religion-based law. Dörthe Engelcke (Chapter 13) analyzes how organized activism of the secular women's rights movement in Algeria failed to bring about new legislation while Nadia Sonneveld (Chapter 14) shows how secular women in Egypt successfully pushed through parliament a law that simplified divorce for women. Instead of insisting on a secular human rights perspective, they presented the new Egyptian divorce law as being in accordance with the principles of Islamic *shari'a*. In the same vein, Yasmine Berriane (Chapter 3) demonstrates how collective activism lead to a significant change in rights of land ownership for women in Morocco. Certainly, one of the most important examples is the Tunisian uprising of 2011 and its effect on women's rights, a topic analyzed by Zoe Petkanas (Chapter 15).

Why North Africa?

Popular Western media frequently present North African and Middle Eastern countries as stagnant nation-states. Even the Arab Uprisings have done little to change the image of the Middle East and North Africa (MENA) as fundamentally religious, conservative, and backward. At closer inspection, however, it is hard to deny the many changes that have taken place in this region, both before and after the 2011 uprisings. In Morocco, large segments of the population met the passing of King Hassan II in 1999 and subsequent ascension to the throne of his son Mohamed VI with great hopes for change, some of which were fulfilled. Mohammed VI introduced a new Moroccan Personal Status Code, or family law, in 2004, giving women some of the most extensive divorce rights in Muslim-majority countries. The king also emphasized Morocco's Jewish heritage and the constitutional recognition of Berber as an official language of Morocco. At the same time, the gradual shift of this North African Kingdom from a migrant sending and transit country to a receiving country has brought other sorts of changes that lead to increased uncertainty and tension.

In neighboring Algeria, the end of more than a decade of internal strife (1991–2002) similarly led to a reform of that country's Personal Status Code reform, yet the women's rights movement there remains stifled due to political stagnation and recurring fear of violence. Further east, the forced departure of long-serving authoritarian leaders in Tunisia and Egypt in 2011 opened the way to new understandings of Islam, the place of Islamic law, and gender relations in these post-uprising nations.

In this volume, we emphasize cases in which ordinary women and men played important roles in shaping social changes, as well as the various forces that have influenced and continue to influence women's lives, primarily in Morocco but also in neighboring countries in North Africa. Clearly, the developments in the MENA region can be viewed and made sense of from different angles. We have taken the perspective of gender, women in particular, as we situate events and seek to elucidate the nature of the social changes that have occurred in Morocco, Algeria, Tunisia, and Egypt in the last decade.

Why Women?

Scholarly literature on gender and Islam is rich. While the term gender often is employed to describe this work, most of these studies actually concern the experiences of women.[16] According to Charrad, this focus is a direct result of the excessive media attention on Muslim women, both before, and especially after, September 11, 2001. In the burgeoning literature on women in the Middle East, the issue of women's agency has garnered much attention. In fact, in interrogating the stereotype "of the silent, passive, subordinate, victimized, and powerless Muslim woman,"[17] studies about the Muslim headscarf and related questions typically reflect this emphasis on women's agency.

By contrast, we do not claim that women are *either* "powerful" or "powerless" or that they are *always* powerless and *never* powerful. Instead, we believe that sometimes, even oftentimes, ordinary actors affect change in their own or other people's lives even when they are not deliberately seeking to do so. Poorly educated and highly religious mothers in Morocco do not choose to be highly religious in order to promote the education of their daughters, for example, even though such a correlation may exist. Nussbaum argues that there is no need to expand the capabilities approach with accounts of agency since agency "can be captured as aspects of the capability/function distinction." "Functioning," she says, "is itself a way of being active, not just a passive state of satisfaction."[18] In our book, we cover some of the ground between capability and functioning as the process leading to change is not always conscious.

Another reason for our critical assessment of the agency of ordinary people is based on the observation that while agency might set in motion changes, the result – "the functioning" – might be quite different from what was initially intended. Everyday realities of ordinary people, women in particular, do not exist in a vacuum, but instead are frequently shaped and informed by the activities of national and international agents, such as policy makers and legislators, as well as various representatives of civil society, including women's rights and human rights associations. Hence, while our main focus is on the daily experiences of ordinary women, some chapters do frame these experiences in interaction with civil society organizations.

We also pay attention to the perspectives of men. Nick Hamelin, Mehdi el Boukhari, and Sonny Nwankwo's conclusions about the gendered dimension of corruption (Chapter 4) is based on interviews with hundreds of men and women throughout Morocco. Similarly, Roukayya Oueslati (Chapter 10) also includes men in her analysis of terminally ill patients. In fact, we hope that this book will encourage scholars to develop a broader and more complete gender analysis and take the study of gender in Muslim-majority countries in new directions.

Organization of the Book

The overarching theme of this volume challenges conventional notions of social change related to women in four fields of inquiry: women's rights, religion, migration, and law.

In the first section, we question conventional notions of social change. Here we address the common practice of domestic and international agencies to assess social change and development using predetermined impact criteria that frequently do not capture subtle, yet sustained, transformations that occur in human behavior and relationships. Such typical measures of advancement have been literacy levels, numbers of women in government or senior positions or increases in income-generating activities. The authors in this first section demonstrate the importance of looking beyond these common predictors of progress and reform.

Section two questions conventional notions of social change as they relate to women and religion. In all North African countries, religion plays a major role in public and private lives. Some women and men may find a rationale for women's agency based on the reinterpretation of sacred texts, leading them to advocate for gender equality in education, law, and the religious and political arenas. Others find that pursuing a religious path empowers them to make personal life choices while at the same time advocating for maintaining a gender hierarchy.

Section three sheds light on issues of gender, migration and social change. Migration today is one of the most pressing vectors of transformation. As Morocco is in the unique position of being a sending, transit, and receiving – even destination – country, change has occurred as a result of the large movement of migrants and refugees from countries south of the Sahara and more recently Syria, Iraq, and Afghanistan. Today, Morocco is more than a point of transit to Europe, but a country where some migrants and refugees hope to establish residence and rebuild their lives, while at the same time, Moroccans continue to leave in search of better economic and educational opportunities abroad, primarily in Europe. There they build new lives that begin to incorporate customs of their host countries that eventually reverberate back to their places of origin.

The fourth and final section deals with various forms of law. Certainly, law is a tangible basis for social transformation and this section contains chapters that assess legal activism, offer legal scholarship and provide a historical perspective on oral and written law. We look at customary oral law among rural Berber communities, Jewish oral law pertaining to women and codified law in Morocco, Algeria, Tunisia, and Egypt. Here we question another conventional dichotomy – between traditional, oral (Berber) and codified (Arab Muslim) law – by showing how Islamic law entered Morocco as oral law and how different legal traditions conflated in time. Likewise, the exodus of the majority of Moroccan Jews left the country without local leadership. Rabbis from beyond Morocco who filled this void took umbrage at some uniquely Moroccan Jewish customs and legal interpretations resulting in conflicting interpretations of Jewish law especially as it relates to women's rights.

What Is Social Change?

Chapter 1, "Capturing Change in Legal Empowerment Programs in Morocco and Tunisia: Shared Challenges and Future Directions," chronicles the experiences of two formidable women's legal rights activists. Stephanie Willman Bordat and Saida Kouzzi have worked for nearly two decades in Morocco and Tunisia in an effort to familiarize rural populations with their rights and at the same time advocate for legal changes at the political level. Their chapter takes a critical look at the way in which national and international agencies and donors assess change; additionally, it documents changes in interpersonal relationships that are not captured in impact assessments yet attest to significant long-term social change.

Chapter 2, "Safe Havens and Social Embeddedness: An Examination of Domestic Violence Shelters in Morocco," is both a scholarly analysis and the product of a labor of love. When Megan O'Donnell came to Al Akhawayn University to speak on the topic of her research, she arrived in Ifrane needing to spend considerable time under a hot shower, taking a nap under clean sheets, and eating a leisurely meal. She had come to the university after spending several weeks living in a Moroccan domestic violence shelter. Determined to infuse her scholarly endeavor with firsthand experience of everyday life in the shelter, she lived with battered women in the shelter rather than merely interview them. Hers is the first in-depth analysis of domestic violence shelters in Morocco based on fieldwork and academic literature on the topic.

In Chapter 3, Yasmine Berriane analyzes the ongoing, highly controversial issue of land ownership by women in "Reforming Gendered Property Rights: The Case of Collective Land in Morocco." Long before urban women's rights advocacy associations took on such cases, rural women battled for their right to own and inherit land. Berriane, too, spent time with the women concerned and examined their claims against the assertions in Moroccan legal texts, international law, and relevant literature. Her research highlights the discrepancy between the aspirations of urban middle class women's rights advocates and their comparatively disenfranchised, semi-literate rural sisters, whose persistence has informed a newly emerging, more inclusive feminist discourse in Morocco.

Chapter 4 offers quantitative and qualitative analyses in "Microcredit, Gender and Corruption: Are Women the Future of Development?" Nicolas Hamelin, Mehdi el Boukhari, and Sonny Nwankwo interviewed hundreds of men and women throughout Morocco to investigate the claim of most micro-finance institutions that women are less likely to offer as well as receive bribes. The authors suggest that this may be due to the lack of opportunities for corrupt behavior of women in highly patriarchal societies as well as their fear of repercussions in small, rural towns. Thus, women's reduced proclivity for corruption may be due less to heightened moral integrity than to the particular circumstances in which they make financial decisions.

Religion and Social Change

Chapter 5, "Morocco's Islamic Feminism: The Contours of a New Theology?" highlights some of the theoretical changes in the gender discourse in Morocco by focusing on the shift from a more secular feminist discourse to a more religiously inspired and referenced reading – one that serves as the basis for new forms of activism and advocacy for equality and justice within an Islamic framework. Doris Gray and Habiba Boumlik describe how these new readings, in fact, challenge notions of patriarchy from within Muslim religious and legal tradition.

In Chapter 6, "Moroccan Mothers' Religiosity: Impact on Daughters' Education," Imane Chaara segues from an intellectual approach to religious texts analyzed in Chapter 5 to the daily, lived observance of highly religious mothers and its impact on their daughters' education. Her field research resulted in the counterintuitive finding that a mother's level of religiosity actually correlates positively with investing in and promoting the education of their daughters. Her findings point to the limits of second wave feminism, which eschews overt displays of religion and regards secular modernity as the way forward in advancing women's rights.

With Chapter 7, we widen the scope from the Maghrib (West) to the Mashriq (East). In her chapter, "Pious and Engaged: The Religious and Political Involvement of Egyptian Salafi Women after the 2011 Revolution," Laurence Deschamps-Laporte argues that women's activism does not always counter existing social norms but can aim at quite the opposite: namely, upholding and strengthening conventional gender roles that are at odds with feminist notions of gender equality. Deschamps-Laporte spent months inside the women's section of Salafi mosques in an effort to understand the motives for young women's involvement, which seeks, as its stated goal, to instill and conform to strict gender nonegalitarian practices.

Migration and Social Change

From Chapter 8 onwards, the focus shifts to migrant populations either transiting or residing in Morocco. In "Morocco at the Crossroads: The Intersection of Race, Gender and Refugee Status," Karla McKanders describes the painful consequences of social class, race, and gender in migrant populations. She also compares Moroccan legal texts to international migration and human rights law and its application – or lack thereof – in Morocco. She addresses the issue of race, the elephant in the room, in the dealings of migrants and asylum seekers with authorities. In this book, we avoid the often-used term "sub-Saharan" as it connotes a distinction between Morocco, an African country inhabited mostly by Arabs and Berbers, and African countries south of the Sahara, mostly inhabited by people with a darker complexion who often are also Muslim.

Chapter 9 continues the theme of migration. Khadija Kadrouch-Outmany, in "Speaking of the Dead: Changing Funeral Practices among Moroccan Migrants in the Netherlands and Belgium," provides an important lens through which to view the personal, interpersonal, social, and legal transformations that result when migrants live in a new culture. Kadrouch-Outmany illustrates how traditional Moroccan funeral practices (and particularly the role of women therein), began to change among Moroccan migrant populations living in the Netherlands and Belgium. These changes reverberated back to the rural areas of Morocco, especially in cases where the deceased was returned to be buried in the soil of his or her birth. As no living being is exempt from death, funerals are a universal human experience. The changes in funeral practices that Kadrouch-Outmany identified are therefore critically important indicators of larger social transformations occurring in Morocco.

Chapter 10 addresses an equally uncomfortable but often unavoidable facet of life. In "Dying with a Clear Mind: Pain and Symptom Control in Palliative Care for Dutch Moroccan Patients in the Netherlands," Roukayya Oueslati shows how the negotiation between medical practices in the Netherlands, where alleviating suffering is paramount and even physician-assisted suicide is legal, and conventional Muslim understandings of noninterference in a process that may include pain, led to altered religious understandings among Moroccan immigrants about the importance of human agency in the process of dying. Due to lack of high-quality end-of-life care, the issue of end-of-life intervention has not yet surfaced in Morocco. Since there is no precedent in the country of origin, Dutch Moroccans are pioneering in the issue of how to deal with pain control and end-of-life-care.

What Is Law? Oral and Codified Law

Social transformations do not occur in a legal void. Therefore, the focus in this last section is on laws pertaining to women in different religious and ethnic communities. Chapter 11, "*Kol B'Isha Erva*: The Silencing of Jewish Women's Oral Traditions in Morocco," explores the side-lining of Jewish women within their own communities following the exodus of Moroccan Jews from the country in the twentieth century. Vanessa Paloma Elbaz explains how orthodox rabbis from outside Morocco entered the country to fill the void left by the emigrating Moroccan Jewish leadership, and began banning and belittling centuries-old Moroccan Jewish customs. She traversed the country in search of remnants of genuine Moroccan Jewish customs and laws pertaining to women and found song. In documenting how women transmitted Jewish customs from one generation to the next – through singing – she unearthed Jewish customs long believed to have died out.

In the same vein, in Chapter 12 Michael Peyron illustrates the importance of "Customary Law and Women's Rights among the Imazighen of the Middle Atlas and South East Morocco." Peyron points to the flawed dichotomy between written Muslim law and traditional oral Berber law, arguing that Muslim law – when it first entered North Africa – was malleable oral law that only much later became codified written law. Peyron, one of the world's foremost experts on Amazigh culture in Morocco, has wandered the Atlas Mountains on foot for more than 40 years. Along the way he collected, preserved, and recited Berber customs and poetry, a small sample thereof is presented. His chapter provides rare insights into oral law and its application concerning women over several generations in the same villages.

From Chapter 13 onwards, we move East. Algeria, Africa's largest country, experienced uprisings in the 1990s that did not result in regime change, but rather descended into civil strife during the so-called "black decade." In "Family Law Reform in Algeria: National Politics, Key Actors, and Transnational Factors," Dörthe Engelcke traces such reforms from the time of independence to the present day. Engelcke spent significant time in Algeria in an effort to untangle the complicated post-independence Algerian history. She conducted her analysis through the lens of the ups and downs of Personal Status Code reform and within the context of former freedom fighters, the black decade, Islamist-secular divides, and the quest for national identity.

Nadia Sonneveld moves further East to Egypt in Chapter 14. In "The Case of Women's Unilateral Divorce Rights in Egypt: Revolution and counterrevolution?" she takes a historic and empirical perspective on the evolution of Egyptian *shari'a*-based family law from colonial to early post-colonial, to pre- to post-2011 Revolution in Egypt. Sonne-veld shows that while the reform of Muslim women's divorce rights through innovative readings of the sources of Islamic law led to revo-lutionary results, when the authoritarian government that supports such reforms is removed from power, a counterrevolution might undo the gains made. The theme of Arab uprisings is again present in the final Chapter 15, "Emerging Norms: Writing Gender in the Post-Revolution Tunisian State." Zoe Petkanas analyzes gender discourse from the state-sponsored feminism of the Bourguiba and Ben Ali eras to the revolution and its aftermath, when secular, urban feminists were at odds with the newly democratically elected Islamist Ennahda party and engaged in embittered battles over the drafting of a new consti-tution. Lending additional weight to her chapter is the fact that the 2015 Nobel Prize for Peace was awarded to the quartet who mediated between the various Tunisian factions to peacefully resolve post-revolution conflicts – many crystallizing in the women's rights discourse.

In sum, this volume provokes readers to reflect on issues of social transformation by engaging with various timely and relevant themes. Readers will gain a window into the realities women face in this part of world, and as a result, develop a fuller understanding of their struggles and successes. At the same time, this volume enables readers to assess mechanisms that may benefit both women and men in the MENA region. In the words of Morocco's most distinguished feminist scholar, Fatema Mernissi: "Either you shut up and you are humiliated or you do what I'm doing. You scream." We hope the "scream" of this book will be heard.

Endnotes

1 Available at www.panorapost.com/article.php?id=11770 (accessed 2 November 2016).

2 Video of Mernissi funeral available at http://fr.le360.ma/societe/diapo-les-funerailles-emouvantes-de-fatima-mernissi-58815 (accessed 2 November 2016).

3 (December 2015). "Afscheid van een Intellectuele Soulmate." *De Stan-daard.* Available at www.standaard.be/cnt/dmf20151202_02001609 (accessed 2 November 2016); (December 2015). "Voor mij was ze de Marokkaanse Simone de Beauvoir." *NRC.* Available at www.nrc.nl/nieuws/2015/12/02/voor-mij-was-ze-de-marokkaanse-simone-de-beauvoir-a1090084 (accessed 2 November 2016).

4 Nussbaum, M. (2000). *Women and Human Development: The Capabilities Approach*. Cambridge University Press.

5 Ibid, p. 7.

6 Ibid, p. 13.

7 Mahmoud, S. (2005). *Politics of Piety: The Islamic Revival and the Feminist Subject*. Princeton University Press.

8 Crocker, D.A. (2008). *Ethics of Global Development: Agency, Capability and Deliberative Democracy*. Cambridge University Press.

9 Bayat, A. (2013). *Life as Politics: How Ordinary People Change the Middle East*. 2nd Edition. Stanford University Press.

10 An important difference between Bayat and James Scott's seminal *Weapons of the Weak* is that Scott focuses on how members of subordinated classes "mitigate or deny claims (for example, rents, taxes, prestige) made on that class by superordinate classes (for example, land lords, large farmers, the state)." Scott, J.C. (1985). *Weapons of the Weak: Everyday Forms of Peasant Resistance*. New Haven: Yale University Press, p. 290. Bayat's analysis focuses not so much on defending already achieved aims but on making fresh demands. Bayat, *Life as Politics*, p. 54.

11 Bayat, *Life as Politics*, p. 56.

12 Abdelrahman, M.M. (2004). *Civil Society Exposed: The Politics of NGOs in Egypt*. Cairo: American University in Cairo Press.

13 Naples, N.A. and M. Desai (2002). *Women's Activism and Globalization: Linking Local Struggles and Transnational Politics*. London: Routledge.

14 For a detailed analysis of unintended, negative consequences of education for women, see Žvan-Elliot, K. (2016). *Modernizing Patriarchy: The Politics of Women's Rights in Morocco*. University of Texas Press.

15 See Bayat, *Life as Politics*, p. 19.

16 See for exceptions Inhorn, M.C. (2012). *The New Arab Man: Emergent Masculinities, Technologies, and Islam in the Middle East*. Princeton: Princeton University Press; Ghannam, F. (2013). *Live and Die Like a Man: Gender Dynamics in Urban Egypt*. Stanford: Stanford University Press; Sonneveld, N. and M. Lindbekk (2015). "A revolution in Muslim Family Law? Egypt's pre- and post-revolutionary period (2011–2013) compared." *New Middle Eastern Studies*. Vol. 5. Available at www.brismes.ac.uk/nmes/archives/1409.

17 Charrad, M.M. (2011). "Gender in the Middle East: Islam, State, agency." *Annual Review of Sociology*. Vol. 37, pp. 417–437.

18 Nussbaum, *Women and Human*, p. 14.

PART I

What Is Social Change?

1 | Capturing Change in Legal Empowerment Programs in Morocco and Tunisia

Shared Challenges and Future Directions

STEPHANIE WILLMAN BORDAT AND
SAIDA KOUZZI

Introduction

This chapter describes local nongovernmental organization (NGO) efforts to promote social change related to women's rights in Morocco and Tunisia through legal empowerment initiatives. Our perspective derives from over 17 years as practitioners and activists working on programs promoting women's human and legal rights in Morocco and Tunisia.[1] The two countries provide both similar and contrasting experiences in lawmaking and civil society development that can be meaningfully shared for their lessons learned.

We take as a starting point the notion that "legal empowerment is the use of law to specifically strengthen the disadvantaged."[2] This idea involves a broader vision of the law beyond just legislation and court decisions and takes a view of empowerment as both a grassroots level-up process and a goal.[3] Under this model, activists promote human rights and social change through a holistic approach combining litigation and legal strategies like legislative advocacy with extra-legal strategies such as community education, services, and mobilization.[4] We examine how the law and legal concepts can serve as awareness-raising and organizing tools that disadvantaged and marginalized groups can use to challenge the status quo and create social change, *outside of the content of the law itself*. We offer examples of micro-level changes, especially in relationships between actors involved. While typically not captured in formal assessments, such changes both constitute significant transformations, and are essential to the success of larger law reform efforts.

Defining Change

While previous decades have witnessed some legislative reforms related
to women's rights in Morocco and Tunisia, these have been limited
in both substance and process. Yet, at the same time, a tendency exists
for international and national actors to applaud what are essentially
nonchanges in both countries, such as long announced but not yet
enacted laws related to women's rights. This criticism of the slow pace
of progress related to women's rights, as well as praise for inexistent
advances, focuses on the macro level of change, that of national legislative reform. In the absence of real, comprehensive legal reforms we
must ask: Where do we look to find social change? How do we define,
capture, and measure it? How do local actors define progress?

These questions are of great practical importance for the broad
range of NGOs that work to promote women's human rights if they
are to ensure sustained support for their work. National and international funders demand "results" from their grantees, and such
donors place pressure on NGOs and national governments to demonstrate indicators of progress toward change. Additionally, understanding past successes is important in planning effective future strategies.

Rather than analyzing how the content of laws can create social
change,[5] we examine how social change can be facilitated or impeded
by the *process* through which law reforms are sought. We illustrate our
analysis with concrete examples from our years of community-level
work with NGOs in Morocco and Tunisia to promote women's rights
through grassroots-level human rights education, legal accompaniment, national lobbying, and international advocacy. We highlight
two national Women's Rights Mobilization Caravans held across
Morocco and Tunisia in 2009 and 2014, respectively.[6] These Caravans
consisted of human rights education sessions with groups of women
and civil society roundtables on violence against women.

A major premise of this chapter is that it is not sufficient for NGO
activists, lawyers, and public actors to work to enact and apply legislative reforms. We argue that they must *transform their own processes
and behaviors* when implementing legal empowerment projects. We
characterize this goal as "relationship change," whereby the aforementioned stakeholders put into practice the human rights values they
purport to promote in order for the eventual legislation to be effective
and for real social transformation to occur.

Defining and Assessing Social Change in Legal Empowerment Programs

NGOs financed by grants, such as our organization and other local associations, are required to submit regular narrative reports to donors justifying the use of funds.[7] Since a major component of these reports is an evaluation of the "results" of our projects, we constantly reflect on how we should define and measure such results. Strikingly, when we come together at workshops or meetings, NGOs often recount detailed, vibrant stories of significant accomplishments that we had not heard before, and that these NGOs never recorded in written reports.

For example, on a visit to one of our partner NGOs we discovered that a sex worker who had previously been a beneficiary of their legal rights and health education outreach programs, had integrated into the Executive Board and become a project manager herself. On such occasions, impact and social change narratives are revealed in all their complexity and richness – in this instance, the individual empowerment of the sex worker and the diversifying and inclusive impact on the NGO management structure.

Yet when we remark to NGOs that they only communicate such information verbally and in social settings, they often reply, "I didn't think it was that important" or "I didn't do anything extraordinary." Such responses represent everyone's loss because they neither validate their experiences for themselves nor share this knowledge with others.

Most frequently, NGOs report results as discrete actions in periodic reports to their funders, rather than engaging in ongoing reflection, analysis, and deliberate learning that would inform future strategies. Trying to fit into various donor formats, NGOs often express the opinion that their reports rarely reflect the realities of their work. Instead, they must respond to funder requests for quantitative data at the output level (such as the number of people trained at a workshop), or for statistics that are related to outcomes but impossible to gather (such as the number of women who have filed a court case as the result of an awareness-raising program).

Given the historically repressive administrative and security context within which NGOs work in Morocco and Tunisia, until very recently it has been a real achievement just to organize an activity such as a conference or a workshop without state authorities banning or canceling it.[8] As a result, for many years the authors conflated merely holding an activity as an outcome in itself, which, given the repressive context, it was and still can be. Moreover, with much energy expended securing official authorizations to hold an activity, or dreading the possibility of mysterious cuts in a conference hotel's water and electricity supply just before an event, local NGOs have only recently begun to have some political space necessary to reflect on and assess the longer-term social progress made by their work.

Time frames for "producing" and assessing change are also problematic within the framework of donor reporting. NGOs point to donor demands for instant results in the one- or two-year life of a standard project grant cycle. As a result, NGOs tend to assess change by reporting outputs, that is, the immediate and countable products of their activities, rather than looking for more subtle but foundational changes in the conditions of peoples' lives.

Finally, NGOs assessing advocacy projects are expected to adhere to traditional understandings of results that frequently focus on or are limited to law reforms. This framework may account for the tendency among many actors, including international donors and foreign diplomats posted in-country, to express impatience and frustration with what they view as a stagnant state of affairs. "Do you really feel like anything has changed?" and "You can't get anything done here," are sentiments we hear frequently.[9] "Why is it taking so long for this violence against women law to get passed?" asked one embassy official in Rabat responsible for funding an NGO advocacy campaign in Morocco.[10] Lack of faith in the rule of law is a dangerous sentiment. Thus, it is imperative that NGOs, governments, and funders develop more nuanced understandings of both the positive effects and limitations of law reform as a social change strategy.

A more complete understanding of the progress made by NGOs also is critical at this point given the current political climate in the region and the difficulty of the tasks faced by NGOs. After more than five years of a Moroccan government led by the Islamist *Parti de la Justice et Développement* (PJD), little real "content" progress – in law and policy – has been made in women's rights.[11] Indeed, many government statements and actions have suggested the risk of further regression in women's status.[12] While several long-pending bills related to women's rights were finally approved in the Government Council and sent to the Parliament for review in a short period in 2016,[13] NGOs and legal analysts have criticized these efforts as merely cosmetic, of passing laws just to pass laws, and not containing the comprehensive and effective reforms on women's rights hoped for. Many NGOs currently describe themselves as demoralized and in a holding pattern.

In post-Revolution Tunisia, local and international actors alike have expressed fears of a backlash against women's rights and a deterioration of women's status given the rising Islamist influence and success of the Ennahda party. The significant increase in the number of women wearing the hijab (headscarf), reports that Ennahda representatives may revisit the longstanding ban on polygamy, and perceived increased violence against women all have raised concerns among women's rights observers and activists.[14]

It is also important to recognize how social change occurs in order to promote a healthier dynamic among NGOs in Morocco and Tunisia. Such knowledge would enable groups to see the collective contributions of many actors rather than focus their attention on one specific NGO. Traditional evaluation models are frequently based on a simplistic vision of causality, such that a specific activity by one NGO is deemed to have directly caused a specific result. In reality, multiple forces, factors, players, and conditions are involved in creating social change.

Whether in social media or at NGO conferences, round tables, and workshops, or donor meetings and receptions, it is common for individual NGOs to take credit for larger achievements. One frequently hears comments such as "Thanks to our NGO, Penal Code article 475 was amended."[15] Donor reporting requirements, whether implied or explicit, often lead grantees to claim their specific project caused a specific outcome, creating attribution problems, competition, and rivalry – instead of much needed collaboration – between NGOs. Indeed, donors themselves often encourage claims of a direct causal link so they can take credit for such achievements in their annual reports, social media, and other publicity and outreach materials.

As a result of and in reaction to these challenges, practitioners and scholars worldwide are increasingly recognizing that traditional evaluation models are inappropriate in both methods and substance for assessing social change efforts, and indeed, can even hamper and discourage such efforts.[16] As a result, an exciting global movement has begun to better define success in the context of social change activism. In this context, we take a multifaceted approach, organized around four outcome areas, to assessing change in our legal empowerment work:[17]

- **Content** outcomes, or changes in *written laws and policies.*
- **Structure** outcomes, or changes in local actors', NGOs', and public institutions' *procedures, operations, systems, resources, knowledge, skills, and capacities* to effectively implement written law and policies.
- **Culture** outcomes, or changes in *public knowledge, attitudes, beliefs, practices, and behaviors.*
- **Relationship** outcomes, or changes in current *hierarchical power relationships* among people and institutions based on gender, age, socioeconomic status, education, ethnicity, and geography, consistent with human rights principles.

These four domains do not necessarily change at the same pace, or even in a similar direction. A thorough systems analysis would examine the interaction between these elements, and how each can feed into social transformation as well as individually support or block the other(s) to either facilitate or prevent comprehensive, sustainable change. For the purposes of this chapter, we focus on the fourth area, relationship outcomes, and the role of legal empowerment projects in Morocco and Tunisia in creating much needed change.

Smoke-and-Mirrors Law Reform in Morocco

If one has followed media reports over the past decade or does online searches, one gets the impression that Morocco has already enacted or is in the process of enacting a plethora of laws protecting women's rights.[18] In response to questions from the United Nations treaty monitoring bodies about the status of these announced laws, the Moroccan government frequently claims that a law is imminent or that a bill is in the last stages of the legislative process.[19] Both the national and international press frequently cite official government declarations that laws on domestic violence, sexual harassment, and abortion are in the works, completed, or "imminent," years before the law's eventual enactment.[20] In reality, often these announced laws then disappear from the radar. Bills may be drafted by the Ministry concerned but then get no farther in the legislative process, stalled by never being approved by the Government Council, withdrawn, or not forwarded to Parliament.

Such public relations statements on the intention to pass a law are often hailed as actual reforms, and the misinformation is widely reproduced and applauded in social media, the press, donor promotional materials, NGO advocacy documents, foreign government human rights reports, and even academic publications. Stated intentions become reality, and announcements become achievements. Thus, laws that exist only in official declarations are equated with actual change, presenting an obstacle to real, sustainable transformation.

A good number of the intended law reforms that were announced years ago have since been (mis)construed by both domestic and international media, scholars, and decision-makers as already implemented. For the national press, reasons for this include the lack of independent or investigative journalism. For the international community, a lack of Arabic language capacity or use of primary source material leads to reliance on third- or fourth-hand French and English language reports. Other reasons include a general lack of understanding of the legislative process, as well as ambitious and misleading official government declarations. Yet, as of this writing, such purported reforms, which include laws on violence against women, sexual harassment, domestic work, and most recently, abortion,[21] have either not been enacted or have taken over a decade to move along in the legislative process.

In a June 2013 case in El Jadida, for example, the press and social media gave substantial coverage to a court decision through headlines declaring, "Marital rape (is) now a crime in Morocco."[22] Putting aside the fact that courts cannot legally create new crimes, the Moroccan government delegation had already affirmed to the United Nations Committee against Torture in November 2011 that marital rape was a crime under the existing Penal Code.[23] In a March 2013 statement, however, the Minister of Justice and Liberties stated that, "it would be impossible to criminalize marital rape,"[24] contradicting the 2011 assertion. It is difficult to work on law reform with such a lack of clarity and consensus among decision-makers themselves over what the current laws actually say.

Resisting Reform

At the same time the Moroccan government conducts public relations campaigns around announced reforms, it also invokes a set code of messages to justify its past, current, and intended future resistance to enacting reforms in areas it deems too sensitive or untouchable. One such strategy the Moroccan government uses to opt out of its obligations to comply with international human rights standards is to make use of qualifier clauses in the Constitution.[25]

In the Concluding Observations to its review of Morocco in October 2015, the United Nations Committee on Economic, Social, and Cultural Rights (CESCR) recommended that "the provision (in the Penal Code) criminalizing illicit [i.e. extra marital] sexual relations be repealed."[26] The Moroccan government responded that, "Concerning ... the aboli- tion of the criminalization of illicit sex, Moroccan authorities do not accept those recommendations related to sexual freedom, being in conflict with the provisions of the Moroccan Constitution, national identity and the conventional practice from Morocco."

Another strategy used by decision-makers and other members of the socioeconomic elite in Morocco to justify not enacting reforms related to women's rights is to claim that "the people are not ready" and "the law is not the problem, people's mentalities are." At the aforementioned Morocco review by the CESCR, for example, when the Committee expressed its concern that polygamy was still legal despite the fact that it constitutes discrimination against women, the head of the Moroccan government delegation replied, "You have to understand that it's normal for a man who can't have a son with his first wife to want to marry a second one, especially given the mental- ities and customs in the rural areas."[27]

Likewise, the previous Minister for Social Development, Family, and Solidarity[28] explained that the prenuptial property agreements allowed under Family Code article 49 "were not very common, probably because couples did not wish to contemplate the possibility of divorce."[29] Under this reasoning, the fault lies not with the law itself, its implementation, or the knowledge and attitudes of public actors responsible for enforcing the provisions,[30] but with "romantic notions" held by couples. The Minister of Justice and Liberties[31] expressed a similar sentiment in the aforementioned meeting with NGOs advocating for a Violence Against Women law. In response to the call for the criminalization of marital rape, the Minister responded, "You can't deprive a man of what is rightfully his."[32] In our Morocco Caravan, we heard again and again in round tables with the local educated elite – lawyers, public actors, and NGO members – that what is needed is not law reform but awareness raising for the "population."[33]

Whether resistance to reforms related to women's rights is based on a desire to protect privilege, justify state inaction, or both, ironically these arguments shifting blame to the ostensibly conservative and ignorant population often contradict social realities. In many instances, current laws in both Morocco and Tunisia are outdated, not responsive to, and not reflective of realities on the ground. Sexuality and violence are two prime examples of widespread social behaviors that the State refuses to acknowledge or address publicly and collectively.

For instance, although sexual relations between unmarried persons are illegal in Morocco[34] and in Tunisia,[35] social realities are quite different. National studies revealed there were 210,434 unwed mothers in Morocco from 2003–2009[36] and 2015 government estimates note 900–1500 births outside of marriage in Tunisia each year.[37] While further information on the topic is anecdotal to nonexistent, one source cites a 2007 Moroccan Ministry of Health study indicating that 36 percent of "young" Moroccan men and 15 percent of "young" Moroccan women admitted to having had sexual relations outside of marriage,[38] and 2014 Tunisian statistics indicate that 80 percent of men and 68 percent of women have had sexual relations outside of marriage.[39]

Further, marital rape is not a crime under the current Penal Codes in Morocco or Tunisia. Tunisian Personal Status Code Article 23 requires both spouses to "fulfill their conjugal duties according to practice and customs," a provision that is generally understood to mean that sexual relations constitute a marital obligation. In contrast to the statements of the Minister of Justice, women across Morocco, including in more remote and rural areas, have spoken openly about and denounced marital rape:

There is a big problem of rape on the wedding night by the new husband, and it is difficult for the bride to protest because people will try and justify this violence by saying that the woman was not a virgin. Women therefore remain silent, and marital rape becomes a habit that women continue to suffer from.[40]

Government statements to the contrary, we have found that people at the local level are eager for and are engaging in profound transformations in social interactions. In this chapter, we go beyond the binary arguments and stale debates about whether we need law reform or culture change, oft-repeated at NGO- and government-organized panels, conferences, and other events related to women's rights,[41] to suggest a more nuanced, interconnected, and interdependent dynamic between laws, their enforcement, and the amorphous concepts of "the public" or "the culture."

Looking for Change beyond the Law

We argue that despite the absence of meaningful law reforms, in both Morocco and Tunisia progress toward change has occurred in other domains, as seen in shifts in social dynamics and relationships in NGO efforts on the ground.[42] The process of implementing legal empowerment projects can itself lead to change, apart from and regardless of any eventual reforms to the content of laws – hence providing an answer to the question of whether "the population" actually resists change. Intangible and invisible changes in the three other aforementioned domains – structure, culture, and relationships – are very frequently not measured, not counted, and overlooked by NGOs, donors, and decision-makers alike.

We also want to temper the prevalent view in both countries that women's rights have stagnated with the current PJD government in Morocco and influence of the first post-Revolution ruling Ennahda party in Tunisia. The general pessimism about women's rights may be due in part to a failure to look for change in the right places. Thus, the challenge for activists and policy-makers becomes how to accurately and appropriately recognize and describe where and how changes have occurred.

For the purposes of this chapter, we will not enter into a description or analysis of *structural* outcomes or *cultural* outcomes of legal empowerment projects. Among the wide array of structural changes discerned from our program assessments, we can cite the enhanced capacities and skills of activists, momentum created around civil society development, and improved implementation of existing laws. Cultural changes include increased public dialogue on previously sensitive or taboo subjects, greater articulation by women of their problems and active solicitation of information and advice, and challenges to previous gender-biased behaviors and practices within communities.

Here we focus on the fourth previously mentioned outcome area, that of *relationship* changes. The Moroccan and Tunisian contexts differ significantly in their contemporary experiences of reform, which occurred in Morocco through a deliberately gradual approach and in Tunisia through a sudden Revolution in 2011 after decades of ostensible stagnation. However, where we find significant commonalities between the two countries is in the hierarchical power relationships among people based on gender, age, socioeconomic status, education, profession, ethnicity, and geography. Due to the top-down and repressive nature of the previous regimes in both countries, similar hierarchical, fear-based relationships have existed between the people and State institutions. NGOs in both countries have, in turn, traditionally assimilated and reproduced internally the hierarchies, power relations, and leadership styles prevalent in the larger society.

James Sater described how pre-1990s Moroccan civil society groups, in their relationship to the State, "were structured by dominant modes of power," and the "inability of organizations of civil society to resist power relations, which were structured through inter-elite conflicts and neo-patrimonial rule ... power relations were omnipresent and shaped particular organizations' activities."[43] We build on this idea to illustrate our findings about how women's rights NGOs in Morocco and Tunisia have begun to shift away from these traditional ways of relating in terms of their: (a) internal NGO relationships, including operations, leadership practices, and dealings with members; (b) NGO-beneficiary relationships, including interactions with and treatment of "beneficiaries"; (c) NGO–NGO relationships, involving dynamics between NGOs; and (d) NGO–government relationships, involving relationships with State actors.

The first two of what we consider to be dysfunctional facets of NGO relationships are particularly sensitive; they seem to be something people know and are aware of but have not written about or publicly addressed. While international actors, donors, and even local NGO members privately express their grievances about an unhealthy civil society dynamic, in open debate or academic discussion, the issue of relationships has been the proverbial elephant in the room.[44]

Below we outline what Moroccan and Tunisian activists have defined as significant changes brought about, at least in part, by their implementation of legal empowerment projects that brought new human rights language and fresh methodologies to their work. We have described these changes under the category of "relationship outcomes" based on our retrospective assessment of descriptions of what was "new" for them. Though the prior baseline situation is implied rather than explicit, the shifts correspond to our prior experiences with the NGOs and findings from our initial needs assessments in both countries.[45]

Internal NGO Relationships

One of the main themes that emerged in our assessments with Moroccan and Tunisian women's rights activists was a shift in internal relationships and dynamics. NGO members cited trends toward more positive and supportive communication, equality among members, autonomy in their tasks, duty-sharing and turn-taking, valuing of each other's contributions, encouragement for creativity and initiative, and transparency, as well as a more horizontal structure. They also mentioned increased participation in decision-making and greater roles and responsibilities among younger members. Indeed, several of the associations taking part in the assessments had been created only recently, the result of younger NGO members having challenged for the first time ever the work methods of their presidents within traditional NGOs and eventually leaving to create their own. As one member commented:

I joined my (predominantly male) association in 2007, and two weeks later I attended my first training on women's human rights ... In 2012 I was the keynote speaker in a big meeting with the male lawyers. That was a big achievement for me because I used to be the secretary and then I took the floor and spoke in front of Embassy representatives and other decision-makers in a big group.[46]

The trends in newer NGOs contrast with the operations in traditional NGO environments, at least those characterized by bureaucracy, hierarchical leadership, top-down authoritarian decision-making, and memberships limited in number and diversity. In Morocco and Tunisia, NGOs typically have been organized around a high profile, longstanding individual president whose personality informs the NGO's identity. In such cases, the accomplishments of the NGO commonly are attributed to the leader. In fact, NGOs are still often referred to as "Ms. So and So's organization" rather than by their proper name.[47] For years, NGO presidents would insist on personally attending events we (or others) organized, regardless of the appropriateness or relevance of their participation to that specific activity. We would distribute big binders full of resource materials at workshops, assuming they would be usefully shared with all of the NGO members upon the participant's return. Yet, in numerous instances we later learned that the NGO presidents considered the workshop materials their own personal property and took them home.

We also recall countless meetings in which younger members of associations would raise their hand, lower their gaze, address the president with the subservient title of "Madame la Présidente," and ask permission to speak. Repeatedly, we witnessed NGO leaders shouting at younger members, "Go on! Speak! What do you have to say for yourself!" and declaring their members "incompetent," in front of everyone present. In one notable incident, an NGO reprimanded us in an official letter and instructed, "All correspondence should be addressed to 'Madame La Présidente,'" and not to "Madame (her last name)," and not cc'd to the junior member responsible for our joint project. Given this context, when NGOs exhibit subtle shifts in behavior, like including a diversity of members as representatives at events, communicating as supportive equals, and sharing information internally, it represents important changes indeed.

NGO–Beneficiary Relationships

A second theme that emerged in our assessments was the shift in relationships between the NGOs and the women they profess to serve, frequently referred to as "beneficiaries," or less frequently as "clients."[48] Many NGO members described "new ways of working, different from the traditional way of doing things," that involved changes in their working methods, the places where they conducted outreach, and the types of women with whom they worked.

One example frequently cited among the Moroccan and Tunisian NGO members we interviewed was how participatory human rights education, used as a community mobilization tool, contrasted with traditional methods in which experts such as lawyers "teach" women about their rights: "In our NGO, we have found new ways of relating to women at the grassroots level, in part by switching to a discourse that says, 'We are here to collectively find a solution together.'"

For NGO activists in Tunisia, the Caravan was the first time they had ever facilitated such an awareness raising discussion with a group of women at the grassroots level. In one notable example from the Tunisia Caravan, a local NGO in a small town had organized a panel following conventional norms for such events: Formal presentations by all-male speakers, microphones on the presenters' table to amplify their voices despite the small size of the room, static noise from surround-sound speakers, a general air of cigarette smoke, and women attendees seated in horizontally lined up rows of chairs as in a classroom. This set-up clearly signaled women's designated role, namely, to sit quietly holding photos of their male relatives martyred in the Revolution and to cry on cue. About twenty minutes into the panel speeches, the members of the Caravan team from NGOs across Tunisia reacted with a mini-revolt. Soon the local women participants followed suit. They all stood up, moved their chairs to form a circle, and asked the men to leave the conference room. The women then proceeded to clearly articulate their sense of the "typical victimization and exploitation of women who suffered under the Revolution," and converted the activity into a lively discussion on women's human rights. The men remained outdoors for the duration of the meeting, smoking, grumbling, and protesting having been kicked out of the activity.

The donor representative present at the activity did not appreciate this turn of events and openly criticized the organizers from the Caravan team on the spot. Though we interpreted the tensions as constructive because they reflected challenges to existing power relationships and described the incident as "social change in action," the donor was not convinced, and deemed the event "chaotic and disorganized."

In a similar vein, a grassroots-level activity for women in a Tunisian village was initially organized as a traditional panel, again with the presenters' table and the participants seated in rows. The NGO President arrived much like a VIP and had planned on giving a speech. Again the women members of the Caravan team changed the chairs from rows to a circle, stopped the panel presentations, and instead conducted a participatory human and legal rights education session that ran an hour longer than planned. The NGO President left the room, reappearing toward the end to take her photo with the village women and post it immediately on Facebook. A few years prior in our Morocco Caravan, a similar shift in the usual NGO-beneficiary relationship occurred. A group of men from one village association had gathered the women to sit in a large courtyard and launched into political speeches for upcoming elections. The members of the Caravan team intervened to ask the participants to show their appreciation for the men's support "by thanking them on their way out" – to which the women responded with laughter and a round of applause.

In addition to adopting such new communication techniques through a specific discussion facilitation methodology, NGOs also reported a shift toward community outreach and grassroots-level direct contact with women. "Now we go to the women where they are, rather than waiting for them to come to the NGO offices," said one NGO member, echoing the frequent remark in our assessments that they have become "open to new communities," begun to access previously remote areas, and spoken with women from "marginalized" communities. NGO members participating in the Tunisia Caravan evaluation described how "it was the first time" they had done outreach work on women's rights beyond the capital city. Under the Ben Ali regime, travel by NGOs promoting human rights outside of Tunis was severely restricted. Additionally, elite urban groups often did not prioritize outreach to rural areas or grassroots-level mobilization as part of their strategies. Some of the NGOs acknowledged during the Caravan that they had never been to certain cities or towns, or to a rural area.

One experience that particularly impacted the activists was an outreach activity in a village with no running water or electricity. Urban NGO members remarked how unaware they were of the challenges, problems, and realities of people in their own country. Residents in this and other villages also commented that it was the first time an NGO had ever come there. Other "firsts" included direct engagement with people in public spaces when handing out literature on the streets, at bus stops, and in public gardens. One activist expressed her excitement about "the first time I've ever gone into the *hammam* (public bath) to speak with women!" On another occasion, an outreach activity planned in a reputedly dangerous Salafist neighborhood in Tunis was almost cancelled because of perceived security concerns. None of the Caravan team had ever been there before, and many hid from their parents and husbands the fact that they went there. Having overcome their fears and concerns, the NGO members remarked after the activity that, "the media has stereotyped this neighborhood," and "in reality it's perfectly safe and normal."

Finally, a staff member of an NGO working in a Moroccan town reputed for its brothels, described a similarly revelatory experience that allowed them to promote a diverse and inclusive beneficiary population:

At first we had conflictual relations with people in the community because we included sex workers in our human and legal rights education programs. Initially the other women didn't want to be in the same groups with them.

But afterwards, with time, they changed their attitudes, and even when one of the sex workers missed a session the other women would inquire after her and go visit her to make sure she wasn't sick or something.

The shift in NGO–beneficiary relationships that we detected in our assessments suggests that NGOs are starting to move away from a vision of themselves as elite lobbying groups or charity providers toward one as a force for social mobilization, strengthening the voices and participation of women in their communities.

NGO–NGO Relationships

A third theme we detected through assessments of legal empowerment projects was a shift in the relationships between NGOs. During the Tunisia Caravan evaluation, team members noted the sharing of both the "credit" and "logistical and programmatic tasks" among the different NGOs represented, citing how they all "rotated speaking time at activities and press opportunities" and ignored typical criteria like age, experience, profession, or NGO affiliation. They also highlighted the networking and collaborative aspects of the project. One NGO member described,

the solidarity and teamwork among Caravan members, despite the fact that we come from different organizations with different ideologies. We felt a sense of community, of a safe space where we were supported and felt like we were accepted, part of a shared voice, and able to make a difference.

The lack of networking and coalition building among women's groups is an issue that has been consistently raised in donor and academic NGO assessments in Morocco and Tunisia. Competition for funds, tensions related to leadership struggles, and political affiliations have prevented collaboration among NGOs. During the Tunisia Caravan, planning disputes arose over the issue of integrating a broader group of local associations in the activities around the country. "How do we know we can trust them? How do we know we share the same values?" asked one NGO member against such inclusion. In a similar vein, Morocco NGOs reported a change in their relationships with lawyers:

At first lawyers were against the legal accompaniment program, they thought we were trying to replace them and steal their clients, and accused us of usurping their work. We held a meeting with the president of the bar association, who then started collaborating with us and helping us *pro bono* with the legal accompaniment project.

NGO–State Actor Relationships

The fourth area where NGOs identified change was in their relationships with State actors, including national decision-makers such as Ministry officials and Parliamentarians, as well as local justice, administrative, and law enforcement authorities. Given the different contexts, this shift seemed to be more prevalent in the Morocco assessments, though the Tunisian activists expressed their desire to develop such collaboration with public actors.

In both Morocco and Tunisia, changes in NGO–State actor relationships are a fundamental issue, both as a means – a necessary condition for any effective law reform – and as an end. After decades of State repression, distrust, fear, and paranoia, a major challenge in post-police state environments is building relationships and trust among people and institutions, particularly with law enforcement and justice system actors such as the police, gendarmes, prosecutors, and judges. Improving relationships is of particular importance in promoting women's rights, where NGOs are advocating for increased State intervention and police powers to fight violence against women, especially in domestic contexts.

Moroccan NGOs noted in our assessments that they have developed relationships with local decision-makers and are now able to hold meetings with them.

One of our successes was when we went with the women in our human and legal rights education program to attend the Municipal council session. Before it was difficult for women to have access to it. The President of the Municipality expressed his surprise, and the women said, it was thanks to the NGO program that now we can talk to you.

They also described improved relationships with justice system actors. This includes the public prosecutor collaborating with them in violence against women cases, and court clerks providing information and assistance to help women with their paperwork.

We also work in the courts, and at first it was difficult to organize activities with judges because they can't do anything without prior authorizations

from the Ministry of Justice. However, thanks to our work and connections
we were eventually able to engage them. Courts sometimes ask us to do
interpretation for Amazigh women who don't speak Arabic.

NGOs likewise reported greater access to courts and case files for
follow-up on individual cases as well as for action research into the
justice system's treatment of women's rights related cases.[49] They
described how local authorities in Morocco have started "treating us
like peers rather than acting superior," giving the example of the
treatment of unwed mothers:

Before, hospital staff would often alert the local police if an unwed
woman came to give birth. Now the local hospital and police authorities
call the NGO instead of arresting the mother, and ask us to come over and
help her.

Finally, NGOs described shifts in their relationships with parliamentarians in their advocacy for a Violence Against Women law in
Morocco. In the first year of the campaign, parliamentary groups
expressed their surprise at NGO requests for meetings, not being used
to lobbying initiated by local NGOs, especially those from outside the
usual privileged urban elite. On one occasion, a parliamentarian's wife
answered his phone and informed us: "My husband doesn't meet with
women." In subsequent years, however, parliamentarians have contacted local NGOs directly to request meetings, provide information
and updates, and propose joint activities.[50]

Conclusions

The examples cited in this chapter illustrate the micro-level impacts
that legal empowerment programs can have outside of and in absence
of any formal changes in the law. We must not underestimate the
significance of seemingly small steps forward toward greater equality
for women in terms of shifts in relationships among diverse stakeholders. Such shifts are significant for two reasons: first, because in
and of themselves they constitute change, and second, because they
will eventually contribute to and inform substantive law reform and
implementation. As Sater observed:

Features of Moroccan society are constantly changing ... [notably social
practices and NGO activity] changes [that] will ultimately increase the

pressure for legal changes despite the structural disadvantages that the women's rights movement is experiencing at the moment.[51]

The micro-level achievements described in this chapter are not likely to satisfy donor expectations, however, despite the reality that such changes in NGO relationships are necessary conditions for and components of the law reform processes that will lead to real social change.

Those seeking to promote law reform must not only advocate for changes to the content of laws, they must avoid reproducing the same practices, dynamics, and power relationships they wish to transform. In their engagement in social change processes, NGO actors must recognize and reject hierarchy, charity, issuing orders, and non-mutual giving and receiving. The *process* by which laws are reformed ultimately will have two major impacts. One is the extent to which the content of the enacted law is well written, responsive to social realities, and appropriate. The other is the extent to which the reforms are accepted by society, and thus, implemented and sustainable. Effective laws depend on the process by which they come into being, or as one activist put it, "Values determine outcomes."[52]

Our assessments in Morocco and Tunisia revealed numerous stories where, over time, changes in structures, culture, and relationships combined to have an impact on the living conditions of individuals and communities, including such actions as:

- Holding a protest in front of a local health center to demand birth control;
- Advocating for local authorities to install public lighting in a zone known for violence against women workers walking to and from their jobs at factories;
- Getting the workday for women agricultural workers reduced from twelve to eight hours and obtaining a minimum wage;
- Getting the public hospital in their town to provide free medical certificates to women victims of violence as a matter of local policy and practice.[53]

These accomplishments would not have been possible, credible, or effective without changes in the NGO capacities to advocate, in grassroots level women's knowledge of their human rights, and in the relationships among NGOs, women, and local public actors. Change in this sense is local and personal, and is often overlooked by international actors, donors, and visitors who frequently remain in the capital cities and focus in their assessments on macro-level, national legal or structural changes. This approach warrants reappraisal, as it neglects opportunities to bear witness to micro-level, incremental, yet sustained shifts that transform daily life in diverse communities across Morocco and Tunisia.

Endnotes

1 Mobilising for Rights Associates (MRA) www.mrawomen.ma.
2 Golub, S. (2010). "What is legal empowerment? An introduction." *Legal Empowerment: Practitioners' Perspectives.* S. Golub (ed.). International Development Law Initiative, p. 13.
3 Ibid.
4 (2006). *Promoting Women's Rights: A Resource Guide for Litigating International Law in Domestic Courts.* Global Rights Maghreb.
5 The 1956 Tunisian Personal Status Code, considered by observers as the most progressive in the region on women's rights, raises interesting questions about the ability of law to create or sustain social change in light of the post-Revolution Islamist rise. On July 26, 2017, the Tunisian People's Representatives' Assembly finally passed the comprehensive law 60/2016 on the elimination of violence against women.
6 In both Caravans the authors, with teams of local NGO members, travelled for twenty-one days and ten days, respectively, to diverse parts of Morocco and Tunisia. Available at http://caravaneglobalrights.bloguez .com/ and www.facebook.com/CaravaneDroitsFemmesTunisie/.
7 This section and the next are based on an on-going initiative we have implemented since November 2013 in Morocco and Tunisia to "Promote Women's Rights through Innovative Impact Assessments." This has involved a series of consultations, training workshops, and implementation of participatory program assessments with thousands of diverse stakeholders from communities across both countries. The results of these experiences and tools developed can be found in our Arabic language Practical Guide: "How Do We Contribute to Change? Methods and Approaches for Innovative Impact Assessments in Human Rights Work," available on the Resources Page of www.mrawomen.ma/.
8 The repressive context surrounding NGOs in Morocco and Tunisia both past and present is documented in Human Rights Watch, www.hrw.org/, Freedom House, https://freedomhouse.org/, U.S. State Department Human Rights reports www.state.gov/j/drl/rls/hrrpt/, and in United Nations treaty monitoring body reviews, www.ohchr.org/.

9 Conversations between the authors and representatives of a foreign embassy and an international financial institution in Morocco and Tunisia. See also www.wrmea.org/2015-january-february/moroccan-women-still-at-the-barricades.html.

10 This specific question was posed to the authors after an advocacy campaign for a Violence Against Women law had been underway for three and a half years. We question the realistic nature of the donor expectations, given that from the time of conception of a draft law to passage, comparatively in Bulgaria it took eight years and in Kazakhstan ten years.

11 In Morocco, Constitutional reforms in July 2011 led to the November 2011 elections resulting in a PJD-led government. The few, quite recent advances on women's issues that have been made since 2011, such as the announced establishment of a commission in Spring 2015 to examine reforms to the restrictive abortion laws, or the November 2015 introduction in Parliament by the Ministry of Solidarity, Women, Family, and Social Development of two bills to implement two Constitutional institutions, the Consultative Council for Women and Children and the Authority for Parity and Fight against all Forms of Discrimination, were royal initiatives.

12 For Morocco, see statements by the current Ministry of Solidarity, Women, Family, and Social Development at www.h24info.ma/maroc/le-top-5-des-declarations-chocs-de-bassima-hakkaoui/25896, the Head of State at www.h24info.ma/h24-tv/lactu-video/le-virage-integriste-dab delilah-benkirane-sur-la-question-de-la-femme/24340 and www.youtube .com/watch?v=QmHPIRLOHo4&feature=youtu.be, and the Minister of Justice at www.mrawomen.ma/sites/default/files/ressources/Le_plai doyer_international/Morocco_Implementation_of_UPR_Reccomendations_ on_Womens_Rights_FINAL.pdf.

13 These include the Draft law #103–13 on the elimination of violence against women, approved in the Government Council on March 17, 2016, voted with amendments in the House of Representatives on July 20, 2016, and pending review in the House of Councilors; Draft law #27.14 on Trafficking in persons, voted by the House of Representatives in May 2016; Draft law 19.12 on the Working Conditions of Domestic Workers voted by the House of Representatives in May 2016; Law establishing the Advisory Council for Family and Childhood Affairs, voted by both houses of Parliament in April and June; and the Law establishing the Authority for Gender Equality and Combating all Forms of Discrimination, approved in May 2016 by the House of Representatives.

14 Examples of a few among the numerous sources include www.lemonde
   .fr/journee-de-la-femme/article/2012/03/08/de-tunis-a-rabat-la-crainte-d-
   un-retour-en-arriere_1653702_1650673.html; Office National de la
   Famille et la Population (2015). "Expérience et vécu des femmes survi-
   vantes à la violence conjugale dans les régions du Kef, Béja et Jendouba:
   résultats d'une étude qualitative." www.onfp.nat.tn/liens/violence_nord_
   ouest_resultats_2015.pdf; (2014). "New law pushes Tunisia to protect
   women." Available at www.al-monitor.com/pulse/culture/2014/08/
   tunisia-women-victim-gender-based-violence.html.
15 February 2014 amendments to Moroccan Penal Code Article 475 eliminated the provision that as applied allowed rapists of minors to escape
   prosecution by marrying their victims. www.nytimes.com/2012/04/06/
   world/africa/death-of-rape-victim-in-morocco-sparks-calls-for-legal-reform
   .html?_r=0.
16 Calhoun, A., E. Whitmore, and M. G. Wilson (eds.) (2011). *Activism
   that Works*. Fernwood Publishing.
17 Significantly inspired by VeneKlasen, L., with Miller, V. (2007). *A New
   Weave of Power, People and Politics: The Action Guide for Advocacy and
   Citizen Participation.* Stylus Publishing; Calhoun et al., *Activism that Works*.
18 Smoke and mirrors was the term used by a foreign diplomat in a
   conversation with the authors in 2006 to describe the Moroccan government's approach to law reform on human rights issues.
19 For the most recent example of this, see http://tbinternet.ohchr.org/_
   layouts/treatybodyexternal/SessionDetails1.aspx?SessionID=968&Lang=en.
20 See www.maghress.com/fr/aujourdhui/72711; www2.ohchr.org/english/
   bodies/cedaw/docs/statement/40Morocco_fr.ppt; www2.ohchr.org/english/
   bodies/cedaw/docs/statement/40Morocco.ppt. These also include January
   2008, March 2008, and November 2011 statements by the Moroccan government to the CEDAW Committee, the Human Rights Council Working
   Group on the Universal Periodic Review, and the Committee against
   Torture, respectively, that a Violence Against Women law was pending.
21 See http://english.alarabiya.net/en/News/africa/2013/11/08/Morocco-
   MPs-drafts-bill-against-sexual-harassment.html; www.huffpostmagh
   reb.com/2013/12/11/maroc-violence-femmes_n_4424725.html; http://
   kvinfo.org/web-magazine/morocco-plans-reform-abortion-law; http://
   lavieeco.com/news/societe/ou-en-est-le-projet-de-loi-sur-les-travailleurs-a-
   domicile-30697.html; www.bayanealyaoume.press.ma/index.php?view=
   article&tmpl=component&id=8571; www.hespress.com/politique/17197
   .html.
22 See www.medias24.com/DROIT/1680-Une-premiere-qui-fera-date-un-
   mari-condamne-pour-viol-conjugal.html and www.al-monitor.com/
   pulse/culture/2013/06/womens-rights-morocco-conviction-victory.html.

23 See www.youtube.com/watch?v=E81HCCNCv_k&feature=share.

24 Written report by NGOs attending a meeting at the Ministry of Justice on March 18, 2013.

25 The supremacy of international conventions over domestic law provided for in the Constitution's Preamble is qualified as "within the framework of Constitutional provisions and laws of the Kingdom, in respect of immutable national identity," while men and women's Article 19 equal rights are conditioned on "respect of Constitutional provisions, and permanent characteristics and laws of the Kingdom."

26 Committee on Economic, Social, and Cultural Rights (October 2015). Concluding observations on the fourth periodic report of Morocco E/C.12/MAR/CO/4.

27 See http://tbinternet.ohchr.org/_layouts/treatybodyexternal/Download .aspx?symbolno=E%2fC.12%2f2015%2fSR.65&Lang=en; http:// lakome2.com/mobile/http://lakome2.com/index.php/politique/5386 .html; http://m.libe.ma/Un-ministre-progressiste-defend-la-polygamie-a-Geneve_a67046.html; www.moroccoworldnews.com/2015/10/ 169408/morocco-progressive-minister-comes-under-fire-for-supporting-polygamy/.

28 Her name is Nezha Skalli.

29 In response to a question posed to the Moroccan government delegation by the Committee on the Elimination of Discrimination against Women during its consideration of Morocco's 3rd and 4th combined periodic reports, at the Committee's 40th Session, held from January 14 to February 1, 2008, CEDAW/C/SR.825.

30 (2008). *Conditions, Not Conflict: Promoting Women's Human Rights through Strategic Use of the Marriage Contract.* Global Rights; (2011). *Promoting Women's Human Rights in Morocco, Algeria and Tunisia through Strategic Use of the Marriage Contract: Researching and Documenting the Use of Marriage Contracts among Local Authorities.* Global Rights; (2012). *Reforming Marriage Contract Procedures to Promote Women's Human Rights: Thematic Working Group Recommendations from Morocco and Algeria.* Global Rights.

31 From the Islamic *Parti de la Justice et développement* PJD.

32 Written report by the associations attending the meeting at the Ministry of Justice on March 18, 2013.

33 See http://caravaneglobalrights.bloguez.com/.

34 Penal Code Articles 490 and 491.

35 Penal Code articles 226 and 236.

36 (2010). *Le Maroc des mères célibataires.* Insaf. www.egalite.ma/attach ments/article/212/INSAF-Rapport%20Etude%20nationale%20"Le%20 Maroc%20des%20m%C3%A8res%20c%C3%A9libataires".pdf.

37 See http://kapitalis.com/tunisie/2015/12/16/les-meres-celibataires-en-tunisie/; www.huffpostmaghreb.com/2015/08/18/tunisie-meres-celiba taire_n_7998814.html.
38 See http://etudiant.lefigaro.fr/les-news/actu/detail/article/au-maroc-les-jeunes-ne-peuvent-toujours-pas-vivre-ensemble-hors-mariage-4318/.
39 See www.baya.tn/2014/03/30/les-tunisiens-et-le-sexe-des-statistiques/.
40 See http://caravaneglobalrights.bloguez.com/.
41 For a good analysis contrasting the secular feminists and Islamists groups in this sense, see Žvan-Elliott, K. (2015). *Modernizing Patriarchy: The Politics of Women's Rights in Morocco*. University of Texas Press.
42 For the purposes of this chapter, since the explosion of the NGO sector in Morocco at the turn of the century and in Tunisia since the Revolution.
43 Sater, J. N. (2007). *Civil Society and Political Change in Morocco*. Routledge, p. 160.
44 Two exceptions to this are Elliott, *Modernizing Patriarchy*, pp. 57–61, and Bargach, J. (2013). "Shortcomings of a reflexive tool kit; or, memoir of an undutiful daughter." *Encountering Morocco: Fieldwork and Cultural Understanding*. Indiana University Press.
45 In Morocco in 2000; in Tunisia in 2003 and 2012.
46 Moroccan NGO member, MRA Workshop, February 2014.
47 Authoritarian, diva style leadership is not a phenomenon limited to the Maghreb.
48 We would refer to them as constituents in English, but there is no equivalent term in French or Arabic.
49 Ligue démocratique de défense des droits des femmes (LDDF) (2007). "Droits des femmes et code de la famille après 4 ans d'application" and (2011). "Promoting women's human rights in Morocco, Algeria and Tunisia through strategic use of the marriage contract: researching and documenting the use of marriage contracts among local authorities." Morocco: Global Rights.
50 Bordat, S. and S. Kouzzi (July 2012). "A violence against women law in Morocco." *Self-Determination and Women's Rights in Muslim Societies*. C. Raghavan and J. P. Levine (eds.). Brandeis University Press.
51 Sater, *Civil Society*, p. 139
52 Personal conversation with Vidya Sri. November 2015.
53 In order to bring an assault and battery complaint, women victims of violence must provide a medical certificate demonstrating that they have suffered injuries resulting in more than twenty days of disability (Penal Code articles 400 and 401). Local NGOs report that hospitals used to require women to pay between 100 and 200 dirhams to obtain the certificate.

2 | Safe Havens and Social Embeddedness

An Examination of Domestic Violence Shelters in Morocco

MEGAN O'DONNELL

In 2004, Morocco presented itself on the world stage as one of the most progressive states in the Middle East and North Africa with regard to gender equality after legally expanding women's rights through significant reforms of the *moudawana al-ahwal al-shakhsiyya* (Personal Status Code).[1] Civil society associations devoted to advancing women's rights received attention and praise for lobbying efforts that long predated the 2004 reform.[2] The Union de l'Action Féminine (Women's Action Union, UAF) for example, was recognized for having initiated the Million Signatures Campaign as early as 1992, which succeeded in collecting over one million signatures in support of the law's reform.[3] Much of Morocco's progressive image regarding gender equality, at least in relation to many of its regional counterparts, has been sustained by the perceived strength and efficacy of the country's women's associations.

Yet, academics and policymakers have evaluated Moroccan women's rights (and the efficacy of women's associations in advancing these rights) almost exclusively on a macro level through the lens of national legislative reforms. Such reforms include the passage of the 2011 Constitution – and particularly Article 19, which expanded constitutional gender equality – as well as the revision of Article 475 of the penal code, which eliminated the ability of a rapist to avoid prosecution by marrying the victim. For their efforts in lobbying for and participating in the drafting of these legal revisions, members of Moroccan women's associations have received further positive attention within and outside of Morocco.[4] Scholars Eve Sandberg and Kenza Aqertit praised the advocacy efforts of these associations in their assertion that, "dedicated, smart, and politically effective Moroccan women worked together since Morocco's independence to alter their country's entrenched gender institution of distinctive male and female obligations and practices."[5] However, the efforts of women's associations to alter Morocco's "entrenched gender institution" have been examined far less on a micro level. Relatively less attention has been directed to the operations and impact of their social welfare-oriented projects, which range from literacy classes to job skills training to legal and psychological counseling, all geared toward Moroccan women.[6]

Even before the passage of the new *Moudawana*, women's rights activists had pointed to violence against women as an issue needing special attention. Women's associations have led awareness campaigns and established counseling centers, legal clinics, and other social welfare services for survivors of gender-based violence, often to compensate for the Moroccan government's lack of such services on a comprehensive scale.[7] In spite of this progress, however, Moroccan domestic violence shelters have not been the subject of thorough research.[8] This study is one of the first of its kind in the academic literature to investigate domestic violence shelters in Morocco, specifically regarding the professed goals of these institutions, the activities they carry out, and their tangible impact on residents. In doing so, it will compare the progressive image of Moroccan women's associations with the results they achieve at a grassroots level, and discuss the challenges that these associations often face in living up to their progressive image.

In *Neopatriarchy: A Theory of Distorted Change in Arab Society*, Hisham Sharabi leaves the reader on an optimistic note when he asserts that civil society organizing may offer the best hope for contesting the ingrained neopatriarchal culture of many Arab countries.[9] He argued that of all civil society-led movements:

Potentially the most revolutionary is the women's movement ... Even in the short term, the women's movement is the detonator which will explode neopatriarchal society from within. If allowed to grow and come into its own, it will become the permanent shield against patriarchal regression, the cornerstone of future modernity.[10]

Since *Neopatriarchy*'s publication in 1988, women's movements across the Arab world have made significant strides. Within Morocco, civil society organizations developed to advance women's rights, have led awareness campaigns, lobbied the Parliament and the King, and offered a variety of grassroots services to Moroccan women. Yet, despite these advances, I have observed that Moroccan women's associations, and particularly those that have undertaken the operation of domestic violence shelters, face obstacles. These obstacles prevent them from achieving their professed goals, exacerbate their hierarchical structures, and impede their ability to live up to the rhetoric praising them as progressive and "transformative."

Instead of imploding "neopatriarchal society from within," the shelters in place to protect and advance Moroccan women's rights are, in effect, heavily constrained in their efforts to combat patriarchal norms and structures. This means that despite the aim of shelter practitioners to operate "transformative institutions" that decrease violence against women and entrenched patriarchy, they frequently fail to achieve their professed objectives, which include job skills training, social integration services, and the overall empowerment of their residents.

What are the factors preventing shelter practitioners from achieving their professed goals? After illustrating the disparity between shelter practitioners' stated objectives and their tangible impacts on residents, I will put forth two overarching explanations for this disparity: (1) the embeddedness of shelters within the Moroccan political and social context; and (2) the internal dynamics that exist between practitioners and residents within shelters. As I will demonstrate, these two types of factors – external and internal – are linked. External constraints create an environment that fosters and substantiates the perceptions of shelter practitioners that they are isolated in their work, in turn influencing the way they interact with shelter residents.

In 2008, Boy and Kulczycki synthesized the academic literature on intimate partner violence in the Middle East and North Africa and spoke to the dearth of such research in these regions. They concluded that, "as a matter of priority, future research should expand the knowledge base," and, "research is needed on interventions that could be successfully offered to victims," such as the services of domestic violence shelters.[11] In the case of Morocco researchers have conducted no systematic review of domestic violence shelters nor of their impacts on the lives of women who seek their help. In a country where, in 2011, 62.8 per cent of women between the ages of 18 and 64 reported having experienced violence,[12] it is crucial to determine how shelters operate, and what, if any, disconnect exists between the needs of women seeking assistance and the support they are provided. The information garnered from this study can be used to shape government and NGO policies regarding the future creation, operation, and financial and institutional support of domestic violence shelters in Morocco.

In bringing an emic perspective to this project, I broadly define domestic violence as any incident of threatening behavior, violence, or abuse (psychological, physical, sexual, economic, or emotional) between individuals who are or have been intimate partners or family members.[13] This definition encompasses a wide range of both violent acts and assailants, a range that represents the cases I encountered in my fieldwork as well as the definitions of domestic violence offered by Moroccan shelter practitioners and residents. The definition includes single, never-married mothers, as it became clear when I discussed domestic violence with shelter practitioners and residents, that many single mothers in Morocco experience domestic violence and are often at greater risk of violence, poverty, and homelessness. In Morocco, where premarital sex is illegal and an unmarried woman's virginity is regarded as an important attribute, single mothers are often shunned by their families, threatened with violence or physically attacked, and left without options for supporting themselves and their children.[14]

My methodological approach comprised three components. I first reviewed the existing literature related to the topic. The second involved semi-structured interviews with a wide range of actors, including 14 shelter residents, 20 practitioners from shelters and women's associations, five government officials and employees, and eight professors and/or nongovernmental organization (NGO) employees and volunteers. Finally, I conducted participant observation at shelters, court tribunals, NGO-led "caravans" to rural areas,[15] and the Moroccan parliament. I lived in and regularly interacted with shelter employees and women and children residents over a period of two months to observe their daily activities and triangulate this data with the information I obtained from the other two components of the methodology.

I conducted case studies at three domestic abuse shelters: Dahlia,* the OFM* shelter, and Dar al-Umhat.*[16] The first two were outgrowths of the *centres d'écoute* (listening/counseling centers) of their organizations. After hearing about the abuse experienced by women seeking assistance from these centers, members of both these groups elected to augment their counseling services by establishing residential shelters for victims of domestic violence. Dar al-Umhat, on the other hand, filled a void left by a European NGO that had operated until the early 2000s. When the NGO ceased operations, Dar al-Umhat was founded to continue providing similar social welfare services, including nursery care and a residential shelter for single mothers.

The Dahlia shelter was a walled compound in a rural area of central Morocco. The residents were locked inside the shelter and not permitted to leave on their own (Dahlia staff members explained that this regulation was necessary for the security of the shelter and its residents), though they could leave if accompanied for a specific purpose, such as a doctor's visit. The shelter's staff consisted of a director, a judicial assistant, two social assistants, a nursery worker, a cook, a night supervisor, a part-time psychologist, and two security guards. During my participant observation period, twelve women, mostly in their 20s–30s but ranging in age from 16 to 65 years, along with ten children, lived at the shelter. The majority of Dahlia residents came from poor backgrounds; few residents had completed secondary school, and about half were entirely illiterate. Ten women were married, many before they reached 18 years of age. Two were unmarried and had been forced to leave home after becoming pregnant out of wedlock. Residents generally were limited to a six-month stay at Dahlia, although staff members shared that in exceptional cases, residents could extend the residence period.

The Organisation des Femmes Militantes, or the Organization of Activist Women, OMF,* ran a shelter in a three-story house located in a major city in central Morocco. The house was within walking distance to local shops and shelter residents were permitted to walk unaccompanied across these short distances. The shelter's staff consisted of its director and two other women who oversaw daily activities and stayed overnight at the shelter. During my participant observation period, four women and three children lived at the shelter and two prior residents had returned for the celebration of the religious holiday known as *'id al-kabir* or *'id al-'adha*. Like the residents of the Dahlia shelter, the women living in OFM's shelter were mostly in their 20s–30s and came from poor backgrounds; none had completed secondary school. Two of the women were single mothers forced to leave home; the other two were married and had escaped abusive partners. The OFM shelter placed no restrictions on the duration of stay of residents, and at the time of my fieldwork three of the four women living in the facility had been residents for over one year.

The Dar al-Umhat* (House of Mothers) shelter was an apartment located in a southern Moroccan city. Dar al-Umhat's shelter and other services exclusively targeted single mothers. Women were permitted to live at Dar al-Umhat's shelter when they were eight months pregnant and allowed to remain until their babies were 40 days old. Shelter residents were locked into the residence unless leaving the apartment accompanied by a staff member. Dar al-Umhat's shelter staff consisted of two women: the shelter director and a woman who supervised the residents overnight. Dar al-Umhat also had a larger staff in another neighborhood across town where it operated a nursery as well as a *centre d'écoute* (listening/counseling center).

When I conducted my participant observation period, three women and one infant were residing in the Dar al-Umhat shelter, although this relatively low number was attributed to exceptional circumstances. The shelter had just reopened after closure due to plumbing problems and subsequent repairs; normally the four-room apartment (living room, kitchen, bathroom and bedroom) housed at least six or seven women and their children, and at times up to ten women, exceeding its capacity. Interviews with three of the residents revealed that all had come from poor backgrounds, none had completed secondary school, and all had begun working as maids or in factories as adolescents. Two of the three were in their late teens or early 20s, and one resident was in her mid-30s. None were married, and all had fled home because of their families' reactions to their pregnancies. Prior to her arrival at Dar al-Umhat, one resident had spent several months in prison for having had sexual intercourse outside of marriage.

Practitioners' Objectives: Socio-Professional Training, Integration, and Empowerment

Shelter practitioners sought to make socio-professional training and integration significant components of the assistance they provided. Socio-professional training refers to the training that shelters seek to provide, from literacy classes to lessons in embroidery, pastry-making, and artisanal crafts that equip women with tangible skills that can be transferred into income-generating activities. Socio-professional integration refers to practitioners' attempts to find women housing and paid work to give them the option of living autonomously and financially supporting themselves and their children instead of having to return to an abusive household.

The stated intention of shelter practitioners to empower residents and provide socio-professional training and integration services is at the centre of my analysis, since these objectives underlie the public image of shelters as transformative places. The practitioners at the shelters I studied distinguished their institutions from traditional shelters of Morocco's past, which the former director of Dahlia referred to as *dar al-mazawaghat* (houses of female beggars or those that depend heavily on others).[17] Yasmina,* the director of a shelter that closed in 2011 due to lack of funding, explained the concept of *dar al-mazawaghat* as:

new and old at the same time. Refuges for domestic violence survivors used to be in central locations, close to neighborhood mosques. Men whose wives came there were judged by their communities and viewed poorly in public. The public shaming was intended as a deterrent for future violence.[18]

Yasmina asserted that these traditional shelters relied on "popular judgment" and did not employ a "human rights–based approach."[19] She stated: "It wasn't really about finding a solution or making women autonomous. It was a context that reinforced their weakness. Even though temporary physical security was achieved, nothing about a woman's mentality would change."[20]

In fact, Yasmina asserted that contemporary domestic violence shelters in Morocco are "new in their norms"[21] because shelter practitioners focus on women's personal development and professional training. She argued that practitioners not only aspire to remove residents from dangerous situations, but to change their aspirations and abilities. Thus, Yasmina asserted that modern shelters have a "different vision"[22] than the old ones. Instead of providing charity, their goal is to increase women's capacity. Her distinction between the *dar al-mazawaghat* of Morocco's past and the domestic violence shelters in operation today was shared by Latifa,* the director of the OFM shelter. Latifa expressed her desire that the shelter serve "not only as a dormitory," solely providing temporary physical security to its residents, but also as a "transformative institution."[23]

Shelter Objectives Versus Results

Statistics on the total number of Dahlia shelter residents and previous residents who were able to find employment and lodging reveal that its shelter practitioners were not meeting their objectives with regard to socio-professional training and integration, and thus empowerment (Tables 2.1 and 2.2).[24]

Table 2.1 *Dahlia residents integrated into professions annually,*
2006–2013

	2006	2007	2008	2009	2010	2011	2012	2013
Number of Shelter Residents	47	90	96	117	127	122	144	64
Number of Residents Professionally Integrated	7	10	14	21	24	14	15	10
Percent of Residents Professionally Integrated	14.9%	11.1%	14.6%	17.9%	18.9%	11.5%	10.4%	15.6%

Table 2.2 *Postshelter residence of women exiting Dahlia, 2014*

Postshelter residence	Number of women	Percent of women
Family home	31	47.7%
Husband's home	11	16.9%
Separate social structure	17	26.2%
Own home	6	9.2%
Total	65	100%

Reflected in the statistics above, Jamila,* Dahlia's judicial assistant, explained that for many of the organization's residents, returning to their husbands or families was, in fact, their only option. Without marketable skills, employment, or savings, the only way for those women to support themselves and their children was to return home.[25]

At OFM's shelter, the lack of a maximum duration of stay for residents, coupled with practitioners' approach to interacting with their residents (discussed below), increased the probability that women would not leave the shelter until years had passed, if at all, since they were not given much incentive to do so. This pattern encouraged residents' long-term dependency on the shelter and stasis in their lives and development.

In the case of the Dar al-Umhat shelter, which identified socio-professional integration as one of its priorities and in its mission statement noted that some of its residents "benefit from educational preparation for work," no such education was provided. The association's employees confirmed that all the residents who found employment worked as maids or domestic servants. That these women found employment only in this sector is problematic, especially since a study published by the National Institution of Solidarity with Women in Distress (INSAF) found that women working as domestic servants in Morocco work an average of 16 hours every day for 250 Moroccan dirhams (about $US 25) or less each month.[26]

Nora,* a Dar al-Umhat resident, explained that she regularly had observed former shelter residents go to the local mosque to beg because their wages as maids were insufficient to cover their expenses.[27] Thus, although Dar al-Umhat residents were not able to financially support themselves and their children when they worked as maids or domestic servants, the shelter did not provide them with education or job skills training that would allow them to secure better employment.

Social Embeddedness: External Constraints Facing Shelters

This section focuses on external factors affecting the work of shelters, aspects of the Moroccan state and society and international donors that limit the ability of practitioners to achieve their professed objectives. Under the overarching category of external constraints, I discuss: (1) shelters' legal insecurities, (2) shelters' resource limitations, and (3) social attitudes adverse to the shelters' work. These factors constitute aspects of the embeddedness of shelters within political and social contexts that restrict their ability to train, integrate, and empower residents.

Karl Polyani, in *The Great Transformation* (1944) was the first to use the concept of embeddedness in relation to economic markets.[28] Michael Woolcock expanded the term's application by asserting that all forms of exchange are inherently embedded in social relationships and that "embeddedness itself could take several distinct forms: Social ties, cultural practices, and political contexts, for example."[29] In their examination of the "Quality Girls' Dormitory" model of the Academy for Educational Development in Morocco, Joshua Muskin, Abdelhak Kamime, and Abdellah Adlaoui used the notion of embeddedness in relation to empowerment.[30] Other studies by Rocha, Monkman, and other researchers also addressed the personal empowerment of the individual[31] or "atomistic individual empowerment" that might be "gained through methods focused on therapy, daily living skills, [and] self-help."[32] Muskin, Kamime, and Adlaoui observe that individual empowerment cannot be disassociated from macro-level forces and particularly from institutions and individuals in positions of power. They state:

> Much of the empowerment literature ... concentrates excessively on the role of those for whom power is sought ... But the ability to obtain and exercise new-found power effectively can depend on many other factors and implies several diverse dynamics that are linked directly to the attitudes, aims, actions and decisions of those persons or institutions that have traditionally been "in control." ... In other words, empowerment is both a bottom-up and a top-down dynamic.[33]

A theoretical framework of embeddedness that breaks down the barriers between micro-level individual empowerment and broader structural forces has not been applied to domestic violence shelter contexts in Morocco. To determine its usefulness in explaining the disparities between shelter practitioners' stated goals and their tangible impact, I applied the theoretical framework of embeddedness to this research, first through a discussion of the external constraints facing shelters and then through an examination of the impacts of such constraints on internal shelter dynamics and the empowerment of residents.

The first impediment to the ability of shelters to achieve their professed objectives is the shifting (and often unclear) legal status of shelters as institutions under Moroccan law. Prior to August 2013, shelters that housed married women who had fled violent household contexts were in violation of the Moroccan penal code, which prohibited the "conscious concealment of a married woman who runs away from the authority to which she is subject (her husband)."[34] Though there is no evidence that this particular penal code provision was ever used to prosecute a domestic violence shelter or its employees, until 2013, Article 496 nonetheless had been in effect since the law's enactment in 1962.

As expressed by shelter practitioners, the relatively recent removal of Article 496 and the longstanding lack of political will to remove it reflect a political culture that remains largely unsupportive of the work of women's associations. Fouzia Yassine, treasurer of the *Association Démocratique des Femmes Marocaines*, or Democratic Association of

Moroccan Women, ADFM, demonstrated the lack of political support for services for domestic violence survivors by referencing a comparable policy change: "When the government decided to focus on family planning, we went from an average of seven children per [Moroccan] family to 2.2. Even the *'ulama* [religious scholars] got on board. Why has this same approach not been applied to protecting women from violence?"[35]

In addition, though drafted and initially debated in Parliament in 2007, a law specifically criminalizing the act of domestic violence took over a decade to be passed. Since 2007, the Ministry of Solidarity, Women, Family, and Social Development has assembled meetings and commissions related to the proposed legislation, but no formal vote was held within Parliament until March 17, 2016.[36] Much like the previous existence of Article 496, the absence of a law specifically related to domestic violence for so long was seen by many shelter practitioners not only problematic for the residents they seek to assist, but also as a signal that their social welfare mission is not entirely supported by the state.

This picture of the relationship between the national government and Moroccan women's associations, and specifically the domestic violence shelters under their purview, stands in contrast to official state rhetoric regarding the government's commitment to advancing gender equality and assisting domestic violence survivors. When I interviewed Sakina Yabouri, Director of Services in Combatting Violence against Women at the Ministry of Solidarity, Women, Family and Social Development, she provided me with a copy of the *Ikram* (Government Plan for Equality), the national plan for advancing women's rights within Morocco between 2012 and 2016. The *Ikram* calls for the "review of Act 14.05 (which focuses on setting up and managing social welfare institutions) considering ... accommodation centers for women and girls victims of violence."[37] Though this objective has an accompanying deadline of 2014, Law 14.05 has to date not been amended.[38]

Sakina Yabouri informed me that her ministry is committed to constructing and financing 40 domestic violence shelters, covering every region of Morocco, by 2016.[39] However, based on the data I was able to gather during my fieldwork, only one shelter, the Batha Centre in Fez, has been built with cooperation from the state, though not with the financial support of the aforementioned.[40]

In contrast to government support provided to shelters in many Western countries (e.g., the United Kingdom, where the organization Refuge operates 45 shelters and is financed primarily by taxpayers through the Home Office and local councils[41]), the Moroccan government has not provided funding to two of the three shelters profiled in these case studies: Dahlia and the OFM shelter. The link between the shelters' relationship with the Moroccan government and resource constraints is straightforward; no government funding means that both shelters must rely on international (and occasional domestic) donors.

Dar al-Umhat is the only one of the three shelters that receives funding from the Moroccan government.[42] As expressed by the organization's employees, however, the government's financial contributions to Dar al-Umhat have been more like symbolic gestures than meaningful, consistent support. This lack of resources was demonstrated in part by the particularly severe financial troubles the organization experienced during the time of my fieldwork. As of August 2014, the Dar al-Umhat staff had not been paid for three months, and according to Soukaina,* Dar al-Umhat's administrator, the staff had been pooling money to ensure that everyone would have transportation to and from work.[43]

Considering the insufficient to non-existent financial support from the Moroccan state, all three shelters turned to international donors. Dar al-Umhat received financial support from the Belgian government and from non-governmental organizations in Germany and Sweden. Dahlia received funding from the Danish government, as well as several Danish nongovernmental organizations. The OFM did not receive direct funding from international donors specifically for its shelter, but received financial support from such donors for its general social welfare and activism activities throughout Morocco. In addition, because many OFM members also had jobs as professors, as parliamentarians and in other fields, many donated their OFM salaries to the organization's shelter.[44]

The downside of the reliance on international donors can be illustrated by the case of a shelter that operated in Agadir from 2010 to 2011. Funded by a Spanish non-governmental organization, the shelter closed its doors when the organization was forced to withdraw from its financial commitment in the wake of Spain's economic crisis. Yasmina, the former director of the Agadir shelter, explained that the shelter was unable to continue operating without outside support.

Hostile attitudes toward shelters were demonstrated most concretely through the organized protests that surrounded them. When Dar al-Umhat opened in 2001, nearby residents took to the streets to voice their opposition to its mission. In recounting the protests, Fatima, founder and president of Dar al-Umhat, explained that when the organization was first created, local residents, whom she characterized as "very conservative," "viewed [Dar al-Umhat] negatively."[45] Aïcha Ech-Chenna, founder and internationally highly decorated director of one of the first shelters for single mothers in Casablanca, not only encountered protesters but also received death threats from religious extremists.[46]

Generally speaking, matters of sexuality, and particularly women's sexuality, are still not discussed openly within Morocco, except to cast women's sexual activity before marriage as forbidden and shameful. Meriam, Dar al-Umhat's shelter director, explained:

There are three words that you will hear all the time when a mother is talking to her daughter about sex: *'ib* (disgrace), *hashuma* (shame) and *haram* (religiously forbidden). Other than that, sex is still not talked about – it's just surrounded by judgment and taboo.[47]

These concepts *'ib, hashuma,* and *haram* inform the attitudes of shelter residents' families. Sarah,* a single mother living at Dahlia, attempted to contact her mother on multiple occasions since giving birth to her son. She said, "I hope my mom forgives me; I know my father and brothers won't."[48] At that point, Sarah's mother still had refused to speak to her because of the shame and dishonor she brought to the family through her pregnancy. Hasna, a single mother living at Dar al-Umhat's shelter, told me that her brother had threatened to kill her because she had become pregnant out of wedlock. Nora, another resident, explained that her father "considered her worthless" and rejected her as his daughter after she became pregnant[49] even though her pregnancy resulted from a gang rape by three men. Frequently, single mothers are threatened with violence and kicked out of their homes by family members. One Dar al-Umhat resident was missing an eye because of her family's violent reaction to her pregnancy.

In certain segments of Moroccan society, the onus for such abuse is placed on the woman herself.[50] Leila, the president of OFM's Agadir branch, explained that in one case she encountered, a man had poured boiling soup on his wife's chest. The burns were so extreme Leila said,

"I cried when I saw her breasts. Even two months later, they hadn't entirely healed."[51] Despite her injuries, the woman's children intervened to pressure their mother not to file charges against their father; when she did, the children testified in court that the incident had been an accident and the husband was ultimately acquitted of all charges. Reflecting on these experiences, Selma, one of Dahlia's staff members asserted, "Moroccan society still won't accept single mothers and they won't accept victims of violence who run away. They think these women shouldn't run away or get divorced. We have a lot of work to do before these attitudes are changed."[52]

Based on my participant observation in three Moroccan courts, oppositional attitudes also exist in local family courts. Mohammed, a social worker working at a southern Moroccan court, explained that most cases the court encounters involve what he termed "cultural violence." He described this in terms of violations that do not meet the legal criteria for a battery or assault conviction, that is, leaving a woman incapacitated for over 20 days, such as when a husband slaps or curses at his wife. Mohammed stated that the court discourages a woman from filing a formal complaint and instead encourages the couple to resolve their dispute independently.[53] This attitude of non-interference reflects a cultural and historical preference for confining certain familial disputes, even those involving violence, to the home.

In the discussion of legal insecurities, resource limitations, and hostile social attitudes faced by domestic violence shelters in Morocco, we observe the impacts of their embeddedness within surrounding political, economic and social contexts. When shelters must devote time and resources to battling legal authorities, lobbying for improved laws of protection, ensuring the daily feeding and clothing of shelter residents, and working to change the hostile attitudes of residents' immediate social networks and those of broader communities, it is likely that their efforts to ensure successful socio-professional training, integration, and empowerment of shelter residents will be neglected or stymied.

Isolation and Over-Personalized Care: The Internal Dynamics of Shelters

Beyond taking up their time and attention, the external constraints faced by Moroccan shelter practitioners result in their isolation and the provision of over-personalized care. The latter works to disempower residents and causes practitioners to fall short of achieving their professed objectives. As discussed above, external constraints directly result in the inability of shelters to achieve their stated goals, as legal insecurity, resource limitations and adverse social attitudes all contribute to diminishing the ability of staff to provide training, integration, and empowerment opportunities to residents. Concurrently, external constraints also lead to additional, internal constraints within shelters; as staff members face external pressures, they also feel increasingly isolated and deliver over-personalized care to residents. (Though highly personalized care may not at face value seem negative, its consequences will be explained in later sections.) The process by which external and internal constraints lead to the failure of shelters to achieve their stated goals is illustrated below:

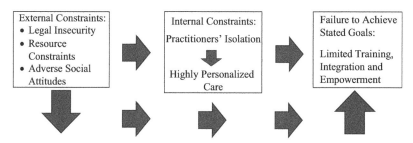

Figure 2.1 Domestic violence shelter constraints.

Striking a balance between empowering residents and maintaining discipline in any domestic violence shelter is no easy task. Why does the Moroccan context compound the challenges practitioners face in negotiating these competing interests? Dekel and Peled, in seeking to understand levels of staff burnout in Israeli domestic violence shelters, concluded that shelter practitioners experienced relatively low levels of emotional burnout in comparison to their counterparts outside of Israel. The political and social context in which Israeli shelters are embedded may explain this disparity:

Israeli shelter workers devote most of their time to delivery of direct services and are rarely involved in advocacy work ... The non-political and less complex job description of Israeli shelter workers may explain the relatively low levels of reported burnout.[54]

Though no studies have measured the levels of burnout among Moroccan shelter practitioners, Dekel and Peled's findings are significant when related to the Moroccan context. This is because shelter practitioners in Morocco also must carry out treatment and advocacy work in a political and social environment that is, from their perspective, particularly unsympathetic or even hostile to their efforts. The corresponding stress they experience may lead shelter practitioners to adopt the perspective that they are working in isolation.

At the Dar al-Umhat shelter, director Meriam explained the rationale for allowing up to ten women to live in the organization's shelter, a number that exceeds the apartment's capacity, by inquiring rhetorically, "Where else can they go?"[55] Similarly, Latifa, the OFM shelter director, justified her reluctance to expel residents from the shelter even when they violated imposed rules and regulations by pointing to the lack of alternative housing options for domestic violence survivors in Morocco.

These feelings of singular responsibility manifest themselves in an interpersonal dynamic between practitioners and residents that more closely resembles a mother–child or savior–victim relationship than one between a service provider and client. Care becomes over-personalized under these circumstances. Shelter practitioners hold the attitude that because the institution has been built with their sweat, and tears it must be governed by their rules, and domestic violence survivors seem to transition from clients to children. References to shelter directors and employees as maternal figures are common. For example, one of the residents in Aïcha Ech-Chenna's Casablanca shelter for single mothers described the founder and director as "our children's grandmother."[56]

Meriam, Dar al-Umhat's shelter director, explained the staff's understanding of the central importance of Fatima, Dar al-Umhat's founder and president, to the organization as a whole when she stated, "You can't talk about Dar al-Umhat without talking about her. She's like a volcano. We need more people like her."[57] Community members living near Dar al-Umhat affirmed this view of Fatima as the centerpiece of the organization. One individual asserted, "There won't be other leaders like her. Things at Dar al-Umhat will fall apart without Fatima."[58] Her reputation is international; Fatima relayed to me that when she visits donors in Europe, they refer to her as "the Mother Teresa of Morocco."[59]

Such statements, on the one hand, give credit to individuals who have worked tirelessly in the face of adversity to operate shelters for domestic violence survivors, work that is often neglected or even openly opposed by their government and social networks. On the other hand, this rhetoric works to reinforce the practitioners' perspective that they alone are responsible for their associations' operations, successes, and failures. When the equation of an entire institution hinges on the work of a single individual – as demonstrated through the laudatory rhetoric of shelter employees – community members, and international donors, a lack of balance results. Shelter practitioners and organization directors may find their effectiveness compromised by the sense of immutable responsibility and power.

Over-personalized care was evident in the actions of shelter staff members, too. One incident at Dar al-Umhat illustrates the power imbalance implicit in the over-personalized care. Practitioners conveyed disappointment and anger at residents' decisions in a particularly personalized and severe manner. I witnessed how Fatima arrived at the shelter and called everyone into the living room, where she proceeded to yell at the three residents, two of whom began sobbing. The night before, a dispute had broken out between these two, Hasna and Najat, because Najat had snuck a phone into the shelter in violation of the association's rules. Days earlier, upon her arrival at the shelter, I had observed Hasna reluctantly hand over her mobile phone to Dar al-Umhat's assistant. After feeling particularly isolated from the outside world, Hasna expressed her opinion to Fatima that what Najat had done was unjust, that Najat should not be allowed to have a phone in the shelter if the other residents were barred from having them.

Instead of focusing on the act Najat had committed – hiding a phone in violation of shelter regulations – Fatima began to insult Najat, referring to the fact that Najat had worked as a prostitute before coming to the shelter: "I know what you've done before coming here and I know what kind of tricks you've learned." After lecturing her, Fatima then dismissed Najat from the living room and Hasna, in tears, proceeded to express her desire to leave the shelter permanently, explaining that she felt suffocated because residents were barred from walking outside on their own. At this point Fatima became very angry, not at Najat, who had broken a rule of the shelter, but at Hasna. Fatima provocatively asked: "Where else are you going to go? Do you have a place to stay? Do you have money?" Hasna explained that she could contact her aunt and ask to stay at her home, to which Fatima responded:

If you go to stay with your aunt, is your aunt going to accept you? Will she allow you to live with her? Even if you weren't pregnant, she'd probably see you as a burden, and on top of that, you're going to have a baby. You and I both know there's no justice for women in Morocco.

Hasna insisted that she did not want to continue living with people like Najat (whether she was referring to individuals who violated shelter rules, had been prostitutes, or something else was unclear), to which Fatima said in turn, "Well, you need to get used to it, because you're going to be living with people like her and worse going forward. It's your parents' fault for not raising you to be prepared to get along with people."

This incident illustrates the over-personalized dynamics evident at Dar al-Umhat. In lecturing and referring to the lack of support Hasna received from family members because of her pregnancy, for example, Fatima emphasized Hasna's dependency on Dar al-Umhat and its services and enacted the underlying hierarchy between staff and residents inherent within any shelter context. By yelling and engaging in personal attacks regarding Najat's previous work as a prostitute and the poor child-rearing skills of Hasna's parents, Fatima positioned herself as a disciplinarian/mother rather than a professional service provider.

I observed that the impact of practitioners' manner of addressing shelter residents, combined with particularly stringent rules and regulations, had the effect of disempowering shelter beneficiaries. Hasna for example, explained that her psychological stress stemmed from her inability to devise a plan for financially supporting her baby: "I want to keep the baby, but I don't know if I can survive and pay for everything. I don't know who is going to hire a single mother."[60] When I asked residents whether they had heard success stories about previous Dar al-Umhat beneficiaries who had gone on to find jobs, all responded in the negative. One emphasized that she had watched other single mothers, though employed at low-level jobs, go to the local mosque to beg. These examples point to a disempowerment of Dar al-Umhat beneficiaries, even with respect to their ability to raise their own children, one that seems connected to the dearth of positive encouragement from shelter practitioners. In fact, Dar al-Umhat's approach may in effect encourage the opposite of what the organization claims to ensure, that is, single mothers feel incapable of raising their children and become even more inclined to give them up for adoption or abandon them.

Though less severe in their treatment of shelter residents, the Dahlia shelter also institutes a rigid hierarchy between employees and residents that results in the disempowerment of residents with strict rules and regulations concerning residents' movement, daily schedules, and parenting decisions. For example, Dahlia has an organized system of regulating women's parenting, to "correct their behavior," according to Selma, one of Dahlia's staff members.[61] Posted on the wall of Dahlia's kitchen is a chart with each woman's name and a series of green checks and red crosses next to each one. Whenever staff members observe a resident "being a good mother," by playing with her children or being affectionate toward them, the resident receives a green check, and such checks can be accumulated for a larger reward. When a resident is observed treating her children poorly (based on practitioners' subjective determination) such as by yelling or being physically violent toward her children, she receives a red cross, and after a certain number of crosses are accumulated, the resident is punished, usually by having to perform additional chores. While having lunch one day, for example, I observed the chef yell at a resident (permitted even though residents themselves are discouraged from yelling at their own children) for feeding her child yogurt, because her child was deemed too young to consume it. The system of rewards and punishments at the Dahlia shelter is complemented by educational sessions on parenting conducted by the shelter's psychiatrist and nursery director. In my observations, these sessions seemed comparable to the parenting classes identified by Harnett and Postmus as a form of social control.[62]

On the other end of the spectrum from practitioners at Dar al-Umhat, those at the OFM shelter tended to err on the side of imposing fewer rules and regulations and interacting with residents in a maternal manner that more closely resembled coddling rather than "tough love." OFM practitioners expressed the same awareness that without their services, residents would risk homelessness or other precarious circumstances. However, instead of adopting the attitude that all residents should be compelled to agree to their terms, OFM practitioners decided to tolerate at times flagrant violations of rules and regulations to avoid expelling residents from the shelter. A severe example occurred when

Raja* a resident at the OFM shelter, put rat poison in another resident's juice. Fortunately, the latter was unharmed. Though OFM practitioners understood the danger of Raja's actions, she was not immediately expelled from the shelter.

Such lack of consideration for the welfare of all shelter residents coupled with the absence of a residency time limit creates dependency as some stay up to four years. Furthermore, residents have few incentives to abide by internal rules and regulations, even those that ensure the minimal safety of other residents. Even though the interpersonal approach at OFM manifests itself differently from that of the other two shelters, the inherent problems stem from the same cause – the embeddedness within a particular environment – and produces the same effect, namely the disempowerment and even endangerment of shelter residents. With little incentive to leave a shelter, OFM residents are unlikely to elect to live independently, financially support themselves and their children, and exercise autonomy.

Conclusions

Domestic violence survivors such as those introduced in this chapter – from Nora, who had been gang-raped, to Najat, who had worked as a prostitute – arrive in shelters after experiencing physical violence and emotional trauma not only at the hands of family members who have shunned, threatened, and physically beaten them, but also at the hands of the Moroccan state and society at large. Women enter domestic violence shelters as a last resort, in need not only of a safe haven, but of the tools and encouragement required to transform their lives.

At the time of this study, however, the transformative capacity of the OFM, Dahlia, and Dar al-Umhat shelters was demonstrably limited by their embeddedness within the social and political contexts that perpetuate the forms of violence committed against their residents. The diversity of forms that the mother–child or savior–victim dynamic can take reflects the over-personalized care that shelter practitioners provide within this Moroccan context. Nonetheless, this level of care by practitioners is linked to their embeddedness in Moroccan social and political contexts that foster feelings of isolation, regardless of the decisions made by shelter directors and staff members. Whether discipline or leniency in the face of flagrant violations of shelter rules, practitioners act more as willful mothers to children than as service providers delivering institutionalized assistance to clients. Thus, whether they are the objects of severe forms of social control or individuals who grow dependent on shelter services with little incentive to integrate into society, such practices disempower shelter residents and limit practitioners' effectiveness in achieving their stated goals. The findings of this study, then, call into question the degree to which shelters as institutions are truly "transformative," despite the rhetoric put forth by shelter practitioners, the Moroccan government, and the international community concerning Morocco's advances in gender equality.

Endnotes

For confidentiality purposes, the names of most shelter practitioners, residents, and government administrators referred to in this chapter, as well as the names of the shelters themselves, have been changed. To indicate use of a pseudonym, I mark a name with an asterisk in its first usage.

1 The revised text is referred to as the Moudawanat Al-Usra (Family Code). Throughout this chapter, I will only discuss the revised version of the law and will use a short form, "the *Moudawana*," to refer to it.

2 "Civil society." World Health Organization. Available at www.who.int/trade/glossary/story006/en/ (accessed 21 March 2016); Sandberg, E. and K. Aqertit (2014). *Moroccan Women, Activists and Gender Politics: An Institutional Analysis*. London: Lexington Books, p. 45.

3 Ibid, p. 88.

4 "Morocco activists target 'marriage rape law.'" *Al Jazeera*. Available at www.aljazeera.com/news/africa/2012/04/201248101924221302.html (accessed 1 April 2015).

5 Sandberg and Aqertit, *Moroccan Women*, back cover.

6 Exceptions include M. Benradi et al. (2007). *Le code de la famille: Perceptions et pratique judiciaire*. Fez: Friedrich Ebert Stiftung and K. Zvan-Elliott (2015) *Modernizing Patriarchy*. Austin: University of Texas Press.

7 La Ligue Démocratique pour les Droits des Femmes (2004). *La Violence à l'Encontre des Femmes*. Casablanca: Centre d'Information et d'Observation des Femmes Marocaines, p. 9.

8 "Morocco's implementation of accepted UPR Recommendations on Women's Rights." The Advocates for Human Rights and Mobilising for Rights Associates. Available at www.theadvocatesforhumanrights.org/uploads/morocco_human_rights_council_women_s_rights_june_2014_english.pdf (accessed 15 December 2014).

9 Sharabi, H. (1988). *Neopatriarchy*. Oxford: Oxford University Press, p. 4. Sharabi conceptualises neopatriarchy in this way: "... over the last one hundred years the patriarchal structures of Arab society, far from being displaced or truly modernized, have only been strengthened and maintained in deformed, 'modernized' forms." In doing so, Sharabi explains neopatriarchy as the continuation of a system of male domination in the public and private spheres.
10 Sharabi, *Neopatriarchy*, p. 154. In Abdelrahman, M. (2004). *Civil Society Exposed: The Politics of NGOs in Egypt*. Cairo: American University in Cairo Press, Abdelrahman articulates the opposite, arguing that civil society organizations in fact reproduce the inequalities in (Egyptian) society.
11 Boy, A. and A. Kulczycki (2008). "What we know about intimate partner violence in the Middle East and North Africa." *Violence Against Women*, p. 65.
12 See endnote 8.
13 "Emic and Etic Approaches." Foundations of Qualitative Research in Education. Available at http://isites.harvard.edu/icb/icb.do?keyword= qualitative&pageid=icb.page340911 (accessed March 21, 2016).
14 INSAF (Institution Nationale de Solidarité avec les Femmes en Détresse) (2010). *Le Maroc des Mères Célibataires*. Casablanca: INSAF and UN Women, p. 6.
15 The term "caravan" refers to trips that NGO employees and volunteers take to rural areas in Morocco in order to disseminate information and supplies related to literacy, health and civil rights.
16 The conclusions reached based on this sample should not be taken as representative of all domestic violence shelters in Morocco.
17 Interview with Dahlia's former director. August 28, 2014.
18 Interview with Yasmina (name changed). September 2, 2014.
19 Ibid.
20 Ibid.
21 Ibid.
22 Ibid.
23 Interview with Latifa (name changed). October 3, 2014.
24 These figures were provided by Dahlia's social assistants based on the shelter's internal records. The figures provided here likely differ from those collected from shelters in developed country contexts, where many shelters' staff are able to focus some of their efforts on helping residents to access public assistance.
25 Interview with Jamila (name changed). September 23, 2014.
26 INSAF, *Le Maroc des Mères Célibataires*, p. 26.
27 Interview with Nora (name changed). September 11, 2014.

28 Polyani, K. (1944). *The Great Transformation*. Boston: Beacon Press.
29 Woolcock, M. (1998). "Social capital and economic development: toward a theoretical synthesis and policy framework." *Theory and Society*. Vol. 27, No. 2, p. 163.
30 This initiative was implemented jointly by USAID and the Moroccan government in an effort to increase rural girls' school attendance beyond the primary level. The authors conclude that the Moroccan state's support of and participation in this project was central to its success, providing an example of macro-level forces' importance for individual empowerment initiatives.
31 See Rocha, E. (1997). "A ladder of empowerment." *Journal of Planning Education and Research*. Vol. 17, No. 1, pp. 31–44; Monkman, K. (2011). "Framing gender, education and empowerment." *Research in Comparative and International Education*. Vol. 6, No. 1, pp. 1–13.
32 Muskin, J., A. Kamime and A. Adlaoui (2011). "Empowered to empower: a civil society-government partnership to increase girls' junior secondary school outcomes in Morocco." *Research in Comparative and International Education*. Vol. 6, No. 1, p. 130.
33 Ibid.
34 "Portant Approbation du Texte du Code Pénal." Adala Maroc Portail Juridique et Judiciaire du Ministère de la Justice et des Libertés du Maroc. Available at http://adala.justice.gov.ma/production/legislation/fr/penal/Code%20Penal.htm (accessed December 12, 2014).
35 Interview with Fouzia Yassine. September 17, 2014.
36 Etezadi, D. "Why domestic violence still plagues Morocco." *Newsweek*. Available at www.newsweek.com/morocco-domestic-violence-not-crime-438595 (accessed October 4, 2016).
37 "ICRAM Government Plan for Equality, 2012–2016." Ministry of Solidarity, Women, Family and Social Development. Available at www.social.gov.ma/MdsfsFichiers/pdf/ikram_anglais.pdf (accessed January 15, 2015).
38 Ibid.
39 Interview with Sakina Yabouri. September 18, 2014.
40 "Modelisation du Centre Multifonctionnel Batha pour l'Autonomisation des Femmes Victimes de Violence Basée sur le Genre." MDG Achievement Fund. Available at www.mdgfund.org/publication/mod-lisation-du-centre-multifonctionnel-batha-pour-l-autonomisation-des-femmes-victimes- (accessed July 15, 2014).
41 "Funding to strengthen accommodation based specialist to domestic abuse service provision." Department for Communities and Local Governments. Available at www.gov.uk/government/publications/funding-to-strengthen-accommodation-based-specialist-domestic-abuse-service-provision (accessed January 15, 2014).

42 Dar al-Umhat receives funding through the National Initiative for Human Development, established by King Mohammed VI in 2005. When asked whether their concerns regarding legal insecurity were assuaged through the King's financial support of the shelter, Dar al-Umhat employees insisted that they nonetheless remain vulnerable under the law and require more legal protection.

43 Interview with Meriam (name changed). September 10, 2014.

44 Interview with Latifa (name changed). October 3, 2014.

45 Interview with Fatima (name changed). September 10, 2014.

46 "Moroccan single moms cope with hostility, shame." YouTube video, 6:13. Posted by Worldfocus. Available at www.youtube.com/watch?v= VYDwU9S21Gc (accessed September 9, 2009).

47 Interview with Meriam (name changed). September 10, 2014.

48 Interview with Sarah (name changed). September 26, 2014.

49 Interview with Nora (name changed). September 11, 2014.

50 Social attitudes held by segments of Moroccan society are certainly not exceptional in this regard. Studies conducted across a range of national contexts conclude that the blame continues to be placed on victims of gender-based violence for the crimes committed against them. See Nayak, M. et al. (2003). "Attitudes toward violence against women: a cross-nation study." *Sex Roles*. Vol. 49, No. 7–8, pp. 333–42.

51 Interview with Leila (name changed). September 5, 2014.

52 Interview with Selma (name changed). September 26, 2014.

53 Interview with Mohammed (name changed). September 2, 2014.

54 Dekel, R. and E. Peled (2000). "Staff burnout in Israeli battered women's shelters." *Journal of Social Service Research*. Vol. 26, No. 3, p. 73.

55 Interview with Meriam (name changed). September 9, 2014.

56 See endnote 47.

57 Interview with Meriam (name changed). September 9, 2014.

58 Interview with community members near Dar al-Umhat. September 9, 2014.

59 Interview with Fatima (name changed). September 12, 2014.

60 Interview with Hasna (name changed). September 11, 2014.

61 Interview with Selma (name changed). September 26, 2014.

62 Hartnett, H. and J. Postmus (2010). "The function of shelters for women: assistance or social control?" *Journal of Human Behavior in the Social Environment*. Vol. 10, No. 2, pp. 289–302.

3 Reforming Gendered Property Rights

The Case of Collective Land in Morocco

YASMINE BERRIANE

Introduction

This chapter aims at contributing to the literature on the struggle to achieve women's rights in North Africa and the Middle East.[1] The focus here is on the changes in women's property rights in Morocco as they are unfolding today, in a context marked by an intensified commodification of land and the emergence of protest movements like the Soulaliyate (from *soulala*, meaning the bond that unites members of an ethnic community) women's movement that started in 2007. This analysis particularly addresses the legal and normative references (including universal human rights, Islamic law, and customary regulations) used to legitimize the inclusion of women among the lists of those entitled to benefit from collective land. Both the gendered character of collective land regulation, as well as the means by which the Moroccan Ministry of the Interior justifies the obligatory inclusion of women among beneficiaries, is examined. Further, I highlight the case of the *Mehdawa* community, which possesses collective land in the surroundings of the coastal city of Mehdia, in order to illustrate how its male delegates have legitimized the implementation of new ministerial directives at the local level by re-adapting arguments put forward by the State.

An extensive literature on women's rights in North Africa and the Middle East has developed over the last two decades, with a focus mainly on the issue of family law. This literature has focused on the State's role in the making of this legislation, its impact on women's lives (via the study of judicial disputes, for instance), and processes of reform, especially in regard to the development of women's rights movements and decades-long advocacy for changes in legislation that disadvantages women.[2] Few scholars have paid attention to women's property rights within "the complex and distinctive forms of land tenure and land rights found in Muslim societies."[3] This gap is all the more surprising given that property rights in these societies have long been gendered and based on unequal access to land ownership for men and women. Moreover, global trends of increased privatization and wholesale land purchase in the Global South have exacerbated and reinforced such inequities.[4] These developments have generated protest movements and incited some governments and international organizations to take measures to reform land laws. For the most part, however, such reforms have generated more criticism than actual effects.[5] This chapter, then, represents a contribution to the literature on women's rights in North Africa and the Middle East by examining changes in women's property rights as they continue to unfold within a context marked by an intensified commodification of land. More particularly, it provides an analysis of regulations recently introduced by the Moroccan government to give its women citizens the right to benefit from collective land.

In Morocco, unequal access to land ownership is, for the most part, grounded in customary practices as well as in *shari'a* based inheritance regulations that set a lower inheritance share for women than men.[6] The unequal distribution of Moroccan land resources varies based on the status of the land in question. As in other Muslim majority countries, different types of property can indeed be distinguished in Morocco: first, individually owned property (referred to as *melk*); second, the private domain of the State; third, properties referred to as *habous*, which is an "institution of Islamic law in which a property is removed from the legally-defined marketplace through its reconstitution for use by religious, charitable, humanitarian, social, and even public arts organizations;"[7] fourth, collective forms of property that are of two main types. The first type is called *ard guish* and refers to land that belongs to the domain of the Monarch but which "the monarchs of the ruling dynasties of Morocco had granted, by way of usufruct, to tribal groups in return for the supply of armed troops, which the monarch used in the suppression of dissident tribes."[8] The second type of collective land is called *ard al-jumu'* and is regulated by a Royal Decree (*Dahir*) that was introduced in 1919, during the French Protectorate. According to this decree, this type of collective land belongs to "ethnic groups, tribes, or villages," which have the right to manage and use the land collectively under the supervision of the Ministry of the Interior.

Today an estimated 15 million hectares[9] of Moroccan land are subject to this latter status. This land tenure system is based on a combination of customary regulations, of religiously inspired law, and of positive law, that refers to state-sanctioned legislation, that does not take its primary sources from religious law and that was introduced during the period of the French Protectorate (1912–1956). Until very recently this tenure system was clearly gendered: land was almost exclusively distributed among the male heads of families. Women generally have remained excluded from actual ownership of this type of land – until recently.

This chapter on gender-based changes in land rights distribution in Morocco focuses mainly on the recent introduction, via ministerial circulars, of state-led measures aimed at giving women the right to benefit from collective land properties like their male counterparts. Moreover, because these government directives represent a break with previous norms, a deep understanding of the government's intention requires an analysis of the manner in which the Ministry of the Interior justified its intervention in an area previously managed by communities. How did state officials justify the introduction of new rules that went against predominant local practices? How were these justifications readapted by local delegates to make them more palatable to the members of the communities owning collective land? What are the concrete implications of this process of adaptation within affected communities?

Using actual examples collected in the areas surrounding the cities of Mehdia, Kenitra, and Meknes, I first illustrate the gendered character of the land tenure systems applied to collective lands in Morocco prior to the changes made by the Ministry of the Interior.[10] Next, I show how the ensuing gender inequalities were exacerbated when the cession[11] of collective land properties to private or public owners intensified in the late 1990s, and how this inequity led to protest actions by the Soulaliyate Movement, a women's movement demanding equal land rights for men and women. In the third section I describe the measures implemented by the Ministry of the Interior to give women the right to benefit from collective land properties, with a focus mainly on the arguments put forward by the Ministry of the Interior to justify the need for women to have the same property rights as men. In the final section, I focus on one particular case study, that of the *Mehdawa* community, which possesses collective land in a semi-urban zone surrounding the city of Mehdia. This case analysis helps to shed light on how the delegates of this community justified a break from former customary practices in response to directives of the Ministry of the Interior.

Gender and Collective Lands: The Exclusion of Women from the Right of Use

The system regulating collective lands puts customary regulations (*'urf*) at the center of the governance of land distribution and conflict resolution. Defined and applied by delegates (*nuwwab*) of each community, these customary regulations vary from one community to another. Despite these differences, a common principle remains: The right of exploitation and usufruct[12] relating to land is generally granted only to male heads of the families.[13] These gender restrictions originated in practices in place in Morocco before it became a French protectorate, but were expanded and rigidified following the Royal Decree of 1919. This decree did not explicitly exclude women from the right of use, but specified that the main beneficiaries of collective land were to be the "heads of the family," a terminology that supported the notion that the "head of the family" refers to a male individual. In 1957, the Ministry of the Interior issued a ministerial circular to standardize the conditions for the sharing of collective lands. In it, "heads of families" were defined as "men married for at least six months, or the widows of members of the collective who have at least one child." This addition extended the status of "head of the family" beyond men but it still perpetuated the notion that the head of the family, by default, must be male, since it was not until his death that his spouse could legitimately claim such status.

Today, the ways in which women are excluded from the rights of exploitation and usufruct of collective lands can vary from one community to another. In the *Haddada* community, for example, which owns collective lands on the outskirts of the city of Kenitra, Rkia, the main representative of the women of the *Haddada* community, described the gender difference in access to land rights:

The tradition was like that ... when a boy got married, he received his share. A girl would receive nothing. Before, the girls of the tribe would often marry boys of the tribe. So, as the boy took his share, the girl would also benefit. A girl who didn't marry would stay with her father. And if she did marry, and lost her husband and only had daughters, she'd lose everything. There'd be nothing left for her, not even her land. The only thing they would do for her is leave her the house and garden, if she had one...But there's no way they would ever give her any land to cultivate.[14]

Among the Ouled Rahhu tribe members, who own land near the city of Meknes, women inherit a third of the olive trees that belonged to their father. In other communities, such as that of the *Mehdawa* community, who have collective land near the city of Mehdia, the widow of a landholder can receive the share belonging to her son, if the son is still a minor. According to Mennana, who represents women of the *Mehdawa* community, "if I have a son who is still very young when his father dies, then at harvest time, they will give me the child's share ... If a woman has no children, she receives nothing."[15]

In this case, the women of the community, especially those who are single, widowed, or divorced, can benefit indirectly from a share of the agricultural yield through their family connection to a male community member (father, brother, or uncle). This indirect access to usufruct was based on intra-community, or more precisely, intra-familial solidarities. Yet, it must be emphasized that this form of solidarity often depends on the goodwill of the other members of the community, especially the family. In certain cases, they may refuse to give a share to women. Even in cases where customary practices would grant a share of the land to the daughters of the deceased, the brothers may refuse to comply, as happened in the case of Fatema, a female farmer originally from the Ouled Rahhu community. She recounted:

When my father died, I went to demand my share from my brother. He told me: 'You have no right to anything, I bought all of our father's land from him.' But how can you buy collective land? I went to see the *qayd*.[16] He chastised my mother, told her: '*You* should have shared the land between your children.' My mother refused and took my brother's side ... My husband is from our tribe...He and his brothers gave their sister the same amount that they received, 17 olive trees each. They shared it all equally![17]

Though limitations on women's access to collective lands was inherent in the system regulating this form of ownership, the phenomenon took on a whole new dimension when the commodification of collective lands started intensifying at the end of the 1990s. This shift led to the emergence of a women-led protest movement in 2007.

The Soulaliyate Movement: Protesting Women's Exclusion From Land Rights

Indeed, collective lands represent a veritable reservoir of property that is increasingly being commodified. Although the Royal Decree of 1919 stipulated that collective lands are "indissoluble, inalienable, and unseizable," subsequent legislation introduced rules and exceptions allowing their cession or rental.[18] Pressure from population expansion and increased large-scale economic projects have accelerated the cession of collective lands to private and public owners, either in the form of a long-term lease or definitive transfer of ownership. Communities have received various forms of compensation in exchange for their land, such as development or infrastructure projects that benefit the whole community or material compensation such as money or plots of land with facilities. Such material compensation is distributed among those identified by the community as beneficiaries. The exclusion from this process of certain segments of the local population has given rise to various kinds of conflict within communities with collectively owned land.

Qasbat Mehdia, a neighborhood of the city of Mehdia located a few kilometers from Kenitra on the Atlantic coast, provides an example of such dealings. Property developers saw the land that was collectively owned by the *Mehdawa* community as highly desirable, with potential for tourist development and housing projects. The representatives of the collective agreed to cede it in three stages, between 2002 and 2010. In exchange for the more than 350 hectares of land sold, beneficiaries in Qasbat Mehdia each received two plots of land with facilities and a monetary sum. Almost all beneficiaries were men.

When an area of land is ceded or rented, compensation is distributed to the members of the community according to a list of beneficiaries established by the community delegates, under the supervision of the relevant local authority and the ministry of the Interior. In most cases, women were excluded from these lists. It should be specified here that although the focus of the article lies on women's rights, women were not the only category excluded from the beneficiary lists. The exclusion from beneficiary lists also applies, for instance, to those unable to prove a patrilineal ancestry linking them to the community, such as adoptees for example.

The *Mehdawa* community provides a case in point. In order to receive compensation after the sales in 2002 and 2006–2007, beneficiaries of the *Mehdawa* community had to be male, descended patrilinealy from one of the community families, and married. The marriage requirement was later replaced by the requirement of having a national identity card, which can be obtained at age 16. This measure increased the number of male beneficiaries, but, apart from a few single women whose fathers had already died, continued to exclude the majority of *Mehdawa* women.

As of 2016, the dispute between women and men community delegates continued to be notorious. In most of the communities where land has been ceded or rented to new owners and investors, the delegates have, in fact, restricted to men only the lists of individuals who can benefit from land compensation. To lend legitimacy to this practice, the male delegates and local authorities overseeing the transfers invoke local customs that exclude women from taking a share in the proceeds from the land. In certain regions where the lands in question are still inhabited and cultivated, transfers enacted in this way have had dramatically negative consequences for women. While men receive compensation allowing them to move elsewhere, women can find themselves in precarious situations of extreme poverty.[19]

As early as 2002, the *Mehdawa* women began protesting against their exclusion from these beneficiary lists. They wrote letters of complaint to public authorities, including the Ministry of the Interior, demanded intervention on their behalf, attempted to enter into direct contact with local authority agents, and lobbied for a candidate in the 2007 election who would support their cause. None of these measures were successful, however. It was in this context that the Soualiyate women's protest movement emerged in 2007 through the collaboration of human rights groups, notably the Association Démocratique des Femmes du Maroc or Democratic Women's Association of Morocco, ADFM, and local women's protest groups. The movement's protests concern women's exclusion from the right to make use of collective lands.

Originating in the Gharb region, where collective land is relatively scarce and the transferal process particularly contested, the movement spread throughout Morocco. Today, it encompasses women from communities as far afield as the southern towns of Errachidia and Ouarzazate to the central region of Meknes. The movement is notable for its protests, which have been widely covered in the media and are intended to put various local disputes on the national agenda. The most spectacular of these were two demonstrations, in 2008 and 2009, when hundreds of women, most of whom had travelled from rural areas, took to the streets outside Parliament in the capital city of Rabat to demand their right to compensation. In March 2009, six women had recourse to the Administrative Court in Rabat to question the role of the State, specifically the Prime Minister and the Minister of the Interior, as the overseer of collective land. National and international media covered these events. In addition, women's rights organizations such as ADFM assisted with negotiations by lobbying public authorities.

The Soulaliyate movement contrasts with elite-based women's activism that has dominated the Moroccan public sphere. The first women's organizations were created in the late 1940s by women from the bourgeoisie within political parties that formed the nationalist movement. They advocated for reforms such as women's access to education and the abolition of polygamy. Until the mid-1980s women's roles in public politics were limited and intrinsically linked to the political parties to which they were affiliated. With the launch of the UN Decade for Women in 1975, women's marginal position in political parties and electoral politics prompted a number of women to establish their own political structures, mainly in the form of women's associations, starting in the mid-1980s. Prominent examples include the above mentioned ADFM, a feminist organization established in 1985 by women who were actively involved in the Party of Progress and Socialism. Throughout the 1990s they were active in various fields, offering services and legal counseling to women while calling for reforms to women's rights and political participation; their main focus being the reform of the Family Code.[20] These organizations were mainly urban and led by educated middle-class women. The Soulaliyate movement, by contrast, brought to the forefront a different kind of female activist: grassroots women with limited access to education, little social capital and without much previous political experience, publicly claiming – for the first time – women's land rights.[21]

When their protests began, the Soulaliyates met violent opposition from within their communities. In Qasbat Mehdia, for instance,

protesters were criticized for turning to the Ministry of the Interior
and to a women's rights organization based in Rabat – which is the
capital and the symbol of the *makhzan* – to seek help from public
authorities and make complaints about the community. The notion
of *makhzan* "is closely associated with monarchy's inner circles of
power" and "has changed over time to mean coercive state apparatus,
as well as the education, health care, administration and economic
services the state provides."[22] This system is built upon a particular
understanding of power that sees the king as the sole supplier of
symbols of authority and the main architect of the dominant political
culture.[23]

The delegates, neighbors, and family members made clear to them
that their demands were unrealistic and would never be met since they
were attempting to change an "ancestral" custom, thus challenging the
fundamental differences between men and women. This last point is
illustrated by one Qasbat Mehdia delegate, who said, "If you ever get
your way, I'll take off my shirt and give it to you, and you give me your
tahtiyya."[24] Apart from the literal reference to clothing as a symbol of
the difference between the sexes, for this man, the idea of allowing
women to benefit from collective land would equate to a fundamental
reversal of gender roles, a possibility he deemed so unlikely that he was
willing to bet the exchange of his shirt for a dress.

Initially, the Ministry of the Interior did not oppose the commonly
used practice of excluding women from the right to use collective land.
During his appearance in a 2009 *Grand Angle* documentary broadcast
on the Moroccan state television channel 2M, the then-Director of
Rural Affairs even claimed that it was impossible for his office to
intervene against the exclusion of women in such situations, as community leaders were unwilling to change their customs. Yet in 2009,
two years after the Soulaliyate protests began, the Ministry of the
Interior published a circular granting women in the Kenitra province
the right to become beneficiaries of compensation when collective land
was purchased from a community. This was followed by two other
circulars that gradually extended these rights in geographical, legal,
and institutional terms. How did the Ministry formulate and justify
this new regulation? How did it legitimize this intervention when it
had previously relinquished such decisions to communities and their
customs? These are questions to which I turn next.

An Evolving Argument: Toward Equality as a Legislative Norm

The three circulars on women's rights to collective land originated in the Directorate of Rural Affairs of the Ministry of the Interior and were addressed to *walis* and governors, the state representatives at regional and provincial levels, respectively, who are appointed by the king.[25] No official information explains why the Ministry decided to intervene in favor of women's land-use rights.[26] Yet, by examining the way this intervention was legitimized and later implemented, we can gain some sense of the way the ministry framed the arguments used to justify women's rights to collective land; gradually moving from a plurality of legal references and norms to a predominant reference to universal principles of equality.

The geographic scope of the circulars expanded gradually, indicating a certain degree of hesitancy by the Ministry to establish new measures regulating the distribution of proceeds from collective land cessions. For instance, the first circular on July 23, 2009 was addressed only to the *wali* of the Gharb-Chrarda-Beni Hssen region, which includes the Kenitra province. The document indicated that the province had been chosen as a pilot area for the introduction of women into the "process of distribution of the products of collective land transfer." It is likely that the choice of Kenitra as the pilot region was based on the high concentration of women's protests there. Indeed, these protests are mentioned in this first circular. The two subsequent circulars issued by the ministry, in October 2010 and March 2012, respectively, extended the directive to all provinces.

Each circular's significance increased not only in terms of geographic area but in scope of the rights it granted. The 2009 and 2010 circulars explained that the policy changes concerned only revenue generated by the cession of collective land rights. In other words, they referred only to women's right to access revenue but not to benefit directly from collective land outside of such cases of land right cession. This approach changed in the third circular (2012), which addressed women's access to the land use rights held by male community members. This circular asserted women's right to the land itself, not simply revenue from its cession. The text distinguishes between two kinds of cases: those involving the distribution of collective land and those involving the distribution of revenue generated from the cession of collective land rights. In both cases, *walis* would be required to ensure that women benefit from the same rights and be subject to the same criteria as men. In the case of distribution of collective land among the community, there was one clause that upheld previous practices. Specifically, women would have the option to formally revoke their right to use a share of the land and transfer it to another member of the family or community.

A comparison of these three circulars sheds light on the gradual changes in the forms of argument and reference points the government used to justify the inclusion of women. Thus, the argument of the first circular was based on the one hand on the perceived gap between "customs" that exclude women as beneficiaries, and on the "developing national and international context and the general progress of women's rights in all areas" on the other. Both the protests of women citizens and the current government policy promoting women's rights were put forward as evidence of the need for change. The second circular, however, presented a different case. Although it also began by referring to the custom that excluded women from beneficiary lists, it contrasted these practices with Islamic principles, stating that:

This state of affairs is inconsistent with the law and with general legal principles, which accord a woman the same status as her brother. Islamic law promulgates the transfer of financial rights from men to women, as in the case of inheritance, *waqf*, legal donation (*al-hiba*), rights of pre-emption (*ash-shafi'a*), payment of life annuities (*al-'omra, ar-ruqba*), and other financial rights.[27]

In the time between the first and second circulars, the Higher Council of *'Ulama* published a *fatwa* (Islamic legal pronouncement) in response to the Ministry of the Interior's request for its expertise on the case of women's right to benefit from collective land property. The Council's pronouncement, published in June 2010 (a few months before the publication of the second circular), stipulated that the exclusion of women as beneficiaries of revenue generated by the sale of land was contrary to Islamic *shari'a* law. Religious law, then, was used to justify the assertion of rights for women identical to those of men concerning transfer of land and financial benefits. Turning to Islam for recourse in questioning the practice of excluding women from financial rights pitted community customs against religious doctrine. Still, the specifics of distributing these rights were not discussed, with the result that different forms of implementation can be observed within different communities

even as of 2016. In some cases, women and men are given an equal
share of land or compensation in deference to the notion of equality
codified in the Constitution. In other cases, women are given only half
a share, in deference to Islamic inheritance law.

A review of the argumentation supporting women's rights in the
2009, 2010, and 2012 circulars points to an interesting shift in content.
In the second circular referencing Islam, the Ministry introduced another
core argument, namely the principle of equality as formulated in the
Constitution and in international conventions signed by Morocco. The
Ministry referred to the idea that the exclusion of women from land
use rights is contrary to the movement towards women's rights and
equality in Morocco. To underline this point, the second circular cited
the 2004 Family Code, which gave equal responsibility to men and
women in terms of household and family management. In addition,
it mentioned various conventions ratified by Morocco (notably the
Convention of the Elimination of all forms of Discrimination against
Women),[28] and stressed the Moroccan Constitution, which stipulates
that all Moroccans are equal before the law.

In the third circular, published in 2012, all references to Islamic law
disappeared and only references to international conventions signed by
Morocco were cited. The 2011 Constitution, which had been reformed
in the intervening period, was prominent in this argument. Passages
pertaining to equality between men and women (article 19) and making
the enforcement of this principle a public task (article 6) were cited.
The disappearance of references to Islamic law in the last circular
was all the more interesting since, as Sait Siraj and Lim Hilary noted,
"Muslim governments have often sought to derive legitimacy for their
land reform or redistribution measures from Islamic first principles of
redistribution, or violation of such principles."[29] Thus, the argumentation in the 2012 circular suggests that, in this later context, references
to universal principles of equality gained more legitimacy than the
argument based on religious norms.

The Ministry's argumentation strategy also attests to a progressive
reassertion of its own role as a body authorized to enforce directives of
this kind. In the first circular, the *wali* was asked to "initiate a dialogue
with communities regarding the distribution of land revenues at the
earliest possible opportunity." By contrast, the second circular was
more authoritative in tone. The circular stated unequivocally that
male-only beneficiary lists would not be accepted. The third circular

went even further: the Ministry asserted that its directives would take precedence over those of local communities. It based this assertion on the Royal Decree of 1919, which established the Ministry's authority and the obligation of community assemblies to respect its directives (article 4) such that "the Ministry of the Interior may, where necessary, act unilaterally on behalf of the communities for which it is responsible" (article 5).

Invoking this passage from the 1919 Royal Decree helped the Ministry to confirm its control over the management of all of its territory; it stood in clear contrast to earlier Ministry pronouncements insisting on its inability to intervene in the matter and turning the decision over to local leaders in accordance with local customs. The Ministry's strong affirmation of its authority in the third circular may be explained, at least in part, by the resistance with which the first two circulars were met and the complete rejection or avoidance by many communities of the measures introduced by the first circulars. The *Mehdawa* community was one of the first to abide by the new ministerial directives.

Justifying a Change in Custom: Social Norms in Qasbat Mehdia

I now turn to the ways in which government-issued directives about land rights were reinterpreted and adapted by the *Mehdawa* community. As mentioned earlier, Qasbat Mehdia, where many members of this community live, is in the Kenitra province, the location chosen by the Ministry of the Interior, in 2009, for a pilot project on its new policy on the inclusion of women. Since the implementation of the pilot project, more than 800 women have received financial compensation, and one plot of land with facilities. How did community leaders deal with the implementation of the new ministerial policy and justify this break with previous customs? In order to explore this question, I mainly rely on interviews conducted in Qasbat Mehdia in May 2012 with the two male delegates of the *Mehdawa* community and their main deputy.[30]

The process of introducing changes to gender-based land laws unfolded in several stages, during which community leaders played key roles as facilitators and intermediaries between public authorities and community members, adapting the official directives in favor of the inclusion of women to fit their local context. The two community delegates of Qasbat Mehdia we interviewed in May 2012 were in their mid-70s and mid-80s and had represented the *Mehdawa* for several decades. The same day, we spoke with a deputy of the two delegates who was instrumental in the change process as well. The deputy, who had close relations with local authorities and had assumed his position only recently, seemed to have been the main negotiator with the local authorities. He appeared well informed about the negotiation process with local authorities and frequently interrupted his elders (the two delegates) to correct them, add details, or remind them not to "veer off the subject" or "talk politics." His role seemed therefore to be central in the process of implementing the Ministry's directives, and provided an example of the way a local government can insert itself indirectly into such communities via intermediaries whose task it is to bridge the gap between government administration and "traditional" community leaders.

According to the testimonies of the male community leaders interviewed, the process of including women on beneficiary lists began well before the receipt of the first circular in 2009 by the *then-wali* of the Gharb region, Abtellatif Bencherifa, a former university professor and expert geographer whose scholarly research focused on environmental issues, resource management, and rural development. Negotiations between him and the community leaders in Qasbat Mehdia began in 2008, indicating that the 2009 circular was an extension of a process that had begun well before. According to the male community leaders of Qasbat Mehdia, the main argument put forward by the *wali* was that the land, when sold, changed its status; it became private property, no longer subject to customary law. As such, Islamic inheritance law should come into force, allowing women to inherit a share of what was inherited by men. The community leaders admitted that they did not pay much attention to the *wali's* recommendations at first, gradually moving to the idea of a half-share by referring to women's inheritance rights in Islam, the argument put forth by Bencherifa. In a subsequent stage, however, negotiations shifted from the idea of a half-share (based on the Islamic inheritance model) to a final decision in favor of equal shares for women. Though the leaders we interviewed claimed they wished to be "innovative" and "set an example," their decision seemed to be influenced by the local authorities. Still, they had trouble convincing the larger community of these new directives:

Giving women the same as men was a big problem for our people! To convince them, we had meetings on a small scale, in cafés. We would explain to the men that one day we were going to include the women, so that they could benefit [from compensation] like the men. It seemed bizarre to them ... We couldn't convince everyone, but eventually, we convinced a majority![31]

When community discussions were brought to a close in August 2009 at a final meeting of community members, two leaders signed the decision (*qarar*) drafted by the deputy. The resulting document does not mention the half-share proposition but rather the need to "respect the rights of all members of the community, whether male or female," women henceforth had the right to the same share as the men of the community.

The document stating the delegate's decision contained three justifications that replicate some of the main arguments put forward by State authorities: (1) the reforms introduced to promote gender equality in the country, such as the 2004 *moudawana* reforms, (2) the recent Ministry circulars, and (3) women's inheritance rights in Islam. In addition, the document stating the delegate's decision was framed as the initiation of a new "custom." If customs had previously been established by way of oral agreements, produced by consensus between community leaders, they would now – according to the two community delegates and their deputy – take the form of written decisions, signed and validated by the delegates. It is interesting to note that for the three interviewed *Mehdawa* leaders, it was the nature of customary law, with its flexibility and roots in consensus, that made the reform possible by bridging the gap between Islamic inheritance law on the one hand (giving women inheritance rights, but only a half-share) and the equal shares ordered by the Ministry. How did the delegates of the *Mehdawa* convince the members of the community they are representing to accept such a break with previous practices?

Economic Motivations and Reproduced Male Dominance

The community delegates in Qasbat Mehdia draw upon different arguments to justify the implementation of the new ministerial regulations. First, they equated the Ministry's circulars with the King's will to give women rights in society: "We listened to Sidna's (i.e. the King's) initiative. He gave rights to women, whether they were Soulaliyates or not. They have the right to enter parliament, to be in the police, to be pilots. So why should we not include our daughters and mothers too?"[32] This statement reminds us of the process we discussed above, in which the *wali*, as the representative of the State, played a key role as initiator. The community leader quoted here, is not only making a link between the changes in Qasbat Mehdia and those affecting the whole country, he is also linking the Ministry's circular to the royal will to introduce gender equality in Morocco. Although the ministerial circular did not have legal force, it developed into a central legal reference point that has come to be associated with the will of the King and that ought therefore to be respected.

The second argument put forward by the two delegates and their deputies to convince the members of the *Mehdawa* community is a combination of both social customs and economic justifications. As previously illustrated, the social custom of men taking care of the women in their family, which relied on goodwill, was an integral part of the normative system that provided the basis for male-only land use rights. The delegates and their deputy describe how they convinced the other male members of the community to accept the changes by explaining to them how including women on the beneficiary lists, then, was a way of respecting this custom without having to do so from one's "own pocket." A community leader illustrated this notion:

I sent my sister some money[33] and she didn't want it. She said, 'That doesn't suit me. I'd rather he pays for me when I have to go to the clinic.' (*Laughter*). But now I'm rid of her! She gives me nothing, I give her nothing. She gets the same share as me. Isn't that convenient!

An interview with another community leader revealed that this was the argument that had most weight in the negotiations with the rest of the community:

Me, for example, I'm going to get a plot of land. My son's going to get a plot, or some money. If I give something to my poor daughter, it'll be a *million*[34] cents or five thousand dirhams. So why shouldn't she get some land rather than me having to pay for her? That way, if I get a million cents, she'll get the same.

Thus, while the duty of men to take care of female family members has been removed from the 2004 Moudawana that codified equal responsibility for the (financial) maintenance of the household, it still seemed to play a central role as a practical and discursive strategy in convincing men that changes in land laws would be beneficial. Yet, for the two male delegates of Qasbat Mehdia and their deputy, it was more particularly the indirect economic benefits linked to that argument that carried the most weight. One former leader who joined the conversation with the two delegates explained, for instance, that he saw the economic implications of the strategy as significant at the household level since – given men's duty to care for women family members – the money women received would return indirectly to men.

If each of your daughters gets 10 [million cents], you'll end up with 40 million cents! You'll get more money if your daughters can get compensation too. They're your daughters. They won't know what to do with [their money] and they'll give it to you. You'll get to invest it for them to get them started.[35]

As they weighed this argument, each of the men referred to their large numbers of daughters. While emphasizing the economic advantages of including women as beneficiaries, the two delegates also highlighted the social implications of the measure, citing the numerous disputes that arise when family members must share compensation:

We sat down with one or two members of the community and we said, 'Look ... many of you have argued with your sisters. Some had even been to court over it, or they don't speak to their sisters any more. Why not think of her and give her a share? These women are your daughters, your wives, your sisters. Or do you want all of it to yourself?'

In combining gendered social norms and economic advantages as justifications for changes to land laws, the leaders reproduced hierarchies and inequalities that had hitherto prevailed. Further, their rationale had significant practical consequences. When the first beneficiary list reserved for women was drawn up, the *Mehdawa* leaders decided to include the names of more than 90 boys who were still minors. This decision was met with opposition by the women, causing several disputes in the community and slowing down the process of awarding compensation to women. In the end, however, the leaders upheld the inclusion of boys on the list, since they saw it as a way to achieve the same two-pronged socioeconomic aim that had led to the acceptance of women as beneficiaries. Including boys would, first, help to meet the needs of the most vulnerable members of the community and second, increase the number of beneficiaries in each family unit.

Based on interviews with women from Qasbat Mehdia and with ADFM representatives, the opinions of women about the implemented changes appear to be mixed. On the one hand, women see the reforms as an improvement of their previous situation, as several communities have applied the new regulations and included women on the lists of beneficiaries. Indeed, according to the Ministry of the Interior, 80,000 women received material compensations totaling approximately 350 million dirhams between 2011 and 2013, accounting for 30 percent of the compensations that have been distributed overall. Yet, in many cases, women received a smaller share than that given to men, and in some cases, women still have not received anything. Accordingly, since the new procedure was instituted, conflicts and negotiations within communities and families have multiplied all over the country and more and more cases are before courts. The Soulaliyate movement is still active, working for both more effective implementation of the new gender-based land rights regulations and a reform of the Royal Decree of 1919.

Conclusion

The findings from the interviews and analysis of documents provide insights into the gender-based changes that are emerging in the context of increased commodification of collective land in Morocco. The issue of inequality of access to collective land for women is not a new phenomenon but the intensified commodification of that land has reinforced and made these inequalities more visible, a process that led to the politicization of the issue. The issue has given rise to new protest movements throughout Morocco by women who are demanding their right to land, and is the subject of increased public awareness. The Ministry of the Interior has responded to these demands by condemning gender-based exclusionary land practices and by issuing new regulations. The official argumentation used to justify this reform shows a gradual shift in normative frame from custom-based justifications to Islamic legal references to universal principles of equality, as enshrined in the Constitution. Above all, the centrality of the state – synonymous here with the monarchy – has been instrumental in promoting social change.

While official government discourse may dismiss customary law as incompatible with modern Moroccan society, traditional systems of diffusion have also played a central role in the application of new land rights directives. Local leaders (or delegates), representing their communities, were significant agents for (re)producing customary law since the 1919 Royal Decree, and continue in this role, now tasked with implementing new gender-based land legislation. In fact, in their public discourse, *Mehdawa* leaders phrased the introduction of the new measures in terms of the flexible nature of *'urf* and continued in this vein in their negotiations with the community. Yet, although the subsequent changes produced new beneficiary practices in Qasbat Mehdia, they ultimately were accompanied by the reproduction of the same social norms that had previously justified women's exclusion from land rights.

Still, regardless of the incompleteness of these changes, they remind us that we are currently witnessing a significant shift in the normative framework for women in Morocco. Previously dominant social norms that disadvantaged women were deemed by many to be resistant to change, yet new norms are being put into place that allow for greater gender equality on such basic, important issues as land ownership. In fact, in 2014, women were named local community leaders for the first time in Moroccan history. When we began our research in Qasbat Mehdia in 2011, this accomplishment seemed unreachable in the eyes of both community leaders and politically mobilized local women. Today, in 2016, five women serve in the Qasbat Mehdia leaders' assembly. It will be interesting to observe the extent to which the entry of women into this decision-making body – hitherto reserved for men – will contribute to the transformation of established gender-based social norms.

Endnotes

1 This is a revised and expanded version of an article first published in French in 2015. "Inclure les 'n'ayants pas droit' : Terres collectives et inégalités de genre au Maroc." *L'Année du Maghreb*. Vol. 13, pp. 61–78.
2 Brand, L. (1998). *Women, the State and Political Liberalization*. Columbia University Press; Charrad, M. (2001). *States and Women's Rights. The Making of Postcolonial Tunisia, Algeria and Morocco*. London: University of California Press; Moghadam, V. and F. Sadiqi (2006). "Women's activism and the public sphere: introduction and overview." *Journal of Middle East Women's Studies*. Vol. 2, No. 2, pp. 1–7; M. Voorhoeve (ed.) (2012). *Family Law in Islam. Divorce, Marriage and Women in the Muslim World*. New York: I.B. Tauris.

3 Sait, S. and H. Lim (2006). *Land, Law and Islam. Property and Human Rights in the Muslim World.* New York: Zed Books.

4 Englert, B. and E. Dalley (eds.) (2008). *Women's Land Rights & Privatization in Eastern Africa.* Eastern African Series. Oxford: James Currey.

5 Whitehead, A. and D. Tsikata (2003). "Policy discourses on women's land rights in Sub-Saharan Africa: the implications of the re-turn to the customary." *Journal of Agrarian Change.* Vol. 3, No. 1, pp. 67–112; Tripp, A.M. (2004). "Women's movements, customary law, and land rights in Africa: the case of Uganda." *African Studies Quarterly.* Vol. 7, No. 4, pp. 1–19; Agarwal, B. (2003). "Gender and land rights revisited: exploring new prospects via the State, family and market." *Journal of Agrarian Change.* Vol. 3, No. 1, pp. 184–224.

6 Daoudi, F. (October 2011). "Droits fonciers des femmes au Maroc. Entre complexité du système foncier et discrimination." *Les Etudes et Essais du Centre Jacques Berque,* No. 4.

7 Filali-Meknassi, R. (1991). "Le Habous." *Code Agraire Marocain.* B. Négib and R. Filali-Meknassi (eds.). Kenitra: ORMVA, p. 59.

8 Mahdi, M. (December 2014). "Devenir du foncier agricole au Maroc. Un cas d'accaparement des terres." *New Medit.* No. 4, p. 4.

9 It is difficult to accurately grasp the extent of the collectively-owned land base, as these lands are not all registered and delimited administratively.

10 The documents and interviews on which this article is based were first collected, in 2011 and 2012, in the framework of a collective research project funded by the French *Agence Nationale de la Recherche.* A second set of data was collected between 2012 and 2014 as part of an individual research funded by the Zentrum Moderner Orient, and the University of Zurich. The cases studied within both research phases are located in a peri-urban context, where collective lands are taken, *de facto,* as private property (even if they maintain the legal status of collective lands). The study has focused on these cases in particular as the first protest movements have started from the Gharb region and as the first attempts to implement the new regulations introduced by the Ministry of the Interior were also observable in that region.

11 As already mentioned, collective land cannot be sold. The members of the community can only – under certain specific conditions – cede their rights for definite or indefinite times, which is different from the process of selling a privately owned property.

12 Meaning here that the families and individuals forming the community have the right to use the land for pastoral or agricultural purposes for example, they can take fruits of it, and benefit collectively from all resources it generates. Yet, they cannot legally sell the land. They can

only cede their land rights under certain conditions specified by the decree of 1919.

13 The right of enjoyment does not depend solely upon the sex of the member of the collective. Age can also be a determining factor.

14 Interview with Rkia Bellot, the main representative of the women of the *Haddada* community. November 2011.

15 Interview with Mennana Shiseh, representing women of the *Mehdawa* community. May 2012, Qasbat Mehdia.

16 Referring here to a state representative heading a rural district called qiyada.

17 Interview with Fatema of the Ouled Rahou community. July 2014, Dkhissa.

18 The transfer of land rights is by no means a new phenomenon. It dates back to the Protectorate when it served mainly as a means to appropriate collective land.

19 Regarding the *Haddada* see Deback, Z. (2009). "Femmes. Au nom de toutes les Soulaliyate." *Telquel.* No. 396.

20 A more detailed description of the development of the feminist movement in Morocco can be found in Sadiqi, F. and M. Ennaji (2006). "The feminization of public space: women's activism, the family law, and social change in Morocco." *Journal of Middle East Women's Studies.* Vol. 2, No. 2, pp. 86–114.

21 A more detailed description of the emergence and development of the coalition between the Association démocratique des femmes du Maroc and grassroots representatives of the Soualilaytes can be found in Yasmine, B. (2016). "Bridging social divides: leadership and the making of an alliance for women's land-use rights in Morocco." *Review of African Political Economy*, pp. 350–364.

22 Maghraoui, D. (2011) "Constitutional reforms in Morocco: between consensus and subaltern politics." *The Journal of North African Studies.* Vol. 16, No. 4, p. 698.

23 Tozy, M. (1999). *Monarchie et islam politique au Maroc.* Paris: Presses de Sciences Po, p. 42.

24 A traditional dress worn by women. Interview with Mennana, female representative of the *Mehdawa* women and chairman of the Ash-Shuruq association. December 2011.

25 Walis and governors are state representatives at the regional and provincial level, appointed by the king. They hold significant power and fulfill a number of functions which are not always clearly defined. Among other things, they reinforce ministerial power over local communities. While governors are appointed at the level of the province and the

prefecture, the walis are heading wilayas, which can regroup several prefectures and provinces.

26 To better understand the factors that played a role in this shift a more detailed study of the process that led to the production of these new regulations would be necessary.

27 Extract from October 2010 ministerial circular.

28 The Convention on the Elimination of all Forms of Discrimination against Women (CEDAW) was adopted by the General Assembly of the United Nations in 1979 and ratified by Morocco (with reservations) in 1993. In 2011 the Moroccan government lifted its reservations to the Convention.

29 Sait and Lim, *Land, Law and Islam*, p. 15.

30 These interviews were conducted, in 2012, with my colleague Fadma Ait Mous as part of a joint research project that focused on the Soualiyates of Qasbat Mehdia. See Ait Mous, F. and Y. Berriane (2016). "Femmes, droit à la terre et lutte pour l'égalité au Maroc: Le mouvement des soulaliyates." *Contester le droit. Communautés, familles et héritage au Maroc.* R. Hassan (ed.). Casablanca: La Croisée des chemins, pp. 87–173.

31 Interview with the two delegates of Qasbat Mehdia. May 2012.

32 Ibid.

33 He is referring to a sum of money which he was given as compensation during one of the land sales.

34 In Morocco, the currency used in daily life is often the cent (100 cents representing 1 dirham). Accordingly, 1 million equates 10 thousand dirhams.

35 Interview with the deputy of the two delegates of Qasbat Mehdia. May 2012.

4 | Micro-Credit, Gender, and Corruption

Are Women the Future of Development?

NICOLAS HAMELIN, MEHDI EL BOUKHARI, AND SONNY NWANKWO

Introduction

In Morocco there exists a general tendency to presume that women are more trustworthy than men. Accordingly, Moroccan micro-credit agencies have largely favored women. In 2006, the non-profit micro-finance organization PlaNet Finance Maroc reported that approximately 75 percent of its micro-credit borrowers were women. PlaNet Finance Maroc was created in February 2002 and is affiliated with PlaNet Finance, a French based non-governmental organization that offers financial and non-financial services. In fact, since 1996 the Zakoura Foundation – the first organization to offer micro-credit in Morocco – reported a repayment rate of nearly 100 percent due both to its intensive coaching and supervision of borrowers as well as women's better repayment practices than men's.[1]

Most micro-financing research provides theoretical arguments to explain the preference for lending to women, but very few of these are based on actual data.[2] One key rationale has been that women are perceived as less inclined toward corruption than men. This notion was challenged by the events leading up to the 2011 uprising in Tunisia, where momentum increased along with the people's growing anger against both dictator Zine el Abinine Ben Ali and also his wife Leila Trabelsi. The public despised Leila Trabelsi for her corrupt lifestyle and her involvement in a multitude of financial scandals.[3] Similarly, following the 2011 Egyptian revolution, Suzanne Mubarak, wife of ousted Egyptian President Hosni Mubarak, attracted public anger and was accused of illegally accumulating wealth.[4] (Of course, first ladies' proclivity for shoes is not unique to North Africa; Imelda Marcos and Elena Ceauşescu come to mind.) Thus, despite the widespread idea that women are less prone to corruption than men, exceptions to this rule suggest that the issue is more complex.

This chapter reports on our study of beliefs about corruption and corresponding gender differences among 200 respondents in Morocco. We surveyed an equal number of men and women in large cities of Marrakech and Rabat, as well as in the rural area of the Middle Atlas Mountains so as to collect an equal amount of data from urban and rural areas. Our sample was representative of the Moroccan population in terms of income with a slight bias toward the more educated strata of the Moroccan population. We used questionnaires to compile data containing questions that addressed differences in men's and women's attitudes toward corruption, definitions of corruption, perceptions of the causes of corruption, and perceptions of factors that are possible deterrents against corruption.

Although this research used a Post-Positivist, quantitative approach to unearth some causal relationships linking Moroccans' corrupt intention to particular socio-cultural traits, it is important to underline that the underpinning philosophy of Post-Positivism is that findings are speculative. The central tenet of Post-Positivism is that hypotheses are not validated, but are "not rejected."[5] Hence in this work we also acknowledge the fallibility of the models, hypotheses were not "validated," rather they were "not rejected." This is an important difference in particular in the case of socio-demographic factors and corruption intention. Using logistic regression, specific factors – such as age, education, and gender – were found to have a significant impact on an individual attention toward corruption. Logistic regression is often used as a predictive tool[6] for example on questions such as: What is the impact of gender on corruption intention? It would be tempting to profile "at risk" individuals based on their socio-demographics yet the consequences of doing so would be dire.

Micro-Credit and Gender

In the past decades policymakers and non-governmental organizations have seen micro-credit as a solution to developing countries' most pressing challenges. In Morocco, for example, such challenges include "poverty eradication and promoting sustainable development."[7] First designed by Dr. Mohammed Yunus for Grameen Bank in Bangladesh in the 1970s, micro-credit was seen as a means to provide credit for people who lacked collateral or a stable employment history. Since that time, governments around the world have launched similar programs to enable those at the bottom of the social class pyramid (less than \$2 per day of income) to gain access to micro-credit funding. World-wide, as of 2010 over 205 million poor people had benefited from financing from over 3,600 micro-credit institutions.[8] In Morocco alone, at least twelve micro-credit institutions were in operation in 2010, providing over 950,000 loans to people in need.[9]

Although Morocco has widely adopted micro-credit as a way to move forward, the country has remained hampered by very modest ratings on global governance indicators.[10] The World Bank defined six such indicators: Voice and Accountability, Political Stability and Absence of Violence/Terrorism, Government Effectiveness, Regulatory Quality, Rule of Law, and Corruption Control.[11] Benhlal compiled data on these indicators for Morocco from 2002 to 2012 and con-cluded that despite legislative and institutional reforms, no notable improvement had occurred in any of these six dimensions of govern-ance.[12] Further, according to Transparency International's Corrup-tion Perception Index, in 2015 Morocco ranked 88 of 168 countries, and its corruption scores rose slightly – to 36 from 39 in 2014 on a scale of 0 (highly corrupt) to 100 (very clean). By comparison, in 2015 Denmark ranked first with a score of 91, Algeria, a neighbor of Morocco, ranked 88th with a score of 36, and Somalia ranked 167th with a score of 8. In addition, on the Global Corruption Barometer, which measures citizen's perceptions and experiences of corruption, 76 percent of Moroccans surveyed in 2015 believed that corruption is a serious problem in their country.[13]

Nevertheless, the general belief in Morocco that women are less corrupt than men, along with the greater tendency of Moroccan women to repay loans, has led not only to more targeting of women by micro-finance lenders but to positive outcomes for the country's economy. Recent findings have confirmed this relationship between micro-credit loans to women and improved economic growth. Research-ers D'Espallier, Guérin, and Mersland, for example, used a dataset of 379 micro-finance institutions from 73 countries and discovered a clear gender bias in most institution's lending procedures, with 73 percent of the loans made to women. Of these 379 institutions, 160 declared they favored lending to women.[14] Various empirical studies support this same preference. For example, Khandker[15] found:

A 100% increase in the volume of borrowing to a woman leads to a 5% increase in the per capita household non-food expenditure and a 1% increase in the per capita household food expenditure, whereas for men such an increase results in only a 2% increase in non-food expenditures and a negligible change in food expenditure.[16]

A 2007 World Bank report similarly concluded, "A dollar loaned to a woman seems to have a greater development impact than a dollar loaned to a man."[17] This observation indicates that women are more likely to participate in projects that benefit society than men.[18] Men also have been found to be less reliable in debt repayment.[19] At the launch of the Grameen Bank, for example, the majority of customers were men, but due to poor repayment practices the bank swiftly moved to women as recipients of their loans. The bank's financing of Bangladeshi women grew from 44 percent in 1983 to 95 percent in 2001.[20]

Some empirical research in Morocco and elsewhere suggests that the reasons why women beneficiaries are better able to repay their loans is because they are generally involved in activities with shorter life cycles[21] and take loans that are within their repayment capacities.[22]

Gender and Corruption

Transparency International has defined corruption as, "the misuse of entrusted power for private gain" and differentiates between "according to rule" and "against the rule" corruption.[23] The former occurs when one pays a bribe to receive preferential treatment for something that a bribe receiver is required to do by law (facilitation payments). The latter occurs when one pays a bribe to obtain services that the bribe receiver is prohibited from providing. In both cases corruption is often perceived as the only way for entrepreneurs to accomplish business objectives and circumnavigate highly bureaucratic systems, as noted by researchers Tulchin and Espach[24] in Latin America and Vorley and Williams[25] in Bulgaria and Romania.

Though models of organizational behavior have variously attributed corruption to bad organization, bad groups, or bad individuals, one may assume that central to corruption is the desire to increase monetary income or gain privileges regardless of legality. Thus, an individual becomes corrupt when the gains from a corrupt practice outweigh the costs,[26] which can be economic, social, and/or moral. Researchers have investigated the relationship between corruption and a wide set of

variables – from economic to legal to religious – in an effort to identify causes. In one key paper, Lambsdorff explored the correlations
between corruption and per capita GDP, inequality, inflation, government size, freedom of speech, religiosity, gender, and other factors.[27] In
regard to the relationship between corruption and gender, Lambsdorff
drew on a study by Swamy, Knack, Lee, and Azfar and another by
Dollar, Fisman, and Gotti – to conclude that an increased role for
women in society would lead to a reduction in corruption.[28] As Dollar
and colleagues stated, "a one standard deviation increase in [female
participation in government] will result in a decline in corruption ... of
20 percent of a standard deviation."[29]

Likewise, in 2007, Transparency International reported that men are
more likely to be the actors (and victims) of corruption than women.[30]
Research has shown, for example, that men are more individualistic
and women are more socially oriented. Eckel and Grossman argued
that women might possess higher moral and ethical principles than
men.[31] Similarly, Branisa and Ziegler[32] concluded, "If one accepts that
women are less selfish and align their actions on higher moral standards than men, having women in important political and economic
positions might lead to less corruption in a country."

In their investigation spanning 66 countries, Dollar and colleagues[33]
found a negative relationship between gender and corruption: the
higher the percentage of women in the labor force and in parliament,
the less the corruption level. They also discovered that gender correlates with overall development (as proxied by per capita income) and
with other indicators of political openness, such as the extent of civil
liberties, average years of schooling, trade openness, and low ethnic
fractionalization. They concluded that the presence of women in parliament, in particular, had a significant impact on the extent of corruption because "women may have higher standards of ethical behavior
and be more concerned with the common good." Similarly, after
analyzing data from a cross-section of 68 countries in the 2009 World
Values Survey, Esarey and Chirillo found that women tended to disap-
prove of corruption more strongly than men, but only in the context of
democratic institutions. They found that women actually had similar
attitudes toward corruption in non-democratic surroundings. In the
same vein, a 2009 survey of more than 60,000 households in 60 countries by Transparency International, women were found to be consistently less likely than men to pay bribes.[34] Swamy and colleagues

analyzed the gender and corruption issue from a macro-level perspective using data from the 1981–1991 World Values Surveys, in which twelve questions among hundreds were asked to men and women about the acceptability of diverse, dishonest, or illegal acts.[35] Averaging the findings across the 18 nations surveyed in 1981 and the 43 surveyed in 1990–91, the researchers discovered a gender gap: 72.4 percent of men and 77.3 percent of women agreed that such acts are "never justified."[36]

Similar finding were reported within American corporations. Analyzing 350 firms in Georgia, Swamy and colleagues[37] found that corruption declined when women constituted a majority of the work force. Companies managed by men were more than twice as likely to give bribes to a government agency (12.5 percent of the occasions). This number fell to 4.6 percent when women were in charge. Yet why this occurred was not entirely clear. The researchers proposed that women may have fewer opportunities to fit into the "bribe-sharing old boy networks" and consequently may be less exposed to situations where they are asked to give a bribe.[38] They also speculated that women may have less personal or collective contact with the labor force, and so have not yet "learned" how to deal with corruption.[39]

An Alternate View of Gender and Corruption

Empirical research[40] has shown that "women are not necessarily intrinsically more honest or averse to corruption than men,"[41] however, women's propensity for corruption is mostly contextual.[42] Using cross-national data from 99 countries or regions, Sung concluded that the relationship between gender and corruption is caused not by women's virtues but by the contexts in which they live.[43] Simply put, in a democratic or "fairer system" there is more control over the crime of corruption and greater promotion of gender equality. Thus, when women are present in government, less corruption exists. For Sung, the statistical connection between gender and corruption is not causal but more likely "coincidental."[44]

Similarly, Goetz argued that the idea that women are innately honest and less corrupt than men is a "myth" and "anecdotal."[45] Goetz even contested the existence of a gender gap in corruption and suggested that women might utilize "informal" payments to access public services or offer sexual favors – voluntarily or under duress – instead of money. Another explanation Goetz offered for the apparent gender disparity in corruption is that in a patriarchal society, where bribery occurs in a male-dominated realm, women can serve as an enticement, and they do so via mediators who are male relatives. Such incidents, then, would be underreported by existing survey techniques and "left off the radar of corruption indices."[46]

Alhassan-Alolo also contested a gender gap in corrupt behavior.[47] Using empirical evidence – obtained from an attitudinal study of public servants in Ghana – he found that women did not prove to be less corrupt. Alhassan-Alolo concluded, "the very gender system, which is used to justify women's inclination to less corrupt behavior and subsequent integration into the public sector, could itself be the source of corruption as women attempt to fulfill their gender roles."[48] Given the relatively new status of anti-corruption scholarship, the disparate findings on the relationship between corruption and gender, and the potential influence of context, the need for more extensive research on gender and corruption, and the impact of culture – the topic to which we turn next – is clear.

The Impact of Culture on Gender and Corruption

Geert Hofstede[49] defined culture as "the collective programming of the mind that distinguishes the members of one group or category of people from others." In the 1970's Hofstede conducted international surveys of 100,000 IBM employees around the world and found correlations pointing to by-country patterns on a variety of dimensions. Ten years later Hofstede published the book *Culture's Consequences*,[50] in which he defined four main cultural dimensions: Power Distance, Uncertainty Avoidance, Femininity/Masculinity, and Individualism/Collectivism. A number of studies have highlighted correlations between these cultural dimensions and corruption. Xiaolan,[51] El Ghoul, Guedhami, and CY Kwok,[52] for example, investigated 3835 banks across 38 countries and found a higher level of corruption in banks in collectivist nations than in individualist nations.

In collectivist cultures like Morocco, the individual exists within the context of a family or a community, and is not easily separable from the extended family. Accordingly, acts of bribery may not be considered immoral since to some extent they benefit the community.[53] Collectivism alone, however, is an insufficient explanation for the gender gap in corruption. Hofstede has asserted that societies with a higher degree of masculinity,[54] such as for example Uganda, are more likely to value success, bravery, and confidence as well as material rewards for success. The "ideal" African man as defined by Bukuluki is a breadwinner, a provider to his immediate family, his wife's family, and his extended family. Corruption may therefore be considered a non-issue since through corruption one serves the interests of the community and, in return, gains social recognition from the family and extended family. Modeling corruption according to cultural dimensions may be inadequate or worse, erroneous, however. Although a collectivist society means that a high level of support between members of a community is the norm, stealing or bribery to help others contravene personal and social values of honesty.[55]

If a gender gap in corruption does indeed exist in Morocco, it has implications for micro-credit lending. In this study, we posed several research questions relevant to this issue: What gender gaps exist among Moroccans in their: (1) attitudes toward corruption, (2) definitions of corruption, (3) perceptions of the causes of corruption, and (4) perceptions of the factors that are possible deterrents to corruption?

Methodology: The Case for a Quantitative, Micro-Level Analysis

Until the mid-90s, quantitative approaches to measure corruption were rarely used. Mauro pioneered the use of perception-based measures to assess corruption.[56] Mauro based his corruption index on the survey of journalists, businesspeople and country experts about their suggestive evaluation of corruption regarding doing business in a given country.[57] Expert Perception-Based Surveys such as Transparency International Corruption Perception Index CPI have rapidly become a preferred tool of assessing corruption.[58] Today, Transparency International's "Corruption Perception Index" is one of the best-known and most widely used indexes to measure corruption.[59] The index is based on surveying the level of corruption perceived either by experts or high or middle-level business managers of international or local corporations.[60] "The index reflects the views of observers from around the world, including experts living and working in the countries and territories evaluated."[61] However, recent findings have questioned to what extent the perceptions of experts reflect the view of the common citizen.[62]

For example, Razafindrakoto and Roubaud,[63] using a common survey in eight African countries that targeted both the general population and experts, discovered that experts would systematically overestimate the weight of petty corruption. Treisman[64] explains this discrepancy by the fact that micro-level data based on experience could be noisier and unreliable. Treisman also hypothesizes that micro-level data may reflect inferences made by experts and accepted beliefs about corruption rather than actual observation by respondents. To date, there has not been much research investigating micro-level corruption using interviews and questionnaires.[65] The particularity of our research is based on micro-level data so as to directly assess Moroccan citizens' perception of corruption in their everyday reality.

Data from questionnaires need to be treated with caution, however, especially when answers to sensitive questions are solicited.[66] Researchers have argued that since the questionnaire is a self-report instrument based on hypothetical choices, an individual who has committed an act of corruption may choose to lessen his or her guilt by stating that corruption is rarely justified.[67] Others may overplay their degree of obedience to the law.[68] In the same vein, Social Desirability Theory suggests that interviewees will tend to avoid socially unacceptable responses or provide answers perceived as matching the interviewer's values system.[69] In Morocco, for example, we found that male respondents were more likely to report that they support relative gender equality with a women interviewer as opposed to opinions expressed towards a male interviewer.

Our study had two objectives. The first was to determine which arguments Moroccan citizens use to justify corruption, and the second was to identify factors that may deter respondents from engaging in corrupt acts. Focus groups, observational research and an intensive literature review were conducted to determine these factors. The investigation was designed to examine which possible values may motivate or deter an individual towards or away from corrupt behavior. To this end, we constructed a three-part questionnaire to measure both respondents' beliefs about corruption as well as their perceptions of various norms that might be used to justify intentions with regard to corruption.

In order to increase questionnaire reliability and secure more honest answers from respondents, the questionnaire minimized direct queries regarding personal participation in corruption.[70] The first part asked respondents to rate their personal beliefs about corruption in terms of possible justifications for engaging in a corrupt action on a 5-point Likert scale where 1 signified that corruption can "never be justified" and 5 signified that corruption can "always be justified." We asked the question, "According to your personal opinion what justifies corruption?" for each of a number of possible justifications: *perceived poverty, household perception* (the feeling that one's household is poorer relative to one's neighbor), *no alternative to afford life expenses, insecurity for the future, "Everybody is doing it," no trust in the government, low career advancement prospects, helping a friend, unfairness in society,* and *"It is normal to accept someone's gift."* We then gave respondents a hypothetical question asking if they would personally be willing to accept a bribe from someone or propose a bribe to an official.

The second part of the questionnaire assessed potential deterrents to corruption. Again, using a 5-point Likert scale, we asked respondents to identify the factors that were most likely to deter someone from a corrupt act. Possible factors were: *higher wages, influence of living abroad, fear of the authorities, personal and moral conviction, influence of family and friends, influence of religion, media scandals,* and *training employees.* The questionnaire also asked about who they thought was the most corrupt out of a list of choices but could also include a category not listed, and if they recently had been solicited for a bribe, and if so, if they had reported this incident to the police or an independent non-governmental organization. The last part of the questionnaire measured respondent demographics, including *level of education, age, monthly income, family status, household number, occupation, gender, marital status* and *work sector.* We also ensured utmost questionnaire reliability by computing the Cronbach Alpha measure for the 200 respondents.[71]

Data Collection and Sampling

Pilot questionnaire. A pilot questionnaire was distributed to 30 respondents in and around the city of Azrou, a middle-sized town in the Middle Atlas region of Morocco. After analyzing the results for each question, we made necessary adjustments and completed the final questionnaire used in the study.

Languages issues. In Morocco around 40–45 percent of the population communicates in one of the three main Berber or Amazigh languages, with one-third of this group speaking exclusively in Tamazight.[72] Darija, or Moroccan Arabic, is a combination of Arabic, French, Spanish, and various Berber languages, and is spoken by about two-thirds of the Moroccan population, yet there are substantial regional variants of Darija.[73] We decided to use French for the questionnaire for two main reasons. First, although three alphabets and three different scripts (Berber, Arabic, and the Roman-letter alphabet) exist in Morocco, French and Modern Standard Arabic are the two official spoken and written languages and are used in official documents.[74] Second, although Darija is increasingly used on billboards, TV, or social media it has no standard writing system, being written in a mix of Arabic and Roman alphabet.[75] Lastly, the interviewers, like many people in Morocco, are more fluent in French than in Modern Standard Arabic, both of the interviewers having studied in a Moroccan university where the main language of instruction is French.

The two female pollsters who were assigned the task of distributing the survey are both fluent in French, but being natives of the Middle Atlas region, they also speak Darija and Tamazight fluently. In rural communities, the illiteracy rate for women averages 70 percent.[76] Hence, the pollsters were often asked to translate and explain the questionnaire and record responses on behalf of the respondents in rural areas who could not read or write. The same procedure had to be carried out for respondents whose languages were only Darija or Tamazight. Distribution of the questionnaire to university students was not difficult as Moroccan universities use French as the main language of instruction.

Dress Code Issues

Regarding the interviewers' dress, Benstead[77] has rigorously demonstrated the impact of an interviewer's dress on a respondent's answers concerning religious questions, with respondents adapting their answer to suit the interviewer's appearance. Less religious answers were given to western-style dressed interviewers and more religious answers were given to interviewers wearing the hijab. Boulanouar's[78] research about the clothing of Moroccan women shows the existence of four main styles sported by Moroccan women in public:

- Western-style tight-fitting garments (Jeans, t-shirts, skirts) without headscarf;
- Western-style clothing with a headscarf/Hijab;
- Loose-fitting clothes without headscarf (i.e. clothes that do not profile the body with a headscarf);
- Loose-fitting outfits with a headscarf/Hijab.

In our case, both interviewers were women. One did not wear a Muslim headscarf while the other did. The difference in attire possibly reduced the impact of the interviewer's appearance on respondent answers. Since corruption is considered "haram," or "forbidden," by Islam[79] pious respondents may be more inclined to reject corruption more strongly in their answer than less religious respondents.

Initially, 30 questionnaires were tested with the participation of students and non-students in the local region of Ifrane. Problematic questions were reworded until they were unambiguous. Back translation, as recommended by Brislin,[80] was used at a later stage to guarantee the accuracy of the English version of the questionnaire for inclusion in this thesis.

Data Collection

In all, we received 200 completed questionnaires. We found that difference in attire (hijab versus no hijab) had no significant impact on responses. Non-probability intercept quota sampling was used. The pollsters were asked to collect answers from an equal proportion of men and women. The questionnaires were distributed in the large cities of Marrakech and Rabat, as well as in the rural area of the Middle Atlas Mountains so as to collect an equal amount of data from urban and rural areas. Marrakech and Rabat are two major Moroccan cities; Rabat is the capital of Morocco and Marrakesh is one of its major tourist destinations, with respective populations of around 600,000 and 900,000. Azrou, Ifrane, and Aïn Leuh are smaller rural towns and villages with populations of approximately 47,000, 15,000, and 5800 inhabitants in 2015, respectively.

The ages of the respondents ranged from 18 to 65. Of the total, 4.5 percent were 18–21; 31 percent were 21–30; 28.5 percent were 31–40; 20.5 percent were 41–50; and 7.5 percent were 51–65.

In terms of education level, 23.5 percent of the sample reported having a high school diploma; 19.5 percent a two-year college degree; 33 pre cent a bachelor's degree; 14 percent a master's degree; and 6 percent a doctoral degree. The sample had a somewhat higher level of education than the Moroccan population as a whole given the estimate of the US Agency for International Development[81] that only 53 percent of Moroccan middle school students continue to high school, and less than 15 percent of first grade students graduate from high school.

In regard to monthly income level, 18 percent of respondents earned less than 1,500 Dirham (dh) per month; 18 percent earned between 1,501 dh and 3,000 dh; 9.5 percent earned between 7,001 dh and 9,000 dh; and 13 percent earned 13,000 dh or more. When asked about the number of individuals in the household, 62 percent reported living in a household of 3 to 5 people and 24 percent in a household of more than 6 people. When asked to compare their household level of income, 24 percent said their households were better off than most households; 60 percent said their households were slightly better off than most households; and none said their households were much worse off than their neighbors.

Data Analysis

For the data analysis, we created three mathematical models.[82] In the first, we analyzed the relationship between socio-demographic factors (*level of education, age, monthly income, family status, household number, gender, marital status* and *sector of work*) and the respondents' willingness to involve themselves in a corrupt act or participate in such an act if offered. In the second, we analyzed the respondents' perceptions about justifiability of corruption given certain personal-societal factors: *poverty, no alternative, insecurity, everybody does it, no trust in the government, no career expectation, help a friend, unfair society, it is normal to accept a gift,* and *household perception (less better off than)*. In the third, we analyzed respondents' perceptions about factors that deter people from becoming corrupt, including *higher wages, impact of living abroad, personal conviction/ moral, influence of family, influence of religion, fear of media scandal* and *training*.

Findings

Definition of Corruption

When asked to choose one or more definitions for corruption, 174 of 200 respondents defined it as *accepting money*, while a slightly smaller number (161) defined it as *giving money*. The definitions *accepting a service* and *providing a service* also were chosen to define corruption, but by a much smaller proportion of respondents, 78 and 79 of 200, respectively. We found no significant gender difference in respondent definitions of corruption.

Who Is Corrupt?

Of the 200 respondents who answered this question, 100 chose "I don't know" and some showed obvious signs of anxiety in refusing to answer. Of the 100 who provided a response beyond "I don't know," nearly half (48 percent) perceived police officers as being the most corrupt, followed by municipal civil servants (14 percent), customs officials (9 percent), and doctors and nurses (9 percent). Respondents perceived teachers and professors (1 percent) as least likely to be corrupt.

199 answered the question about having been solicited for a bribe. Sixty male respondents (51.7 percent) and 39 female respondents (47 percent) admitted to having been solicited for a bribe. However only four respondents – two male and two female – said they had reported this demand for a bribe to a non-governmental organization like *Agence Marocaine des Droit de l'Homme* (Moroccan Association for Human Rights), a local group involved in the fight against corruption.

Gender and Corruption Intention

Respondents were asked to rate their corruption intention on a binary scale: 0 for not considering corruption at all, and 1 for potentially considering corruption. The overall corruption intention was low for both genders, but lower for women. In fact, over twice as many men (20.5 percent) as women (8.4 percent) stated that they could be tempted by corruption.[83]

A test of the relationship between corruption intention and the socio-economic factors (Table 4.1) showed significance in the model

Table 4.1 *Corruption intention by gender*

| | Corruption intention | | |
| | Mean (0 = no intention, 1 = could consider corruption | Standard deviation | Number of respondents |
Gender			
Male	0.20512821	0.40553204	117
Female	0.08433735	0.27958241	83
Total	0.155	0.36281285	200

Table 4.2 *Corruption intention by sociodemographic factor*

Corruption intention	Coefficiency	$P>|z|$	%
Level of education	−0.28340	0.037	−24.7
Age	−0.07107	0.714	−6.9
Gender	0.99989	0.033	−63.2
Household number	−0.00520	0.987	−0.5

overall (p value = 0.0336 < 0.05). Level of education and gender were most significantly correlated to corruption intention, but inversely. Thus, as the education level of a respondent increased, his or her intention to accept corruption decreased (by 24.7 percent). Regarding gender, based on the binary variable we created (0 = Male, 1= Female) we found a negative correlation between gender and the intention to accept corruption. The probability for a female respondent to consider corruption was 63.2 percent less than that of a male respondent (Table 4.2).

Causes of and Justifications for Corruption

The factors most frequently identified as justification for corruption were *helping a friend* and *accepting a gift*. Although we found no significant gender difference for *helping a friend*, men more than women rated *accepting a gift* as a justification (F(1,195) = 3.92,

p value =0.0491). The factor least cited as justification for corruption was *everyone does it*. Men more than women, however, rated this as a justification (F(1,198) = 5.01 p value = 0.0264).

Corruption Causes and Justifications

The second model studied the relationship between societal factors and the tendency toward corruption. Using logistic regression we independently tested the correlation between corruption and gender.

For women, the overall model was significant (Prob > Chi2 = 0.0174), indicating with 95 percent confidence that at least one of the independent variables contributed to predicting corruption intention (see Table 4.3). For women, *accepting a gift* and *household perception* were factors correlated to corruption intention. Women who believed that accepting a gift is a cultural norm and women who felt that their household is less well-off had a greater corruption intention, by 507.2 percent and 97.5 percent ($P>z < 0.05$), respectively.

For men, the overall model was significant. In this case, *injustice in society* was the only significant factor and was positively correlated to corruption intention. Men who rated society as unfair had a 15.6 percent higher probability of contemplating corruption than those who did not.

Table 4.3 *Factors associated with corruption intention for females*

Corruption intention (female) Prob > Chi2 = 0.0174, pseudo R2 = 0.4374, n = 72 observations	Coefficiency	Std. Err.	$P > z$
Poverty	−1.024455	0.6307008	0.104
Insecurity for the future	0.3016107	0.7581585	0.691
Everybody does it	−0.5594378	0.7911621	0.479
No trust in the government	0.1807548	0.5784489	0.755
Low career advancement prospects	−0.3148612	0.600361	0.6
Help friend	−0.4719043	0.4005182	0.239
Injustice in society	0.099104	0.4399288	0.822
Normal to accept a gift	1.803757	0.754855	0.017
Household perception	−3.690431	1.691432	0.029
Constant factor	2.759188	2.305798	0.231

Deterrent Factors

The third model tested the correlation between deterrents factors such as *higher wages, living abroad, fear of authority, personal conviction, influence of family/religion, fear of scandals, training,* and *intention not to be cor*rupt. For women, the model was not significant (Intention with Prob > Chi2 = 0.226), while for men the overall model was statistically significant at a *p* value of Prob > Chi2 =0.0001 (Table 6). Thus, at least one of the independent variables contributed to the prediction of the intention to be corrupt at the 95 percent confidence level. Only three variables were found to have a significant impact on the intention not to participate in corruption (*p* value less than 0.05). These variables were *higher wages* (*p* value < 0.05) and *the influence of religion* and *training of employees* (*p* value < 0.05).

Conclusion

Our results pointed to an important gender gap in beliefs and intentions related to corruption, one that substantiates the privileging of women over men by Moroccan micro-financing agencies. This gender gap in corruption supports the notion that gender, education, and development are key factors to combating corruption in a country plagued by social problems.

Our results revealed an important gender difference in regard to corruption intention, with 74.2 percent men and only 25.8 percent women reporting that they would be tempted by corruption under certain circumstances. Similarly, 61 percent of respondents who said they would offer a corrupt opportunity were men. Similarly, our findings showed a gender gap in the perceived causes of corruption. Men were more likely to consider corruption if they deemed society as unfair, while women were most likely to consider corruption as an exchange of gifts.

One explanation for these results can be found in Moroccan society, where women's sphere of influence is within the private space while men dominate the public space.[84] Women also constitute the least educated segment of the Moroccan population. As of 2002, official statistics put the illiteracy rate among Moroccan women at 60 percent, with 48 percent in urban areas and 95 percent in rural areas.[85] Even by 2011, 56 percent of women above 15 years of age were illiterate.[86]

Greater literacy gives men increased awareness of societal issues; thus corruption is seen as a way to remedy social inequalities. Conversely, for women, who manage the family's resources, offering or accepting gifts in exchange for services is seen as a way to remedy the lack of state services.

Offering gifts and providing reciprocity are both common practices in societies composed largely of communitarian solidarity networks of family or extended family. Such networks are necessary when citizens do not to trust the state to deliver basic services, as in Morocco, where the state provides only weak support for local needs, for example, in its lack of infrastructure for both health care and education. In 2011 Morocco ranked 130 of 186 countries in HDI (Human Development Index) and the poverty level remained high, with 9.0 percent of the population below the poverty line.[87] For example, in the 1990s only 70 percent of the Moroccan population had access to some sort of health care,[88] and although progress had been made by 2011, a quarter of the population still resides more than 10 km away from a rudimentary health facility. In 2006, the illiteracy rate in rural areas was also high – at an average of around 50 percent. For women this figure peaked at 70 percent and in the Middle Atlas region,[89] at 97 percent.[90]

Morocco remains a largely patriarchal society. Since the 2004 family law reform (*moudawana al usra*), women have had more legal rights in theory.[91] Prior to that time, Moroccan women could not legalize contracts without male consent and were subject to discriminatory practices in marriage, divorce, and child custody.[92] Traditionally, Moroccan women are the nucleus of the family; they take care of most personal matters relating to marriage, household spending, child health, and schooling, while the men have authority in public spaces.[93] In a country that struggles to provide basic funding for services, particularly housing, health, and education,[94] women must rely on solidarity networks to provide for their family. Lack of infrastructure and government presence has led to a large trust deficit – even a sense of abandonment.[95] Consequently, women have little choice but to find help within traditional solidarity networks such as the extended family, and within these networks, exchanges of gifts are the norm.

If development and corruption are correlated, education and gender are key catalytic factors. Our study showed that the more educated respondents were, the less likely they were to take part in corruption. Further, within Morocco's male dominated society, micro-credit loans to women give them greater control of household resources and consequently more resources dedicated to children, food, health, and education. A higher level of education for women, then, could reduce corruption.

This study is an initial attempt to answer some of Morocco's development challenges. Our findings suggest that education and development are key factors to combating corruption. Further, because women in Morocco are at the center of extended family structures and bear the weight of a deficient social system, they play a crucial role in development. Our findings corroborate the idea that women are less tempted by corruption than men, and seem to justify the predilection of micro-credit organizations for women. Certainly, one might question the causes underlying our results. Are gender differences attributable to women's greater sense of moral behavior? Or is it that Moroccan women have less access to corrupt opportunities than men based on the limited roles in society that are available to them? Are Moroccan women more subdued within their male-dominated society and more fearful of the consequences of corrupt actions?

Other important questions arise from our findings. From the mathematical models used it would be tempting to profile "at risk" individuals based on their socio-demographics. For example the RAND Corporation, a "non-profit institution that helps improve policy and decision making through research and analysis," initiated in 1945 by the Douglas Aircraft Company,[96] used logistic regression to predict suicide attacks.[97] Similarly, Hamelin et al.[98] used logistic regression as a tool to profile potential terrorists in Morocco. Schneier[99] shows how such mathematical models have been used to build disputable discriminatory lists, such as the "no fly list" established by the Terrorist Screening Center (TSC), barring individuals from flying in and out of the US on commercial airlines. Moroccan micro-credit agencies are already using discriminatory practices by favouring women and policy makers use such models to exclude men from access to funding. High rates of male unemployment inevitably result in increased social tension and domestic violence in a country where violence against women is rife. While our research provided some answers, further research is needed to address these questions.

Endnotes

1 Sabra, M. (2007). "Microcredits in Morocco: formula for success against poverty?" Available at http://en.qantara.de/wcsite.php?wc_c=6509.
2 Armendariz, B. and J. Morduch (2005). *The Economics of Microfinance*. Cambridge: MIT Press.
3 Manji, F. and S. Ekine (2012). *African Awakening: The Emerging Revolutions*. Fahamu/Pambazuka.
4 BBC (2011). "Egypt: Suzanne Mubarak detained in corruption probe." *BBC*. Available at www.bbc.co.uk/news/world-africa-13392099 (accessed 17 May 2011).
5 Creswell, J.W. (2013). *Research Design: Qualitative, Quantitative, and Mixed Methods Approaches*. Sage publications.
6 Harrell, F. (2015). *Regression Modeling Strategies: With Applications to Linear Models, Logistic and Ordinal Regression, and Survival Analysis*. Springer.
7 ICDF Annual Report 2002.
8 Maes, J.P. and L.R. Reed (2012). *State of the Microcredit Summit Campaign Report 2012*. Washington, DC: Microcredit Summit Campaign.
9 Morvant-Roux, S. et al. (2012). "Explaining heterogeneity in microcredit take-up rates and repayment defaults in rural Morocco: the role of social norms and actors." *Rural Microfinance and Employment*. Paris.
10 Transparency International (2007). "Gender and corruption: understanding and undoing the linkages." *Transparency International*. Working Paper # 03/2007. Available at http://unpan1.un.org/intradoc/groups/public/documents/un-dpadm/unpan044385.pdf (accessed 17 May 2011).
11 Kaufmann, D., A. Kraay, and M. Mastruzzi (2010). "The worldwide governance indicators: methodology and analytical issues." *Policy Research*. Working Paper #5430. World Bank Group, p. 4.
12 Benhlal, M. (2014). "Governance in Morocco: discourse, policies and reality." *Arab Reform Initiative*.
13 See www.transparency.org/gcb2013/country/?country=morocco.
14 D'Espallier, B., I. Guérin, and R. Mersland (2013). "Gender bias in microfinance." A later version of this paper is published in *Journal of Development Studies*. Vol. 49, No. 5, pp. 589–608.
15 Khandker, S. R., B. Khalily, and Z. Kahn (1995). "Grameen Bank: performance and sustainability." World Bank Discussion Paper 306. Washington, DC: World Bank.
16 D'Espallier, B., Guérin, I., and Mersland, R. (2009). "Women and repayment in microfinance." *Elsevier*. Vol. 39, No. 5.
17 World Bank (2007). "Finance for all? Policies and pitfalls in expanding access." World Bank Policy Research Report. Washington, DC: World Bank.

18 Armendariz, B. and J. Morduch (2005). *The Economics of Microfinance.* Cambridge: MIT Press.

19 D'Espallier et al., "Gender bias."

20 Armendariz and Morduch, *The Economics of Microfinance.*

21 Freeman, L. A. and N. A. Tran (May 2000). *Morocco: Appropriate Microfinance Model for the Rural Areas of the Sous-Massa-Drâa.* USAID/Morocco.

22 D'Espallier et al., "Gender bias."

23 Archive.transparency.org (2015). Available at: http://archive.transparency .org/news_room/faq/corruption_faq (accessed 11 October 2015).

24 Tulchin, J. S. and R. H. Espach (2000). *Combating Corruption in Latin America.* Woodrow Wilson Center Press.

25 Vorley, T. and N. Williams (2015). "Between petty corruption and criminal extortion: how entrepreneurs in Bulgaria and Romania operate within a devil's circle." *International Small Business Journal.*

26 De Graaf, G. (2007). "Causes of corruption: towards a contextual theory of corruption." *Public Administrative Quarterly,* pp. 39–86.

27 Lambsdorff, J. G. (1999). "Corruption in empirical research: a review." *Transparency International.*

28 Swamy, A., S. Knack, Y. Lee, and O. Azfar (2001). "Gender and corruption." *Journal of Development Economics.* Vol. 64, No. 1, pp. 25–55.

29 Dollar, D., R. Fisman, and R. Gatti (2001). "Are women really the "fairer" sex? Corruption and women in government." *Journal of Economic Behavior & Organization.* Vol. 46, No. 4, pp. 423–429.

30 Transparency International, "Gender and Corruption."

31 Branisa, B. and M. Ziegler (2010). "Reexamining the link between gender and corruption: the role of social institutions." *Courant Research Centre "Poverty, Equity and Growth in Developing and Transition Countries."* Georg-August-Universität Göttingen, Discussion Paper #24.

32 Ibid.

33 Dollar, Fisman, and Gatti, "Are women really the 'fairer' sex?"

34 Transparency International (2015). "Transparency International – Country Profiles." Transparency.org. Available at www.transparency .org/country/#MAR_DataResearch (accessed September 17, 2015).

35 Dollar, Fisman, and Gatti, "Are women really the 'fairer' sex?"

36 Ibid.

37 Swamy et al., "Gender and corruption."

38 Ibid.

39 Ibid.

40 Ibid.

41 Frank, B., J. G. Lambsdorff, and F. Boehm (2011). "Gender and corruption: lessons from laboratory corruption experiments." *European Journal of Development Research.* Vol. 23, No.1, pp. 59–71.
42 Esarey, J. and G. Chirillo (2013). "'Fairer sex' or purity myth? Corruption, gender, and institutional context." *Politics & Gender.* Vol. 9, No. 4, pp. 361–389.
43 Sung, H. (2003). "Fairer sex or fairer system? Gender and corruption revisited." *Social Forces.* Vol. 82, No. 2, pp. 703–723.
44 Ibid.
45 Goetz, A. M. (2007). "Political cleaners: women as the new anti-corruption force?" *Development and Change.* Vol. 38, No. 1, pp. 87–105.
46 Ibid.
47 Alhassan-Alolo, N. (2007). "Gender and corruption: testing the new consensus." *Public Administration and Development.* Vol. 27, pp. 227–237.
48 Ibid.
49 Hofstede, G. (2011). "Dimensionalizing cultures: the Hofstede model in context." *Online Readings in Psychology and Culture.* Vol. 2, No. 1, p. 8.
50 Hofstede, G. (1980). *Culture's Consequences: International Differences in Work-Related Values.* Beverly Hills, CA: Sage.
51 Zheng, X. et al. (2013). "Collectivism and corruption in bank lending." *Journal of International Business Studies.* Vol. 44, No. 4, pp. 363–390.
52 Hofstede, "Dimensionalizing cultures."
53 Bukuluki, P. (2013). "'When I steal, it is for the benefit of me and you': is collectivism engendering corruption in Uganda?" *International Letters of Social and Humanistic Sciences.* Vol. 5, pp. 27–44.
54 Hofstede, *Culture's Consequences.*
55 Bukuluki, "When I steal."
56 Mauro, P. (1995). "Corruption and growth." *The Quarterly Journal of Economics,* pp. 681–712; Leon, C.J., J. E. Arana and J. De Leon (2013). "Correcting for scale perception bias in measuring corruption: an application to Chile and Spain." *Social Indicators Research.* Vol. 114, No. 3, pp. 977–995.
57 Ibid.
58 Treisman, D. (2007). "What have we learned about the causes of corruption from ten years of cross-national empirical research?" *Annual Review Political Science.* Vol. 10, pp. 211–244.
59 Leon et al., "Correcting for scale perception."
60 Andvig et al., *Corruption.*
61 Transparency International (2011). Transparency International Annual Report 2011. Available at www.transparency.org; Eurobarometer (2012). Corruption (Special Eurobarometer 374). Available at http://ec.europa.eu/public_opinion/archives/ebs/ebs_374_en.pdf; GCR (2012). Global

Competitiveness Report 2011–12. World Economic Forum, Geneva. Available at www3.weforum.org/docs/WEF_GlobalCompetitiveness Report_2012-13.pdf.

62 Lee W. S. and C. Guven (2013). "Engaging in corruption: the influence of cultural values and contagion effects at the microlevel." *Journal of Economic Psychology.* Vol. 39, pp. 287–300.

63 Razafindrakoto, M. and F. Roubaud (2010). "Are international databases on corruption reliable? A comparison of expert opinion surveys and household surveys in sub-Saharan Africa." *World Development.* Vol. 38, No. 8, pp. 1057–1069.

64 Treisman, "What have we learned."

65 Dong, B., U. Dulleck, and B. Torgler (2012). "Conditional corruption." *Journal of Economic Psychology.* Vol. 33, No. 3, pp. 609–627; Lee and Guven, "Engaging in corruption."

66 Oloo, I. et al. (2012). "Effect of gender of the recorded voice on responses to sensitive sexual behavior questions: use of Audio Computer-Assisted Self-Interview (ACASI) in Kisumu, Kenya." *Field Methods.*

67 Dong, B., U. Dulleck, and B. Torgler (2009). "Social norms and corruption." In Proceedings of the European Economic Association and the Econometric Society European Meeting. A. Ciccone (ed.). Catalonia, Spain: Barcelona Graduate School of Economics, pp. 1–48.

68 Torgler, B. and N. T. Valev (2010). "Gender and public attitudes toward corruption and tax evasion." *Contemporary Economic Policy.* Vol. 28, No. 4, pp. 554–568.

69 Benstead, L. J. (2013). "Effects of interviewer-respondent gender interaction on attitudes toward women and politics: findings from Morocco." *International Journal of Public Opinion Research.*

70 Torgler and Valev, "Gender and public attitudes."

71 Questionnaire reliability was tested through computing the value of Cronbach's Alpha for the totality of the variables included in the study for a sample of 200 respondents.

72 Ajabili, M. (2015). Alarabiya.net. Available at www.alarabiya.net/articles/2011/04/09/144873.html.

73 Hall, J. L. (2015). "Debating Darija: language ideology and the written representation of Moroccan Arabic in Morocco." PhD dissertation. University of Michigan.

74 Dodson, L. L., S. Sterling, and J. K. Bennett (2013). "Minding the gaps: cultural, technical and gender-based barriers to mobile use in oral-language Berber communities in Morocco." *Proceedings of the Sixth International Conference on Information and Communication Technologies and Development: Full Papers.* ACM. Vol. 1, pp. 79–88.

75 Hall, "Debating Darija."

76 Amaghouss, J. and A. Ibourk (2015). "Les inégalités dans le domaine de l'éducation au Maroc: Une approche spatial." *European Journal of Development Research.*
77 Benstead, L. J. (2014). "Does interviewer religious dress affect survey responses? Evidence from Morocco." *Politics and Religion.* Vol. 7, No. 4, pp. 734–760.
78 Boulanouar, A. (2010). "Myths and reality: meaning in Moroccan Muslim women's dress." Doctoral dissertation. Available at http://otago .ourarchive.ac.nz/handle/10523/1748; Bachleda, C., N. Hamelin, and O. Benachour (2014). "Does religiosity impact Moroccan Muslim women's clothing choice?" *Journal of Islamic Marketing.* Vol. 5, No. 2, pp. 210–226.
79 L'Economiste (2012). "Eviter la corruption, car elle est haram." Entretien avec Mustapha Ramid ministre de la Justice et des Libertés – Leconomiste.com. Available at www.leconomiste.com/article/900382-eviter-la-corruption-car-elleest-haram-entretien-avec-mustapha-ramid-ministre-de-la- (Accessed 18 November 2015).
80 Brislin, R. W. (1980). "Translation and content analysis of oral and written material." Handbook of Cross-Cultural Psychology. H.C. Triandis and J.W. Berry (eds.), pp. 389–444.
81 USAID (2015). Available at www.usaid.gov/morocco/education.
82 In the first model, we wrote an equation for a prospective relationship between demographic factors and the intention toward corruption. In the second model, we analyzed the respondents' perceptions about justifiability of corruption. In the third model we analyzed respondents' perceptions about deterrent factors.
83 The mean for males was 0.20 while the mean for females was 0.08 (see Table 1). An ANOVA test confirmed that the difference in means was statistically significant. A similar gender difference was seen in response to questions about accepting corruption, with 74.2 percent of males and 25.8 percent of females reporting that they would accept a bribe.
84 Direction de la Statistiques (2002). Available at www.hcp.ma/Direction-de-la-statistique_a716.html.
85 WHO (2011). Available at www.who.int/countryfocus/cooperation_strategy/ccsbrief_mar_en.pdf.
86 Ibid.
87 Obermeyer, C. M. (1993), "Culture, maternal health care, and women's status: a comparison of Morocco and Tunisia." *Studies in Family Planning.* Vol. 24, No. 6, pp. 354–365.
88 Moghadam, V. (1997). "Women's NGOs in the Middle East and North Africa: constraints, opportunities, and priorities." *Organizing Women: Formal and Informal Women's Groups in the Middle East.* D. Chatty and A. Rabo (eds.). Oxford: Berg.

89 Zouini, M. et al. (2009). "Etude de la morbidité maternelle et du recours aux soins de la population rurale du Haut Atlas Occidental (vallées d'Azgour, d'Anougal et d'Imnane, Province d'Al Haouz, Maroc)." *Biométrie humaine et anthropologie*. Vol. 27, No. 3–4.

90 Eisenberg, A. M. (2011). "Law on the books vs. law in action: under-enforcement of Morocco's reformed 2004 Family Law, the *Moudawana*." *Cornell International Law Journal*. Vol. 44, p. 693.

91 Benstead, "Effects of Interviewer."

92 Eisenberg, "Law on the Books."

93 Pennell, C. R. (2003). *Morocco: From Empire to Independence*. Oxford: Oneworld Publications.

94 Zaki, L. (2008). "Maroc: dépendance alimentaire, redicalisation contest-ataire, répression autoritaire." *Alternatives Sud*. Vol. 15, No. 4, pp. 83–88.

95 Truex, R. (2011). "Corruption, attitudes, and education: survey evidence from Nepal." *World Development*. Vol. 39, No. 7, pp. 1133–1142.

96 RAND.org (2016). RAND Corporation Provides Objective Research Services and Public Policy Analysis. Available at www.rand.org/ (Accessed February 14, 2016).

97 Perry, W. L. et al. (2013). "Predicting suicide attacks: integrating spatial, temporal, and social features of terrorist attack targets." *RAND Corporation*.

98 Hamelin, N. et al. (2011). "Trigger factors of terrorism social marketing analysis as a tool for security studies – a Moroccan case study." *EMUNI Press*. Vol. 24, No. 3, pp. 223–250.

99 Schneier, B. (2015). "Data and Goliath: the hidden battles to collect your data and control your world." *WW Norton & Company*.

Religion and Social Change

5 | Morocco's Islamic Feminism
The Contours of a New Theology?

DORIS H. GRAY AND HABIBA BOUMLIK

Introduction

The religion of Islam is one of the pillars of Moroccan identity, and King Mohamed VI is a strong advocate of an "open, moderate Islam"[1] based on the Maliki school of Islamic jurisprudence and Sunni Sufism. Since 2013, the Moroccan government has actively sought to train imam students from Tunisia and Libya as well as several West African countries, thus exporting Morocco's Islam as a counterpoint to more radical or fundamentalist versions. In his dual capacity as Head of State and Commander of the Faithful (*amir al mu'minin*), the king is in the unique position of shaping religious discourse concerning women without resorting to authoritarian state-imposed feminism, as was the case in pre-revolution Tunisia.[2] There, the government repressed religious discourse on women's rights, a course that was later reversed when, in the first free and democratic post-uprising elections, the religiously based Ennahda party was elected to government, allowing for a religiously inspired discourse on gender equality.

An important component of Morocco's moderate Islam is support for women's rights. The official discourse is based on the notion that Islam is a dynamic religion, the eternal message of which needs to be adapted to changing historical circumstances. Commonly referred to as Islamic feminism, the Moroccan variant conforms to the royal position, which combines the conventions of the Maliki school of jurisprudence with advocacy for gender equality based on the interpretation of sacred texts. This interpretive process, called *ijtihad* (independent reasoning of the sources of Islamic law) involves the sacred texts of the Qur'an, *sunnah* (sayings and doings of the Prophet) and *hadith* (sayings attributed to the Prophet). Interpretation also occurs within the context of domestic and international pressures for gender parity and advancement of women's rights.

In this chapter, we focus on Islamic feminist ideas that challenge predominant androcentric, absolutist theological concepts of authority. Certainly, the term "Islamic Feminism" is problematic. Feminism is based on universal notions of human rights without including religious notions. Those who emphasize religion as a major source of knowledge and inspiration will find the secular term "feminist" unacceptable. However, to date no better term has been coined to capture this approach and therefore we use it. With reference to Morocco, we also use the term "Third Way" to acknowledge the problems inherent in "Islamic Feminism" and in recognition of the King's support for reinterpreting the Qur'an to be congruent with the advancement of women's rights. We explore the work of the most vocal proponents of Islamic feminism in Morocco, as well as their use of new communication technologies. In so doing, we show that women who are appropriating religious authority contribute significantly to a Third Way in Morocco, one that bridges western feminism and women's rights advocacy grounded in references to Islam while also expanding the royal project, and thus propose a new vision for their societies and beyond.

Our discussion of this Third Way refers to an approach that initially emerged in the wake of the 1995 Bejing Conference on Women. At that time, tensions arose between secular feminists, who insisted on the universality of human rights, and conservative Muslim women, who insisted that the Qur'an granted them all the rights they needed and, therefore, rebuffed Western feminism that was perceived as rejecting religion and insisting on a dominant role for Western feminists. Caught in the middle were reformist Muslim scholars and activists, who emphasized that Muslims were not a homogeneous community and that it was possible to be both "pro-faith" *and* "pro-feminism,"[3] thus laying the groundwork for Islamic feminism.

We describe Fatema Mernissi's groundbreaking scholarship and her "Digital Ummah" model as well as the career trajectories of Third Way Islamic feminists Asma Lambrabet and Amina Wadud, who have used new communication technologies to promote their ideas and connect with Muslim feminists around the globe. Digital Ummah captures the phenomenon of a like-minded community that is not limited by geography but exchanges ideas via internet-based communication tools. In recent decades, these three women have had the most marked impact on reformulating the scholarly gender discourse in Morocco.

We contend that Third Way Islamic feminism can serve as an alternative Muslim theological framework for a gender egalitarian society.

Further, because the Moroccan gender discourse is embedded in a broader quest for social and economic justice for women – as elaborated in the other chapters of this volume – we point to its resemblance to liberation theology that emerged among Catholic scholars in Latin America in the 1950s and 1960s.

Liberation Theology and Justice

Catholic liberation theology, much like Islamic feminist exegesis, is concerned with the concept of justice in our times. One of its central questions, then, is what is justice? According to Bell,[4] justice may broadly be defined in terms of the ancient phrase *suum cuique*: "to each what is due," or more commonly, "to each his own." What one individual or a group of people is due may be ascertained according to a variety of criteria, such as social rank, gender, merit, legal entitlement, and more. In the words of one of the founders of liberation theology, Leonardo Boff:

Justice, in the classical definition, consists in giving to each his own. Evidently "his own" presupposes a given social system. In slave society, given to each his own consists in giving to the slaves what is theirs and to the masters what is theirs and to the workers what is theirs; in neo-capitalist systems it means giving to the magnates what is theirs and the proletarian what is theirs.[5]

Liberation theology challenges classical theology with the argument that the task of theology is to struggle with issues located within human history. As Tombs noted, "Theology does not take place in a social vacuum but always arises in relation to particular historical contexts and social situations."[6] Thus, as Bell asserted, Catholic social justice teaching, out of which liberation theology evolved, has changed throughout the ages:

It is the story of the gradual and subtle move away from justice as the principle of a community's solidarity, in a robust sense of the common good, to justice as a fundamentally distributive force that secures rights in societies distinguished by the absence of anything but the thinnest of conceptions of common good.[7]

The point here is not to compare Christian with Islamic conceptions of justice and the evolution of such concepts throughout the centuries. It is rather to assert that theologians and religious scholars must necessarily wrestle with changing mores if they are to continuously promulgate inclusive, religiously based contemporary notions of justice. As will be shown below, Asma Lamrabet has referred to liberation theology as a source of inspiration for her exploration of a modern Islamic understanding of justice, including gender justice.

In his *Islamic Liberation Theology*, Iranian-American scholar Hamid Dabashi, argued against the binary of Islam and the West. For Dabashi an Islamic liberation theology is primarily concerned with an alternative notion of what is commonly referred to as political Islam. In the interest of resisting "globalized imperialism," Dabashi laid the groundwork for a new conception of Islam, yet he does not advance a comprehensive position on gender justice. Islamic Feminism, therefore, breaks new ground by generating a theology focused on gender equality and social and economic justice.

Islam as a Dynamic Religion

Because of some unique aspects of Morocco's approach to women's rights, we use the term Third Way[8] interchangeably with Moroccan Islamic feminism. While in the past, Moroccan women's rights associations have emphasized the universal – and secular – character of gender equality, other Moroccan women have come to the fore in the last decade, insisting on an alternative feminist discourse that includes religious perspectives. The voices of these religious feminists in Morocco are new. In the past, a cleavage existed between the positions of secular, urban elite feminists and the positions often espoused by conservative Islamist movements.[9] The new religious feminists, however, have emphasized the need for gender, social, and economic justice as have secular feminists, but in a different way by arguing that equality can be derived from a reading of sacred texts. Naturally, there are critics of Islamic Feminism such as Ibtissam Bouachrine who argues that Islamic Feminism is not transformative but merely explicative.[10] Other critics point to the fact that Islamic feminism does not offer one coherent theory but is rather heterogeneous. Al-Sharmani argues:

Islamic feminism emphasizes the importance of the connection between text and context, and the multidimensionality of the interpretative process, notions that were also implicitly present in Islamic religious sciences and are reflected through the diversity in classical exegetical and juristic interpretations.[11]

Moroccan Islamic Law scholar Aïcha El Hajjami is an advocate for the Third Way. She observed:

In Morocco, the rights of women to equality as understood in the light of new approaches, especially that of gender, is questioned and contested, placing the issue of women at the center of the problem of identity.[12]

El Hajjami distinguished the Maliki School of Islamic jurisprudence from the other three Sunni schools by its adoption of innovative methods of exegesis and the use of *al-masalih al-mursala* (considerations of public interest) and *istihsan* (principle of judicial preference) as paradigms for the general concept of *maqasid al shari'a* (the ultimate goal or purpose of the law). According to El Hajjami there needs to be:

a balance between fundamental values of sacred texts while taking into account the needs of reality and social changes...The tradition of the Prophet, too, bore a vision of profound social transformation...The Prophet's approach brought about a profound reversal of the socially established divisions of gender roles and rethinking of separations between the public and private sphere.[13]

Thus, social transformation in the tradition of the Prophet, rather than adherence to a status quo, lies at the heart of feminist theological inquiry.

Proponents of Third Way Feminism in Morocco

Sociologist Fatema Mernissi (1945–2015) was one of the earliest and most important pioneers of Muslim feminist scholarship in Morocco. She was among the first to turn to the Qur'an to advance a reformist interpretation of the sacred texts with a view of supporting gender equality. In addition, Mernissi placed women's rights within a larger context of social and economic justice. Ironically, it was only after Mernissi's death that she became widely known in her home country and finally was publicly acknowledged for her contributions.

Today, Asma Lamrabet, a Moroccan medical doctor and activist, and Amina Wadud, a US-born Professor of Islamic Studies, are prominent proponents of Third Way feminism in Morocco. Lamrabet currently serves as the Director of the Research Center on Women's Studies in Islam for the Rabita Mohammadia des Oulémas du Maroc (Royal Council of Religious Scholars of Morocco), an institution that operates under the auspices of the king, after whom it is named. In most of the world, feminist thinkers and activists stand in opposition to official discourse and power structures rather than being part of them. In Morocco, by contrast, new religious discourse on gender equality is part of a royal project. For her part, Amina Wadud writes in English and does not directly address the North African context. Nevertheless, she is frequently referenced in Morocco, where translated versions of her works are widely read in scholarly circles. Thus, Mernissi, Lamrabet, and Wadud represent important alternative voices in Moroccan scholarly discourses on gender and Islam. A review of their personal trajectories, intellectual production, and active roles in transnational Islamic feminist organizations allows for a deeper understanding of the complexity, diversity, and dynamics of the Islamic feminist movement and the challenges it has posed to traditional understandings of male authority. Still, while their scholarship is locally and internationally recognized, women's rights associations within Morocco have yet to incorporate this new knowledge production into their activism.

Fatema Mernissi

Fatema Mernissi was adamant for decades that women's rights need to be embedded in larger economic, social, and political projects and cannot be achieved in isolation. As a sociologist, her interest was in examining broader societal changes and developments. Her books have been translated into more than 30 languages and are considered classic texts outside of Morocco; in fact, she is the most widely read Moroccan author worldwide.[14] For Mernissi, the first step towards gender equality and social justice is the achievement of individual autonomy:

The emergence of the individual is one of the single most important trends that have become apparent in the past decades. But people have to get used to being individuals and being treated as such. Because of our authoritarian culture, we are not used to thinking for ourselves. For substantial change to take place, we need to reflect on what it is we want and not just criticize what is.[15]

Well before social media became ubiquitous, Mernissi coined the phrase Digital Ummah (community of believers) to refer to a community that transcends regional and national boundaries because it is connected in cyberspace.[16] She argued that new communication technologies allow for the swift exchange of ideas across geographic and national divides. In addition, such technologies easily facilitate the creation of new alliances among those seeking to re-interpret sacred texts in order to challenge the conventional (though presumably divinely sanctioned) patriarchy. In her many books, Mernissi also pioneered a new hermeneutics of sacred Islamic scriptures.

Islamic feminist hermeneutics considers the Qur'an as a historical text, revealed at a particular time and place. Over time, then, certain interpretations need to be reconsidered or refuted in accordance with the principles and egalitarian spirit of the texts.[17] As Mernissi has repeatedly argued, sacred texts have been used as a political weapon to uphold laws that treat women as legal minors. This action is possible because traditional Islamic theological scholarship lacks fundamental historic contextualization, fails to acknowledge that knowledge production always occurs within a given historical context, and downplays the possibility of human fallibility in any hermeneutics. Recognizing such limitations is an important element of Islamic Feminist thought.[18] Inasmuch as Mernissi critiqued the gender inegalitarian reality, she also was critical of promoting women's rights without simultaneously advocating for social and economic justice.

Asma Lamrabet

Asma Lamrabet initially appeared on the international scene via her website (www.asma-lamrabet.com), where her biography and other features are translated into four languages.[19] Lamrabet's website describes her work as a medical doctor in Morocco after several years of volunteering in hospitals in Chile, Spain, and other Latin American countries where her husband served as a Moroccan diplomat. During her tenure in Latin America, Lamrabet came into contact with the ideas of liberation theology. Initially much despised by the Catholic Church hierarchy, liberation theology was grounded in an interpretation of the Gospels that emphasized social and economic justice for the poor through fundamental change and challenges to existing power structures. This exposure led Lamrabet to ponder the possibility of an alternate reading of Islamic sacred texts with a view to creating a more just society.

From 2004 to 2007, Lamrabet coordinated the Research Group on Muslim Women and Intercultural Dialogue in Rabat. In 2008 she became president of the International Research Group on Women in Islam (GIERFI) and in 2011 she received a royal appointment to be the Director of the Center of Feminine Studies in Islam within the Rabita Mohammadia des Oulémas (Royal Council of Religious Scholars). As the appointed director of an institution established by King Mohammed VI, she found her place within the official discourse on gender issues. Though this position lends weight to her assertions within Morocco, it also limits her exploration beyond the royal project.[20]

Like Mernissi, Lamrabet received no academic training in theology. She educated herself in Islamic Studies and, in the process, authored several books on Islam and women.[21] At the time of this writing Lamrabet is a ubiquitous presence in the Moroccan public sphere. She appears on television, her face graces magazine covers, and she is a frequent speaker on Islam and gender, contemporary Islam, and modernity. As a women's rights advocate and public personality, she falls in line with those seeking to cultivate the image and substance of Morocco's moderate Islam while at the same time placing the discourse on women's rights within a reformist religious context. In this way, she has avoided the binary distinction between secular feminists and religious women's rights advocates that has ravaged neighboring Algeria and Tunisia (as elaborated in Chapters 13 and 15 in this volume).

Through the effective use of online media technologies, Lamrabet is questioning concepts that structure traditional Islamic thought and reference points that govern the conception of the sacred. In so doing, she is contributing to the formulation of a new theological discourse in Morocco. Her use of Internet portals amplifies her approach, enabling her to build bridges, widen the conversation, raise awareness, and lift taboos that have prohibited challenges to Islamic authority and patriarchy.

Lamrabet's research focuses on certain pertinent concepts in Islamic legal scholarship that most directly affect the daily lives of women and men. In this, she selectively analyzes concepts, deliberately limiting herself to aspects of the religion with immediate relevance to practical realities. In a recent publication, Lamrabet argued:

It is not fair to expect the prophet to have been a feminist at a time when feminism, as a social movement, did not exist. The other option is to accept

Prophet Muhammad in the patriarchal context in which he lived, all the while looking for indications of his resisting patriarchy in even the smallest ways possible.[22]

Consequently, Lamrabet has argued that "to reduce *wilayah* to male guardianship over dependent wards, or *quiwamah* to an assumed authority of the husband, amounts to violating the spiritual principles of the Qur'anic messages regarding the ethics of marriage and family life." We will explore this more closely later in this chapter.[23]

Amina Wadud

Lamrabet's critique of patriarchy and advocacy for women's empowerment is consistent with the work of Amina Wadud. A trained theologian, Wadud taught Qur'anic Studies from 1989 to 1992 at the International Islamic University in Malaysia and served as a professor of Islamic Studies at Virginia Commonwealth University from 1992 to 2008. Additionally, she has been a consultant on Islam and gender at the International Center for Islam and Pluralism in Indonesia. Wadud rose to international prominence when she dared to lead Friday prayers, first in South Africa in 1994 and then again in New York City in 2005, a practice strictly reserved for men. She has written extensively on ethnicity and Muslim identity but is best known for her works on gender.[24] She has called for an inclusive Islam in opposition to a fundamentalist/traditionalist Islam, and advocates reading the Qur'an from a gender mainstreaming perspective, that is, one that recognizes and, indeed, emphasizes a woman's identity as an individual – not primarily as a relative, mother, sister, daughter, or wife.[25]

Over the course of her career, Wadud has evolved from reclusive scholar focusing on hermeneutics (*tafsir*) to a scholar-activist with a feminist interpretive orientation.

Like Lamrabet, Wadud has used social media like blogs, personal websites, and Facebook to propagate her messages and interact with readers through responses to queries and comments on current events related to women in Islam. Both women are now part of Musawah (Equality in Arabic), an international network of scholars, activists, and lawyers who, in scholarly works and activism, challenge patriarchy within Muslim legal traditions. Musawah grew out of the groups Sisters in Islam and Karama (Dignity), both of which promote understandings of Islam that foster justice, equality, freedom, and dignity, especially for women. Founded in 2009 in Malaysia, Musawah's headquarters moved temporarily to Morocco in 2015 where it is beginning to gain recognition among women's rights activists. Thus, Malaysia and Morocco can be said to form the bookends of a reformist, moderate Islam.

Challenging Male Authority within a Religious Framework

Mernissi, Lamrabet, and Wadud, at different times, have been at the forefront of a creative dialogue between theology and feminist theories that challenge androcentric theological conceptions of authority. The elaboration of new Islamic feminist theories runs parallel with their advocacy for more involvement of women in legal knowledge production and decision-making. In personal interviews, Lamrabet has acknowledged her lack of training as a religious scholar and explained her approach to exegesis, "I ask the questions that I think scholars should focus on and find answers to."[26] In recent years, however, she has proposed alternative interpretations herself. In the following sections, we highlight several important Islamic concepts that directly impact the lives of women, along with their re-interpretations by Lamrabet and Wadud.

Qiwamah

The Qur'anic concept of *qiwamah* (variously rendered as guardian, protector, maintainer) is at the root of male-female relationships among Muslims. It is a concept that historically has been used to establish the superiority and authority of men over women and husbands over wives, based on Qur'anic verses 4:34, 4:135, and 5:8. Lamrabet has argued that multiple translations of *qiwamah* are possible, but the one that is most common – erroneously, according to Lamrabet – is "authority." According to Lamrabet, renditions such as "provider" and "supporter" are more in keeping with *maqasid*, that is, the ultimate goal of the revealed text.[27] Lamrabet has maintained that the Qur'an instructs that all human life be guided by the ethical values at its heart. Further, she has urged that when applied to gender relations, *qiwamah* should be read alongside notions of *ma'ruf* (common good), just as *quiwamah* should be read in reference to justice when alongside *istikhlaf* (appointing, successor, trustee) and *wilayah* (guardianship). Lamrabet has asserted, "These three key concepts embody the spiritual message of Islam and encapsulate the shared responsibilities on earth of women and men: managing the affairs of the world, enjoining good and forbidding evil, and doing justice.[28]

On her website, Lamrabet developed her argument against traditional literal understandings of the crucial legal concept of *qiwamah*. In another text published on her website, Une relecture du concept coranique de Qiwamah ou autorité de l'époux (A Re-Reading of the Qur'anic Concept of Qiwamah or the Authority of the Husband), she explored the etymology of the word and its polysemy, or multiple meanings, which number more than thirty. She argued that her rendering of *qiwamah* is more congruent with joint responsibility, sharing within the family, and the concept of justice among all believers, regardless of gender. Thus, Lamrabet analyzed a significant Qur'anic concept that has been long used to justify male superiority, made a case for its obsolescence, and then offered a rendition that is congruent with contemporary notions of gender equality. In so doing, she, like other reformers, built her assertions on an implicit assumption – that the Qur'an was revealed in a given socio-cultural context. Any attempt to reproduce this context, then, amounts to manipulation for political rather than spiritual ends.

According to Lamrabet, the Qur'an speaks of the moral and material responsibility of a man to his family and not of superiority or authority of one over the other. To further prove her point, she linked the idea of *qiwamah* to *wilaya* (guardianship). Inspired by the work of the Egyptian reformist Mohamed Abdou (1849–1905), Lamrabet argued that *qiwamah* and its corollary, *ta'a* (the principle of obedience) are legal interpretations that have contributed to the disparagement and belittlement of women.[29]

Hijab

"I say it loud and clear. There is no obligation in the Qur'an concerning the headscarf,"[30] proclaimed Lamrabet on her website, though she herself does wear the Muslim headscarf, commonly known as the hijab. Lamrabet has stated that hijab "means separation, not veil," and at the time of the Prophet, women wore coverings for modesty, piety, or social convention. When the Qur'an mentions such coverings, it remains true to its original context:

For me and some reformist thinkers, hijab is a recommendation not an obligation. In religious texts, when there is a prescription, non-compliance is generally accompanied with a punishment. In the case of the verse that refers to the hijab, no punishment is mentioned, which proves that wearing it is not mandatory.[31]

Lamrabet has asserted that the wearing of the Muslim headscarf is the choice of an adult believer, and one that loses its meaning and value when imposed from beyond the self. While the hijab is almost an obsession in Western public discourse, both Lamrabet and Wadud, like their colleagues at Musawah, have moved beyond discussing the veil. Instead, they believe that issues of gender relations and women's rights, and specifically, the reformation of laws to obtain complete legal equality for women, are of paramount importance.

On her website, under the title "The 11 Key Concepts of Female-Male Equality in the Qur'an," Lamrabet wrote:

The Qur'an calls for equality between the faithful – women, and men (*al-muslimun wa l-muslimat*). This spiritual equity, initiated by the creation story, is found throughout the text, although formulated in masculine language. This did not hinder some Muslim women at the time of the Prophet, inspired by the breath of liberation of the new message, to complain directly to the Prophet about the overly masculine tone. In response to these women's demands there was a quick reaction and new verses were revealed.[32]

Irth

The matter of *irth* (inheritance) is one of the most complex and controversial topics in contemporary Muslim majority countries. Unlike other verses that lend themselves to multiple renderings and interpretations, the Qur'an is explicit about inheritance in *surat an-nissa* 4:11:

Allah instructs you concerning your children: for the male, what is equal to the share of two females. But if there are [only] daughters, two or more, for them is two thirds of one's estate. And if there is only one, for her is half. And for one's parents, to each one of them is a sixth of his estate if he left children. But if he had no children and the parents [alone] inherit from him, then for his mother is one third. And if he had no brothers [or sisters], for his mother is a sixth, after any bequest she [may have] made or debt. Your parents or your children – you know not which of them are nearest to you in benefit. [These shares are] an obligation [imposed] by Allah. Indeed, Allah is ever Knowing and Wise.[33]

This unambiguous language has prevented Moroccan women's associations from openly advocating for changes to inheritance laws that would enable women to obtain legal equality in inheritance matters. Even in Tunisia, where polygamy was abolished with the 1956 Personal Status Code reform, inheritance laws have continued to reflect original interpretations of sacred scriptures and therefore, continue to be unequal. Yet, Lamrabet places this verse in its socio-historic context. She argued that Islam introduced inheritance laws at a time when women had very few rights, so providing for even limited inheritance rights was revolutionary, if not transformative.

Lamrabet went even further by demonstrating that a contextualized exegesis actually promotes gender equality in inheritance laws. For instance, *sura* 4 continues in verse 32 to say, "For men is the share of what they have earned, and for women is a share [*nassib*] of what they have earned."[34] In Lamrabet's reading, this verse establishes the basis for equality of inheritance between men and women. She explained, "We see through these two verses the Qur'an establishes a basic rule, which is that of equality in units (*nassib*)...We note the insistence of the Qur'an on 'duty' of the egalitarian distribution (*nassiban mafroudan*)."[35] Considering explicit Qur'anic prescriptions about inheritance to be open for interpretation is a bold stance, and one that the Musawah network has taken on. Like Lamrabet, Musawah upholds the idea that historic interpretations allow for the possibility of equal inheritance.

Marriage of Muslims and Non-Muslims

Another controversial topic in Islam is marriage between Muslims and non-Muslims, especially when the husband is not a Muslim. Contrary to Judaism, where Jewishness is matrilineal, Islam is patrilineal, so anyone born to a Muslim father is considered a lifelong Muslim.[36] Thus, a non-Muslim man wishing to marry a Muslim woman must convert to Islam, while a Muslim man can marry a non-Muslim woman of one of the monotheistic religions. This inequality has been explained as a response to the fear that Muslim women may leave the *ummah* upon marriage to a non-Muslim. This prescription, however, can be questioned when reading *sura* 2:221, which admonishes Muslim men and women to marry believers, including other people of the book (*Ahl al-Kitab*), that is, Jews and Christians.

Lamrabet takes issue with this marriage provision in Moroccan law by demanding that men and women be free to choose a marriage partner without insisting on abandoning their religion and adopting another. She refers to *Tafsir al-Tahrir wa t-Tanwir* by Tunisian scholar Mohamed Tahar Ben Achour (1879–1973), who concluded that no Qur'anic text explicitly prohibits marital union between a Muslim, Christian, or Jewish person or makes it contingent on conversion. Considering that about ten percent of the Moroccan population resides and works abroad, the legal status of inter-religious marriage is a pertinent legal issue.

Lamrabet has relied on multiple sources for her gender-egalitarian interpretations of Islam with a view to promoting social change. Amina Wadud, on the other hand, has focused singularly on situating the status and role of women as expressed in the Qur'an. Yet, both have come to the same conclusions. Wadud's views are based on her reading of the scripture and her exploration of hermeneutics.[37] She sees gender equality as so essential to a contemporary reading of the scripture that she uses the term "gender jihad" to describe her work:

Islam, which is nothing unless lived by people, must be lived by its people today, people who are no longer isolated from pluralistic chaos and consequences of modernity and the after-effects of colonialism...As a Muslim woman living and working with other Muslim women worldwide, I have encountered enough to understand how many seek to find their identity and full voice through continued struggle in the gender jihad, whether consciously or coincidentally.[38]

Wadudian Hermeneutics[39]

In her groundbreaking 1992 book *Qur'an and Woman*,[40] Wadud presented a hermeneutical approach to reading the Qur'an that is inclusive of women's perspectives. As a religious scholar, Wadud claims the right to *ijtihad* (interpretation of scripture). Of course, Wadud's Qur'anic methodology is not entirely new. She has situated herself among reformist theologians like Farid Esack,[41] a South

African Islamic theologian and erstwhile anti-apartheid activist who has long advocated an Islam that demonstrates solidarity with the marginalized. Like Catholic liberation theologians, Esack's reading of sacred scriptures emphasizes a contemporary concept of justice, including social and economic justice. He has called for an end to all forms of oppression, including environmental degradation. Recently, Esack has turned his focus to Morocco.[42]

What is new about Wadud's work, however, is her attempt to pursue an answer to "the woman question" by examining the concept of woman in the Qur'an. According to Wadud, hermeneutics that include female experiences will lead to a greater appreciation for the concept of gender justice in Islamic thought. In contributing this new hermeneutical model, Wadud has expanded and moved beyond an intellectual legacy dating back fourteen hundred years.[43] She has arrived at a new interpretive methodology for understanding the Qur'an from the perspective of a contemporary world in which women deserve to have equal rights. Instead of considering verses on women in the traditionally fragmentary way, she extracted from the Qur'an the complete body of verses concerning women – and then situated them within their larger scriptural context. Thus, Wadud employed a hermeneutics based on *tawhid* (monotheism, or the unity or unicity of God) in which the unity of the Qur'an, or God's word, permeates all of its parts, and verses about women fall into a larger holistic framework of Qur'anic coherence.[44]

In interpreting the first verse of the *sura* entitled "Women," for instance, which discusses the creation of Adam and Eve, Wadud applied her hermeneutical approach to the narrative of creation and concluded it is Qur'anically justified to argue that Eve was *not* born from the "crooked bone" or "rib" of Adam. Since the Qur'an states that everything in creation is paired, Eve must have been created from the same soul as Adam. This led Wadud to conclude that Eve, like Adam, is to become God's vicegerent.[45]

For historical and socio-cultural reasons, however, in the early years of Islam women were excluded from the foundational discourse on what it means to be Muslim. The exegesis of the original text, then, is marked by the absence of women's voices. According to Wadud, this gendered voicelessness in the traditionally interpreted Qur'an is not to be equated with gendered voicelessness in the Qur'anic text itself.[46] Aware also of the discrepancies in gender equality in the *sunnah* and the Qur'an, Wadud chose to use the Qur'an as a source in order to evaluate the difference between "text" and "context," that is, between what is stated in the Qur'an and what is actually practiced in Muslim societies.

Tawhidic *Paradigm*

In her work "Engaging *Tawhid* in Islam and Feminisms,"[47] Wadud outlined the importance of the *tawhidic* (oneness) paradigm for developing new Islamic understandings and policies in specific nation-states as well as the global arena. *Tawhid* is the key term that refers to monotheism in Islam, as it contains the meaning God (Allah) is one. *Tawhid* is taken from the Qur'an, which states that all sins can be forgiven except for *shirk* (the practice of idol worship or polytheism), which is the opposite of *tawhid*. Wadud proposed that *tawhid* is a more dynamic term than the simple translation of monotheism suggests. She instead translated *tawhid* as unicity, meaning God is one, God is unique, God is united, and God unites all things. In the latter part of this definition rests the basis for non-discrimination and challenges to patriarchy within Islamic worldviews. As Wadud explained:

Since God is the highest conceptual aspect of all, then no person can be greater than another person, especially for mere reasons of gender, race, class, nationality, etc. The *tawhidic* paradigm then acts as a basic theoretical principle for removing gender asymmetry, which is a kind of satanic logic or shirk, positing priority or superiority to men. Instead, women and men must occupy a relationship of horizontal reciprocity, maintaining the highest place for God in His/Her/Its uniqueness.[48]

The *tawhidic* paradigm represents a reformulation of the Qur'anic concept of *tawhid*, denoting the oneness of God, in which a radical vision of equality between all human beings, under one God, is articulated.

Thus, consistent with her belief that women's use of Islamic primary sources is a "fundamental strategy for empowerment,"[49] Wadud has utilized Qur'anic notions of equality as a basis for developing symmetrical and reciprocal relations between men and women in all areas of society, including in the familial, political, and spiritual realms:

If human beings really are horizontally equal, independent, and mutually co- dependent, each has the same potential for performing any social, religious, political, or economic task. The cultural and historical precedent of exclusive male leadership in the role of religious ritual is not a requirement. Although it has served as a convenience which later became legally inscribed, it was merely customary and should not be prescribed as religious mandate. Women's *tawhidic* humanity allows them to function in all roles for which they develop the prerequisite qualifications.[50]

Khalifah

Another key term for gender equality is *khalifah*, representative, successor, or vice-regent. In a geo-political sense, this concept arose in the context of succession, after the death of the Prophet Mohamed. No one else could take on Mohamed's theocratic leadership identity since his followers believed he was called by God to fulfill both a transcendent and politically immediate mission. Subsequent leaders assumed the title Khalif to mean "successor" to the legacy of Mohamed.

When it is stated in the the Qur'an: "Inni jaa'ilun fi-l-'ard khalifah," ("Indeed, We will create on the earth a khalifah"), Wadud argues that this verse refers to "the responsibility of each human being to establish social justice as a representative of the divine will or cosmic harmony."[51] According to Wadud, *khalifah* comprises a specific ethical dimension for existence, that is, that humans are created to be moral agents. Further, the Qur'an makes no distinction between males and females in terms of this divine mandate. Humans are held equally accountable for their actions, individually and collectively.

As an ethical term, *khalifah* summons up the primordial ontology of human creation. Wadud has argued that humans are assigned the task of constructing systems of justice and equality on earth, a nuance that has been pivotal in global reform movements related to Muslim Personal Status Codes. Such laws and codes often have served as the basis for the second-class citizenship of women in Muslim-majority countries, as well as explicit discrimination against them. In Wadud's formulation, once proponents of women's rights can demonstrate the existence of religious authority behind the movement to eradicate gender-based discrimination and establish full human rights for women, then the oppression of women can no longer be justified by Islam.[52]

Each in her own way, then, Mernissi, Lamrabet, and Wadud have arrived at positions from which to advocate for religiously sanctioned gender equality. For Lamrabet this means ending patriarchy and gender hierarchy so as to experience fully the unity of God and human submission to the divine. The Qur'anic concept of *insan* (human) and its vision for human existence demand equality and justice for all men and women.[53]

The Significance of Wadud's Gesture (*Salat*) and Sermon (*Khutba*)

After leading Friday prayers in New York City in 2005, Wadud delivered a sermon in Arabic, with extracts in English chosen for their relevance to contemporary gender discourse. She selected the verses of *sura* 33.35: "The men who surrender and the women who surrender, the men who believe and the women who believe ... Allah has prepared for them forgiveness and a vast reward," as well as a verse from *Surat al-nisa'* 4.1 as the basis for the equality of creation of humankind: "He has created you from a single *nafs* [a living being, a soul] and created from it, its mate."

Wadud's selection was meant to illustrate the *tawhidic* paradigm and point to the horizontal reciprocity between humans, particularly men and women. Her elaboration on the *tawhidic* paradigm had the effect of re-inscribing gender symmetry – the equal significance of both men and women. She concluded that male leadership in prayer is not a theological requirement, but merely the result of custom, of historical and cultural precedents. In these ways, Wadud, like Lamrabet, uphold the feminist tradition emphasizing male and female equality.

Lamrabet and Wadud as Representatives of a Transnational Third Way

Videos on Lamrabet's website serve as an indication of her connection with feminist scholars throughout the world. An example is her video, "Equality *Inch'allah*," which documents some of the November 2010 Fourth Annual International Congress on Islamic Feminism in Madrid, Spain. In the video, Lamrabet stated that all religions are in essence, patriarchal, because their spiritual message is grounded in patriarchal cultures that instrumentalize the spiritual message of a religion to sustain the patriarchy. She goes on to contend that Muslim feminists call for reading and reinterpreting sacred texts from a feminine[54] perspective because of the invisibility of females in the field of hermeneutics (*tafsir*), and that her advocacy for Third Way feminism is based on the notion that women can achieve peace with themselves only when they are no longer undervalued by religion.

Lamrabet has argued for pluralistic interpretations of sacred scriptures as a means by which global feminists can establish a dialogue based on the deconstruction of traditional knowledge that is masculine and patriarchal. She has said that Third Way Islamic Feminism allows for the reconciliation of Islam and modernity and goes beyond the false dichotomies of Muslim and secular, modernist and traditionalist, East and West.

Lamrabet's and Wadud have advocated for transnational women's rights discourse. They have taken their messages to universities, grassroots civil society organizations, and government and non-government forums throughout the United States, the Middle East, Southeast Asia, Africa, and Europe.[55]

Wadud and Lamrabet as Islamic Feminist Reformers

Lamrabet and Wadud's writings enjoy wide popularity, especially among young, intellectual Muslims in Morocco who want to find answers to the question of what it means to be a Muslim in the modern world. Faced with increasingly conservative and radical interpretations of sacred texts, these scholars offer a religious perspective on modern religiously inspired identity formation. They exemplify how Muslim women can re-appropriate sacred texts, a fundamental strategy of their empowerment and personal development. Certainly there are other important authors who have explored new forms of feminism in Morocco such as Fatima Sadiqi and Zakia Salime but they have not primarily focused on the theological aspect.[56]

Both Lamrabet and Wadud have addressed head-on an age-old question: Who has the authority to interpret the sacred texts? Each woman in her own way is appropriating authority over textual analysis and, in doing so, is creating a new voice, a new way of approaching gender and women's rights within an Islamic context. Together, their work exists within the larger context of challenges to religious authority in contemporary Muslim societies. The role of the traditional 'ulama' (Islamic scholars) has been challenged by the rise of alternative sources of religious authority that claim equal legitimacy, as evidenced by the existence of many Internet fatwas and satellite TV imams.[57] If men with limited scholarly theological training can exert influence – uncontested by conservative scholars – why would alternative interpretations by women not fit into this colorful landscape of religious authorities?

Lamrabet and Wadud represent new models of Islamic leadership. Each in her own way refers to *taqwa*, or God consciousness, as the basis of her personal and scholarly endeavors. Each refers to her faith as the foundation for engendering a type of thinking about God and a divine plan (insofar as any human can conceive of God's intentions), which for each of them translates into advocacy for social, political, economic, and legal reforms. Such reforms, then, aspire to both spiritual and worldly liberation.

By speaking publicly, writing, and propagating their ideas via new communication technologies and social media, Lamrabet and Wadud have created a distinctive female presence in Morocco, the Muslim world, and beyond. More importantly, they are claiming space within Islamic orthodoxy by assuming the role of exegete, thereby introducing a female orientation to the scriptural and legal interpretative process. At the time of this writing, however, it is too early to assess the extent of their contribution to reshaping the larger framework within which scriptures are being reinterpreted.

They are shaking the foundations of Islamic knowledge, of what constitutes "truth" in regard to gender. Their epistemological shift in the lens through which religious knowledge is viewed means that such understandings need not be considered authoritative and incontestable, but rather constructed and context-specific. Further, in the process of engineering this shift, they have dismantled the traditional androcentric paradigms that have kept women out of the interpretive process.

Conclusions

Liberation theology emerged in Latin America at a time when social inequalities there were glaring and the Catholic Church in that region was aligned with corrupt ruling elites. In Morocco, as in other North African countries, conservative Islamists have articulated the most strident regime critiques based in part on equally glaring social inequalities that are perceived as un-Islamic. Similarly, some Third Way proponents are incorporating their gender egalitarian discourse within the larger context of other inequalities, much like the first liberation theologians. In Morocco, however, Third Way feminists have not overtly critiqued the state, nor the monarchy. Neither Wadud nor Lamrabet sees herself as a rebel like Brazil's Dom Hélder Câmara or Leonardo Boff, who were early proponents of liberation theology. Instead, they believe that religiously inspired gender equality can come about through dialogue and the engagement of men and women in a new discourse about sacred texts. They believe the Qur'an can become a pillar of social change that lays the groundwork for greater fairness and justice and encompasses political and economic issues. Mernissi, Wadud and Lamrabet each aims to liberate Muslim women from archaic and limited roles with negative social and economic consequences. Their ideas are consistent with the notion of a Third Way Islamic feminist liberation theology, disseminated through networks on the ground and through powerful, contemporary social media.

Endnotes

1 See, for example, Moroccan weekly *TelQuel* February 6, 2016, "Mohamed VI ordonne une révision de l'enseignement religieux."
2 Murphy, E. (2003) "Women in Tunisia: between state feminism and economic reform." *Women and Globalization in the Arab Middle East*. D.E. Abdella and P. Posusney (eds.). Boulder: Lynne Rienner.
3 Wadud, A. (2015). "The Ethics of Tawhid over the Ethics of Quiwamah." *Men in Charge?: Rethinking Authority in Muslim Legal Tradition*. Z. Mir-Hosseini, M. Al-Sharmani and J. Rumminger (eds.). Oneworld, p. 263.
4 Bell, D.M. (2001). *Liberation Theology: After the End of History*. London: Routledge, p. 101.
5 Quoted in ibid, p. 101.
6 Tombs, D. (2002). *Latin American Liberation Theology*. Leiden: Brill, p. 121.
7 Bell, *Liberation Theology*, p. 103.
8 Gray, D.H. (2014). *Beyond Feminism and Islamism – Gender and Equality in North Africa*. London: I.B. Tauris.
9 Ibid.
10 Bouachrine, I. (2015). *Women and Islam: Myths, Apologies, and the Limits of Feminist Critique*. Lanham, MD: Lexington.
11 Al-Sharmani, M. (December 2014). "Islamic Feminism: transnational and national reflections." *Approaching Religion*. Vol. 4, No. 2, p. 86.
12 El Hajjami, A. (2009). "Gender equality and Islamic Law: the case of Morocco." *New Directions in Islamic Thought – Exploring Reform and Muslim Tradition*. London: I.B. Tauris, p. 101.
13 Ibid, p. 108.

14 Mernissi, F. (1987). *Beyond the Veil: Male-Female Dynamics in Modern Muslim Societies*; (1992). *The Veil and the Male Elite: A Feminist Interpretation of Women's Rights in Islam* (with Mary Jo Lakeland); (1995). *Dreams of Trespass: Tales of a Harem Girlhood*; (1996). *Women's Rebellion and Islamic Memory*; (1997). *The Forgotten Queens of Islam* (with Mary Jo Lakeland); (2001). *Schehrezade Goes West*; (2002). *Islam and Democracy: Fear of the Modern World*.

15 Personal interview with Fatima Mernissi by Doris Gray as cited in Gray, *Beyond Feminism*, p. 33.

16 Mernissi, F. (2004). "The satellite, the prince, and Scheherazade: the rise of women as communicators in digital Islam." *Transnational Broadcasting Studies*, p. 12.

17 Badran, M. (2009). *Feminism in Islam: Secular and Religious Convergences*, Oneworld Publications; A. Hidayatullah (2014). *Feminist Edges of the Qur'an*. Oxford University Press.

18 Tais, A. (2015). "Islamic perspectives in post-revolutionary Tunisia: the work of Olfa Youssef." *Journal of Religion and Society*. The Kripke Center. Vol. 17, pp. 1–12.

19 www.asma-lamrabet.com.

20 Moroccan Constitution, Article 46: The person of the King is inviolable, and respect is due Him.

21 Lamrabet, A. (2002). *Musulmane tout simplement*; (2004). *Aïcha, Epouse du Prophète ou l'Islam au féminine*; (2007). *Le Coran et les femmes: une lecture de libération*; (2011). *Femmes – Islam Occident: chemins vers l'universel*; (2012). *Femmes et hommes dans le Coran: quelle égalité?*

22 Lamrabet, A. (2015). "An egalitarian reading of the concepts of Khalifah, Wilayah and Quiwamah." *Men in Charge?: Rethinking Authority in Muslim Legal Tradition*. Z. Mir-Hosseini, M. Al-Sharmani and J. Rumminger (eds.). London: Oneworld, pp. 65–87.

23 Ibid.

24 Wadud, A. (2003). "American Muslim identity: race and ethnicity in progressive Islam." *Progressive Muslims*. O. Safi (ed.), pp. 270–285; (1999). *Qur'an and Woman: Rereading the Sacred Text from a Woman's Perspective*. Oxford University Press; (2006). *Inside the Gender Jihad: Women's Reform in Islam*. Oxford: Oneworld.

25 Gender mainstreaming is not a goal in itself but a strategy to achieve equality between women and men. It is used to integrate gender concerns into policies, programs, and, in this case, hermeneutics.

26 Interview with Asma Lamrabet. September 23, 2013.

27 Lamrabet, "An egalitarian reading," p. 82.

28 Ibid, p. 85.

29 Ibid.

30 www.Asma-Lamrabet.com.

31 Ibid.

32 Lamrabet, Asma. "Les 11 concepts clés de l'égalité femme – hommes dans le Coran." www.asma-lamrabet.com/articles/les-11-concepts-cles-de-l-egalite-femme-hommes-dans- le-coran/.

33 http://legacy.quran.com/4.

34 Ibid.

35 Lamrabet, "Les 11 concepts."

36 There are Muslim majority communities that are matrilineal such as certain Tuareg Hassaniya, Serer and some coastal peoples in Tanzania.

37 Wadud, A. (1999). *The Qur'an and Woman: Rereading the Sacred Text from a Woman's Perspective*. Oxford University Press.

38 Wadud, A. (2006). *Inside the Gender Jihad: Women's Reform in Islam*. Oxford: Oneworld.

39 Abugideiri, H. (Winter 1996). "Allegorical gender: the figure of Eve revisited." *The American Journal of Islamic Social Sciences*. Vol. 13, No. 4, pp. 524–526.

40 Wadud, *The Qu'ran and Woman*.

41 Esack, F. (1996). *Qur'an, Liberation and Pluralism: An Islamic Perspective of Interreligious Solidarity against Oppression*. London: Oneworld.

42 See Esack, *Qur'an, Liberation*; (1999). *On Being a Muslim: Finding a Religious Path in the World Today*. London: Oneworld.

43 For a discussion of the different historical Qur'anic methodological approaches to the Qur'an from classical to contemporary times, see B. Stowasser (1998). "Gender issues and contemporary Qur'anic interpretations." *Islam, Gender and Social Change*. Y. Haddad and J. Esposito (eds.). Oxford University Press, pp. 30–44.

44 Abugideiri, H. (Spring 2001). "The renewed woman of American Islam: shifting lenses toward 'Gender Jihad?'" *The Muslim World*. Vol. 91, pp. 1–18; A. Wadud (2015). "The ethics of Tawhid over the ethics of Qiwamah." *Men in Charge? Rethinking Authority in Muslim Legal Tradition*. Z. Mir- Hosseini, M. Al-Sharmani and J. Rumminger (eds.). Oneworld.

45 Abugideiri, H. (2001). "Hagar: a historical model for 'Gender Jihad.'" *Daughters of Abraham*. Y. Haddad and J. Esposito (eds.). Gainesville: University Press of Florida, p. 91.

46 Wadud, *The Qur'an and Woman*, p. 2.

47 Wadud, A. (December 2008). "Engaging Tawhid in Islam and Feminisms." *International Feminist Journal of Politics*. Vol. 10, No. 4, pp. 435–438.

48 Ibid, p. 437.

49 Wadud, A. (2007). *Inside the Gender Jihad: Women's Reform in Islam*. Oxford: Oneworld, p. 9.
50 Ibid, pp. 168–169.
51 Ibid, p. 35.
52 Wadud, A. (2015). "The Ethics of Tawhid over the Ethics of Qiwamah." *Men in Charge?: Rethinking Authority in Muslim Legal Tradition*. Z. Mir-Hosseini, M. Al-Sharmani and J. Rumminger (eds.). London: Oneworld, 2015.
53 Lamrabet, "An Egalitarian Reading," p. 84.
54 Interestingly, both Lamrabet and Wadud were reluctant to consider themselves as feminists in their early work. In her blog on *qiwamah*, Lamrabet explains that the feminine interpretation of religious texts has revealed the existence in the Qur'an of a true divine pedagogy of women's liberation. Since the citadel of religious knowledge has almost always been monopolized by male scholars, she adds, men self-appointed themselves as guardians of the sacred and banned women from the right to access religious knowledge in order to perpetuate their domination of that sacred.
55 Some of Wadud's speaking engagements have included the keynote address "Islam, Justice, and Gender" at the 2008 international conference Understanding Conflicts: Cross-Cultural Perspectives, held at Aarhus University, Denmark; a paper titled "Islam Beyond Patriarchy Through Gender Inclusive Qur'anic Analysis" at the 2009 Musawah (www.musawah.org) – Equality and Justice in the Family conference; the Regional Conference on Advancing Gender Equality and Women's Empowerment in Muslim Societies, hosted by United Nations Development Fund for Women (UNIFEM) and the International Centre for Islam and Pluralism (ICIP) in Jakarta, Indonesia, in March 2009. Her talks and workshops in universities include Norway, Australia, and the US.
56 Salime, Z. (2011). *Between Feminism and Islam: Human Rights and Sharia Law in Morocco*. Minneapolis: University of Minnesota Press; F. Sadiqi, M. Ennaji and K. Vintges (2016). *Moroccan Feminist Discourses*. Africa World Press.
57 Kramer, G. and S. Schmidtke (eds.) (2006). *Speaking for Islam. Religious Authorities in Muslim Societies*. Leiden: Brill.

6 | Moroccan Mothers' Religiosity
Impact on Daughters' Education

IMANE CHAARA

Introduction

Raising school enrollment in developing countries is a universally praised policy objective and a focus of the United Nations Millennium Development Goals and Sustainable Development Goals. The World Bank has repeatedly recognized in its World Development Reports the importance of primary schooling as an impetus to social and economic progress. The education of girls has received special attention due to its important positive impact on children and adult health, fertility, and infant mortality. Raising school enrollment may depend, however, on the relative importance of school supply and household demand factors. On one hand, the educational infrastructure must be present and affordable. On the other, parents must be willing to send their children to school.

Handa[1] showed that in the case of Mozambique, for instance, building more schools or raising adult literacy would have a larger impact on primary school enrollment than interventions that raise household income. Huisman and Smits[2] looked at the effect of household and district level factors on school enrollment in 30 developing countries and found that in addition to the effects of socio-economic factors, family demographic characteristics, and characteristics of educational facilities at the district level, the empowerment of women was an important determinant of primary school enrollment. Moreover, the strong positive effect of a mother's education indicates that mothers with more knowledge are in a better position to get their children into school. Huisman and Smits have argued that since many mothers in developing countries are illiterate, a major way to make them aware of the benefits of education for their children is through the media. The aim of such communication would be to stimulate public discussion about the importance of education and pass along information that would serve to widen mothers' horizons.

In this chapter, I use quantitative and qualitative evidence to show that, in the context of Morocco, mothers' involvement in household decisions leads to better educational outcomes for girls and religious mothers are more likely to be involved in educational decisions, especially those with limited or no formal education. I therefore argue that religion may play a similar role as education regarding consciousness-raising about the importance of children's education and self-valuation of women with respect to their capacity to play a key role within their household. I further argue that the positive social message on the importance of education and the role of women in society conveyed by the women's section of an influential religious movement may have played a critical role.

The decision to invest in a child's education is made primarily at the household level. Because households are complex structures, more knowledge of the way decisions are made by its members is crucial for understanding household outcomes. In regard to the education of children, then, a natural question is, who makes the decisions? Given previous research, a better sense of the role played by mothers in the decision-making process appears to be of particular importance. In analyzing data I collected in Morocco in 2008, I observed that when mothers participated in decisions concerning the education of their daughters, the latter were more likely to stay in school after primary education in urban areas and more likely to enroll in primary school in rural areas.[3] These findings led to a subsequent question: What triggers mothers' involvement in decisions concerning the education of their daughters?

Research on the participation of women in household decisions generally is framed in terms of their bargaining power within the household.[4] The household economics literature often characterizes bargaining power in terms of control over tangible resources, but in my research in Morocco, I focused on an unconventional factor: the religiosity of mothers. Some psychologists[5] have argued that, in addition to tangible resources, certain behavioral traits can lead to more influence and power if valued by family members.[6] Further, cultural anthropologists have emphasized that in addition to economic valuations, social or religious valuations may play a role. Based on these considerations, I began to suspect that religious faith may be a factor in the relative power of each household member, and that women may strategically use religion in order to gain more control, play an important role in their family, and access public life.[7] In this chapter I present the results of research I conducted to examine this proposition.

In discussing the results of this research, I argue that in the Moroccan context, socially influential religious movements are important because they may represent an underlying factor influencing both religious practice and decision-making within the household. I examined two major religious movements and associated organizations. One is the illegal but tolerated Jama'a al 'Adl wa-l Ihsan (al-'Adl) or Justice and Spirituality movement, as well as its associated women's section. The other is the political Party of Justice and Development (PJD) and its associated organization, the Organization for the Renewal of Feminine Consciousness (ORCF – Tajdid al-Wa'i al-nisa'i). These groups are influential across a wide spectrum of the population and are especially popular in the low and lower-middle classes thanks to the social services they provide. However, my interest resides more specifically in al-'Adl. In addition to providing assistance, the members of al-'Adl transmit messages about their own vision of education and the allocation of roles within the family. Understanding the actions and discourse of this influential religious group and its affiliates may, therefore, be useful in identifying how religion plays a role in the division of tasks between spouses in the household, particularly in decisions concerning children's education. In fact, I contend that religious movements may represent an alternative way to make mothers aware of the benefits of education for daughters and raise the perceived value of women by framing them as important actors in the private sphere and society.

Exploring Mothers' Participation in Educational Decisions for Daughters

The evidence presented in this chapter is based on both quantitative and qualitative data collection and analyses. The quantitative component of the project is based on survey data; it is very briefly summarized here and more intensively presented in a companion paper.[8] Based on this data, I present a statistical analysis of the relationship between the mother's religiosity and her participation in educational decisions for daughters. The qualitative component includes data derived from interviews with local women activists and was designed to expand my understanding of the potential social influence of religious movements and how this influence may explain the main results of the quantitative study. To my knowledge, there is no previous study on Muslim societies, and in particular on countries in the Maghreb, that use precise micro-data on religiosity and household decision-making that could inform the present research project. This study is therefore a first attempt to empirically address the role of religiosity in household decisions, and in particular decisions concerning education of girls.

Quantitative Component of the Analysis: Mothers' Religiosity, Household Decision-Making, and Daughters' Education

Methodological Aspects

A quantitative analysis was based on survey data that I and my research team collected in 2008 in 3 of the 16 administrative regions of Morocco:[9] Tangier-Tetouan, Casablanca, and Souss-Massa-Draa (in the Ouarzazate province). The regions were not randomly selected but were chosen on the basis of relevant socio-demographic characteristics (conservatism of Tetouan, national immigration for Casablanca, and Ouarzazate for being mostly rural and composed of Amazigh – Berber populations). The choice of these regions allowed for the inclusion of people who have been subject to a variety of influences in the course of their history. The inclusion of regional dummies in the analysis enabled me to control for unobserved differences across regions.

A total of 542 randomly chosen individuals were interviewed in both rural and urban areas. Of those interviewed, 283 (51 percent women and 49 percent men) were married with children and were the focus of the analysis. In each family visited, a questionnaire was randomly administered to either the husband or wife.

The central question was whether religiosity played a role in the involvement of mothers in their daughters' schooling decisions. I estimated the religiosity of mothers using a multidimensional proxy measure of the intensity of their religious practice, that is, their faith and religious devotion. I also tested whether the role of religiosity differed between educated mothers and mothers with limited or no formal education. In other words, I tested whether the effects of education and religiosity reinforced or substituted for each other in regard to mothers' involvement in decisions concerning the education of their daughters.

Intensity of religious practice. Each respondent was asked if he or she obeyed a series of practices (such as praying, fasting, tithing, etc.). For affirmative responses, each respondent was asked about the frequency of that religious practice. The questions that were used to construct this index concerned particular practices: the obligatory prayers (five per day), the prayer at dawn (*fajr*), the prayer at night (*qyam layl*), the nonobligatory prayers (*nawafil*), the supplementary prayers of Ramadan (*tarawih*), the fasting beyond Ramadan, the tithing duty (*zakat*), ownership of the Qur'an, ownership of the prophetic traditions (*hadith*), ownership of books about Islamic thought, and finally, whether the respondent shared her knowledge of religious principles with her circle of kin, friends, and neighbors.[10] There was no significant difference in terms of the intensity of religious practice between urban and rural populations, while women appeared to be significantly more religious than men.

The use of a multidimensional measure of religiosity represents a real improvement with respect to measures that were used in the relevant literature (see for instance, the World Value Survey or the Arab Barometer Survey). Most of these measures focus on religious beliefs or on one particular practice (i.e. attendance of religious services), and therefore do not take into account the diversity of practices and the subjective importance attached to different practices.

Formal education level. The measure of education that was used in the analysis was based exclusively on formal education and excluded religious teaching or any form of educational training respondents may have received outside the formal education system, particularly from religious movements. This decision had two rationales: first, formal education is easier to identify and measure, and second, education received by religious movements is probably less consistent and more difficult to compare.

Respondents were asked if they had ever been to school. If yes, they were asked about the highest level of education completed. Respondents also were asked to report the same information about their spouse. In a majority of households there was a match in terms of the education of husbands and wives (176 households out of 274, i.e. 64.2 percent of households). When there was no match, it was more likely that the husband was more educated than his wife (83 households out of 98, i.e. 85 percent of the cases). About 42 percent of the sample was composed of noneducated spouses (115 households out of 274).

Empirical Results

In a companion paper,[11] I discussed in great detail the relationship between mothers' involvement in educational decisions for their daughters and their intensity of religious practice, while taking into account the variables of socio-economic status, level of education, spouse and family characteristics, location (urban vs. rural) and institutional factors that may impact women's bargaining power. Here it suffices to say that the analysis revealed a positive relationship between the intensity of the religious practice of mothers and their participation in the decisions concerning their daughters' education. In other words, the more religious the mother, the more likely it was that she participated in decisions concerning the education of her daughter. I also found that women who had completed at least primary school and women who engaged in an income generating activity were more likely to take part in educational decisions.

I also tested the hypothesis that intensity of religious practice, hereafter referred to as religiosity, acted as a "substitute" for education. The central question here was whether religion played the same role as education regarding consciousness-raising about the importance of children's education and self-valuation of women with respect to their capacity to play a key role within their household. Interestingly, I found that the positive relationship previously identified between the religiosity of the mother and her involvement in educational decisions occurred mainly among mothers with limited or no formal education, i.e. those who did not complete primary education or never went to school. Educated women also were more likely to participate in educational decisions, though in this case it was the factor of education, rather than religiosity, that drove their participation.

For educated women, then, religiosity did not play a complementary role, but among mothers with limited formal education, religiosity increased the likelihood of their participation in educational decisions for their daughters. These results indicate that religiosity served as a compensating factor for the lack of education in regard to mothers' educational decision-making. Thus, educated women were more likely than uneducated women to participate in educational decisions, but among uneducated women, the more religious they were, the more likely they were to take part in decisions concerning the education of their daughters.

I also looked at the same indicators when it comes to the education of boys. The same results are observed but the correlation between women's religiosity and the likelihood to participate in educational decisions is weaker and less statistically significant than in the case of decisions concerning daughters' education. Moreover, it appears that the correlation is robust only in families composed of daughters and sons but not in families where children are all boys. My interpretation of this result is the following: a spillover effect may exist, which means that women participate in educational decisions concerning their sons when they are already involved in decisions concerning their daughters. In fact, if the involvement of women in educational decision when more religious is partly explained by the influence of a religious movement such as Al-Adl wa-l Ihsane, priority may be given to daughters since the educational discourse of the women section is focused on the significant social role of women and the importance of their education. As a consequence, women who have only sons may be less affected by the educational discourse of the movement. I explore this possible interpretation in more detail in the following section, which is based on a qualitative analysis of the quantitative research findings.

By using the sub-sample of men I found that the religiosity of the father is not related to the involvement of mothers in educational decisions.[12]

Qualitative Component of the Analysis: The Role of Influential Religious Movements in Mothers' Participation in Education Decisions

The results described above emphasized the existence of a robust positive relationship between women's religiosity and the likelihood of participating in education decisions concerning their daughters. One mechanism may help to explain the greater involvement of mothers in education decisions in the Moroccan context and warrants further exploration: the influence of religious movements. Religion is expected to shape parental values, just as education does. In addition, it can influence a number of life decisions.[13] I have argued that the nature of the impact of religion on the involvement of women in educational decisions is not clear, and depends on perceptions concerning the role that women should play in the private sphere as well as the importance attached to children's education, especially for girls. I hypothesized that these perceptions are likely to be directly or indirectly shaped by the discourse of religious authorities and religious movements.

Though I could not establish whether the surveyed women in 2008 were directly connected to any religious movement, I believe that this information would have, in any case, underestimated the influence of religious movements for two reasons. First, the interviewed women may not have been directly connected to a religious movement but may have had close relatives, neighbors, friends who were connected, thus requiring a network analysis for the full picture. Second, the interviewed women may have been connected to local associations where members of religious movements operate and convey their messages without necessarily being labeled as official members of a specific movement. Accordingly, I chose to explore how religious movements may influence the lives of women, especially the most religious ones. I therefore interviewed local activists associated with two religious movements that were important and influential at the time the data was collected.

Methodology

In September 2014,[14] I conducted eight one-on-one interviews with current and former members of Al-Adl wa-l Ihsane women's section[15] with the goal of better understanding the group's messages, strategies, and actions on the ground.[16] I sought to understand more fully how female members of the movement interacted with the large female population in their regions. I was particularly interested in the actions of the women's section in the period preceding the surveys I administered in 2008.[17]

I conducted interviews in Casablanca, Rabat, Marrakech, and Tangier both with members who had important positions of responsibility in the women's section and members who were at the bottom of the hierarchy. The interviews were semi-structured; I introduced a limited number of primary questions and a series of secondary questions about the organization of the women's section, as well as its strategy, actions, and targeted population. Other information emerged spontaneously in the course of the interviews. Before presenting the results, I will provide more context on the two major religious movements in Morocco in existence in 2008 with a focus on the Al-Adl wa-l Ihsane movement.

Religious Movements in Morocco

In the last three decades, the socio-political landscape of Morocco has grown to include two important religious movements,[18] the Justice and Spirituality movement (Jama'a al 'Adl wa-l Ihsane or Al-Adl), and the political Party of Justice and Development (PJD) associated with the socially conservative Movement for Reform and Unity (Haraka al-Islah wa-l Tawhid). Both are nonviolent organizations that originated in the late 1960s-early 1970s, though the two groups never formed a coalition because of their differences. On an ideological level, the PJD has taken a much more conservative line on social issues like the place of women in society.[19] Differences also exist at a strategic level: the PJD accepted co-optation by the authorities and decided to participate in official political life.[20] To the contrary, Al-Adl has stayed out of the political system and decided instead to act as a critic of the regime by challenging the monarchy. Understanding the main philosophy, structure, strategic approach, and social involvement of these two religious movements can help illuminate their impact on educational decision-making for daughters, especially among mothers.

I focus on Jama'a al 'Adl wa-l Ihsane, and in particular on its women's section because they appear to be more active among the female population at the local level and better organized. Moreover, members of ORCF (Organization for the Renewal of Feminine Consciousness – Tajdid al wai al nisai), the women's association linked to the PJD, have more conservative views about family structure: they are favorable towards polygamy, guardianship of the father, and marriage for women from the age of 15.[21] This organization also has been known to support the idea that women should not work outside the home if the husband has the financial means to maintain the family.[22] ORCF is attached to a traditional vision of society with a clear division of roles between men and women. During an interview with the president of ORCF, she emphasized that women should know their duties and rights, defined by prioritizing the protection of the family.[23] In the same vein, Gray[24] found that ORCF members felt that women's rights need to be first and foremost grounded in safeguarding the rights of children and the family. Unlike the women's section of Al-Adl, however, the ORCF has had no well-defined educational project.

Jama'a al 'Adl wa-l Ihsane (Al-Adl)

Al-Adl was founded by a former school inspector, Abdessalam Yassine, who was a member of a Sufi brotherhood named Boutchichiyya.[25] Sheikh Yassine believed that the social, political, and economic problems of the kingdom stemmed from the State's insufficient attention to Islam,[26] and that change must come through social activism and criticized the constitution, the concentration of political powers, and the "sacred" status of the Monarch in Morocco. Because the movement was constructed around the ideas of Sheikh Yassine and is based upon Sufi principles,[27] priority is placed on the inner-transformation of the individual as a means for changing society. This bottom-up approach stresses the importance of education and the transformation of society along Islamic lines at the individual level so as to establish an ideal political system.

Since the 1980s, the main concern of Al-Adl has been social justice, and it gradually has become more engaged in various social services such as schooling and medical care while at the same time providing religious and spiritual guidance to its beneficiaries.[28] In supplying these social services, Al-Adl acts as a substitute for the state, and at the same time, disseminates its own educational plan. The foundation of the organization's work is the *da'wa* ('making an invitation' to Islam, or an act of proselytizing): each member makes an effort to become a better Muslim and attempts through example to turn others into better Muslims, so that individual behavior can slowly affect the society as a whole.[29] *Da'wa* implies missionary activities in as many areas as possible of social life.

Despite being officially illegal, Al-Adl is tolerated by Moroccan authorities. As of 2016, Al-Adl is the largest and most well-organized movement in Morocco; it has a sophisticated pyramidal structure and branches throughout the country.[30] Al-Adl seems to benefit from the support of a large segment of the population, but its number of members is unknown.

Al-Adl women's section. Women have been active in Al-Adl since the 1980s, the women's section of the organization was officially created in 1998 by Nadia Yassine, daughter of Sheikh Yassine. Members of this section accepted the rejection of polygamy in certain cases,[31] and favored the model of the nuclear family, including the belief that women can have a profession outside the home. Al-Adl members may be seen as militants who support a feminist interpretation of the religious texts as well as the emancipation of women through education.

The education of women was central to the women's section of Al-Adl and represented the basis of their model. The women's section supported the egalitarian involvement of men and women in family matters, though it did not defend a model of clear equal rights and responsibilities. Rather, the group used the notion of "complementarity" to characterize the preferred roles of men and women – despite the elusiveness of a definition of the concept.[32] Though gender complementarity emphasizes the role of women as wives and mothers, the female leaders of the movement insisted on the importance of education for women and their right to pursue a professional career.[33] They favored the concept of gender justice over gender equality,[34] a preference that appears to have been mainly a terminology issue, since the improvement of women's rights was a common objective.

Naciri[35] has argued that some women are receptive to Muslim movements because they value their social roles within the family, in part because Muslim movements envision the gendered division of roles not in terms of hierarchy, but as noble tasks that are the responsibility of the Muslim woman. Moreover, Merieme Yafout, a former member of Al-Adl who wrote a thesis on women in Islamist movements, argued that Islamist movements offer greater prospects for self-realization and advancement than many secular feminist associations that are characterized by rigid power structures.[36]

Sisters for eternity. Al-Adl women's section established the Sisters for Eternity project in order to increase the "consciousness" of women and advise them about the "right path" to follow in life. Though the project no longer exists, at the time it functioned, Sisters of Eternity offered life guidance with the goal of helping women get closer to God through a return to religious sources. It involved organizing all-women gatherings led by women, and these gatherings sent a strong empowering signal, according to Gray.[37] Though initially open only to members of Al-Adl movement, according to one member of the women section I interviewed, the project rapidly grew in importance.

Sisters for Eternity trained women with good communication skills to lead sessions all over Morocco. They were taught basic principles of the movement and how to organize gatherings, to which women interested in the philosophy of the movement were invited. In these sessions, they talked about women's enlightenment, that is, a certain level of consciousness and agency that can only happen through education.[38] The Sisters of Eternity asserted that women in Morocco have a self-esteem problem, and emphasized that women should learn to respect themselves and be confident. They viewed the process of increasing women's agency as a difficult one, and believed that women could change more easily if they associated changes in their behavior with their relationship with God. The Sisters contended that the changes women made would be valued by God and would allow them to get closer to God. Though they used religious references in order to induce social change, they believed that change could occur only when people understand their religion and see change as a way to become closer to God.

Religious Movements and Social Influence

Though a rigorous evaluation of the social influence of these religious organizations is beyond the scope of this discussion, it seems obvious that Al-Adl is very well organized and has been quite active on the ground. The movement chose to adopt a bottom-up approach, starting at the grassroots level, in order to change society. To this end, it has provided residents with social services, helping people while educating them. Secular education is important – as one of their members asserts, they "have no complex about learning from the Western world."[39] At the same time, they believe moral education and spiritual teaching must accompany education.

Al-Adl attaches importance to the education of women; those with formal education are strongly encouraged to pursue their studies and/ or go back to school and university. For those without formal education, Al-Adl organizes literacy courses beside moral and spiritual teachings. They describe women as the basis for the development of future generations and, in turn, for the ideal society they hope to construct.

The PJD chose another strategy, arguing that in order to change society, the organization must be involved in the political system. Even if they are also active on the ground, particularly through different associations linked to the party, their approach is more top-down. Nevertheless, since their existence as a party, the PJD has won a great deal of political support from the voters and achieved very good results since the 2002 legislative elections. In November 2011, the PJD emerged as the largest party in parliamentary elections. Their leader, Abdelilah Benkirane, became prime minister and was chosen by the King to lead the new government. As of 2016, the PJD remained in power and the king maintained Benkirane in his position as prime minister after parliamentary elections of October 2016.

What Do the Discourse and Projects of Women Activists Teach Us?

The interviews I conducted with current and former members of the women section of Al-Adl provided a number of relevant insights that supported my hypothesis about the influential role of this religious movement among women. Members of the women's section had a positive influence on female education and women's empowerment. Several main patterns emerged from my interviews with these women activists.

Gender Justice, Re-Reading of Sacred Texts

Those I interviewed from Al-Adl women's section generally felt that women are the victims of unequal treatment in the name of religion. They stated that in order to change the status quo it is urgent to correct biased interpretations of religious prescriptions. They considered gender justice to be derived from a scholarly re-reading of sacred texts. According to those interviewed, women should play an active role in such reinterpretation efforts and should be involved in important debates on such questions. They emphasized the need to study religion in order to distinguish between the message conveyed by original sources and the message interpreted by the 'ulama' (religious scholars). Accordingly, they initiated theoretical work of their own in order to challenge the dominant Islamic jurisprudence about women's rights.

The women I interviewed believed that both an interpretation problem and a selective reading of religious prescriptions have led to the diffusion of messages that reinforce patriarchy, which they perceived as a major obstacle to the advancement of women's rights. They emphasized the need for highly educated women in several disciplines in order to challenge the dominant patriarchal view. Mainly, they wanted women to specialize in social sciences and jurisprudence and become competent to engage in the reinterpretation of religious prescriptions.

Education, therefore, appeared as a central element in their fight against the lack of justice for women.

In fact, they highly encouraged women members of the movement to pursue an education.[40] One important project they discussed is the 'Alimat (knowledgeable women) project, aimed at motivating members to undertake more advanced studies. They described education as the only way for individuals in society and for society itself to evolve, and thus, as a responsibility and a duty for all believers. According to members of the women's section, women who do not make effort to acquire education and educate their children are thought to be failing in their commitment to God. One of the members stated that education is a religious duty: "Failing to educate yourself or educate your children is to fail in your commitment to God. Education is a responsibility, a religious duty as praying and fasting are."[41]

Here, it is worth quoting the words of Nadia Yassine as reported by Gray:[42]

It is by meeting the challenges here on earth with a serene mind that we ultimately effect change. We are striving for women to become experts not just in the domain of religion but also in areas such as psychology, political science, law, medicine, etc. By doing this, we revive the prophetic tradition which elevates the value of human beings. We have to remember the history of Islam and reject the paternalistic readings and interpretations that have marginalized women. It is necessary for women to have their own interpretations.

Social Action and Education

The women I interviewed indicated that the actions of the women's section were motivated by three main objectives: to fight against poverty, address illiteracy, and remedy injustice. They privileged their proximity with people and action at the local level, encouraged the involvement of local people, and offered training. This latter strategy may have increased the participation rate of women in projects initiated by Al-Adl. In fact, women might have felt more confident when other women from their region implemented the projects, a strategy that provided the additional benefits of a widespread network and a decentralized structure. The movement conducted discussions about the needs of each region at the national level, making it possible to define specific strategies based on knowledge of the reality on the ground. In this way, members of the women's section worked with women in neighborhoods, teaching and speaking to them about justice and rights and the importance of education as well as giving them a religious education.[43]

Projects of Al-Adl women's section included targeting poorly educated women and/or women from lower socio-economic backgrounds, ostensibly because these women generally were characterized by poor mental and physical health and poor spiritual knowledge. Local sections organized meetings in neighborhoods to discuss issues related to women and children's education with the objective of offering a platform where women could share their needs and difficulties in life and engage in a dialogue with others. Members of Al-Adl women's section, then, sought to increase the consciousness of other women on a number of family and social issues, as well as listen to these women and encourage them to take action in structured and efficient ways.

Sisters for Eternity: In Search of Women's Enlightenment
The Sisters for Eternity gatherings represent an ambitious project initiated and organized by members of the women's section of Al-Adl. According to two former members of the women's section leadership,[44] education was central in the Sisters for Eternity discussions. The Sisters defined education in a broad sense and emphasized three dimensions: learning, spiritual teaching, and physical/mental health. They maintained that even if a mother is not educated, if she is conscious of the importance of education, she can play an important role in encouraging her children. According to one, "the mother even if she is not educated, if she knows the message of Islam, she will focus on the education of her children because she understands that this is her responsibility. The child is a 'present' in her hands."[45]

Also central to their approach was a willingness to question and point out to women the patriarchal nature of dominant interpretations of religious prescriptions. They typically explained the historical origins of these interpretations and argued that there is no reason to think these interpretations should be unique and unchangeable. Moreover, they sought to engage in jurisprudential questions and believed that such questions should not be dissociated from political motivations. They incentivized women to work for a reinterpretation of religious prescriptions by returning to the sources. They called this approach *tajdid*, or renewal.

The End of an Influential Era?

The Sisters for Eternity project became so popular that opposition arose from Al-Adl leadership, who were mainly men. One of the interviewees, a former member of the movement, characterized those men as "inflexible minds" who felt threatened by the "feminist" approaches adopted by women of the movement. The leadership, on the other hand, criticized women who dared to challenge the current interpretation of religious prescriptions and accused them of adopting attitudes similar to those of secular feminists. Consequently, women with important positions of responsibility in the women's section as well as women in charge at the local level decided to leave their positions in order to avoid conflict. These events occurred following the death of Al-Adl founder and leader, Sheikh Yassine in 2012. Interestingly, his daughter, Nadia Yassine, has completely disappeared from the public scene. According to former members, she has since dedicated her time to writing about the women's section and the philosophy of the movement as conceived by her father.

The former members of the women's section I interviewed believe that Sheikh Yassine's 1990, *Guide to Believing Women*, has been decisive for women members because it provided a theoretical framework that enables them to develop arguments, philosophies, and justifications for their strategies and actions. The departure of women members from the women's section of the movement created a large vacuum in the women's section. Those who left believed they could not be involved without respect for two main principles: the acknowledgment of the uniqueness of the women's condition and the independence of their actions. They felt that without such independence, they could not produce change.

As of 2014, the actions of the women's section were decided by a committee composed of women members of the section and men members from the leadership of the movement. This committee was in charge of defining strategies and projects that should be implemented. Given that the leaders of the movement no longer acknowledge women's unique condition and independence, most women in responsible positions ended their involvement. Those I interviewed still considered themselves part of the movement, however, given that they are faithful to its philosophy. Unlike the women's section, the leadership of the Al-Adl movement has no clear strategic plan for improving the position of women in society. In fact, one of the former members of the women's section believed that the movement had not reached a sufficient level of maturity to be able to take advantage of the actions of the women's section. Even if the Sisters for Eternity project was disrupted by the departure of many leading women, local activists still considered their actions on the ground to be motivated by the same objectives and based on the same philosophy. Without the support of their leadership, however, one must wonder how effective their current and future actions can be.

Limitations and Possible Extensions

The results of this research may have been hampered by some limitations, mainly related to data availability.

Firstly, only one spouse in each household (either the wife or the husband) was interviewed, and for interviewed women I did not gain data on their husbands' religiosity. As a result, I could not determine whether the mother's participation in educational decision-making was reinforced or reduced when the husband was very religious. However, I did gather enough information about husbands to control for their level of education and the age distance between spouses. Future research should consider interviewing both spouses within a household and following a detailed matching perspective format in analyzing family decisions. One may explore how bargaining takes place and how decisions are made when spouses are similar/dissimilar along a series of characteristics. Moreover, when it comes to the influence of religious movements, men and women are subject to different influences characterized by distinct discourses. For instance, the progressive discourse of the women section of Al-Adl is mainly addressed to women.

Secondly, it is quite complicated to establish a clear causal link if one considers that the influence of the movement may be indirect as well. To obtain a full picture of the influence of religious movements on mothers' participation in educational decisions, it would be necessary to conduct a network analysis to uncover influences of neighbors, friends, and family members who may have a direct link with the movement. Such a breakdown would require a more complex analysis than one could conduct with the available data. I assert, however, that data on respondents' direct links to religious organizations could at least provide a lower-bound estimate of the potential influence of religious movements (minimum effect).

One might assume that if religious movements indirectly influence people, their impact may be more spread out over the population. An analysis focused on direct links would not capture potential spillover effects. My interviews with local women activists from Al-Adl indicated that people with whom they work in neighborhoods through local associations do not necessarily know about their affiliation with a specific movement. Women activists tended not to reveal their affiliation with Al-Adl due to its illegal status. Thus, women could be connected to members of Al-Adl without being aware of it.

Thirdly, there is probably an underlying self-selection process at play. Women who are attracted by the discourse of the women's section and who adopt their recommendations may share certain characteristics. They may be inclined to challenge existing domestic relations and advocate for improvement of their status in the family and society at large. If this is true, the effect of religious movements in which they are involved may be overstated. One can assume, however, that even if these women are more favorable to a change of the status quo, social change is likely not to happen without a support system. Religious movements that offer encouragement and support may play a significant role in triggering social change. Furthermore, religious movements, and in particular the women's section of Al-Adl, provide women with a religious justification for agency within the household, which makes their aspirations for change more socially acceptable and reduces the potential psychological cost of deviating from the dominant social norm. In order to clearly discern the impact of the religious movements on social change for women, a more rigorous empirical strategy may be needed.

Conclusion

The results of this research support the notion that in regard to mothers' participation in educational decisions for daughters, the role of religion, particularly through the influence of religious movements, is more nuanced than widespread views suggest. In an analysis presented in details in a companion paper[46] and summarized in the present chapter, I found a positive relationship between the religiosity of mothers – mainly with limited or no formal education – and their participation in decisions concerning the education of their daughters, as well as improved school attendance rates for daughters whose mothers so participated.

The results also support the idea that improvement of female education outcomes, and more generally women's rights and standards of living, is not necessarily the result of a secularization of society, as argued in the literature on modernization.[47] The relation between modernization, secularization and women's rights is complex. A few recent studies have discussed these complexities in Muslim societies and have shown that despite modernization, religious values could remain strong and, under specific conditions, socially conservative religious movements can have socially progressive effects, especially on educational outcomes.[48]

I argue that in Morocco, one of the drivers of the results of my research may be the existence of influential religious movements. The influential Al-Adl movement – and especially its women's section – has attempted to help followers reach "spiritual awakening" through education. They emphasized that women's education is a key condition for the development of future generations, thus conferring upon women a social role in the construction of their ideal society. Leaders of the women's section even describe education as a religious duty. Moreover, the women's section defends the egalitarian involvement of women in family matters. Thus, they spread a message about the importance of education for girls. They also confer an important social role on women based on their action within the household. Moreover, the women's section of the movement launched a series of actions and projects, most importantly the ambitious Sisters for Eternity project that aimed to increase women's self-confidence and agency.

The role of the women's section grew in importance thanks to the support of Al-Adl founder Sheikh Yassine. Recently, disagreement between current Al-Adl leadership and former leaders of the women's section has limited the role of women within the movement. It remains to be seen how persistent past initiatives and actions will be. Those I interviewed felt that their actions were motivated by the same objectives and based on the same vision concerning the empowerment and education of women. Without support of the current leadership, however, the effectiveness of their local actions is drawn into question.

Given that religiosity has a positive effect on mothers' involvement in girls' education decisions among mothers with limited or no formal education, I contend that religiosity leads to similar effects as mothers' educational level. More specifically, my research indicates that a mother's religiosity is connected to greater awareness of the importance of her children's education and greater self-valuation with respect to her capacity to play a key role within her household.

Interestingly, these results were not replicated when I looked at the relationship between fathers' religiosity and mother's involvement in their daughter's educational decisions. This is consistent with my hypothesis that the main driver of affirmative educational decisions for daughters is the influence of the women's section of Al-Adl.

Endnotes

1 Handa, S. (2002). "Raising primary school enrolment in developing countries: the relative importance of supply and demand." *Journal of Development Economics.* Vol. 69, pp. 103–128.

2 Huisman, J. and J. Smits (2009) "Effects of household – and district-level factors on primary school enrolment in 30 developing countries." *World Development.* Vol. 37, No. 1, pp. 179–193.

3 Chaara, I. (2015). "Women as decision-makers within households: does religiosity matter? Evidence from Morocco." Working Paper. Another important factor appears to be the father's education. The latter positively influences daughters' participation in the education system.

4 Hashemi, S.M. and S.R. Schuler (1993). *"Defining and studying empowerment of women: a research note from Bangladesh."* JSI Working Paper 3. Boston: JSI Research and Training Institute; N. Kabeer (1999a). "The conditions and consequences of choice: reflections on the measurement of women's empowerment." UNRISD Discussion Paper, No. 108; (1999b) "Resources, agency, achievements: reflections on the measurement of women's empowerment." *Development and Change.* Vol. 30, pp. 435–464; A. Malhotra, S.R. Schuler and C. Boender (2002). *"Measuring women's empowerment as a variable in international development."* Background paper prepared for the World Bank Workshop on Poverty and Gender: New Perspectives. Gender and Development Group, World Bank, Washington, DC. Nevertheless, as pointed out by Kabeer, "The conditions and consequences," only a few cultures operate with starkly dichotomized distributions of power, with men making all the decisions and women making none (see also A.R. Quisumbing (ed.). (2003). *Household Decisions, Gender and Development. A Synthesis of Recent Research.* Washington D.C.: Ifpri. Ch. 4). Kabeer in "The conditions" reports that usually, a hierarchy of decision-making responsibilities exists, certain areas being reserved for men, others for women. For instance, in

South Asia, women seem to be mainly in charge of decisions concerning food purchases and children's health while men are in charge of children's education, children's marriage, and market transactions for major assets. Further, Quisumbing does not consider decision-making to be a measure of power but believes that the relative power of spouses is an underlying factor that likely effects decision-making.

5 See E. Foa and U. Foa (1980). "Resource theory: interpersonal behavior as exchange." *Social Exchange: Advances in Theory and Research.* K. Gergen, M. Greenberg and R. Willis (eds.). New York: Plenum Press, pp. 74–97.

6 For instance, M. Johnson (2000). "The view from the *Wuro*: a guide to child rearing for Fulani Parents." *A World of Babies: Imagined Childcare Guides for Seven Societies.* J. DeLoache and A. Gottlieb (eds.). Cambridge, UK: Cambridge University Press explained that among the Fulani tribes of Western Africa (who are primarily Muslims), family members, especially women, can increase their power in the family by practicing the traditional Fulani custom of conjuring the spirits of dead ancestors.

7 Carvalho, J.P. (2013). "Veiling." *The Quarterly Journal of Economics.* Vol. 128, No. 1, pp. 337–370; Platteau, J.P. (2017). *Islam Instrumentalized: Religion and Politics in Historical Perspectives.* New York, NY: Cambridge University Press.

8 Chaara, "Women as decision-makers."

9 I supervised the survey, conducted a large number of interviews on my own and worked with the help of three teams of enumerators, a small team in each region.

10 I decided not to keep questions about readings as they may have biased the scores for respondents who could not read. I also decided to remove the question concerning visits to the mosque since this question may have biased the scores in favor of men.

11 Chaara, "Women as decision-makers."

12 I did not look at the role of men's religiosity in their participation in educational decisions. This question was not relevant because most of the fathers in my sample were involved in educational decisions whatever their level of religiosity (low variance in responses). So, in most of the cases, either the father was the only family member to be involved or both the father and the mother were involved. The cases where only the mother is involved are pretty rare (about 7 percent of the cases in my sample).

13 Lehrer, E.L. (2004). "Religion as a determinant of economic and demographic behavior in the United States." *Population and Development Review*, Vol. 30, No. 4, pp. 707–726.

14 I interviewed six current members (two members from the leadership and four local activists), and two former members from past leadership.

15 Some of the interviewees refused to be named. I therefore do not mention any family names.

16 I also had an interview with the president of ORCF and other women from a network of women associations. However, these interviews were not very helpful.

17 I also briefly comment on the fact that the women's section became less influential after 2012. Current members claim that the women's section still exists but former members explain that it cannot act as an autonomous section anymore.

18 Geertz (1968, introduction written in 1991). *Observer l'islam: changements religieux au Maroc et en Indonésie*. Paris: Editions la découverte; M. Willis (2007). "Justice and Development or Justice and Spirituality? The challenge of Morocco's nonviolent Islamist movements." *The Maghrib in the New Century. Identity, Religion, and Politics*. B. Maddy-Weitzman and D. Zisenwine (eds.). University Press of Florida.

19 Willis, "Justice and Development."

20 The co-optation consists of an official recognition of the movement by the authorities on the condition that the movement explicitly recognizes the authority and legitimacy of the monarchy.

21 Dalmasso, E. (2008). "Family code in Morocco. State feminism or democracy." Unpublished; Ramírez, A. (2006). "Other feminisms? Muslim associations and women's participation in Morocco." *Etnográfica*. Vol. 10, No. 1, pp. 107–119.

22 Gray, D.H. (2013). *Beyond Feminism and Islamism: Gender and Equality in North Africa*. London: I.B. Tauris.

23 Interview with Saïda Maarouf. September 2014.

24 Gray, *Beyond Feminism*.

25 The Boutchichiyya brotherhood grew in importance under the reign of King Mohamed VI, after the Casablanca bombings of 2003. The brotherhood re-established the order's link to scriptural Islam and its followers are mainly found among educated youth. K. Bekkaoui and R. René Larémont (2011). "Moroccan youth go Sufi." *Journal of the Middle East and Africa*. Vol. 2, pp. 35–36.

26 Willis, "Justice and Development."

27 However, mainstream Sufi figures have argued that Yassine's knowledge of Sufism is superficial. Ibid, p. 166.

28 Pruzan-Jorgensen, J.E. (2010). "The Islamist movement in Morocco: main actors and regime responses." Danish Institute for International Studies (DIIS) Report.

29 Cavatorta, F. (2006). "Civil Society, Islamism and Democratization: the case of Morocco". *Journal of Modern African Studies*. Vol. 44, No. 2, pp. 203–222.

30 Willis, "Justice and Development."

31 Merieme Yafout, former leader of the women's section, goes one step further considering that monogamy should be the norm and polygamy only the exception. Gray, *Beyond Feminism*, p. 89.

32 Ramírez, "Other feminisms?"

33 Gray, *Beyond Feminism*.

34 Ibid.

35 Naciri, R. (1998). "The women's movement and political discourse in Morocco." Occasional Paper 8. United Nations Research Institute for Social Development.

36 Gray, D.H. (n.d.). "The many paths to gender equality in Morocco." Oxford Islamic Studies Online.

37 Gray, *Beyond Feminism*.

38 According to a current member of the women's section, 90 percent of the activities of the section are educational and professional training activities (the figure comes from an internal report). They aim to increase the autonomy of women. They prefer to use the term 'autonomy' instead of 'independence' to distinguish themselves from the discourse of secular feminists.

39 Willis, "Justice and Development," p. 168.

40 The example they gave mainly concerns women with a high level of formal education, that is, women who finished secondary education or women with some university education.

41 Interview with Limia. September 14, 2014.

42 Gray, *Beyond Feminism*.

43 See Ramírez, "Other feminisms?"

44 Interview with Aziza. September 13, 2014; Interview with Limia. September 14, 2014.

45 Interview with Limia. September 14, 2014.

46 Chaara, "Women as decision-makers."

47 See for instance, Inglehart, R. and P. Norris (2003). *Rising Tide: Gender Equality and Cultural Change Around the World*. New York: Cambridge University Press.

48 See for instance, Myersson, E. (2014). "Islamic rule and the empowerment of the poor and pious. *Econometrica*. Vol. 82, No. 1, pp. 229–269, for a discussion on the case of Turkey, and C. Binzel and J.P. Carvalho (2013). "Education, social mobility, and religious movements: a theory of the Islamic revival in Egypt." *The Economic Journal*, forthcoming, for the case of Egypt.

7 | Pious and Engaged

The Religious and Political Involvement of Egyptian Salafi Women after the 2011 Revolution

LAURENCE DESCHAMPS-LAPORTE

Introduction

The Salafi Call (al-Daʻwa al-Salafiyya,[1] or simply "the Daʻwa" in this chapter) is currently Egypt's largest Salafi movement.[2] Since its creation in Alexandria in the 1970s, men have led the movement, and its activities and discourses have targeted men. However, the 2011 Egyptian Revolution represented a critical juncture in the movement's history. At that point, the Daʻwa abandoned its political quietism[3] and decided to create a political party, the Salafi Light party (al-Nur). This new organization presented an opportunity for women to become more visibly involved, and some Salafi leaders encouraged this involvement for strategic electoral reasons. Women, they thought, would mobilize voters and supporters in this new sphere of electoral politics for Egypt.

Yet beyond the brief electoral period, women have remained involved in the Daʻwa. In this chapter, I argue that the Daʻwa's leadership began to permit and even encourage women's involvement for calculated electoral reasons, motivated by their desire to compete with the Muslim Brotherhood (who more actively recruited women members and voters) and to be portrayed in a favorable light by national and international media. In addition, I contend that the women who have entered Daʻwa male spaces and become involved in the public life of the movement have done so not primarily to satisfy the aims of the party, but to fulfil their own social, familial, and spiritual needs. In fact, as I argue in this chapter, the presence of women in Salafi community spaces allows them to expand the boundaries of their network, take control of their religious knowledge and practices, and obtain more social choices, especially in marriage.

My argument is based on ethnographic accounts and observations I gathered during several periods of fieldwork conducted in Alexandria and Cairo between 2012 and 2015. I begin this chapter by reviewing the relevant literature on women in Islamist movements and then compare women's roles and duties in the Da'wa prior to the Egyptian Revolution and after the creation of the al-Nur party. To illustrate my arguments, I focus on a specific case study of a Salafi community in Alexandria where women have taken on new roles and used previously male-only spaces to fulfil their social needs. This research is significant because it examines the understudied subject of the Da'wa, Egypt's second largest Islamist organization after the Muslim Brotherhood. Just as important, it addresses the less studied topic of the role of women therein.

The Da'wa was founded in the late 1970s in Alexandria and the creation of its political party al-Nur in 2011 surprised both local and foreign media who had not anticipated that the Da'wa would turn to politics. But pundits were even more astounded at the results of the 2011–2012 parliamentary election in which al-Nur captured 27 percent of the vote, coming in second only to the Freedom and Justice Party, the party of the Muslim Brotherhood. During my fieldwork, even though al-Nur politicians and Da'wa shaykhs publicly declare that their political party and religious organization are two separate entities, they were actually one movement. When conducting fieldwork, I often observed that leaders from al-Nur and the Da'wa were in constant communication and aligned their strategies. Even more telling, in the early 2013, some of al-Nur's leaders attempted to act independently from the Da'wa, sparking a tense conflict with the Da'wa's most powerful shaykhs and leading to the eventual creation of the split-away party, The Nation (al-Watan).[4] Following these events, the Da'wa leadership made sure that new leaders of al-Nur were loyal Da'wa figures. Therefore, I use "the Da'wa" to refer to the wider religious umbrella organization which includes the political party al-Nur.

Scholarship on Gender and Islamism

While the literature on gender and Islam is rich, more research on the relationship between women and Islamism is needed.[5] Saba Mahmood's (2004) *Politics of Piety* was one of the first academic books to discuss

pious women's subjectivity in depth, and it was widely read and debated after its publication.[6] Mahmood questioned the liberal premise that
individuals always work to assert their autonomy and human action
is first and foremost directed at contesting rather than applying social
norms.[7] Her challenge to the existing assumptions about pious women
is relevant to this case study of Egyptian Salafi women. Mahmood contested the dominant discourse, according to which one's desire for piety
and religiosity had to be explained and argued against "the assumptions of secular modernity."[8] Her research is a significant contribution
to the study of Islamic piety by expanding on Bourdieu's theory of the
habitus and applying it to the reality of pious urban women.

Yet, Mahmood did not explicitly report on her informants' attitudes or
formal involvement in politics, nor their possible affiliations to Islamist
movements. Accordingly, this chapter builds on her work and addresses
this gap by carefully analyzing Islamist women's subjectivities, intentions, and relationships to the political and religious movement they have
joined - in this case the Da'wa.

The work of Humeira Iqtidar on Islamist groups in Pakistan which
touches on women's involvement is similarly relevant to my argument
that women's motivations for joining Islamist movements might be complex and are often different from men's motivations to include them.

In Iqtidar's case study, like mine, the competitive environment in
which the Islamist organizations evolved influenced the meaning and
consequences of women's involvement. Indeed, the motivations of
women to participate in these groups transcended electoral politics
and extended far beyond male leaders' arguments about involving
them. Iqtidar's study focused on the competition between the Islamist
Jama'at e-Islami and Jama'at ud-Da'wa groups in Pakistan and the role
of this competition had "not only in shaping their strategies, but also in
the impact they have."[9] Iqtidar also claimed that this competition has
led to a gradual *secularization* of Pakistani society, that is, as gradually
reducing religion to carefully selected texts and practices which are
interpreted and practiced towards distinct political aims.

The intense rivalry between Jama'at e-Islami and Jama'at ud-Da'wa
has not only led to objectification and *secularization* of Islam, but
to the creation of ready-made and cohesive religious solutions for
dealing with modern society. In other words, each group has developed
different pre-interpreted, packaged amalgams of creed in order to distinguish itself from rivals and enhance recruitment. Accordingly, the

Da'wa's competition with the Muslim Brotherhood has led it to become more involved in a socially and politically contingent process of functionalization of religious symbols and language to justify its political actions and decisions. Thus, Da'wa shaykhs have attributed to Islamic symbols and language political meanings and functions that work towards their social and political aspirations.

As Iqtidar has noted, "Islamism is widely defined in part through its misogyny." Indeed, the "dislike of, contempt for, or ingrained prejudice against women"[10] has been perceived as a defining feature of Islamist movements by non-Islamists inside Muslim-majority countries as well as by pundits, scholars and the broader population in much of the world. In this context, for Iqtidar and for me the question arises: Why do women join Islamist parties? As I noted previously, academics such as Mahmood have explored the circumstances in which women choose a life of piety in Islam,[11] but few, besides Iqtidar, have looked at women's incentives inside Islamist groups. Despite the paucity of research on this topic, I should note that Mahmood, Iqtidar's and my research all take root in the broader legacy of debates on feminism, "third world" feminist, gender and Islam and Islamic feminism (which includes the work of Spivak,[12] Mohanty,[13] Ahmed,[14] Mir-Hosseini,[15] Kandiyoti,[16] Al-Ali,[17] Keddie[18] and Gray[19]). And while some of this literature is not always directly addressed, this body of literature has advanced the academic debates on women and Islam and should be recognized as such.

This gap in the literature on women in Islamist movements has meant that over the past decades, women's desire to support, affiliate with, and campaign for Islamist groups and parties has sometimes been described as motivated by a "false consciousness."[20] Accordingly, Islamist women are assumed to be victims of ideological deceit, rather than making educated conscious decisions to join a movement. This popular discourse on Islamist women transcends Egypt and has emerged in various forms over the past decades. For example, around the time of the 1979 Iranian Revolution, Islamist women were described in western media as hysterics, and dubbed *"Les Folles d'Allah."*[21]

Yet, much of the recent ethnographic work on women's subjectivity and agency, including on their experience as part of piety movements, has challenged this problematic assumption.[22] The principal alternative approach that feminist scholars have embraced when confronted with such women who join Islamist movements is simply to take the women's explanations at face value,[23] that is, to accept their validity and contextualize them. Therefore, in this chapter, I report on my findings in regard to women's intentions and motivations mostly as they are presented to me by my informants and put them in perspective.

Salafi Women Before and After the Revolution

In 1977 a split occurred in the university-based al-Jama'iyya al-Islamiyya, an Islamist group which embraced and later renounced violence.[24] One faction of the Gama'a Islamiyya affiliated with the Muslim Brotherhood while the other formed the Madrasa Salafiyya, a scholarly group focused on interpreting the Qur'an *(tafsir)* and the study of the works of specific scholars, particularly Ibn Taymiyya. In the late 1980s, however, the Madrassa Salafiyya became an organization focused on proselytization and it began spreading its teachings more widely and became known as the Da'wa Salafiyya. Modern Salafi groups such as the Da'wa Salafiyya are part of a global Islamic religious trend that emerged in the twentieth century. Such groups encourage their followers to "purify" their ritual practices and live in accordance with the behaviors and beliefs of the First three generations of Muslims (the *salaf*). They differentiate themselves from their Islamist rivals such as the Muslim Brotherhood, in that they typically are more concerned with defining and policing "correct" ritual practices than controlling the means of political power. The expansion of the Da'wa's activities in the 1980s led to competition and conflict with the Muslim Brotherhood. At the Faculty of Medicine of the University of Alexandria, Brotherhood members tried to break up Da'wa meetings – and neither did Da'wa leaders shy away from attacking Brotherhood members.

At the inception of Da'wa, the salafization of both men and women was important, but there was no mention of having a women's section per se. In fact, until the Egyptian Revolution, women's involvement in Da'wa was limited, sporadic, and mostly informal. Dr. Hannan Alam, the representative of women in both al-Nur and the Da'wa was the most prominent Salafi women's leader during the years of my fieldwork. In an interview, Dr. Hannan stated that she has been involved in the movement since the late 1980s, when she was a student in the Faculty of Medicine. She began to engage in proselytization (*da'wa*) in different social clubs in Alexandria,[25] and later worked for the Christian organization Caritas as a physician.

In the early 1990s, Hosni Mubarak's repressive regime made social and charity work generally difficult but even more challenging for Salafi women. Dr. Alam's other Salafi women friends were discriminated against at the university. For example, every time a woman wearing a niqab (face veil) had to sit for an examination, she was required to first get permission from the deans, a bureaucratic hurdle the university imposed to discourage women from covering their face. The charity and *da'wa* work of Salafi women was therefore informal, underground, and poorly organized.

After the 2011 Revolution, however, the Da'wa adopted a more organized approach for actively involving women in the movement and providing them with formal roles within the organization. This is the case for example, in the Da'wa's geographic base in Egypt where the city of Alexandria was divided into 16 electoral districts. In 2011, al-Nur offices were opened in each district for campaign purposes, and committees for women were also created. Dr. Hannan and Fatma, Dr. Hannan's deputy director and a leader in many mosques of the neighborhood of Abu Suleiman (where the Da'wa is the dominant Islamist organization), both argued that Salafi women's intensified participation was not necessarily due to a change in attitude within the Salafi movement, but rather, to the opening of the public space that has followed the Revolution. This renewed sense of publicness is similar to what Moors described as emerging in several Muslim-majority countries in the 1990s.[26] Fatma alluded to this opening of the public sphere:

> The isolation was imposed. We did not choose to stay indoors. Women wearing niqab were discriminated against, were searched at the gate to the University. They were not welcomed outside. But after the Revolution it was different, we decided it would be beneficial to go out.[27]

After the Revolution, the male leadership of al-Nur decided to give formal female leadership roles to specific women. At the time of the foundation of the party, Imad Ghafour had called on Dr. Hannan Alam to be the woman representative of the party nationally. According to Alam, this decision was uncontroversial – no tensions existed among the men of the party or its religious organization in regard to increasing and formalizing women's involvement.

Despite Dr. Hannan's claims, however, the transition was not all that harmonious: according to al-Nur leaders, shortly after the Revolution there were contentious discussions and negotiations with the hard-liners on the acceptable level of female involvement in the movement. In a 2012 meeting, Yusri Hammad, the secretary of al-Nur (Who joined al-Watan in 2013) presented a simple explanation for the involvement of women in electoral politics: the 2011 Egyptian electoral law required all parties to have women on their electoral lists. Thus, the inclusion of women was not an earnest move toward equality, but more of a formality. The 2011 parliamentary electoral law required all party lists to include at least one woman, but did not require placing women in winnable positions on the list.[28] Indeed, al-Nur typically placed female candidates at the bottom of its electoral lists making it nearly impossible for them to win seats in the predominantly proportional representation system that is the Egyptian parliament. A further act of limiting women's role in the electoral process, was the party's decision to use posters featuring photos of its male candidates, while displaying a rose or the party logo instead of images of its female candidates. Ultimately, not a single female candidate of al-Nur was elected to serve in parliament following the 2011 elections.

Yet, al-Nur needed Salafi women to campaign for them. Hammad stressed that because the party wanted women's votes it needed Salafi women to reach out to other women. To this end, every district party office opened a parallel women's section, at least in Alexandria, the Da'wa's stronghold. Salafi leaders also knew that they were mainly competing against the Muslim Brotherhood for Islamist votes. The Muslim Brotherhood has had an active women's section since the creation of the movement in the 1930s. Even though women had never held equal positions in the Brotherhood's leadership, they ran in the 2005 and 2010 parliamentary elections with more formalized institu-tions in place.[29] Also, during the 2011–2012 parliamentary elections, al-Nur politicians gradually became used to speaking to non-Salafi audiences: journalists, diplomats, researchers, and think tanks. Since they often had to answer questions about women in their community, they came to understand that involving women and making them more visible could be positive for their party's image.

Dr. Hannan and other women leaders confirmed that following the 2011 Revolution, every district office has had an active women's section. In fact, in my research I met six women leaders who introduced them-selves as representing various district committees. Many of these offices had dedicated opening hours for men and women so that they do not use the rooms at the same time. After the July 2013 military coup that brought down the Muhammad Mursi government, Salafi women have remained active in charity work, educational activities, preaching, and sometimes even political activities.

According to the Da'wa's women leaders, women's participation in the movement even exceeds men's participation. While Dr. Hannan denied the existence of tensions between women and men leaders of the Da'wa, she reiterated numerous times that it is the men's responsibility to care for and support the women:

Women and men have the same training in our organization, the same capabilities, the same mind. But when it comes to political positions and so on, we look around and we see that there are capable men and if we are asked to help we will. But now, there are men in the men's section who can do the work. It comes from the idea that men have to care for women and help women.[30]

In reality, beyond "not having to" take on political positions, the leadership of the women's section did not usually justify the existence of the Salafi political party in political terms. Both Dr. Hannan and Fatma maintained that the party and their public involvement were necessary because it would enable them to reach out to more people and "help them out of poverty, sickness, and ignorance" through official means, unlike working unofficially, as they did before the Revolution. They justified most of their actions using charitable arguments, and emphasized the source of their motivation: "You know Madam Laurence, this is labor of love! ['*amal al hub*]."

Because of these women's deep commitment to doing work with pious and charitable intentions, it can be said that they engage in activism of the heart - *jihad bi-l-qalb*.[31] Likewise, this commitment conforms with the Da'wa's dominant narrative about what Salafi women should do. Toth has noted that most Salafi women and men are such activists of the heart: "Their own personal practices, beliefs, and identity are subjectively re-oriented to conform to the movement's definition of what is correct."[32] Charity and social work as well as Da'wa are the women's main activities; they explain their involvement not as a protest against the preconceptions of Western media, or against what Mahmood interlocutors might assume to be pure compliance with social norms. Rather, Salafi women have said that they participate in the movement to fulfill their social, personal, and family needs. Dr. Hannan and her colleagues also publically emphasize a discourse of charity and use the language of *da'wa* to make themselves acceptable and attractive to other Salafi women.

During our meetings, Dr. Hannan and Fatma often dodged questions about politics, and brought the conversation back to da'wa and helping "the less fortunate." In the Da'wa's context, women's political activism seemed to be displayed mostly through public activities rather than conversation and debates. When I was in Alexandria, groups of Salafi women visited sick children in hospitals and orphanages, provided financial assistance to widows, distributed food to poor families, and organized various educational activities. These activities were charitable but also deeply political as their political affiliation was worn, shown, and embodied. Women wore pins of al-Nur or the Da'wa, posted pictures on the groups' Facebook pages, and asserted publicly that their primary motive was charitable. Overall, the women I spoke with conveyed that proselytization must outweigh politics, and it is this same sense that has shaped the way women Salafi activists discuss their activism.

Generally, Salafi women's political positions did not differ greatly from their male counterparts. Moors noted a similar tendency among Islamist women in the context of family law reform. She argued that the reason for women's apparent acquiescence to men's positions is that Islamist movements are usually opposition movements struggling against larger forces, making it difficult for them to present dissenting views.[33]

Even though for Salafi women, *da'wa* generally took precedent over politics, their increased public activism in the post-Revolution era has at times seemed utilitarian. Both male leaders and women used images of Salafi women to publicize and promote their political positions. Salafi politicians were well aware of the widespread pejorative perception of Salafis in Egyptian society. Since the ouster of President Mursi, when Salafi leaders have taken up new strategic positions, they often have involved women in organizing activities and events, or simply took pictures to share widely on social media. These types of pictures attracted the attention of Salafi and non-Salafis alike because they showed active and politicized Salafi women. These images were mostly popular on social media, rather than in mainstream Middle Eastern or Western media that rarely present images that challenge pre-existing framing of Salafi women and men.

In sum, between the founding of the Da'wa in 1977 and the founding of al-Nur in 2011, women's involvement was at best sporadic.

Salafi women's presence in the public space was discouraged, and seldom did religious and educational activities target Salafi women. However, starting in 2011 with the formation of the Nur party and the shift in Egyptian political life, the number of Salafi women leaders increased, and Salafi women became more visible in public spaces in Alexandria and also online. Party offices and mosques started welcoming women, and parallel religious and political committees were formed to involve them. As I show in the case study that follows, through their increased presence in the Daʻwa, women have been able to support and promote the party's political positions as intended by their male leaders. More significantly, however, they have taken this opportunity to transform their public life and embrace new social practices.

Mosques at the Heart of Women's Involvement

The locus of the Daʻwa's religious and political activities is their mosque-based networks, and this is especially true for women. Fatma provided an example: her own peri-urban neighborhood of Abu Suleiman southeast of Alexandria has several mosques where the Daʻwa is active.

There were 21 mosques in Abu Suleiman, all of which were affiliated with the Daʻwa. Six were very active mid-size mosques; the remaining 15 were smaller corner mosques. Most Daʻwa mosques had suboptimal facilities for women. Women sections tended to be equipped with a sound system, or both a sound and TV system, to broadcast the sermon or class that is happening in the men's section. Almost always, the women's sections I visited were smaller than the men's sections.

Despite women's emphasis on charity and *daʻwa* and their usual discomfort with political conversations, there was no doubt that prestige was attached to being associated with al-Nur or having a husband who holds a high position within the party. For example, for Friday prayers in Abu Suleyman, Fatma wore the al-Nur pin on her black *ʻabaya*, setting her apart as a representative of the party. In mosques in al-ʻAgamy (a suburb west of Alexandria), women whose husbands held positions on an al-Nur committee would always make sure to share this information when they introduced themselves. I also witnessed gossiping and competition among women in some mosques in Alexandria about the influence of their husbands within the party. For example, one woman bragged about her husband being on a committee in one district, which prompted another woman whose husband also was involved in al-Nur to quietly tell a friend, "He does not have an important position in al-Nur! What is she saying!" These and other observations I made during my fieldwork indicate that political action and involvement in al-Nur produced an additional layer of power and prestige above participation in Da'wa activities. The creation of the Da'wa political arm introduced new power dynamics, even among the women of the movement. As highlighted by Iqtidar, "the changes in structures of authority with which Islamism is linked contain the paradox of rationalized and individualized practice within a hierarchical organizational structure."[34] Thus, in their pious activities, which were embedded in their new political identity, Da'wa women created a public community, but this community was inherently demarcated by power relations and the emergence of new hierarchies of prestige.

Salafi Female Social and Religious Practices after the Revolution: The Case of Umm Al-Mu'minin

Egyptian Salafi women were also involved in an array of new post-revolutionary practices that warrant examination, such as charity activities, public demonstrations, increased mobility between Alexandria and Cairo, or the formation of proselytization groups. Yet, it seems most illuminating to study a type of involvement that has been especially popular since the Revolution and showed no sign of dwindling: religious classes and sermons targeting women within the Da'wa.

In this section, I report on my analysis of the classes that took place in the Umm al-Mu'minin (Mother of the Believers) mosque in the neighborhood of Bacchus, in the center of Alexandria.[35] Bacchus is known to be one of the more underprivileged neighborhoods of Alexandria. Umm al Mu' minin is a mid-sized mosque, considerably smaller than the large historic mosques in central Alexandria.

When I discussed the role of Salafi women with young Salafi men who attended Umm al-Mu'minin and other Da'wa mosques, they often explained that the norm is for women to pray at home, but women often like to attend special prayers such as *tarawih*, the long prayers that take place on specific nights of the holy month of Ramadan. In fact, both the women and men told me that prayers at the mosque are in no way an obligation (*wajib*), but that Friday prayers are *wajib* for men – a fairly mainstream religious view held by Salafis and other Muslims. Regular attendance at the mosque is a comparatively new practice for Salafi women in Alexandria, however, and it was gradually becoming more accepted and encouraged by male Da'wa leaders.

It is unlikely that Salafi women attending Da'wa educational activities would expect to easily listen or watch the sermon from the women's section, or to develop a mentorship relationship with the shaykh, because of the physical barriers. In all Salafi mosques with a dedicated space for women, the women's section was separate (on a different floor, in the basement, or in a different building) from the men's section. Thus, at best, women watch the lecture on a screen, or at worst, have no way of knowing what is happening in the men's section.

The most popular events at Umm al-Mu'minin, are the classes given by Muhammad al-Ghaliz, an shaykh who leads prayers and events at that mosque. Analyzing al-Ghaliz's classes illuminates Salafi women's post-revolution communal practices and sheds light on the evolving nature of religious authority within the Da'wa. The involvement of new charismatic shaykhs in the Da'wa is reminiscent of the broader phenomenon of Islamic revivalism reflected in consumerist practices. Haenni has noted that such practices are palpable in the media landscape and include the emergence of "superstar" Islamic televangelists, Islamic TV stations, and the popularization of online platforms managed and promoted by these famous shaykhs.[36]

At Umm al-Mu'minin, al-Ghaliz's rising popularity as a shaykh is a phenomenon that cannot be dissociated from the increasing presence of women in Da'wa mosques. Such young charismatic shaykhs have some responsibility in attracting women to mosques and contribute to the way women embody their relationship with the institution of the Da'wa. Understanding al-Ghaliz and his message is a crucial part in understanding why young Salafi women want to spend time at Umm al-Mu'minin.

While at Umm al-Mu'minin, I observed that al-Ghaliz purposefully targeted the youth, and for specific events, young women in particular. He worked to attract them to the mosque and more generally, to the Da'wa movement. Al-Ghaliz's Thursday classes were targeted specifically at women; his Saturday classes were targeted at youth in general, but women were still strongly encouraged to attend.

Despite this, on Thursdays, the men's section of the mosque was also generally quite full. The average age of the women in the Thursdays and Saturdays classes was about 25 years old.

Al-Ghaliz's style more closely resembled famous Egyptian TV evangelists than that of other Da'wa shaykhs. Al-Ghaliz was 29 years old, preached in Egyptian Arabic, and wrote in colloquial language on his social network pages (other Da'wa shaykhs tried to speak in classical Arabic). His parents were not particularly religious; they were, as he told me, "an ordinary family."[37] His father passed away when he was in his second year of university, and his death was a deeply traumatic event for Al-Ghaliz. He subsequently became more religious and embraced Salafism.

In contrast to Muslim Brotherhood members who often have been part of the organization since primary school, Salafis most frequently speak of being "self-made," and coming to Salafism after a traumatic or life-changing event. The community of Umm al-Mu'minin, like al-Ghaliz, was mostly made of such "self-made" Salafis.

Al-Ghaliz started preaching after the Revolution, and his classes were so popular, especially his lessons for women, that the Da'wa moved him to ever larger mosques. Several women followed al-Ghaliz to attend his lessons, sometimes even embarking on long bus commutes to do so. Al-Ghaliz usually preached wearing t-shirts, polo shirts, or sweaters and jeans. Yet, he still wore the typical Salafi beard, with no mustache and a very short haircut.

Al-Ghaliz acknowledged that he wanted to attract young women to the mosque, something that older Da'wa shaykhs have not been successful at, but he also wanted to emphasize the local Egyptian character of Salafism. As he put it, some Da'wa preachers "read Salafism through Saudi eyes ... We are not Saudis, we are Egyptians – this is very different. It does not have to be so formal all the time." When al-Ghaliz commented on adopting a more casual dress code, his comments pertained only to men, whom he does not expect to come to the mosque wearing Saudi garb. Ironically, however, most women still wore the black niqab, *'abaya*, and white gloves, and only removed their gloves and uncovered their face in the women's section.

In his classes for women, al-Ghaliz addressed topics such as rituals, worship, purity of intention in actions, covering and modesty, obedience to one's husband, love and fear of God, and generosity of a husband towards his wife. Al-Ghaliz represents a new style of preaching to young men and women, which has not been typical of Salafi preaching in the past. One specific lesson I attended took place on a Thursday night in March 2014, when al-Ghaliz held classes for women that were broadcasted live from the men's section to a TV on the women's floor. The topic that night was modesty and the hijab, and the lecture was provocatively titled, "Is that all?" (*huwwa kida bass?*).[38] Al-Ghaliz began by telling his congregation that "the class tonight is directed mainly at women ... in fact, at women only." Al-Ghaliz recalled the story of a young woman who is about to begin university and who has decided to "become veiled (*muhajjaba*)." (He used the word *muhajjaba* rather than *munaqqaba,* which refers specifically to the niqab.) When she tells her father about her intentions, he, in turn, presses her to reflect on the matter seriously. After reflection, she announces to her father that she is convinced about her decision. He then encourages her and gives her money to buy new clothes. Later that day, the young woman returns home with a small plastic bag. Eventually, her father asks her about her purchases, and she shows five scarfs (*turah*). Her father is surprised: "Is that all?" (*huwwa kida bass?*), he asks. At this point the story turns into a lesson about the meaning of covering or veiling and its significance beyond "simply covering of the hair." Al-Ghaliz's message, then, was that women must embody modesty beyond "simply" covering. He suggested that "simply covering of the hair" might not be enough and that women should embrace full Salafi dress and become *munaqqabat.*

In warning women against lying to themselves and to God, by veiling wrongly or with inauthentic intentions, al-Ghaliz presents an argumentation that was not entirely new, but it was his delivery that was distinctive for a Salafi shaykh. Trying to convince women to reflect on their modesty and intentions is not surprising in Egyptian society today, where *muhajjabat* are the norm. Rather, in the Salafi context, it was the other aspects of his preaching that stood out, such as his conscious effort to exert charisma and connect with his audience. He paced his speech carefully, feigned timidity, and changed his tone to give urgency to his argument. He repeated lines rhetorically, such as, "The *muhajjaba* is something else (*haja thaniyya*)!" He sighed dramatically, looked up at the ceiling, and smiled widely with eyes closed, then suddenly continued his speech with a quotation from the Prophet that he deemed to be related to his point. His delivered his stories with a wide smile, sometimes as if he was making eye contact with his

audience. Thus, he distinguished himself from the sometimes mono-
tone, or often angry and screaming mainstream Salafi preachers. He
also addressed young women directly, rather than their husbands or
fathers, to try to convince them to purify their practices. Throughout,
he worked to make the atmosphere of the mosque convivial and
welcoming.

Al-Ghaliz's style was not unlike the style of other famous young
Egyptian TV evangelists[39] who engage in proselytization of youth
(*du 'wa shabiyyin*). Yet what separated al-Ghaliz's from other young
TV evangelists was that he did not try to simply Islamicize the youth,
but targeted already highly pious youth. In fact, as mentioned, most
women wore niqabs, *'abayas*, and gloves in the Salafi mosques I visited.
A minority of women wore "only" the *hijab* and long skirts. Al-Ghaliz
was popular with the already puritanical, because these Alexandrian
Salafi young people had become Salafi by their own volition. Attending charismatic preaching like that of al-Ghaliz's helped them keep
their identity and commitment alive and nurtured, and their sense of
belonging fervent.

Al-Ghaliz created a sense of renewed fervor among the women who
attended his events. At the end of the lesson, Wafaa', Basma, and Sara –
three young women who sat close to me – began to passionately tell me
about their niqab. Wafaa' turned to me and said, "I love my niqab!
I love it because I love Allah." For these and other women, the sermon
was not so much about convincing them to veil appropriately with the
right intentions – as they believe they already have the right intentions
and do exactly that – but was an opportunity to confirm their decision
and women seemed to appreciate the emphasis on a woman's agency in
showing her love of God.

The prominence of the notion of women's pious agency towards
God in al-Ghaliz's lecture was not the only reason women valued these
gatherings. In these Alexandrian mosques, women viewed the gatherings as an opportunity to foster a community and participate in a
public life outside their homes. The atmosphere at these lessons was
warm, and women sat close together, leaving part of the room unoccu-
pied except for some young children playing. They put their arms
around each other and around me on many occasions, kissing each
other on the cheeks or the head. These lessons were a time for women
to come together, mingle, gain strength and validation from each
other. They looked forward to this bi-weekly occasion, where they

also discussed weddings in their Salafi community, Sara's upcoming religious ceremony, exams, and university life. Al-Ghaliz's classes, then, offered a unique opportunity for a large group of women to get together and socialize - unlike smaller gatherings at individuals' homes.

Al-Ghaliz's decision to preach to women has become accepted by older and more puritanical Da'wa shaykhs. The established shaykhs have agreed, though reluctantly in some cases, that women may become involved in political and religious life in order to compete in elections and increase their base of voters. Since women have become a larger part of the life of the Da'wa, a situation has developed that cannot easily be overturned. The "old guard" Da'wa leadership is responsible for involving women, and now they must come to terms with the fact that women have embraced and shaped the life of the movement far beyond the electoral period.

In the time I spent at Umm al-Mu'minin during the presidency of 'Abd al-Fattah al-Sisi, women were present not to organize politically or campaign but to fulfil their religious aspirations. They clearly valued these events, for they provided a space where women of different social classes could mingle, organize, build community, and enrich their social life. Both for unmarried Salafi women who do not necessarily come from families as pious as themselves, or for newly married women who live in small apartments – sometimes in distant neighborhoods in Alexandria – large gatherings with like-minded Salafi women are not frequent and difficult to recreate outside of the mosque.

This conclusion is consistent with Iqtidar's findings on Islamist groups in Pakistan. Iqtidar observed that women involved in the Jama'at al-Da'wa in Pakistan may have greater choices in society because of their involvement in the organization. They may become more involved in their choice of husband, for example, and rely less on their family's connections. In some ways the situation of women involved in the Da'wa is similar to what Iqtidar described. Through their activities in Da'wa mosques and al-Nur party offices, Egyptian Salafi women have had the opportunity to expand their social network and meet new women.

My interpretation of some of the benefits to women of participating in these mosque networks is shared by the Salafi women I met in Alexandria. Sara, for example, was getting married to a young man who attended al-Ghaliz's classes. Both Sara and her husband-to-be had been exposed to the same values through the lessons. To a certain extent, then, they can expect to have a shared understanding of gender roles in their relationship and of a woman's prescribed attire. They expect to social, religious, and cultural worldview even though they have not spent much time together before marriage. This kind of network can be reassuring for women who do not come from Salafi families but intend to start a family with someone who also identifies as Salafi and is affiliated with the Da'wa.

This is not to say that women in the Muslim Brotherhood, or ordinary Muslim women who go to non-affiliated mosques in Egypt, do not also attend mosques in order to participate in religious educational activities for religious, personal, and social reasons. What I have described in this chapter is not a uniquely Salafi phenomenon. It is beyond the scope of this research, however, to investigate why women get involved in educational activities in non-Salafi contexts, though it is likely their reasons also are manifold and specific. What this case study revealed is that the Revolution was a turning point for Salafi women that allowed them to get involved in political activities, and that beyond the ephemeral electoral campaigns that represented their entry point, women have continued their participation. Further, the long-term effect has been that women now inhabited and used new and public spaces, not just for political or purely religious reasons, but also to fulfil their social aspirations.

Conclusion

In this chapter, I discussed the transformation of the Da'wa since the Egyptian Revolution, not simply in regard to the creation of the al-Nur party, but also in terms of the renewed involvement of women in the movement's activities. Following the Revolution, the Da'wa began to give a greater role to women like Dr. Hannan Alam and Fatma for formalistic and strategic political reasons. Yet, even after the short period around the elections, women's activities in the Da'wa mosques and al-Nur offices continued – becoming the new norm as their participation expanded from political, charitable, or social activities to educational and religious Da'wa activities focused on women.

One example of such educational activities are the classes offered by al-Ghaliz. Even though al-Ghaliz's intention may be to purify and educate Salafi women about modesty, women actually value these events not only because of their desire to increase their religious knowledge, but also to enrich their social life. Da'wa activities allowed women to enter into a broader Salafi network, discuss student and professional challenges, and importantly, plan their Salafi family.

Without necessarily wanting to engage in political discussions, these Salafi women supported the Da'wa's political aspirations, because they saw this Salafi project as enabling their growing presence in Alexandrian public life. In these new women's communities, political affiliation and party hierarchy were revered and the emerging dynamics of power were palpable.

My research aligns with Mahmood's conclusion that human action, and more particularly, female agency, is not always directed at contesting social norms. Da'wa women do not contest the definition of women imposed by the Da'wa shaykhs or preachers like al-Ghaliz. The Salafi social norms they embrace are deeply conservative rather than mainstream. Accordingly, their piety and behavior can be interpreted from an alternative perspective as a contestation of norms outside their Salafi circles or even in their own non-Salafi families, that is, a challenge to what it means to be a woman in Egyptian society. My interviews revealed that they did not want equal gender representation in all Da'wa committees or leadership positions. This perspective did not mean, however, that they chose to participate in the Da'wa activities because of a "false consciousness." They did not contest the shaykhs, and accepted Salafi norms, but in this period of changing gender dynamics within the movement, they were eager to occupy new spaces in the mosques and party offices. Their participation, then, went beyond some shaykhs' expectations that their involvement would be limited to the electoral period, or purely religious, as they found ways to shape their community and use Da'wa activities to pursue their own social interests.

Endnotes

1 Note that most names except those of prominent and public political or religious figures for which I have not included last names have been replaced by pseudonyms for confidentiality.
2 While many groups identify as Salafi, Salafism is also modern revivalist identity embraced by Muslims around the world even though they might not formally affiliate with a political or religious movement in their country.

3 Political quietism is a term used to refer to Islamist parties that refuse to participate in organized political action because of a specific interpretation of Islamic law that cautions against "defying the ruler."

4 However, al-Watan expressed some support for the Muslim Brotherhood-led protests in the summer of 2013.

5 While Islam and Islamic refer to the religion more broadly, Islamism denotes an interpretation of all spheres of public and private life, especially of politics, through the lens of Islamic concepts and values.

6 Mahmood, S. (2004). *Politics of Piety: The Islamic Revival and the Feminist Subject*. Princeton University Press.

7 Sassoubre, B. (2005). Review of *Politics of Piety. The Islamic Revival and the Feminist Subject*, by S. Mahmood. Princeton University Press; (November 2008). "Langues, religion et modernité dans l'espace musulman." *Revue Des Mondes Musulmans et de La Méditerranée*. No. 124, pp. 316–319.

8 Hamdy, S. (August 2008). Review of *Politics of Piety: The Islamic Revival and the Feminist Subject*, by S. Mahmood. *American Ethnologist*. Vol. 35, No. 3, pp. 3063–3067.

9 Iqtidar, H. (2011). *Secularizing Islamists? Jama'at-E-Islami and Jama'at-Ud-Da'wa in Urban Pakistan*. University Press Scholarship Online. London: University of Chicago Press, p. 2.

10 Pearsall, J. (July 2003). "Misogyny." *The Concise Oxford English Dictionary*. Oxford University Press.

11 Here the term puritanical, despite its Christian etymology, is used to connote strict personal (particularly sexual) and social morals, an interpretation of Muslim modesty that usually entails covering the body and the face, and strict ritual observance.

12 Spivak, G.C. (2010). "Can the subaltern speak?" Revised Edition. From the "History" chapter of *Critique of Postcolonial Reason*. New York: Columbia University Press; (2010). "Féminisme et Déconstruction." *Tumultes*. No. 1, p. 179.

13 Mohanty, C.T. (October 1998). "Under Western eyes: feminist scholarship and colonial discourses." *Feminist Review*. No. 30, pp. 61–88.

14 Ahmed, L. (1992). *Women and Gender in Islam: Historical Roots of a Modern Debate*. Yale University Press; (1982). "Feminism and feminist movements in the Middle East, a preliminary exploration: Turkey, Egypt, Algeria, People's Democratic Republic of Yemen." *Women's Studies International Forum*. Special Issue Women and Islam. Vol. 5, No. 2, pp. 153–168.

15 Mir-Hosseini, Z. (2000). *Islam and Gender: The Religious Debate in Contemporary Iran*. I.B.Tauris.

16 Kandiyoti, D. (1991). *Women, Islam, and the State*. Temple University Press; (1996). *Gendering the Middle East: Emerging Perspectives*. I.B. Tauris.

17 Al-Ali, N. (2000). *Secularism, Gender and the State in the Middle East: The Egyptian Women's Movement*. Cambridge University Press.

18 Keddie, N.R. (2012). *Women in the Middle East: Past and Present*. Princeton University Press.

19 Gray, D.H. (2015). *Beyond Feminism and Islamism: Gender and Equality in North Africa*. Reprint edition. I.B. Tauris.

20 In works such as Afshar, H. (1996). *Women and Politics in the Third World*. Taylor & Francis; Hale, S. (1997). *Gender Politics in Sudan: Islamism, Socialism, and the State*. Boulder: Westview Press.

21 Adelkhah, F. (2000). *La Révolution sous le voile : Femmes islamiques d'Iran*. Paris: Karthala, p. 11; Bracke, S. (2003). "Author(iz)ing agency - feminist scholars making sense of women's involvement in religious 'fundamentalist' movements." *European Journal of Women's Studies*. Vol. 10, No. 3, pp. 335–346.

22 Most notably Mahmood, *Politics of Piety*; Abu-Lughod, L. (1989). *Veiled Sentiments: Honor and Poetry in a Bedouin Society*. Berkeley: University of California Press.

23 Iqtidar, *Secularizing Islamists?*, p. 135.

24 The movement *al-Gama'iyya al-Islamiyya* was a violent Islamist group (which later renounced violence) born in Egyptian universities. See Kepel, G. (1985). *The Prophet and Pharaoh: Muslim Extremism in Egypt*. London: Al Saqi Books.

25 Many of these social clubs are relics of the colonial days, but remain popular with Egyptian elites. Dr. Hannan spoke of the Smouha club and the Sporting club.

26 Moors, A. (2003). "Introduction: public debates on family law reform participants, positions, and styles of argumentation in the 1990s." *Islamic Law and Society*. Vol. 10.

27 From a meeting with women of the *Da'wa Salafiyya* at party headquarters. March 2014, Alexandria.

28 International Foundation for Electoral Systems (January 2011). "Elections in Egypt: Analysis of the 2011 Parliamentary Electoral System." Available at www.ifes.org/publications/analysis-egypts-2011-parliamentary-electoral-system.

29 Hamed, E. (2013). "Egypt's 'Muslim Sisterhood' moves from social work to politics." *Al-Monitor*. Available at www.al-monitor.com/pulse/originals/2013/11/egypt-muslim-sisterhood-social-work-politics.html# (accessed March 22, 2015).

30 Interview with Hannan Alam about the work of al-Nur and the Da'wa Salafiyya. March 2014, Alexandria.

31 Toth describes the three types of jihad that shape Islamist movements. He argues that *jihad* is not only a holy struggle, but also all activities and attitudes that pertain to activism, he proposes three forms of iihads: (1) *jihad bi-l-qalb*: activism of the heart, (2) *jihad bi-l-kalima*: activism of the word, (3) *jihad bi-l-haraka*: jihad of action, that could include violence and militancy.
   Toth, J. (November 2003). "Islamism in Southern Egypt: a case study of a radical religious movement." *International Journal of Middle East Studies*. Vol. 35, No. 4, pp. 547–572.

32 Ibid, p. 551.

33 Moors, "Introduction," p. 8.

34 Iqtidar, *Secularizing Islamists?*, p. 151.

35 Even if some describe this area as Zizinia, the neighborhood, which is the next one over – is a little bit more affluent and home to more commerce. The boundary between the two areas is not clear and in some of al-Ghaliz's advertisements Umm al-Mu'minin is said to be in Zizinia.

36 Haenni, P. (2005). *L'Islam de marché: L'autre révolution conservatrice*. Paris: Seuil.

37 Interview with Muhammad al-Ghaliz about preaching in the Umm al-Mu'minin Mosque. March 2014, Alexandria.

38 M. al-Ghaliz's class "Huwwa Kida Bass?" Available at www.youtube .com/watch?v=OaShhe-IitI.

39 Islamic evangelists is a term used in the literature on Islamic revival to draw parallels to the mediatic Christian phenomenon in the United States as used and studied in the Middle Eastern and Egyptian context by Moll, Y. (2010). "Islamic Televangelism: Religion, Media and Visuality in Contemporary Egypt." *Arab Media & Society*. Vol. 10, pp. 1–27; Thomas, P.N. and P. Lee (2012). *Global and Local Televangelism*. Palgrave Macmillan; Høigilt, J. (2011). *Islamist Rhetoric: Language and Culture in Contemporary Egypt*. Routledge.

PART III

Migration and Social Change

8 Morocco at the Crossroads

The Intersection of Race, Gender, and Refugee Status

KARLA MCKANDERS

Introduction

For centuries, Morocco has been a country of emigration[1] and transit. Its proximity to the European Union and to the Spanish territories of Ceuta and Melilla on the northern border of Morocco has led migrants to attempt transit through Morocco to gain access to the European Union. Despite its history as a country of transit, Morocco now faces unprecedented challenges regarding increased immigration[2] and its corresponding international obligations to protect the human rights of migrants within its borders. As a new destination country, Morocco has experienced increased pressure from national and international nongovernmental organizations to adhere to its obligations as a signatory to two important documents: (1) the 1951 Refugee Convention, a legal document defining which migrants may be considered refugees and outlining the rights and the legal obligations of states; and (2) the 1967 Protocol, which removed the geographical and time limits that were part of the Refugee Convention.[3]

As of November 2015, the United Nations High Commissioner for Refugees, UNHCR, estimated that there were approximately 830 refugees and 3,776 asylum seekers residing in Morocco.[4] A migrant is an individual who, either temporarily or permanently, moves from one place to another.[5] Thus, a refugee is considered a "forced" migrant. According to Chapter One, Article IA(2) of the Refugee Convention, a refugee is someone "unable or unwilling to return to their country of origin owing to a well-founded fear of being persecuted for reasons of race, religion, nationality, membership of a particular social group, or political opinion."[6]

The variables of race and gender influence the UNHCR and the Moroccan government's decisions as to whether to grant an individual or a group refugee status. In this chapter, I argue that Morocco's issues with the legal designation of refugee status, the processing of asylum seekers and the treatment of refugees and asylum seekers signifies the need to reconstruct how the Refugee Convention is applied. The issues Morocco faces as a new destination country, attempting to apply the Convention in a nondiscriminatory manner, evinces the contemporary reality that countries in the Global South have become destinations for greater numbers of forced migrants than ever seen in recorded history.

Most of the existing scholarly literature on migration in Morocco is grounded in a social science framework. Scholars have analyzed interviews and other data in order to draw conclusions about the future of Morocco as a destination country and the flaws in its migration policies.[7] Hein de Hass, for example, has focused on migration patterns in Morocco and current trends in immigration to Morocco.[8] Other scholars have assessed the impact of the European Union's border policies on Morocco. This chapter, on the other hand, is written from a normative and reformist legal perspective. As a legal scholar and practicing refugee lawyer, I examine the normative precepts, or how the drafters of Refugee Convention envisioned the Convention would be applied and implemented, and propose reforms that are in line with the contemporary applications of the Refugee Convention. This legal analysis addresses gaps in the literature on forced migration trends in Morocco, what these trends portend for the Global South, and the need to consider focus on Morocco as it is at critical juncture as it is creating new refugee laws and procedures.

The goal of this chapter, then, is to critically analyze the vulnerable situation of refugees and asylum seekers at the intersection of race and gender in Morocco. Accordingly, the chapter contains four major parts. In the first part, I give background information on the 1951 Refugee Convention, the obligations of nation-states that are signatories to the Convention, and how nation-states make legal determinations to distinguish between migrants, asylum seekers and refugees. This section recounts the historical background of the Refugee Convention from 1920 to 1951 to facilitate understanding of how the Convention is applied today. In the second part, I review the historical and legal context behind Moroccan migration and refugee laws. In the third part, I highlight the historical and legal context in which the Convention is being applied in Morocco. In the fourth part, I analyze the contemporary problematic of the application of the Convention in

Morocco focusing on how individuals with gender based reasons for fleeing persecution and asylum seekers of African descent may be precluded from presenting their cases to obtain refugee status under existing legal frameworks.

This analysis utilizes both primary and secondary data to examine, from a legal perspective, gaps in the protection of refugees under the Refugee Convention, to which Morocco is one of the first and few Muslim and Arabic countries to be a signatory.[9] Sources of data included UNHCR statistics, existing immigration laws related to refugees and migrants in Morocco, social science research on mixed migration in Morocco, policy briefs, and data on global migration flows as well as current trends in litigating and processing refugees across the globe. After using these data to approach Morocco as a legal case study, I found support for the conclusion that international actors must rethink collaboration to ensure refugees protections under the Refugee Convention – especially given that countries of the Global South are becoming new destinations for migrants.

Implementing the 1951 Refugee Convention

The 1951 Refugee Convention imposes a duty, on countries that sign, to provide protection from removing an individual to a country where they will be subjected to persecution. The Convention is the key legal document that provides for who constitutes a refugee, what protections a signatory is required to provide to refugees, and the signatories' legal obligations.

Eligibility for Refugee Status

A refugee is someone "unable or unwilling to return to their country of origin owing to a well-founded fear of being persecuted for reasons of race, religion, nationality, membership of a particular social group, or political opinion."[10] An asylum seeker, by contrast, is an individual who claims to be a refugee who awaits an individual legal determination, by a nation-state or UNHCR's refugee status determination process, to be classified as a refugee. Until there is a legal determination that an individual or group of asylum seekers are refugees, the asylum seeker is not entitled to lawful status that protects their right to not be removed back to the country where they fear persecution.[11] The varied presumptions about which migrants constitute refugees hinder the nondiscriminatory implementation and global consensus of who is a refugee under the Convention.[12]

The history of the development of international protections for refugees has transitioned through many stages. The first two stages, from 1920 to 1935 and 1935–1939, were grounded in a *juridical perspective* that was based on treating people as refugees because of their membership in a group of persons who were effectively deprived of formal protections by the government of their state of origin.[13] From 1935 to 1939, the international community extended protections to groups of individuals who lost the protections of their government because of social and political upheavals. The legal terminology for this concept is *de facto* refugee status. Such people came to be known as *prima facie* refugees.[14]

Around 1939, during World War II, international protections for refugees were based on the abrogation of *personal freedoms*. This definition forms the basis for the definition under the 1951 Refugee Convention. From this contemporary perspective, a refugee is "a person who seeks to escape from perceived injustice or fundamental incompatibility with her home states" that leads to persecution by state or nonstate actors.[15]

Morocco's Obligation as Signatory to the Refugee Convention, Nondiscriminatory Application

Morocco signed the Refugee Convention in 1956.[16] The changes in immigration demographics in Morocco and the politics surrounding migration in the region for the past ten years have led Moroccan policymakers to reevaluate the treatment of migrants and the legal protections to which they are entitled under the Refugee Convention. The Convention, in particular, obliges the signatories to the Convention to apply provisions "without discrimination as to sex, age, disability, sexuality, or other prohibited grounds of discrimination."[17] For example, refugees and asylum seekers are guaranteed: The right not to be expelled (except under certain, strictly defined conditions); the right not to be punished for illegal entry into the territory of a contracting State; the right to work, to housing, to education, to public relief and assistance, to freedom of religion, to access the courts, to freedom of movement within the territory and to be issued identity and travel documents. These rights, however, are not guaranteed to refugees and asylum seekers who are reasonably regarded as a danger to the security of the country, or having been convicted of a particularly serious crime, are considered a danger to the community.[18]

Morocco's obligations under the Refugee Convention must be analyzed in light of several competing aspects: Its 2013 changes to migration and refugee laws; Morocco's geographic proximity to Europe; and the intersection of race and gender which impacts public perceptions about who qualifies as a refugee and the rights to which they are entitled. These issues highlight both contemporary global challenges and special challenges faced by the Global South.

Although the Refugee Convention clearly defines refugees as a distinct class of individuals, the distinction between refugees and migrants who leave their countries for other reasons remains controversial. Like many countries, Morocco has struggled with defining which migrants can establish eligibility for relief under the Convention.[19]

Asylum Seekers and Refugees in Morocco: Historical and Legal Context

Throughout its history, Morocco's geographic location and proximity to Europe have made it a natural country of migration.[20] Some African migrants have used Morocco as a point of transit before attempting to enter Europe, generally through the Spanish enclaves of Ceuta and Melilla or by boat.[21]

Morocco's 2003 Migration Law

The 2003 Migration Law represented an attempt by the Moroccan government to identify and protect migrants seeking refugee status. The law enacted provisions that enabled asylum seekers to seek residency rights; request asylum at the Moroccan border when denied entry; and gain protection against removal from Morocco when warranted.

In general, in 2007, the UNHCR signed an agreement known as *accord de siège* with the Moroccan government with the intention of "expanding and deepening cooperation between the Moroccan authorities and the UNHCR operation in the country."[22] The *accord de siège* outlined the process by which individuals with refugee claims could apply for asylum,[23] and resulted in limited improvements for refugees and asylum seekers.[24]

UNHCR, and Convention signatories, implement some sort of refugee status determination (RSD) process through officers or their court systems, to review asylum applications. The 2007 law[25] involved many complicated legal steps of submitting an asylum application or registration to the *Bureau des Réfugiés et Apatrides* or the office of the UNHCR in Rabat; having an interview with a UNHCR protection officer for the purpose of gathering biographical information and more detailed information about the request.[26] If the officer believes the asylum seeker had established a preliminarily claim to refugee status,[27] then UNHCR schedules an interview for the asylum seeker to relay the facts of his or her case.[28]

Though the UNHCR refugee certificate was supposed to be honored by the Moroccan government to prevent deportation from Morocco, many journalists and human rights organizations have documented the deportation of African refugees without regard to their refugee status.[29]

2013 Migration Reforms: Morocco Taking Back Legal Processing of Asylum Seekers

In June 2013, asylum seekers, migrants, and refugees gathered outside the UNHCR Office in Rabat to protest alleged Moroccan government mistreatment.

In September 2013, Morocco's National Council of Human Rights released a report criticizing the country's migration policy. The report alleged that the government repeatedly failed to consider the human rights of migrants and made policy recommendations, which addressed the concerns of both migrants and refugees. The proposals targeting refugees ensured that they would have rights and a way to obtain lawful status once they obtained refugee status. The Royal Cabinet, an independent body appointed by King Mohammed VI, quickly endorsed the Council's report. Still, more criticisms of Morocco's existing migration policy followed.

In September 2013, the Moroccan government announced it would adopt comprehensive immigration reform in response to the criticisms and the actions of the Royal Cabinet. Under the new law, six categories of migrants could apply for a one-year residence permit that would authorize them to work and give them access to social benefits some of which included spouses of Moroccan citizens, foreign couples who have lived together in Morocco, children from marriage of couples, immigrants with work permits and individuals with serious illnesses.[30]

Many scholars and activists critiqued the new law as a political move. It was passed at a strategic time, when Morocco was attempting to strengthen its diplomatic ties to Western African countries in order to build power and influence within the region. Thus, the reforms were seen as an opportunistic attempt for Morocco to position itself for economic gain via the temporary legalization of African migrants. The adoption of the new migration policy occurred in December 2013, and was closely followed by King Mohammed VI's diplomatic tour through Western African countries in February 2014. Around this time, scholar Katharina Natter observed, "the deepening of African-Moroccan relations seemed at odds with the denial of African migrants' rights in Morocco … Like in any other political system, various potentially contradictory interests in foreign policy and domestic affairs are shaping the issue of migration control."

Based on the 2007 *accord de siège*, the UNHCR had assumed the sole responsibility for Refugee Status Determinations until 2013. Under the new 2013 law, the Moroccan government took over this process[31] and re-opened the Bureau de Protection des Réfugiés et Apatrides (Protection Office for Refugees and the Stateless) to assume the UNHCR's function.

Morocco's geographic proximity to Europe and its corresponding attractiveness to African migrants seeking to enter Spain has created diplomatic and foreign policy issues between Morocco and the European Union.[32]

Contemporary Problematic in the Application of the Refugee Convention

As described above, in Morocco, the recent historical shift from a transit to destination country impact its ability to fully actualize and implement its obligations under the 1951 Refugee Convention. This section discusses how the intersection of gender and race also impact the nondiscriminatory application of the Refugee Convention.

Gender-Based Asylum Claims

Nation-states' legal systems for processing refugees around the world have begun to acknowledge the role of gender-based violence in forced migration and the unique issues it creates for those fleeing persecution and seeking protection under the Refugee Convention. Gender-based violence is typically perpetrated by nonstate actors, who a government is unwilling or unable to control, and includes such acts of persecution as domestic violence, rape, forced marriage, female genital cutting, and other gender-based violent acts.[33] UNHCR and various governments have begun to recognize such nonstate actor persecution on account of gender.

The use of the juridical perspective, as described above, has typically disadvantaged women and others experiencing gender-related persecution who are seeking protection outside their country of origin where gender related asylum claims are often connected to persecution by nonstate related actors that the government is unwilling or unable to control.

Further, the Convention defines a refugee as "a person who has suffered persecution or who has a well-founded fear of future persecution due to race, religion, nationality, membership in a particular social group, or political opinion."[34] The plain language does not mention gender, which may lead advocates, laypersons and asylum seekers alike to assume that gender-related persecution is not protected under the Refugee Convention.

Individuals with gender related asylum claims, however, have used the social group category to establish they are entitled to refugee status.[35] The social group category is a protected category in the Refugee Convention. Social group is not specifically defined in the Convention. There are two main theories under which refugee lawyers have defined social groups: (1) protected characteristics approach (sometimes referred to as an "immutability" approach) and (2) social perception approach. The protected characteristics approach "examines whether a group is united by an immutable characteristic or by a characteristic that is so fundamental to human dignity that a person should not be compelled to forsake it. An immutable characteristic may be innate (such as sex or ethnicity) or unalterable for other reasons (such as the historical fact of a past association, occupation or status)."[36] Whereas the social perception approach "examines whether or not a group shares a common characteristic which makes them a cognizable group or sets them apart from society at large."[37]

The social group category has been applied to protect individuals who fall within the groups of "women, families, tribes, occupational groups, and homosexuals," under the 1951 Convention.[38] Gender, as it is an immutable characteristic that is socially visible, has been interpreted by many signatory states to fit within the formulation of a social group.

Recognition of gender as a social group developed in 2002 when UNHCR issued a report that acknowledged, "historically, the refugee definition has been interpreted through a framework of male experiences, which has meant that many claims of women and of homosexuals, have gone unrecognised." Importantly, the report also acknowledged that although women and men both can suffer gender-based persecution, "women are disproportionately affected."[39] In order to respond to this problem, the report provided signatory countries with an expanded definition of gender, guidelines for dealing with gender-related persecution, and commentary on gender-related claims:

Gender refers to the relationship between women and men based on socially or culturally constructed and defined identities, status, roles and responsibilities that are assigned to one sex or another, while sex is a biological determination. Gender is not static or innate, but acquires socially and culturally constructed meaning over time. Gender-related claims may be brought by either women or men, although due to particular types of persecution, they are more commonly brought by women.[40]

Gender-related claims have typically encompassed, although are by no means limited to, acts of sexual violence, family/domestic violence, coerced family planning, female genital cutting, punishment for transgression of social mores, and discrimination against homosexuals.[41] Despite the promulgation of the report and UNHCR's acknowledgement regarding the lack of economic, political, civil, and social rights afforded to women within their home countries facilitates their migration, very few countries have applied gender-based standards to refugee status determinations.

At the University of California Hastings Center for Gender and Refugee Studies, scholars have compiled the decisions and laws of eighteen countries (Argentina, Australia, Belgium, Canada, Costa Rica, the European Union, Germany, Ireland, Mexico, The Netherlands, New Zealand, Norway, Romania, South Africa, Spain, Sweden, Switzerland, and United Kingdom) that have implemented gender-related provisions in processing refugees.[42] Some of the published accounts of the application of gender to refugee status are explored below.

South Africa. Between 2009 and 2011, South Africa had the largest number of asylum seekers, both male and female, in the world.[43] In 2005, the last year data is available on South Africa from UNHCR, there were approximately 86 percent male and 14 percent female asylum seekers.[44] In 2008, South Africa passed legislation containing procedures for implementing the Refugee Convention. One of the protected categories in implementing the Convention extended beyond the Convention's enumerated grounds and includes gender as a protected category.[45] Despite these progressive measures, however, in South Africa there have not been any cases granting refugee status based on the protected category of gender.

A 2012 study on the processing of South African asylum seekers noted that both a "woman who fled Kenya to avoid forced circumcision" and a "Ugandan man who fled persecution for being a homosexual" were rejected.[46] In a critique of the South African asylum process, the authors stated, "South Africa's asylum system exists only to refuse access to the country and makes no attempt to realize the goal of refugee protection … [but] functions solely as an instrument of immigration control."[47] Further, they found that the asylum officers there "limited their definition of persecution to political grounds and only considered a history of persecution as evidence of future risk."[48]

Romania. Despite being a developing country, Romania has published cases recognizing and granting refugee status based on gender. In the case *Minor Appellant L.A.A. v. Decision of the National Refugee Office*, 8945/2003, "a 16-year-old girl from Somalia was granted refugee status in Romania after the murder of her family members and multiple rapes by members of the paramilitary forces."[49] The court acknowledged that she was subjected to gender-based violence and cited community opinions about "women and single girls, especially if they were victims of sexual attack, in which case there is a risk for feminine genital cutting enforced by the members of her own community."[50] The court granted refugee status based upon several factors: the applicant was subjected to persecution by a nonstate agent, the authorities were unable to offer protection, and the persecution was based on the claimant's gender and ethnicity.[51]

Mexico. Mexico, much like Morocco, is a traditional country of transit and a new destination country. In its refugee determination process, Mexico treats gender as a protected category. Its laws require that vulnerable asylum seekers – including women, pregnant women, victims of torture, victims of sexual abuse and gender-based violence, and children and adolescents – receive special attention as well as procedural and institutional measures established for their benefit."[52] UNHCR reported that in a Mexican asylum case, the government granted refugee status to a Nicaraguan woman who was the victim of domestic violence. She fled to Mexico because she felt that there were no organizations or government institutions to protect her. In 2014, the Mexican government granted her asylum application based on the Nicaraguan government's inability to protect her from her abuser.[53]

The United States. Progress has been made in the United States in recognizing gender as a basis for refugee status under the social group category. The 1996 opinion, *Matter of Kasinga*, was one of the first cases to recognize gender as a category under which an individual could obtain immigration relief. In this case, a United States Administrative Court held that a young Togolese woman fleeing female genital cutting had a well-founded fear of persecution on account of her membership in a particular social group. The attorneys defined the social group as "Young women who are members of the Tchamba-Kunsuntu Tribe of northern Togo who have not been subjected to female genital cutting, as practiced by that tribe, and who oppose the practice."[54] This group fits within the social group category because young Togolese women who are tribe members and subjected to female genital cutting are all immutable characteristics.[55]

More recently, US immigration courts have recognized domestic violence victims who cannot obtain protection from their government as members of a group with a gender-based claim. In the 2009 case *Matter of R-A-*, which was litigated over fourteen years, a Guatemalan woman fleeing her husband's severe domestic abuse was granted asylum by the US immigration court.[56]

After having set this precedent, in the 2010 case *Matter of L-R-*, the immigration court granted refugee status to a Mexican domestic violence victim who was abused by her children's father. When Ms. L-R- was 19 years old and a student in Mexico, her school's 33-year-old sports coach raped her at gunpoint. For the next two decades, he kept her in virtual captivity, using physical force and beatings, and threatened death to her and her family members to prevent her from leaving. He raped her regularly and tormented her mentally and verbally. Ms. L-R- was not able to obtain assistance from police as going to the police placed her at risk for retaliation.[57] In this case, the United States Administrative Court acknowledged that gender, combined with the individual's status in the family and in society, satisfied the requirement for a defined social group.

Evaluating Gender-Based Asylum Claims in Morocco

The court cases from Mexico, Romania and the United States demonstrate substantial progress towards recognizing gender-based asylum claims. While South Africa is a leader in implementing legislation and including gender as a protected category, its courts have yet to grant asylum based on an applicant's gender. Over the past twelve years, nation-states have implemented gender as a protected category extending protections even further than the Refugee Convention. Further, various courts holdings that gender is a category for which an individual can obtain protection is a significant development as the precedent court cases and legislation in other countries can inform decisions about women migrants with gender-based asylum claims in Morocco who may seek refugee status.

The acknowledgment that the refugee status determination process may, in some instances, be a highly individualized legal analysis, requires an analysis of how the legal definition under the Convention was developed and a willingness to understand the political and cultural impact of the operation of the Convention in different countries. This understanding may in turn impact the treatment of gender related asylum claims and African migrants in Morocco and more globally.

Under the social group category, we can extrapolate circumstances under which women with gender-based asylum claims in Morocco would possibly qualify for refugee status. For example, women asylum seekers from Ivory Coast and the Democratic Republic of the Congo (DRC), the largest group of asylum seekers, may have claims based on being subjected to gender-related persecution that their government is unwilling or unable to control.[58]

As documented in the Ivory Coast, women may face individualized gender related persecution that results from the lack of protection from nonstate actors who subject them to rape, domestic violence, female genital cutting, dowry deaths, forced marriage to a dead husband's brother, and for children forms of child abuse.[59]

Similarly, in the DRC rape survivors were commonly pressured by family members to remain silent, even in collaboration with health-care professionals, to safeguard the reputations of the survivor and her family and avoid significant social stigma. As in many countries, women and girls in the DRC who survived a sexual assault typically were seen as unsuitable for marriage, and husbands frequently abandoned wives who had been assaulted. Some families forced rape survivors to marry the men who raped them or to forgo prosecution in exchange for money or goods from the rapist.[60] In addition, as of 2012 there were no laws in the DRC to protect the reported 64 percent of women who experienced domestic violence.[61] In both the Ivory Coast and the DRC, women fleeing gender based violence may be able to present individualized asylum claims that may be overlooked through *prima facie* refugee designation that typically recognizes refugees who are persecuted by government actors.

In addition, human trafficking as a form of gender-based persecution requires particular attention and individualized evaluation in Morocco, not least because of the large number of Nigerian women who are trafficked through Morocco.[62] Trafficked women or minors may have valid claims to refugee status that may not be traditionally recognized under the Refugee Convention.[63] The forcible or deceptive recruitment of women or minors for the purposes of forced prostitution or sexual exploitation is a form of gender-related violence or abuse that can be considered a form of torture or cruel, inhuman or degrading treatment or even death. Further, the abduction, incarceration, and/or confiscation of passports or other identifying documents that are frequent hallmarks of human trafficking can impose serious restrictions on a woman's freedom of movement. Trafficked women and minors often face serious repercussions after their escape and/or upon return to their country of origin (such as reprisals or retaliation from trafficking rings or individuals). When returning to their countries of origin, victims of trafficking face the real possibility of being re-trafficked, severe community or family ostracism, or severe discrimination. In individual cases, then, being trafficked for the purpose of forced prostitution or sexual exploitation can be another basis for a refugee claim when the State has been unable or unwilling to provide protection against such harm or threats of harm.[64]

Similarly, the US State Department Trafficking Report of 2014 warned that "unaccompanied children and women from Cote d'Ivoire, the Democratic Republic of the Congo, and Nigeria are highly vulnerable to sex trafficking and forced labour in Morocco."[65] Through access to individualized refugee status determinations, such women and minors may be eligible for refugee status in Morocco, a group-based frame may inherently exclude trafficked women without adequate consideration of their individual claims.

Race and Refugee Exceptionalism in Morocco

Until recently, African migrants[66] who may be eligible for refugee status have remained largely invisible due to the Moroccan government's failure to consistently differentiate between migrants, asylum seekers and refugees. In fact, most Moroccan citizens, government officials, and lawyers believe that African migrants leave their home countries solely for economic reasons. This designation fails to consider the diverse and complex reasons that compel individuals to flee as refugees or become *refugees sur place*. *Refugees sur place* are individuals who leave their own country for nonrefugee related reasons but develop a fear of persecution in their country of origin following their departure – typically when conditions in their country have changed.[67]

Accordingly, migrant advocates in Morocco have engaged in more thorough evaluations of the reasons why migrants initially leave their countries of origin. Their work has resulted in a variety of insights. A substantial minority of migrants in Morocco, for example, are fleeing violence or persecution in their home countries or are afraid to return to their home countries for fear of future persecution. [68] According to the definition established by the Refugee Convention, these migrants are refugees, no matter their race, gender, or geographic location of origin. As de Haas observed in 2015, "the African immigrant population in Morocco also includes asylum seekers and refugees fleeing conflict and oppression in their origin countries."[69]

In addition, in an earlier study, Lindstrom[70] interviewed recognized refugees and learned that though some had come to Morocco as students, they "found themselves unable to return home become of the outbreak of violence in their countries of origin ... [particularly those] from Congo, Sierra Leone, Liberia, and the Sudan."[71] These migrants are categorized as *refugees sur place*. Similarly, in 2013, refugees and asylum seekers in Morocco who were from the Ivory Coast were mostly fleeing a civil war in their country.[72] Even after the civil war had ceased, however, the country still contained warring groups that were targeting civilians, thus inhibiting repatriation. In the same way, most refugees and asylum seekers in Morocco from the Democratic Republic of the Congo-Kinshasa in 2015 were fleeing conflict in the eastern side of their country.[73]

Race also impacts public perception and official treatment of asylum seekers, as well as their access to the refugee status determination process. Xenophobia is a phenomenon that immigrants throughout the world confront today. Some Moroccan scholars attribute the difficulties that African migrants experience in Morocco to a deep-seated fear and ignorance of an unknown "other." The racism faced by migrant populations in Morocco is both historical and political in nature, and has been the subject of debates about North Africa, xenophobia and racism, and the effects of the European Union's attempt to "externalize the migration problematic."[74]

For example, *Maroc Hebdo*, a Moroccan news magazine, published a cover with the face of an African immigrant and the title *Le Peril Noir* (The Black Peril).[75] The magazine cover led to mass mobilization by the immigrant community and Moroccan nongovernmental organizations against racist media discourses. Further, in July 2013, the television station *France 24* covered a story about Casablanca landlords who systematically refused to rent to Africans. A sign bearing the message "Il est strictement interdit de louer les appartement aux Africains," ("It is strictly forbidden to rent apartments to Africans") was posted in both French and Arabic in the lobbies of apartment buildings throughout a Casablanca neighborhood.[76]

It is within this context that African migrants in Morocco have not availed themselves of existing UNHCR due process mechanisms, nor opportunities to obtain refugee status through the Moroccan government. Racism creates fear and discriminatory treatment that can cause migrants to retreat underground and avoid governmental entities that might otherwise help them to gain legal assistance with their immigration status.

Further, racism may account for broad categorizations of potential asylum seekers as economic migrants without regard for the individual circumstances that may have caused them to migrate from their countries of origin. Until recently, the Moroccan government, lawyers, and non-legal actors have perceived all African migrants in Morocco as economic migrants.[77] Not infrequently, countries intentionally use the label "economic migrants" to justify their failure to respond to the complex and diverse reasons why individuals immigrate to their country.[78]

Such is generally the case in Morocco. The broad categorization of African migrants as "economic migrants" marginalizes and stigmatizes this group, and limits their ability to gain access to institutions that may provide a means to legalize their status. This practice ultimately hinders the government from adhering to Convention's basic requirement that it administer the provisions without discrimination based on race or gender.

In part, misconceptions about economic migrants are created because asylum seekers often utilize the same unauthorized means to enter a country as other migrant populations. Like other categories of migrants, asylum seekers use smugglers and fraudulent documents to escape persecution or the fear of persecution in their home countries. Yet, the Moroccan government's failure, and refusal, to develop procedures to identify asylum seekers at its border perpetuates the conflation of migrants with asylum seekers in contravention of the Convention.[79]

Still, some scholars have asserted that it is divisive to categorize and segregate refugees from economic migrants.[80] Many have argued that the distinction is a political tool used by nation-states to categorically deny certain populations from the protections of the Refugee Convention. The distinction is important, however, so that signatories to the Convention can provide specific international protections and due process rights to prevent *nonrefoulement* – the return of refugees to countries where they have been persecuted or face a reasonable possibility that they will face persecution.[81]

These examples demonstrate systematic barriers, stereotypes and other preconceived notions that prevent the implementation of legislative, administrative and judicial strategies for protecting the rights of refugees under the Refugee Convention. Thus, the failure of the 2013 refugee law to bring about true reforms may be remedied by educating lawyers, migrants (especially women) and nonlegal actors in Morocco about who constitutes a refugee. In fact, many refugees will only gain the protections they deserve when Morocco addresses widespread prejudices and misconceptions that have inhibited identification of African migrants who have fled their countries because of fear of persecution or future persecution.

Migrants in Morocco often fall into multiple categories based on racial identity, immigration status, gender and economic status. All of these intersect and interact with existing legal institutions in Morocco, which historically have failed to offer protections to vulnerable populations. Such failures make clear the need to critically evaluate and reform the procedures for implementing the Refugee Convention in order to address key questions about the shift in migration patterns that has resulted from restrictionist immigration policies in the Global North.[82]

Prima Facie Refugees and Cultural Compatibility

In contrast to gender based asylum claims and African asylum seekers, the Moroccan government collectively categorized Syrians as refugees and gave them refugee status in 2014.[83] The Moroccan government extended lawful status to approximately 5,000 Syrians fleeing civil war in their country, categorically designating them *prima facie* refugees – unlike individual asylum seekers who have cases pending before UNHCR.[84]

The term *prima facie* refugees refers to the designation of a group of migrants from one country as refugees without individualized determinations as to whether the migrants meet the criteria outlined in the Refugee Convention.[85] The UNHCR has explained:

During mass movements of refugees (usually as a result of conflicts or generalized violence as opposed to individual persecution), there is not – and never will be – a capacity to conduct individual asylum interviews for everyone who has crossed the border. Nor is it usually necessary, since in such circumstances it is generally evident why they have fled. As a result, such groups are often declared '*prima facie* refugees.'[86]

The Moroccan government, however, has never categorically recognized asylum seekers from the Ivory Coast and the Democratic Republic of the Congo, who also faced life-threatening circumstances at home. Many Moroccans argued that there was "cultural compatibility" with Syrian refugees who speak a dialect of Arabic and have many of the same customs. This criticism is not intended to diminish the plight of Syrian refugees who are fleeing widespread and systematic violence, of course, but to highlight how race, gender, geographic home of those in need and political goals impact a country's decision to recognize refugee populations, even if their situation meets the Convention definition of refugees. Further, the categorization of refugees without a system that provides individualized asylum determinations deprives asylum seekers of due process rights and tends to marginalize both women and individuals from certain racial groups.

Conclusion

The voices of the most vulnerable populations often point towards social constructs in dire need of systemic change. This critique points to the intersectionality of race and gender in the treatment of African migrants, especially women migrants, in Morocco in order to formulate ways to reform the current implementation of the Refugee Convention in the Global South.[87] In Morocco, many migrants have fled repression and human rights abuses in their home countries, such as those from the Ivory Coast and Congo-Kinshasa,[88] only to find themselves in a place where they are not able to gain access to legal institutions where they can assert claims for refugee status, and where they sometimes face even more human rights abuses.

Scholars, lawyers, and policymakers have largely overlooked the overall growth in the number of nations in the Global South that have become destination countries for refugee and asylum-seekers.[89] As Freedman has noted, "Those who bear the costs of hosting refugees and displaced people are not the rich states of the West (although these states do make contributions to UNHCR budget), but largely the poorer states of the Global South."[90] Accordingly, the Global North must be held accountable for the shifts in migration that its policing policies have created in destination countries within the Global South and actively participate in solutions to address this issue instead of externalizing its borders.

As Morocco transitions from a country of emigration and transit to a destination country, there needs to be a corresponding shift to Moroccan lawyers, policymakers, migrants and the general population about who is a refugee, how to access the refugee status process for obtaining refugee status, and how to assess, on an individualized basis, eligibility based on gender-related persecution. Widespread education and continued advocacy also will help Morocco adhere to its obligations under the 1951 UNHCR Refugee Convention and 1964 Protocol while ensuring the rights of refugees and asylum seekers to *nonrefoulement*. This task is already in process with many of the migrant advocacy organizations in Morocco. Despite the promise of the 2013 Moroccan immigration law, the country's failures and delays in implementing a new system for processing asylum claims raise concerns for the future of refugees in Morocco. In addition, these problems deepen the need for advocates and lawyers who will continue to lobby

European Union neighbors – not solely for support for Morocco's border policing policies, but for assistance for Morocco itself, as it fast becomes a primary destination country for migrants.

Endnotes

1 Webster's Dictionary. Merriam-Webster.com. Emigrate is defined as "to leave one's place of residence or country to live elsewhere." Available at www.merriam webster.com/dictionary/emigrate (accessed May 10, 2015).

2 Webster's Dictionary. Merriam-Webster.com. Immigrate is defined "to enter and usually become established; especially: to come into a country of which one is not a native for permanent residence." Available at www .merriam webster.com/dictionary/emigrate (accessed May 10, 2015). Destination migration is another term for "immigration" involving the action of coming to live permanently in a foreign country.

3 UN General Assembly (July 1951). *Convention Relating to the Status of Refugees*. United Nations. Treaty Series. Vol. 189, p. 137. Available at www.refworld.org/docid/3be01b964.html (accessed January 15, 2016); UN General Assembly. *Protocol Relating to the Status of Refugees*. January 31, 1967. Available at https://treaties.un.org/doc/Publication/ MTDSG/Volume%20I/Chapter%20V/V-5.en.pdf (accessed February 5, 2016).

4 Ibid. The terms "refugee" and "asylum seeker" are often confused.

5 Black's Law Dictionary Free 2nd Ed. "The Law Dictionary: What is MIGRATION?" Available at http://thelawdictionary.org/migration/ (accessed January 14, 2016).

6 See endnote 3.

7 See generally (September 2015). "Revisiting Moroccan migrations." *Journal of North African Studies*. Vol. 20, No. 4.

8 De Haas, H. (March 2014). "Morocco: setting the stage for becoming a migration transition country?" *Migration Policy Institute*. Available at www.migrationpolicy.org/article/morocco-setting-stage-becoming-migra tion-transition-country (accessed February 2, 2015).

9 Elmadmad, K. (July 1991). "An Arab convention on forced migration: desirability and possibilities." *International Journal of Refugee Law*. Oxford Journals. Vol. 3, No. 3, pp. 461–481.

10 See endnote 3.

11 Freedman, J. (2007). *Gendering the International Asylum and Refugee Debate*. Palgrave Macmillan. Defining *nonrefoulement*.

12 Ibid, p. 4, stating "for some there is a clear difference between an asylum seeker and an economic migrant, one fleeing persecution and the other

leaving their country of origin 'voluntarily' for economic motives. This distinction is often made in a form that is not neutral, classifying the two groups of migrants within a particular political schema with the real asylum seeker or genuine refugee as a 'good' migrant, a poor victim of persecution or oppresion worthy of support and protection, and the economic migrant a 'bad' [...]."

13 Hathaway, J. (April 1984). "The evolution of refugee status in international law: 1920 – 1950." *International and Comparative Law Quarterly*. London. Vol. 33, pp. 350–351.

14 McKanders, K. (October 2015). "Responding to the refugee crisis, can lawyers help?" *JURIST – Academic Commentary*. Available at http://jurist.org/forum/2015/10/karla-mckanders-refugee-convention.php (accessed February 7, 2016).

15 Hathaway, "The evolution of refugee," pp. 348–380, 378.

16 UN High Commissioner for Refugees (UNHCR) (June 2014). *State Parties to the 1951 Convention relating to the Status of Refugees and/or its 1967 Protocol.* Available at www.refworld.org/docid/51d3dad24.html (accessed March 15, 2016).

17 United Nations Convention Relating to the Status of Refugees 1951. April 22, 1954.

18 UNHCR (September 2011). *The Legal Framework for Protecting Refugees*, p. 4. Available at www.unhcr.org/4ec262df9.pdf (accessed January 15, 2016).

19 Ibid.

20 Information provided in March 2015 interview with Maude Depresle, Directing Lawyer of Droit et Justice. Translated from French. Interview on File with Author.

21 De Haas, "Morocco: setting the stage."

22 UNHCR (July 2007). *Morocco and UN refugee agency sign agreement to strengthen cooperation.* Available at www.unhcr.org/print/46a0ccb14.html (accessed January 15, 2016).

23 See endnote 42.

24 De Haas, "Morocco: setting the stage."

25 The 2007 iteration of the refugee status determination process provides the basis for the 2013 proposed process that has not yet been implemented in Morocco. The described process is a process that UNHCR currently uses in other countries and refugee camps globally and is not unique to Morocco.

26 UNHCR (2006). Available at www.unhcr.org/publications/sowr/4a4dc1a89/state-worlds-refugees-2006-human-displacement-new-millennium.html.

27 In legal terminology, this is called establishing a *prima facie* case, which is "Latin for 'at first sight.' Prima facie may be used as an adjective meaning 'sufficient to establish a fact or raise a presumption unless disproved or rebutted;' e.g., prima facie evidence. Wex Legal Information Institute at the Cornell Law School. Definition of Prima Facie Case. Available at www.law.cornell.edu/wex/prima_facie (accessed November 6, 2015).

28 See endnote 26.

29 Axelrad, J. (November 2013). "For African refugees in Morocco, a perilous path to asylum." *Christian Science Monitor*. Available at www.csmonitor.com/World/2013/1130/For-African-refugees-in-Morocco-a-perilous-path-to-asylum (accessed June 4, 2015).

30 International Organization for Migration (2014). Available at www.iom.int/.

31 Global Detention Project. (February 2014). *Morocco Detention Profile*. Available at www.globaldetentionproject.org/countries/africa/morocco/introduction.html (accessed May 30, 2015).

32 De Haas, "Morocco: setting the stage."

33 Center for Gender & Refugee Studies University of California Hastings College of the Law. (May 2014). *Review of Gender, Child, and LGBTI Asylum Guidelines and Case Law in Foreign Jurisdictions: A Resource for U.S. Attorneys*. Available at http://cgrs.uchastings.edu/sites/default/files/Review_Foreign_Gender_Guidelines_Caselaw_0.pdf (accessed November 6, 2015).

34 United Nations Convention Relating to the Status of Refugees 1951. April 22, 1954. Article 1A (2), 189 U.N.T.S. 150.

35 See endnote 33.

36 UNHCR (May 2002). Guidelines on International Protection No. 2: Membership of a Particular Social Group within the Context of Article 1A(2) of the 1951 Convention and/or its 1967 Protocol Relating to the Status of Refugees. Available at www.refworld.org/docid/3d36f23f4.html (accessed March 15, 2016).

37 Ibid.

38 Ibid.

39 See endnote 33.

40 UNHCR (May 2002). Guidelines on International Protection: Gender-Related Persecution within the context of Article 1A(2) of the 1951 Convention and/or its 1967 Protocol relating to the Status of Refugees. Paragraph 3. Available at www.unhcr.org/3d58ddef4.html (accessed May 30, 2015).

41 See also UC Hastings Gender Asylum Guidelines in Foreign Jurisdictions. Citing UNHCR Gender Guidelines and Office of the Special Adviser on

Gender Issues and Advancement of Women. Department of Economic and Social Affairs of the UN. Concepts and Definitions. Available at www.un.org/womenwatch/osagi/conceptsandefinitions.htm.

42 See endnote 40.

43 Amit, R. (January 2016). "African refugees in South Africa are often unable to access their rights." *Africa London School of Economics and Political Science Blog*. Available at http://blogs.lse.ac.uk/africaatlse/2016/01/29/african-refugees-in-south-africa-are-often-unable-to-access-their-rights/ (accessed February 5, 2016). States that "before the Syrian crisis, South Africa was the world's top recipient of asylum seekers for six years in a row." See also Integrated Regional Information Networks (IRIN) (April 2013). "South Africa's flawed asylum system." Available at www.refworld.org/docid/5187a9f74.html (accessed November 7, 2015). South Africa had 222,000 refugees in 2009 and107,000 refugees in 2011.

44 UNHCR. 2005 Statistical Year Book, South Africa. Available at www.unhcr.org/4641bebd0.html (accessed January 15, 2016).

45 Refugees Amendment Act 33 of 2008, art.1 § 1 (xxi), art. 4(a). Available at www.refworld.org/docid/4a54bbd4d.html. States that "the Amendment Act also explicitly incorporates gender-related persecution claims by including gender as one of the possible bases for a "particular social group" as well as by adding gender as a separate ground for refugee status."

46 See IRIN, "South Africa's flawed." See also endnote 33.

47 Ibid.

48 Ibid.

49 UC Hastings Gender Asylum Guidelines in Foreign Jurisdictions, p. 47. Citing Minor Appellant L.A.A. v. Decision of the National Refugee Office, 8945/2003, Romania: Bucharest Sector II Court. November 24, 2003. Available at www.unhcr.org/refworld/docid/4104e5784.html.

50 Ibid.

51 Ibid.

52 Ibid. citing Ley Sobre Refugidos y Proteccion Complementaria, Mexico (January 2011). Art. 8, p. 35. Available at www.unhcr.org/refworld/pdfid/4d4293eb2.pdf.

53 Ibid. citing Mariana Echandi (September 2009). "A new start in Mexico: leaving domestic violence behind." UNHCR. Telling the Human Story, p. 35. Available at www.unhcr.org/.

54 Kasinga, F. (June 1996). United States Department of Justice, Executive Office of Immigration Review, Board of Immigration Appeals. Interim Decision #3278. Available at www.justice.gov/sites/default/files/eoir/legacy/2014/07/25/3278.pdf (accessed November 6, 2015).

55 UNHCR (2002). *Guidelines on International Protection No. 2.*

56 *Matter of R-A-*, United States Department of Justice, Executive Office of Immigration Review, San Francisco Immigration Court (October 2009). Available at http://graphics8.nytimes.com/packages/pdf/national/20091030asylum_brief.pdf (accessed November 6, 2015).

57 *Matter of L-R-*, Brief of the Department of Homeland Security (April 2009). Available at http://cgrs.uchastings.edu/sites/default/files/Matter_of_LR_DHS_Brief_4_13_2009.pdf (accessed November 6, 2015). (Articulating the US government's acknowledgement of protection for victims of domestic violence as refugees under the social group category). See also University of California Hastings, Gender and Refugee Studies, Summary of *Matter of L-R-*. Available at http://cgrs.uchastings.edu/our-work/matter-l-r (accessed November 6, 2015).

58 United States Department of State 2014 Human Rights Report on the Democratic Republic of the Congo. June 2015. Available at www.state.gov/j/drl/rls/hrrpt/humanrightsreport/index.htm#wrapper (accessed October 6, 2015).

59 Human Rights Watch. World Report 2015 Côte d'Ivoire: Events of 2014 (2015), p. 174. Available at www.hrw.org/sites/default/files/world_report_download/wr2015_web.pdf (accessed February 7, 2016). See also United States Department of State, 2014 Human Rights Report on the Ivory Coast. June 2015. Available at www.state.gov/j/drl/rls/hrrpt/humanrightsreport/index.htm#wrapper (accessed October 6, 2015).

60 United States Department of State, 2014 Human Rights Report on the Democratic Republic of Congo. June 2015. Available at www.state.gov/j/drl/rls/hrrpt/humanrightsreport/index.htm#wrapper (accessed October 6, 2015). See also Human Rights Watch. World Report 2015 Democratic Republic of the Congo: Events of 2014 (2015), p. 187. Available at www.hrw.org/sites/default/files/world_report_download/wr2015_web.pdf (accessed February 7, 2016).

61 United Nations Commission on the Status of Women: The Democratic Republic of Congo. Available at www.humanrightsvoices.org/EYE ontheUN/un_101/figures/?p=1039 (accessed February 7, 2016). Citing United States Department of State, 2014 Human Rights Report on the Democratic Republic of Congo. June 2015.

62 United States Department of State (June 2014). *2014 Trafficking in Persons Report – Morocco*. Available at www.refworld.org/docid/53aab9c6d.html (accessed May 31, 2015).

63 See generally Stepnitz, A. "Human trafficking and asylum: problematic overlap," pp. 1–4. Available at www.refworld.org/pdfid/5021497a2.pdf (accessed February 7, 2016).

64 Christensen, T.M. (April 2011). "Trafficking for sexual exploitation: victim protection in international and domestic asylum law." Available

at www.unhcr.org/4d9c7c869.pdf (accessed February 7, 2016). "A significant source of protection for victims of trafficking is the Convention
and Protocol Relating to the Status of Refugees (1951 Convention)."

65 Ibid.

66 I will use the terminology "African" migrants to acknowledge that "sub-
Saharan" is a divisive and often perceived as racist term. The designation
sub-Saharan Africa is commonly used to indicate all of Africa except
northern Africa, with the Sudan included in sub-Saharan Africa. See
generally United Nations Statistics Division (October 2013). But see
J. Butty (September 2010). "Campaign launched to drop 'Sub-Saharan-
African-Phrase.'" Available at www.voanews.com/content/butty-sub-
saharan-africa-campaign-onyeani-20september10-103260644/155853
.html (accessed June 4, 2015).

67 UNHCR. *Refugee Protection and International Migration*. Available at
www.unhcr.org/4a24ef0ca2.pdf (accessed January 14, 2016).

68 De Haas, H. (October 2013). "Smuggling is a reaction to border
controls, not the cause of migration." Available at http://heindehaas
.blogspot.com/2013/10/smuggling-is-reaction-to-border.html (accessed
February 2, 2015).

69 De Haas, "Morocco: setting the stage."

70 Lindstrom, C. (October 2002). "Report on the situation of refugees in
Morocco: findings of an exploratory study." Available at www.aucegypt
.edu/GAPP/cmrs/reports/Documents/ChanneOct_000.pdf (accessed October 6, 2015).

71 Ibid.

72 Palmisano, L. (May 2013). "Repatriation of refugees from Liberia
to Côte d'Ivoire picks up this year." Available at www.unhcr.org/
519e29256.html (accessed October 6, 2015).

73 UNHCR. *2015 UNHCR country operations profile – Democratic Republic of the Congo*. Available at www.unhcr.org/pages/49e45c366.html
(accessed October 6, 2015).

74 Khachani, M. (2009). "Les Marocains et les Subsahariens, quelles relations?" *Red Cross/Red Crescent*.

75 Elboubkri, N. (September 2014). "Uncertain future: racial discrimination against African migrants in Morocco." *Fair Observer*. Available
at fairobserver.com.

76 (July 2013). "Casablanca landlords try to ban renting to Africans."
The Observer. Available at http://observers.france24.com/content/
20130719-landlords-casablanca-ban-renting-africans (accessed May 30,
2015).

77 Freedman, *Gendering the International*.

78 McKanders, K. (2010). "The unspoken voices of indigenous women in immigration raids." *Journal of Gender, Race and Justice*. Vol. 14, No. 1, pp. 1–40. Critiques United States policies wherein migrants are categorized as "economic" without detailed consideration being given to the complex reasons, push and pull factors and why individuals flee their countries of origin.

79 Riera, J. (December 2006). "Migrants and refugees: why draw a distinction?" *United Nations Chronicle*, pp. 31–32.

80 Ibid. See also Freedman, *Gendering the International*.

81 Riera, "Migrants and refugees."

82 American critical race and intersectionality theories can provide a relevant theoretical framework to analyze the treatment of sub-Saharan refugees in Morocco and the failure of Moroccan laws to provide them with protections. See generally Crenshaw, K. (1991). "Mapping the margins: intersectionality, identity politics, and violence against women of color." *Stanford Law Review*. Vol. 42, No. 6, pp. 1241–1300. (Discussing how women of color are marginalized in racism and feminist discourse). See also Browne, I. and J. Misra (2003). "The intersection of gender and race in the labor market." *Annual Review of Sociology*. Vol. 29, pp. 487–488. A. P. Harris (1990). "Race and essentialism in feminist legal theory." *Stanford Law Review*. Vol. 42, No. 3, pp. 581–616; K. Johnson (1995). "Public benefits and immigration: the intersection of immigration status, ethnicity, gender and class." *UCLA Law Review*. Vol. 42, No. 6, pp. 1509–1576.

83 UNHCR 2015 demonstrating that "the Government of Morocco wished to process non-Syrian refugees (issuance of national refugee card) separately from Syrians (status and document to be determined). See also A. Smith (July 2014). "Seeking refuge in Morocco." *The Middle East Monitor*. Available at www.middleeastmonitor.com/articles/africa/12886-seeking-refuge-in-morocco (accessed May 30, 2015).

84 Stitou, I. (September 2015). Translated by Ö. Pınar. "Shattered dreams of Syrian refugees in Morocco." Available at http://eng.babelmed.net/cultura-e-societa/74-marocco/13400-shattered-dreams-of-syrian-refugees-in-morocco.html (accessed January 14, 2016).

85 McKanders, K. (October 2015). "Responding to the refugee crisis, can lawyers help?" *JURIST – Academic Commentary*. Available at http://jurist.org/forum/2015/10/karla-mckanders-refugee-convention.php (accessed February 7, 2016).

86 UNHCR Website defining *Prima Facie* Refugees. Available at www.unhcr.org/pages/49c3646c137.html (accessed January 16, 2016). See also UNHCR (October 2014). *International Protection Considerations with*

regard to people fleeing the Syrian Arab Republic, Update III explaining why most Syrians qualify for refugee status.

87 McKanders, "The unspoken voices."

88 See endnotes 58–64 explaining why individuals from the Ivory Coast and the Democratic Republic of the Congo flee persecution.

89 Freedman, *Gendering the International*. States that sixty percent of the world refugee population in 2005 were in Africa, Asia, and the Middle East according to a UNHCR 2006 report.

90 Ibid, p. 3.

9 | Speaking of the Dead

Changing Funeral Practices among Moroccan Migrants in the Netherlands and Belgium

KHADIJA KADROUCH-OUTMANY

Introduction[1]

When my husband died, I joined in the funeral procession [in the Netherlands]. I walked along in the cemetery as his coffin[2] was being carried to his grave by his brothers, friends, and father. There were a lot of men present, family members of course but also colleagues and neighbors. My sister also participated, as did several of my [male and female] best friends and my mother. My family had no difficulty with the presence of women and non-Muslims in the funeral procession. However, the imam who led the procession objected. I still see him before me, yelling at all the women and non-Muslims to leave the cemetery! For a moment there, I thought of throwing him into the grave! You just cannot deal with those kinds of people at that particular moment. There I was, in my twenties, with my newborn baby, burying my husband. I just wanted to say farewell to my husband without that imam upsetting everything. On the spot, my father politely requested the imam to leave and we proceeded without the imam.[3]

Muslims hold various opinions about the presence of Muslim women at burial rituals. In some cases, these attitudes can lead to distressing situations, such as the one that Najia and her family endured. Najia's father did not hesitate to intervene and ask the imam to leave, not only because the imam's behavior incited an emotionally charged quarrel in a cemetery but because the imam, as a Surinamese Hanafi, held opinions that differed from those of the bereaved family, who were Moroccan Maliki adherents. This case illustrates the topic of this chapter: How the coming together of various Islamic denominational ideas in

215

the Netherlands and Belgium – a phenomenon I refer to as a fusion of denominational ideas – has effected the participation of Moroccan Muslim women in funeral rituals both in their host and home countries. The phenomenon of Muslim burial rituals is little researched in general, let alone in a context of migration. As far as I know there are only two other studies in relation to the burial of Moroccan French Muslims in and outside of France.[4] Furthermore, none of these studies includes the coming together of various denominational ideas and the effect thereof.

In order to analyze this fusion of ideas, I focused on Islamic burial rituals and the changing participation of Moroccan women in these rituals. I decided to focus on this aspect of life events, because Islamic burial rituals tell us much about how power-relations and identity are explained, embedded, second-guessed, and eventually challenged by Moroccan-Dutch Muslim women. I chose to compare the situation of Moroccan women with other Muslim women from different ethnic and denominational backgrounds. Although Moroccan women's denominational background generally forbids them to attend or participate in funeral processions, change is omnipresent. In this chapter I argue that two variables play an important role in changing Islamic burial rituals: a migration context and the diversity of Islamic communities in a host country. Interaction of these variables brought up questions about why, how, and especially, by whom burial preparations are to be performed. The consequence of the fusion of ideas the Moroccan women experienced, then, led them to confront issues of inclusion and exclusion based on gender and religious adherence.

Methodology

I conducted explorative research in the Netherlands and Belgium in order to gain insight into a phenomenon that to date has not been studied in detail, that is, changing Islamic burial rituals in the Netherlands and Belgium and the participation of Moroccan women living there. Respondents were selected using a purposive sampling technique also known as judgment sampling. This sampling method made it possible to select respondents who had experiences with Islamic burials within their circle of relatives and acquaintances in the Netherlands, Belgium, and/or in the countries of origin.

This chapter reports on the results of 35 interviews I conducted. Respondents between the ages of 20 and 45 were asked about their experiences with Islamic burial rituals and their own ideas and opinion. The respondents all had been born in the Netherlands or Belgium or had come to these countries before the age of 12. Respondents included individuals from four Islamic religious denominations: Sunni, Shiite, Ahmadiyya, and Alevi. In order to offer some representative results, respondents were selected from within these religious communities, to tally with the number of their presence in both the Netherlands and Belgium. Often research dealing with Muslims in Europe is limited to research among the largest Muslim communities: Turks, Moroccans and Surinamese. Although this approach might be useful for policy-making, from an academic point of view, it is impossible to ignore the smaller communities, especially in a discussion of changing religious practices. Between July 2012 and January 2013, 22 Sunni, 6 Shiite, 4 Alevi and 3 Ahmadiyya respondents were interviewed. They came from various ethnic backgrounds: Moroccan (11), Turk (12), Surinamese (3), Sudanese (1), Iranian (2), Iraqi (2), Afghani (1), Pakistani (1), Indonesian (1) and one convert. Of these, 17 were female and 18 were male respondents. My focus is on the six Moroccan female respondents. In order to understand how their experiences were shaped by a fusion of denominational ideas I compare their experiences to those of the other 11 women. Of those 11, 5 had a Turkish background, and the others were Indonesian (1), Surinamese (2), Iranian (1), Sudanese (1) and Belgian (1) – this last a convert to Islam.

Data also was collected through participant observation. During the fieldwork period I attended four burials as an observer (two in the Netherlands, one in Belgium, and one in Morocco), participated in three corpse washings and shroudings (one each) in the Netherlands, Belgium, and Morocco, and attended three funeral prayers (two in the Netherlands and one in Belgium). In all cases, except one involving a Bosnian funeral, bereaved Moroccans allowed me to attend and participate.

As this multidisciplinary research was qualitative in nature, my aim was not to generalize the results to all Muslims in the Netherlands and Belgium. Rather, my primary purpose was to ensure as much variation in funeral experiences as possible. I sought to describe and explain opinions and changing practices specifically around death, dying, and burial, and more particularly, around the participation of Moroccan women and how it compares to that of other Muslim women of various ethnic and denominational backgrounds.

In the first part of this chapter I provide a background to the study through demographic statistics on Muslim communities in the Netherlands and Belgium that highlight their diversity. I then discuss Islamic burial preparations as *rites de passage* and apply theories developed by Arnold van Gennep and Victor Turner[5] to shed light on the ambiguous "betwixt and between" nature of the liminal phase in the transition from life to death. Literature on women and rites of passage is abundant, but this chapter opens the door to theorization in the field of women and funeral rituals. I argue that the liminal phase during which burial preparations occur can be characterized by vulnerability, conflicting opinions, and time pressures, owing in part to the Islamic prescription for burial within 24 hours after death. In the next section I examine the four elements of burial rituals: the washing, the shrouding, the funeral prayer, and the funeral procession. How these rituals are to be performed, by whom and where is discussed in detail in the various jurisprudence (*fiqh*) manuals. I pay special attention to the issue of gender, Moroccan women's participation in burial rituals, and the fusion of denominational ideas, illustrated by excerpts from interviews I conducted. Finally, I conclude with observations about how trends in burial rituals in the Netherlands and Belgium have reverberated back to Morocco.

Diversity among Muslims in the Netherlands and Belgium

Islam and its adherents cover a wide spectrum of normative beliefs and cultural backgrounds. In studying the fusion of different Islamic denominational beliefs and corresponding changes in the burial rituals of Muslims in the Netherlands and Belgium, and the resulting "fusion of denominational ideas," some insight into this diversity is useful. In addition, it is helpful to understand the migration context for Moroccans living in the Netherlands and Belgium.

Large-scale settlement of Moroccan and Turkish Muslims in the Netherlands and Belgium began in the 1960s, when they were recruited as guest workers (*gastarbeiders*). Today, Muslims living in the Netherlands and Belgium vary in regard to their ethnic and cultural backgrounds, adherence to different Islamic denominations, schools of law, and understandings of various modern Islamic ideas. Moroccan and Turkish ethnic groups represent about 80 percent of the Muslim population of these countries, with the other 20 percent from various countries and regions, including Surinam, Indonesia, Iraq, Iran, South Asia, the Balkans, and Africa south of the Sahara. To these can be added small groups of native Dutch and Belgian converts to Islam.[6]

In 2011, the estimated number of Muslims in the Netherlands varied between 857,000 and 950,000 out of a total population of 16 million inhabitants and in the same year an estimated 410,000–628,000 Muslims lived in Belgium out of a population of 11 million.[7] The geographical distribution of the Muslim population in the Netherlands and Belgium is quite uneven. In the Netherlands, a great majority of the Muslims live in the western part of the country, with large concentrations in the cities of Amsterdam, Rotterdam, The Hague, and Utrecht.[8] In Belgium more than 40 percent of Muslims live in the Brussels-Capital Region[9] and account for 17 percent of the region's population, resulting in the fact that Brussels today has one of the largest Muslim populations in the Western world.[10]

An estimated 85 percent of Muslims worldwide follow the Sunni branch of Islam, and this is also the case in the Netherlands and Belgium.[11] In addition to Sunni Muslims, adherents of Shiite, Alevi, and Ahmadiyya Muslim denominations also are found in both countries. Shiite Muslims form a significant part of the Iranian and Iraqi communities, Alevi Muslims are a significant part of the Turkish community, and Ahmadiyya Muslims are a prominent part of the Surinamese and Pakistani communities.

Muslims also follow the teachings and opinions of various schools of law (*madhhab*). A school of Islamic Law is a school of thought within *fiqh*, (Islamic jurisprudence). In Sunni Islam the four major schools are Maliki, Hanafi, Hanbali, and Shafi'i, while in Shiite Islam the major school is the Ja'fari.[12] Sunni law schools differ in their treatment of what is known as subsidiary matters (*furu'*), which extend to a large variety of topics, including burial practices and regulations. The *madhab* to which one belongs is principally determined by the country or community to which one belongs. Moreover, many prominent scholars of contemporary Sunni Islam, such as Yusuf al Qaradawi, head of the European Council for Fatwa and Research, reject *madhhabism* in principle and prefer a return to an original doctrine of Islam that can be shared by all Muslims. Their position predominates in many of the scholarly opinions (fatwas) issued within what is known as Jurisprudence for Minorities (*fiqh al-'aqalliyyat*).

Islamic Burial Rituals as *Rites de Passage*

Because Islamic burial rituals are neither eternally nor universally fixed in their form and content, it is difficult to define them with precision. For the purposes of this research, then, I considered burial preparations to be rituals within the specific genre of life events known as *rites de passage*. Using this approach, I examined Islamic burial preparations performed in the "liminal phase" of dying. In analyzing the practice of Islamic burial preparations in this liminal phase, I focused especially on inclusion and exclusion based on gender and religious denomination. In this way, I was able to touch on the issue of how normative conditions surrounding burial practices in Morocco were subject to change.

Rites de passage are life-cycle rituals that mark changes of place, state, social position and age during a person's life. The French anthropologist Arnold van Gennep identified a tripartite form inherent in all *rites de passage*: the phase of separation, the phase of transition, and the phase of incorporation.[13] The separation phase emphasizes detachment of the subject from "either an earlier fixed point in the social structure, from a set of cultural conditions (a "state"), or from both."[14] In the transition phase that follows, the characteristics of the subject (in this case, the individual undergoing the burial ritual) are ambiguous, as he or she belongs neither here nor there. Finally, in the third phase, the subject is incorporated into her or his new state.

Islamic burial preparations can be considered rituals performed in the phase of transition with the purpose of guiding the deceased through the transition from one world to the other. Those involved in performing the rituals are expected to be aware of the deceased's state of uncertainty and the need for a rapid and correct effectuation of the burial preparations. This imperative is consistent with the work of Victor Turner,[15] which builds on van Gennep's threefold structure by emphasizing the dynamic nature of *rites de passage*. Turner characterized the second phase, that of transition, as a phase in which people are "betwixt and between." Turner called this a "liminal" or period in which the subject does not have a status, making it highly desirable to keep this phase as short as possible. Thus, this liminal phase is of great importance in the burial practices of Muslims.

In Islamic practice, helping the deceased through the perilous journey from life to afterlife involves at least four important obligatory elements prior to burial: the washing, the shrouding, the funeral prayer, and the funeral procession. In Van Gennep's terms, the actual burial occurs in the final phase of incorporation. As long as a person lies unburied, he or she is considered to be "betwixt and between." Herein lies the principal reason why Muslims emphasize the correct and rapid effectuation of burial preparations and of the actual burial itself. From a religious perspective, the soul will not rest until the body is buried and enters into its next phase; that of incorporation. Thus, the longer the period between death and burial lasts, the more heavily the burden of the deceased lies on the bereaved. Accordingly, burial preparations usually are performed carefully and within a very short period of time (mostly within 24 hours after death) in order to shorten the precarious liminal period. Certainly, because this phase typically involves the mourning of a loved one it also is marked by an explosion of emotions, conflicting expectations, and various opinions about how the rituals should be performed.

Outside their context of *rites de passage*, burial preparations can also be viewed as an activity that expresses a strong sense of belonging to a specific denomination. Certain people are allowed to perform burial rituals, and others are not. Participation is predicated not only on knowledge and expertise, but also on religious background and gender. For this reason issues of identity come to the forefront during the performance of burial preparations. Further, individuals are included and excluded from these rituals based on various decisions that must be made within a very short period of time. Thus, the "liminal period," also is a time when the identity of the bereaved is underscored, particularly in regard to belonging or not belonging to a preferred gender or Islamic denomination. Again, issues related to being betwixt and between come to the fore – not for the deceased, but in the assessment of those who are or are not allowed to attend or perform the burial preparations.

Changing Burial Rituals in the Netherlands and Belgium

Analysis of the interviews and participant observation revealed that the processes of inclusion and exclusion in Islamic burial rituals were subject to change. In seeking to understand how to explain these changes, I looked to the social and legal settings of the host country as well as the influence of the different Islamic regulations and beliefs held by Muslims of various denominations in the Netherlands and Belgium. In order to illustrate this fusion of denominational ideas, I focused on the washing and shrouding of the corpse, the funeral prayer, and then the funeral procession and on the viewpoints of Islamic scholars from various schools of law. Overall, the findings suggest that in the context of immigration to the Netherlands and Belgium, changes in the participation of Moroccan women in Islamic burial rituals may be attributable less to the influence of the larger non-Muslim community than of adherents to other denominations and schools within Islam.

Washing the corpse (ghusl al-mayyit). In various manuals of Islamic jurisprudence (*fiqh*), the washing of the corpse is described in detail, and there is some variation between the different Islamic denominations and the *maddhabs*. Just as in the other aspects of burial preparations, the washing of the corpse is considered to be a communal obligation (*fard kifaya*).

The washing is to be performed by a Muslim who knows the procedure. Although the *fiqh* calls upon immediate family members to perform the ritual, in practice the washing is often done by volunteers from a "washing group" from the local mosque. The washers can either be men or women, though as a rule, deceased men are washed by men and deceased women are washed by women. An exception to this rule is when an individual washes his or her spouse.[16]

Halima, a Moroccan respondent living in Belgium, told me how her father forbade her from attending the washing of her deceased baby boy, who had died only three weeks after birth due to heart problems:

No, I was not allowed to participate according to my father. Although I knew that in the case of babies, gender is not an issue. I took Salmane with me before he was washed. My father wanted me to go home after Salmane died, but I refused. I insisted that I had to stay with my child.

When I asked Halima about her father making this decision for her she emphasized that she regretted not arguing with him, especially since both her husband and the Maliki regulations did not prohibit her from being present at the washing. At that time though, she agreed to follow her father's wishes and was relieved that her husband could wash their son under the supervision of trained washers. She recounted how the hospital nurses sought to help her with her grief:

While Salmane was taken away to be washed the nurses in the hospital really helped me and they made me a little box with some of Salmane's belongings. His hospital bracelet, a lock of his hair, and the report they had been filling in since he came in to the IC.

Lukewarm water is used during the washing and the washers must handle the deceased very carefully, as if she or he still were alive. It is a general belief that the deceased is still aware of what is going on around him or her and is able to feel the washing as it is performed.[17]

This story was reflected in a 2012 washing in Belgium in which I participated. When I arrived at the mosque in Antwerp to interview Majda, a Moroccan woman who was part of a professional washers group, she informed me that a woman was coming in shortly to be washed. She asked me if I would assist. When I asked Majda what I needed to do, she explained that I mainly would assist her and the other two women who would participate in the washing and that they would talk me through the process. After performing my ablutions (*wudu'*) along with Majda and the other women, we went into the washing room of the mosque and waited for the coroner to bring in the deceased woman.

Before beginning the washing, I remember all the washers quietly apologized to the deceased woman for the trouble we had moving her from the coffin onto the washing table. They emphasized that the deceased is in a vulnerable state after the process of dying, and if a washing is to be performed easily there must be enough people present to turn the deceased gently from one side to the other. Under no circumstances, they explained, should the deceased be turned face down.[18]

Of the six Moroccan women I interviewed for this study, none was present at the washing and shrouding of their deceased. Ilhame and Mouna shared their stories of the deaths of their fathers. Ilhame's father died in the Netherlands and was buried in Morocco. Mouna's father died while on vacation in Morocco. Mouna and her siblings traveled from the Netherlands to Morocco as soon as they received the news of their father's heart attack. Wisaal shared with me the story of traveling to Morocco with other relatives after the death of her older brother, who died while working in Belgium and was transported to Morocco for burial. Najia shared her story about the death of her husband, who died in the Netherlands in a car accident and also was buried in the Netherlands. Nora shared the story of the death of her mother, who died in the Netherlands after being sick and was transported for burial to Morocco, where Nora and her relatives then traveled. Finally, Halima related the story of the death of her baby boy, who died only a few weeks after birth due to heart problems and was buried in Belgium.

The first three testimonies about the deaths of two fathers and a brother reflected the Islamic prohibition against women participating in the washing and shrouding of their fathers and brothers. The respondents explained that they were at peace with this regulation and understood the idea behind it, which had to do with the concept of *'awra* (the intimate parts of the body).[19] Mouna added:

The men really kept me, my sisters, and my mother out of the whole thing. We were told not to interfere. But I said that my mother was allowed to wash her husband! I knew this because I had read about it and also heard about widows who had been allowed to wash their husbands.

Mouna understood that Islamic regulations allow for exceptions to the rule that men are washed by men and women by women in the case of spouses and infants. Najia explained that, in her case, she was mentally unable to attend to her deceased husband as she was so distressed by his loss and had to take care of her newborn baby. Nora, as we discussed earlier, did not participate in the washing of her mother because of her need to care for her children and the condolence visitors. Her sisters and her father, however, did attend and participate in the washing. Halima was aware that according to the Islamic regulations, she was allowed to wash her baby boy, but as she explained, she "lost the battle with my father. He allowed me to either attend the funeral prayer or nothing at all. So I chose for the first option."

The situation of these six Moroccan women diverges from those other eleven women I interviewed. These were mostly allowed to attend the washing (unless there was a gender restriction) and most of them did so.

Takfin: Shrouding of the corpse. The requisite shroud (*kafan*) consists of at least one cloth that covers the entire body.[20] However, various denominations and *madhahib* have different preferences for the number of cloths and the *kafan*.

Regardless of the nuances, the shrouding procedure typically proceeds as follows: The garments are laid down one on top of the other, the largest garment at the bottom. The deceased is then placed on top of the garments to be enshrouded. Before shrouding, a piece of cloth with some fragrance is placed between the buttocks to prevent any impurities seeping out onto the *kafan*.[21]

Islamic *fiqh* prescribes that the *kafan* be purchased with the deceased's own money.[22] In practice, however, a mosque organization or the funeral director usually provides it. During one washing and shrouding I attended in Belgium, the *kafan* was made on the spot from a large role of fabric. Measuring the height and width of the deceased woman, we cut the five pieces of her *kafan*. I held the large role of fabric while one of the other women measured the *kafan* with her hands.

The respondents indicated that their last chance to see the deceased and say their goodbyes occurred after the shrouding ritual, and in some cases before the washing and shrouding. Halima, the mother of the deceased baby boy recounted:

After the washing had taken place, I took Salmane alone with me again. We spent maybe an hour together. I kept kissing him and praying for him. I still remember how he looked, so beautifully wrapped in his white *kafan*. I said my goodbyes to him, and told him how much I love him.

Mouna's testimony about her father's death and funeral in Morocco:

After the washing my father was to be transported to the cemetery. My uncles had put him in the ambulance that was going to bring him to the cemetery. We didn't get the time nor space to say goodbye and I knew that this was our very last moment with him. He was so close and yet so far. It was so frustrating, also because my younger brother was allowed to do everything, and we were forbidden everything. Eventually after I argued, pleaded, and screamed at my uncles, my mother, my sisters, and me were allowed into the ambulance to say our farewells. It was bittersweet. I said goodbye in my own way, touched his corpse and then I insisted that we would drive with them to the cemetery. My uncles were furious, but I just stayed in the ambulance.

These testimonies correspond with a study by Venhorst[23] on the ritualization of death among Muslims in the Netherlands. Since both cleaning and shrouding are not public, the hours before or after the washing and shrouding provide a suitable private moment and space for bereaved to pay their last respects. As Venhorst noted, "Particularly for women and children – who, due to gender and age restrictions, are often not permitted to attend the burial – it is the last opportunity to say their goodbyes."[24] Halima took both moments as

an opportunity to say farewell. She explained to me how she took her
baby son with her both before and after he was washed and shrouded:

It was hard to say goodbye to Salmane. I didn't want to forget the feeling of
holding him. I knew that after he was washed and shrouded, I would never
hold him again, because he was going to be buried. So I took my time to
say goodbye. We were alone, just him and me, and I tried to say goodbye.
But it was hard.[25]

Funeral prayer (salat al-janaza). After the corpse is washed and
shrouded, the last ritual to be performed before the actual burial takes
place is the funeral prayer. According to *fiqh*, praying for the deceased
is considered to be a collective obligation for Muslims. The guidelines
are the same as for the obligatory daily prayers. Participants should be
in a state of ritual purity – meaning that they have performed ablutions
(*wudu'*) – and they should cover their *'awra* and stand facing in the
direction of the *qibla*.[26]

Since the funeral prayer typically is held after a daily prayer, anyone
present at the mosque can join in. My analysis of relevant texts did not
yield statements concerning the desirability or undesirability of women
and children attending a funeral prayer. Consequently, this practice
differs from case to case. All the funeral prayers I attended in the
Netherlands, Morocco, and Belgium, I was in the mosque for the daily
prayer when the imam announced that we should not leave after the
prayer because there would be a funeral prayer. In each of these cases
women and children were participating, albeit in the separate women's
section of the mosque.

The interview data indicates that funeral prayers that took place in
the Netherlands and Belgium were performed mainly in the mosque or
outside in a square near the mosque (57 percent), or at a funeral parlor
(20 percent) or the cemetery (23 percent). The attendance of women at
funeral prayers is the subject of an ongoing discussion among Muslims
who have migrated to Europe, and the Netherlands and Belgium are
no exception.[27] Half of the Moroccan women I interviewed (Najia,
Ilhame, and Halima) participated in the funeral prayer even though
they did not attend the washing and shrouding. On the other hand, the
relatives of two of the women, Mouna and Wisaal, forbade them from
attending the funeral prayer. Nora was absent during the funeral
prayer because she had to care for her children and the visitors who
came to console her.

Shiite, Alevi, and Ahmadiyya respondents considered attendance of women at the funeral prayers and the actual burial as normal. Thus, prohibitions against the attendance of women at funerals seemed to be most vigorous among Sunni Muslims. Some female Moroccan respondents saw this exclusion as being unfounded, however. Mouna shared the story of the funeral prayer for her father which took place in Morocco:

I thought it was ridiculous that I was not allowed to attend the funeral prayer! Islam does not forbid women to attend the funeral prayer. I know that because I personally know a widow who participated in her husband's funeral prayer. She is an Iraqi from the Shia. But that doesn't matter, she is also Muslim. She wears *hijab* and goes to the mosque. So then why can she attend and not me? When my sister, brother, and I arrived in Morocco, my father had already passed away. The next day was his burial and a funeral prayer was held. I was not allowed to attend or to participate. I was so angry. According to my brother, the mosque was full of people. People who never knew him, and I, his daughter, was forbidden to be there! I was also sorry that my mother didn't help me to confront my uncles, she was so distressed by her loss.

By contrast, Ilhame, a Moroccan living in the Netherlands, spoke of her surprise at seeing how normal it was for Surinamese Ahmadiyya Muslim women to participate in the funeral rituals of their deceased:

I think it's such a traditional thing for Moroccans in the Netherlands, to exclude women from attending and participating in funeral rituals! It has nothing to do with religion, or with halal and haram. For example, I live close to an Ahmadiyya mosque. I actually go there quite often because I'm friends with several women in this community. Whenever someone dies in their community, a lot of people come together in the mosque, men, women, and even children, to participate in the funeral prayer. I remember once an aunt of one of my friends had passed away. The deceased woman was the imam's wife. After the prayer, they took the coffin in the hearse and drove to the cemetery. Everyone, including women and children, got into their cars and joined the deceased at the cemetery. I saw them! Later I spoke to my friend and she said, everyone present at the cemetery also participated in the funeral prayer. Maybe it has to do more with cultural traditions than with religion that Moroccan women are so absent during funeral rituals. Personally, I do not participate in those stupid halal and haram (allowed and forbidden) discussions. You just have to think for yourself as a Muslim what makes sense for you, and what doesn't. I totally understand that as his daughter, I'm not allowed to see my fathers naked body, and therefore I cannot participate in the washing and shrouding. But I am certainly allowed to join the funeral procession and the actual burial!

Ilhame's assertion illustrates how Moroccan women in the Netherlands and Belgium come to learn of different Muslim customs and try to incorporate these into their own beliefs. Hence the fusion of denominational ideas mentioned previously in this chapter. Whether or not they actually participated in the funeral prayer, Mouna and Ilhame clearly changed their views on the participation of women due to their exposure to other denominational practices in the context of migration.

Another respondent, Halima, was allowed to attend the funeral prayer for her baby son after she reached a compromise with her father. As noted earlier, he had strictly forbidden her from attending the washing, shrouding and burial. When it came to the funeral prayer, she agreed on a compromise with him. She would not make a fuss about the washing and shrouding and in return, would be allowed to attend the funeral prayer. She explained:

I really pleaded with my father to be there at the funeral prayer. He thought I was making a fool of him in front of other people. I demanded that if I were not allowed to participate in the funeral at the cemetery, I would go along to the *salat al janaza* and see with my own eyes how the coffin would be taken from the mosque into the car. I went to the mosque with a friend of mine. I saw my child leave the mosque in his coffin.

Participation of Moroccan Women in Funeral Processions and Burials

Like visiting the sick, accompanying the funeral prayer and burial (*janaza*) of a deceased person is seen as an obligation that Muslims owe their fellow Muslims.[28] Yet, while some elements of the etiquette for the funeral procession are widely accepted, others may be frowned upon. For example, there is a range of scholarly opinions about who may join in the procession. Concerning attendance and participation of women, scholars from the various schools of law (*maddhahib*) vary greatly. Where Hanbalites and Shafi'ites hold the opinion that it is undesirable (*makruh*) in some situations, Hanafites are convinced that the presence of women at the funeral procession is undesirable under *all* circumstances.[29]

Further, among the Malikites, participation in the funeral procession is open to old women as well as any young woman who is appropriately covered and whose presence will not lead to any temptation.[30] Thus, in the Maliki school (to which Moroccans generally adhere), women are not strictly forbidden from attending funeral processions, suggesting a more open-minded approach than some other schools of law.

Nevertheless, while some of the Moroccan women in this study had been present at the funeral procession of their loved one, the majority had not. Though they offered different reasons for their absence, the primary one was that their relatives or the imam forbade their participation. In the following, I discuss these various situations separately in order to elucidate the respondents' different considerations in agreeing or disagreeing with the prohibition.

Halima, who was not allowed by her father to attend the washing, shrouding and funeral of her baby son, made a deal with her father to get him to go along with her presence at the funeral prayer in the mosque. For Halima, it was of utmost importance to see her child, in his coffin, leave the mosque to be buried. By the time she started the negotiations with her father, she was aware that her religious denomination permitted her to be present at all the rituals, since gender was not an issue with an infant. Therefore, though she could have emphasized her religious right, she chose to select the one ritual that was most important to her, namely the funeral prayer. Halima explained, "It's such a special moment. All those people come to pray for the deceased. I wanted to see that and share the communal power of prayer with my fellow Muslims."

Halima told me that the experience of her child's death made her aware of her responsibility and position within Islam. Previously, she would take her father's word for truth. Unlike Halima, who gained a broader sense of her position and understanding of Islam *after* the funeral rituals for her son, for Mouna the moment of awareness came when she insisted on her presence and participation *prior* to the funeral rituals. As noted earlier, Mouna, after arguing with her uncles, refused to leave the car carrying her father's body to the cemetery.

While Halima argued and negotiated with her father in Belgium, where her son was born, Mouna's struggles occurred in Morocco. She had developed her ideas about the presence of women at funeral rituals in the Netherlands, in part because of her interaction with Muslims from different denominations and ethnic backgrounds. She took this altered sense of religious practices around funeral rites back to her country of origin. This dynamic is significant in that it serves as an indicator of larger religious and social changes taking place among Moroccan Muslims in the Netherlands and Belgium as well as Morocco. Mouna told me that she and her sister were the only women present at her father's funeral.

My sister and I attended the funeral from a distance. We were not allowed to join and carry my father to his grave, although my brother was allowed to perform this special act. I really regret that we were forbidden. It is said that people who carry the deceased to his grave earn *hasanat* (good deeds). Aren't women aloud to earn *hasanat* through this act? My Islamic right to fully participate was denied by my uncles, not by Islam.

Mouna's anger at her uncles and Moroccan funeral practices were evident when I spoke with her. She recounted her experience with great bitterness. This is in contrast to Nora and Wisaal, neither of whom attended the funeral procession. Neither Wisaal nor Nora argued about their role in the funeral rituals. They both spoke about the trust they had in the people that did attend and performed the rituals for the deceased. The same was true for Ilhame, although she emphasized that she did not agree with what she called "Moroccan panic" when it comes to women attending and participating in funeral rituals. Ilhame explained:

I was not allowed to join in the procession or in the funeral according to my male relatives in Morocco. I felt sorry, but didn't make a problem of it. I went up to our roof terrace and saw how the group of men carried my father's coffin to his grave. It felt as if I was there, with them. I found my own way of participating, and no one could deny me this right from my own roof terrace. If my father had been buried in the Netherlands, I would definitely have joined in the funeral procession and funeral. I feel more at ease in the Netherlands and know my way around. Because we were in Morocco, I didn't feel comfortable breaking traditions and the way people obviously do things. I trust that the imam who joined in the procession knew what he was doing, I just don't agree with how he manages women at funerals. He acted so panicked when I asked if I could join.

Ilhame found her own way of attending her father's procession and funeral. Najia's husband died and was buried in the Netherlands, in a cemetery located in a city different from the one where Najia and her family lived. Because they did not know anyone there, her father contacted an imam in that city via the cemetery manager. This imam had a different view about the attendance of Najia and other women at the funeral procession and at the funeral:

My family is very open-minded. I grew up in a non-Muslim environment, so we as a family are used to having non-Muslims for dinner and joining them and inviting them in weddings, baby showers, and funerals. We are also a very religious family, we pray, we fast, we do everything. But we were not expecting the imam to behave the way he did. My father was very disappointed in him, and he never ever visited that mosque again.

When confronted with the imam's attitude, Najia's father responded by taking over the ceremony. At this personal and painful moment, Najia's father had to ask the imam to leave, and the family proceeded without him. Nevertheless, Najia recounted a beautiful ceremony:

Once the imam left, it was so much better. My father said some prayers at the grave, and then he and my husband's brothers, friends, and father each threw three hands full of soil into the grave. Then I did the same, and my sisters, my mother, and all the others followed. We buried him together. We all lost someone that day. We all had and have the right to say our farewells in our own way.

Although the Maliki school to which Najia and her family belonged is more liberal on the issue of the attendance of women and widely followed in Morocco, it is certainly not common for Moroccan women to attend funerals.

Opinions about the attendance of women can lead to distressing situations such as the one that Najia had to endure, as cited above and at the beginning of this chapter. Without much hesitation, the respondent's father decided to intervene and ask the imam to leave, prompted not only by the emotionally charged situation resulting in a quarrel in a cemetery, but also by the fact that the imam's opinions differed significantly from those held by the bereaved family. The imam was a Surinamese Hanafi, whereas the bereaved where Moroccan Maliki adherents. As discussed earlier, scholars differ in their opinion on the permissibility of the attendance of women at funeral rituals.

Both in theory and practice Moroccan Sunni Muslims seem to be less accepting of the participation of women in funeral rituals than Shiite,

Alevi and Ahmadiyya Muslims. Instances of changes are evident in the experiences of several of the Moroccan Sunni female respondents who had accompanied a funeral procession and even the funeral itself. They emphasized that although imams or male relatives made clear that they were unwelcome, they decided to attend anyway.

One of the most interesting underlying reasons for this change in participation can be traced to a fusion of denominational ideas. Through meeting and interaction with other Muslims in the migration contexts of the Netherlands and Belgium, the Moroccan women I interviewed came to know other Islamic customs related to the attendance of women in funeral rituals. Especially Mouna and Ilhame, but also Najia, referred to the different approaches of various Islamic denominations and how they embraced some of these rulings within the scope of their own Maliki views. Ilhame summarized this most succinctly:

The prohibition of women at funerals and processions has nothing to do with *halal* or *haram*, or with Islam. It's just tradition and culture. I don't want to follow tradition and culture in that way, I want to know what Islam says about our attendance in general. In that regard, if other Muslim women from other denominations are allowed to participate, then why shouldn't I? They are Muslims, and so am I. So yes, sometimes I just like other customs better than what I was told from within the Moroccan community. So I follow what suits me, whether it's Shiite, Hanafi, Shafii, or Ahmadiyya regulations.

Conclusions

This study reveals that some Moroccan women with a migration background are becoming more aware of their rights in Islam with regard to their participation in Muslim burial rituals. This awareness may have been catalyzed by a personal experience of exclusion at a particularly painful moment in their life. The Moroccan women in this study referred to friends and acquaintances from different ethnic backgrounds and Islamic denominations. "If they are Muslim and are allowed to participate, then why shouldn't I?" The women carried their changed ideas back to their country of origin.

It is important to mention that all the families discussed in this chapter hail from rural Morocco where traditions are more closely observed. Changed attitudes of those who migrated to Europe are especially noteworthy because they were not introduced top-down by the Moroccan government or through civil society associations in urban Rabat and Casablanca. Daughters of migrants from rural villages and towns held on to their new understandings upon their return to the country of their parents' origins.

The Moroccan women described in this chapter reflected deeply about their roles in funeral rituals. They took in the legal and social contexts of their host countries. Equally influential was their contact with the Islamic customs from denominations other than their own. The women skillfully fused these various influences and evaluated them against their own backgrounds, resulting in an altered understanding. Since no one is exempt from witnessing death and being confronted with the in- or exclusion in funeral rituals, these rituals serve as a significant indicator of larger religious and social changes taking place within Moroccan communities. One of the most important outcomes is the fact that young women of Moroccan origin in Europe dare to challenge the authority of male elders and family members. In a context of migration to non-Muslim countries, it is not the funeral rituals of non-Muslims and the participation of women therein, but the funeral rituals of fellow Muslims from other minority denominations (Shiites, Ahmadiyya and Alevites) that the Moroccan women looked to. They derived strength for defending their new convictions based on their understanding that they were claiming their religious rights. This new awareness not only changed funeral rituals in the host country but also in the country of origin. Though this study is based on a small sample, it nonetheless documents an important cultural and social shift and offers starting points for further exploration of changing senses of women's agency.

Endnotes

1 This chapter is based partly on chapter 3 of my 2014 PhD dissertation: "Islamic burials in the Netherlands and Belgium. Legal, religious and social aspects."

2 As a rule, Muslims are not to be buried in a coffin but in shrouds unless there is a necessity to do so. All women referred to in this chapter had participated in a funeral which involved burial with coffin. In the case of Najia, her husband had a car accident and the body was very damaged so they decided to bury in a coffin. Halima did not know of the possibility of burying without a coffin and Belgian law is still vague on this issue.

The cases of the other four women in this chapter involved repatriation in which the body is transported in a coffin which is sealed and cannot be opened.

3 Interview with Najia. January 2013.
4 Aggoun, A. (2006). *Les musulmans face a la mort en France*. Vuibert: Espace éthique; Chaib, Y. (2000). *L'émigré et la mort*. Aix en Provence: Edisud. There are some studies done on Turkish, Bengali and Surinamese burial rituals, but the latter fall outside the scope of this chapter.
5 Turner, V. (2002). "Liminality and communitas." *A Reader in the Anthropology of Religion*. M. Lambek (ed.). Oxford: Blackwell Publishing, p. 359.
6 De Koning, M. (2011). "The Netherlands." *Yearbook of Muslims in Europe*. J. Nielsen et al. (eds.). Boston: Brill, pp. 401–402; Fadil, N. (2011). "Belgium." *Yearbook of Muslims in Europe*. J. Nielsen et al. (eds.). Boston: Brill, p. 70; FORUM Verkenning (2012). "*Moslims in Nederland*." Utrecht: FORUM Instituut voor Multiculturele Vraagstukken, p. 8; Sengers, E. and T. Sunier (eds.). (2010). *Religious Newcomers and the Nation State: Political Culture and Organized Religion in France and the Netherlands*, p. 115.
7 De Koning, "The Netherlands," p. 401; Fadil, "Belgium," p. 69; Berger, M. (2012a). "Nederland en zijn Islam. Een kijkje in de spiegel." *Kerk en Buitenwereld. Opstellen over de kerk in de samenleving voor Marius van Leeuwen*. K. Holtzapffel, J. Magliano-Tromp, and M. Tolsma (eds.). Zoetermeer: Uitgeverij Meinema, pp. 15–31; FORUM Verkenning, "Moslims in Nederland," pp. 6–8; Hertogen, J. (2008). "In België wonen 628.751 moslims" [In Belgium there are 628,751 Muslims]." *DeWereldMorgen*, pp. 1–4.
8 Berger, M. (2012b). "The Netherlands." *Oxford Handbook of European Islam*. J. Cesari (ed.). New York: Oxford University Press, p. 2.
9 Fadil, "Belgium," p. 71.
10 Ibid.
11 Shadid, W. and S. Van Koningsveld (2008). "Islam in Nederland en België." *Religieuze institutionalisering in twee landen met een gemeenschappelijke voorgeschiedenis*. Sunni Muslims accept the legitimacy of the first four successors of Muhammad. See Esposito, J.L. (2003). *The Oxford Dictionary of Islam*. New York: Oxford University Press, p. 306. Whereas Shiite Muslims believe that Muhammad's religious and political authority was passed on to his descendants. See Esposito, *The Oxford*, p. 292. Alevis is a term which is used to cover a number of heterogeneous socio-religious communities in Turkey and the Balkans, who in the twentieth century began to share a common trans-regional Alevi identity called Alevism. See Dressler, M. (2013).

"Alevīs." *Encyclopaedia of Islam, THREE.* K. Fleet et al. (eds.). Available at http://dx.doi.org.ezproxy.leidenuniv.nl:2048/10.1163/1573-3912_ei3_COM_0167 (accessed January 17, 2017). The Ahmadiyya is a controversial messianic movement founded by Mirza Ghulam Ahmad in Qadian (India) in 1889. See Esposito, *The Oxford*, pp. 11–12.

12 These schools of law came into existence during the ninth and tenth century. Different scholars applied different methods of interpretation when explaining the Qur'an and *hadith* (traditions of the Prophet Mohammed). The Hanafi school was established by Imam Abu Hanifa (700–767 CE) in Kuffa, Iraq. It is the first and largest school. The Hanafi school is prevalent in central Asia, Afghanistan, South Egypt, Syria, Lebanon and Iraq. Second is the Maliki school, founded by Imam Malik Ibn Anas (710–795 CE) in Medina, Saudi Arabia. The Maliki school spread over North and West Africa. Third is the Shafi'i school, founded by Imam Muhammad al-Shafi'i (767–820 CE) in Medina. The Shafi'i school prevails in central and north Egypt, Palestine, Jordan, Indonesia and Malaysia. Finally, the Hanbali school was founded by Imam Ahmad Ibn Hanbal (780–855 CE) in Baghdad, Iraq. In both Saudi Arabia and the United Arab Emirates the teachings of the Hanbali school represent the main source of legislation.

13 Van Gennep, A. (1960). *The Rites of Passage.* Chicago: University of Chicago Press.

14 Turner, "Liminality and communitas," p. 359.

15 Ibid.

16 This exception is derived from prophetic traditions such as the following: "Aisha reported that when the Prophet returned from a funeral at al-Baqee, she was suffering from a headache and said, 'Oh my head.' The Prophet replied, 'No, it is I who is in pain from whatever hurts you. If you were to die before me, I would wash you, shroud you, pray for you and bury you.'" Philips, A.A.B. (2005). *Funeral Rites in Islam.* 2nd edition. Riyadh: International Islamic Publishing House, p. 33.

17 A well-known *hadith* on this matter: "By God, O washer, take off my clothes gently, for I have just escaped the torture of the Angel of Death (...) By God, O washer, do not make the water too warm or too cold because my body has endured much pain when the *ruh* left her (...) By God, O washer, do not hold me too tight for my body has suffered much when the *ruh* left her (...) By God, O washer, do not tighten the *kafan* around my head so that I can see the faces of my family and my children and my relatives." (1872). *Kitab Ahwl al-Qiyama.* Edited and translated by Monitz Wolff. Leipzig: F.A. Brockhaus, p. 26.

18 See also Al Jaziri, *Islamic Jurisprudence*, p. 680.

19 '*awra* is the area from the navel to the knees in the case of a man, and the whole body of a woman with exception of the hands and face. Ibid, p. 672; A. Sabiq (1991). *Fiqh us-Sunnah. Funerals and Dhikr.* Indianapolis: American Trust Publications, p. 29.

20 Al Jaziri, *Islamic Jurisprudence,* p. 684; Sabiq, *Fiqh us-Sunnah,* p. 31; M. Muhammed Ali (2005). *De religie van de Islam. Een uitgebreide verhandeling van de bronnen, beginselen, wetten en voorschriften van de Islam.* Den Haag: Ulamon, p. 354.

21 Al Jaziri, *Islamic Jurisprudence,* p. 687.

22 Ibid, p. 634.

23 Venhorst, C. (2013). *Muslims Ritualizing Death in the Netherlands. Death Rites in a Small Town Context.* University of Nijmegen.

24 Ibid., p. 35.

25 In the Netherlands burial in a shroud is allowed. In Belgium it is not although it is expected that these rules will be amended. See (July 2012). "Voorstel van ordonnantie tot wijziging van de wet van 1971 op de begraafplaatsen en de lijkbezorging om de plaatsing van het stoffelijk overschot in een ander lijkomhulsel dan een doodskist toe te staan" [Proposal of ordinance to amend the law of 1971 regarding cemeteries and corpse disposal, allowing the placement of the remains of the body in a different body wrapping than in a coffin]. Brussel Hoofdstedelijk Parlement.

26 Sabiq, *Fiqh us-Sunnah,* p. 38. Only Shiite scholars state that ritual purity of the participants is not a condition for the validity of the prayer. See Sistani, *Al fiqh li l-mughtaribîn,* Dialogue 5.

27 Dessing, N. (2001). *Rituals of Birth, Circumcision, Marriage, and Death among Muslims in the Netherlands.* Leuven: Peeters, pp. 156–157.

28 Muhammed Ali, *De religie van de Islam,* p. 354; Al Baghdadi 2005, 192.

29 Al Jaziri, *Islamic Jurisprudence According to the Four Sunni Schools,* p. 713; Sabiq, *Fiqh us-Sunnah,* p. 59

30 Sabiq, *Fiqh us-Sunnah,* p. 59. Based on the sample that I studied for this chapter, we can see that a significant part of the women challenged the dominant discourse with regard to religious authority. It seems to be a trend which is not limited to burial practices. In my current fieldwork in Mecca during the Hajj I found that women there also challenged the dominant male discourse with regard to religious regulation within their own group of pilgrims.

10 Dying with a Clear Mind

Pain and Symptom Control in Palliative Care for Dutch Moroccan Patients in the Netherlands

ROUKAYYA OUESLATI

Introduction

During the past decades, palliative care has developed rapidly in the West due to an aging population and an increasing prevalence of noncommunicable diseases.[1] Palliative care starts when the focus of a treatment process changes from curing a life-threatening disease to improving the quality of life of patients and their relatives, shifting from cure to care. Part of this comfort-oriented care might include end-of-life decision making.[2] Two of these end-of-life decisions related to pain and symptom control are the focus of this chapter: Pain and symptom management and palliative sedation.[3] The latter is defined as the deliberate lowering of a patient's consciousness in the last stages of life in order to relieve suffering.[4]

While such end-of-life treatment decisions are difficult for all patients and their relatives, they are especially challenging for populations with a migration background. Different religious and cultural norms come to bear on end-of-life decisions at a time when families are least equipped to navigate between contradictory expectations. A study conducted by Buiting et al[5] found that pain and symptom management with a potential life-shortening effect was used less frequently among non-Western immigrants in the Netherlands, which suggests that cultural factors may affect end-of-life decision-making.[6]

Dutch Moroccans form a major ethnic minority in the Netherlands, comprising 2.3 percent of the total population.[7] Due to the aging of the first generation, whose immigration was officially encouraged by the Dutch government during the 1960s, it is expected that in coming years there will be an increasing recourse to healthcare among Dutch Moroccans in general, and to palliative care in particular.

The concerns of Dutch Moroccans may challenge Dutch physicians because many are not yet familiar with the specific concerns of this Muslim minority population. Recent studies show that religion plays an important role in medical ethical decision-making among Dutch Moroccans, who are usually Muslim.[8] And although scholars have given increasing attention to Islamic bioethics,[9] few have studied the issue of pain and symptom control in a medical context.[10]

In order to better understand the dilemmas Dutch Moroccans may encounter in palliative care, and to fill a gap in the available literature, this chapter examines how Dutch Moroccan patients and their physicians negotiate pain and symptom control at the end of life. This is done on the basis of three cases from the Dutch context derived from publications in medical journals. The cases were presented by medical teams who faced a moral dilemma because their views on pain and symptom control did not correspond with the views of their patients or their patients' relatives.

This chapter opens with a description of two common end-of-life treatment decisions, pain and symptom management and palliative sedation, and then continues to discuss three particular cases in which these treatment decisions raised religious concerns for Dutch Moroccan patients and their relatives. These three cases were selected because they illustrate the difficult choices faced by patients and their relatives. I then discuss the dilemmas faced by physicians whose opinions about these treatments diverge from those of such patients or their relatives, and analyze the compromises reached by consultation with a third, intermediary party. Last, I explore the status of palliative care in Morocco, where this specialty has only recently begun to develop.[11] By comparing the perspectives of those in the Netherlands who are involved in this decision-making process, and by discussing pain and symptom control in Islamic thought and in Morocco, I hope a comprehensive picture of the complexity of the subject will emerge.

Pain and Symptom Management and Palliative Sedation in Dutch Palliative Care

In order to describe the dilemmas faced by Dutch patients of Moroccan origin, I begin with describing pain and symptom management and palliative sedation, the two end-of-life decisions related to pain and symptom control that are explored in this chapter.

The first is the management of pain and other symptoms such as vomiting and suffocation.[12] Dutch physicians usually use the pain ladder developed by the World Health Organization (WHO)[13] according to which different types of drugs are administered in relation to the severity of the patient's pain. At the top of the ladder are opioids such as morphine.[14] Depending on the severity of pain, higher doses can be administered, but the doses should always be in proportion to the pain.[15] However, pain and symptom management at the end of life is not uncontroversial: there can be a thin line between alleviating suffering (a good and intended effect) and the possible shortening of life (a harmful and unintended effect) that this type of pain and symptom control may cause. In weighing such a dilemma, the principle of double effect (PDE) is often used by physicians to morally justify acts that may cause harmful, unintended effects as long as they intend good effects. According to the PDE, pain and symptom management with a life-shortening effect is not morally wrong if the intention is to relieve pain and suffering and not to cause death.[16]

The second end-of-life decision distinguished in this chapter is palliative sedation which over the past few years has been considered a separate end-of-life decision in the Netherlands.[17] Palliative sedation is applied in exceptional cases when symptoms for which conventional models of treatment are ineffective or induce unacceptable side effects (refractory symptoms), continue to exist. Palliative sedation is accomplished through the administration of sedative drugs in order to relieve a patient's suffering and can be superficial or deep, intermittent or continuous. The latter can only be administered when a patient's life expectancy is less than two weeks.[18]

Proportionality is also important in the case of palliative sedation. The degree of symptom control determines the dosage, the combinations of medication and the duration of the treatment.[19] To ensure a safe administration of palliative sedation, national guidelines were drafted by the Royal Dutch Medical Association (RDMA) in 2005 and revised in 2009.[20] The European Association for Palliative Care (EAPC) drafted guidelines for palliative sedation in 2009 which show strong similarities with the RDMA's guidelines. However, the EAPC mentions a small potential risk that palliative sedation accelerates death for individual patients.[21]

Both pain and symptom management and palliative sedation are considered a regular medical treatment for which the permission of the patient is needed.[22] If the patient is not able to give permission, it should be discussed with a patient's representative, usually a relative, as is stipulated in the Dutch Medical Treatment Contracts Act.[23] In practice, the situation is not so clear-cut, and relatives are often involved in the decision-making process.[24]

Dutch Moroccan Cases in the Dutch Context

The end-of-life treatments described above may raise ethical concerns in general,[25] but they may raise particular concerns for Dutch Moroccans. The following three cases illustrate how religious concerns regarding pain and symptom control resulted in divergent visions regarding "good care." These cases were discussed in detail in medical journals and offer insight into the conflict between medical teams whose views on "good" palliative care conflicts with the views of their patients or their patients' relatives. In two of the three cases, an outside intermediary helped the differing parties to find a compromise. Though these cases are not representative of the Dutch Moroccan population in general, they are indicative of the larger concerns over pain and symptom control at the end of life for Muslim patients. Naturally, there are cases where pain and symptom control do not lead to ethical dilemmas.

Case I

The medical team shared their story because they encountered transcultural differences with their patient regarding religion and faith that strongly influenced both parties' understanding and policy of palliative care.[26]

A 26-year-old Dutch Moroccan woman suffered from a spinal bone tumor that caused her severe pain and kept her hospitalized. She begged her physicians to do whatever they could to alleviate the pain, but eventually the medical options were exhausted and further prolongation of life was seen as only increasing her suffering. The medical team could not add anything to her analgesic regimen and expected her to request information about end-of-life decisions like palliative sedation or euthanasia, which has been legal in the Netherlands since 2002.[27] When she did not, her physicians considered palliative sedation[28] the only remaining option, for at least a couple of hours a day to make nursing care possible without pain. The members of the medical team, who felt powerless because they could not alleviate her suffering by means other than palliative sedation, decided to consult an imam to ask whether they were allowed to administer palliative sedation from an Islamic point of view. The imam explained that sedation would be acceptable as long as the patient was awake intermittently to perform the five daily prayers of Islamic practice.

As a result, sedation was initiated in the mornings so nursing care could be delivered without pain. This regimen worked well for the patient and enabled her to return home, where she died peacefully seven months later, surrounded by relatives.[29]

Case II

This case was presented by physicians in order to verify whether they acted in accordance with the law.[30]

A 63-year-old Dutch Moroccan woman[31] suffered from colon cancer and severe respiratory problems that made her dependent on artificial respiration. She told her relatives that she wanted to continue treatment. However, after she slipped into a coma, the medical team decided not to resuscitate her should a life-threatening event such as a cardiac arrest occur, because they considered this a medically futile treatment. The eldest son, who presented himself as the patient's spokesperson, rejected this decision for religious reasons. Mediation efforts by a family-appointed imam did not succeed.

After the patient had been unconscious for eight months, the medical team concluded that the time had come to stop the artificial respiration and to administer morphine to prevent pain and shortness of breath in the process of dying. The patient's eldest son and a daughter rejected the use of morphine because they did not want their mother to "appear dazed before God," which they considered unacceptable from a religious point of view. At the same time, however, three of her other children did not object to its use. The situation was further complicated by the fact that the woman's wishes regarding the administration of morphine were unknown. Because the eldest son uttered threats against the medical team, the physicians decided not to administer morphine. Five hours after the artificial respiration was stopped, the woman died with significant shortness of breath.[32]

Case III

This case was presented to show how "good" culture sensitive care can be delivered by using a health care consultant.[33]

A 60-year-old Dutch Moroccan man suffered from pancreatic cancer that caused him severe pain in his upper abdomen. Since he did not speak Dutch well, his eldest son acted as translator and mediator. The patient's pain was treated with morphine, but it was not sufficient to relieve his suffering. When the pain became unbearable, the patient stopped eating and drinking. He could recognize people but had become unable to communicate.

Since his death was imminent, the medical team suggested palliative sedation to help relieve his suffering. The relatives opposed this measure, arguing that according to their Islamic faith, patients should "undergo suffering and die consciously." The medical team then faced a moral dilemma, based on their belief that their treatment was a matter of beneficence, a principle in medical ethics requiring that physicians contribute to positive health benefits and prevent and remove harmful conditions to the best of their ability.[34] Yet, at the same time, they wanted to respect the wishes of the relatives. After mediation with a Dutch Moroccan healthcare consultant, the physicians and relatives came to a solution in the use of a particular local anesthesia technique that would alleviate suffering without sedating the patient. This enabled him to utter the declaration of faith (*shahada*) before dying.[35]

Perspectives of Patients and Their Relatives

The cases above illustrate how religious beliefs can influence end-of-life decision making, based on the value some of them attached on dying with a "clear mind." In their understanding, this is religiously required and therefore their decisions regarding pain relief were based on the avoidance of measures that would cause drowsiness or unconsciousness.

De Graaff et al.[36] found that among their Moroccan and Turkish respondents pain and symptom control should not lead to the patient losing consciousness. In their study, staying conscious was important as it gave the patient the opportunity to say goodbye to their loved ones and forgive them, but also so to answer for themselves before God.[37]

The cases described above illustrate additional reasons to avoid pain and symptom control that affects the patient's consciousness. The patients and relatives appear to believe that the absence of a clear mind was undesirable because it would: (1) hamper the performance of Islamic rituals, and (2) challenge religious understandings of pain and suffering. A third concern that was not mentioned in the cases, but that I wish to address – because it has a prominent place in Islamic normative literature regarding end-of-life decisions – is the concern to (3) transgress a religious ban by accelerating death. This latter concern was also found by de Graaff et al.[38]

Because these particular concerns have a religious character, the following sections discuss them in the broader context of theological debates. This will allow us to generate a better understanding of how religion and palliative care in general, and pain and symptom control, in particular, intersect, not only in the lives of Dutch Moroccan patients but also in those of the medical specialists who treat them.

Performance of Rituals before Death

The wish or perceived need – to die with a clear mind, that is, with full consciousness – is closely related to the performance of religious rituals. Through the use of a particular local anesthesia technique, the 60-year-old Dutch Moroccan man in Case III could remain a conscious believer until the end of life. This allowed him to express his utterance of the declaration of faith (*shahada*) as his last words. The *shahada* is whispered at the beginning of life in a newborn's ear, and devout Muslims strive to make these the last words as well, in order to complete their life cycle. Doing so is believed to open the doors to paradise.[39]

In addition, attitudes about unconsciousness as a means of pain relief are influenced by the beliefs of Muslim patients and relatives about their religious obligation to perform the five daily prayers. For example, the imam in Case I found sedation acceptable as long as the patient was awake intermittently to fulfill the daily prayers.

The general ruling within Islam regarding prayer is that everyone who is Muslim, sane, and mature is obliged to perform the five daily prayers, and when prayers are missed, one should make up for them at a later date (*qada*). Yet, differences of opinion exist when prayers are missed due to unconsciousness. Some Muslim scholars in the past have dropped the *qada* for unconscious persons, while others believe it should be maintained and that an unconscious person should make up a symbolic number of prayers after regaining consciousness. At the center of this disagreement is the question of whether unconsciousness is similar to sleeping or to insanity. Those who have equated unconsciousness with sleeping seem to impose *qada*, while those who have equated unconsciousness with insanity drop it.[40] A marked difference between the unconsciousness described in classical jurisprudence (*fiqh*) and pain and symptom management and palliative sedation, however, is that the latter two are treatments that are consciously decided upon. A modern religious opinion (*fatwa*) on this issue was issued by the Egyptian mufti 'Atiyya Saqr (1914–2006). He argued that one who missed prayers due to unconsciousness as a result of anesthesia was exempt from *qada*, regardless of the duration of the unconsciousness.[41]

Religious Understandings of Pain and Suffering

Beside the wish to perform certain rituals before death, pain and symptom control may raise concerns regarding religious understandings of pain and suffering. The relatives in Case III argued that a patient actually should undergo suffering based on their understanding that Islam requires patients to undergo pain and suffering consciously. Simply put, the basis for this belief is that enduring pain and suffering in this life leads to rewards in the afterlife. Does the religion of Islam, then, forbid the possibility of relief from severe pain? To answer this question, we need to look into certain Islamic theological traditions that adhere to a holistic conception of the human being. In Islam, health and illness do not encompass only a physical and biological dimension, but also a psychological and spiritual one.[42] Some believers consider pain and suffering to be a trial that contributes to the expiation of sins. The Qur'an (2:153–57) suggests that pain can demonstrate God's purpose for humanity by reminding humans that they ultimately belong to God and will return to Him,[43] and several prophetic traditions (*ahadith*)[44] indicate that any manifestation of pain can lead to the expiation of sins. At the same time, however, suffering is not exalted. The Qur'an indicates that it was not revealed to be a distress (20:2), and that no soul will be burdened except with that within its capacity (2:286). Consequently, suffering can be alleviated and one does not have to endure unbearable pain. Thus, although suffering is not needless according to religious texts because it expiates sins, it is also encouraged to alleviate suffering.[45] However, if the only option for pain relief is to lose consciousness, some prefer to endure the suffering, as Case I and III illustrate, although it is not clear what the patient's wish was in Case III. In the end, however, in both cases pain relief was accepted in a way that did justice to the wishes of the patient(s) and relatives.

Fear of Accelerating Death

Although not mentioned in the above-cited cases, the possible life-shortening effect of pain and symptom control is another concern found by de Graaff et al.[46] Van den Branden and Broeckaert,[47] in contrast, found that pain and symptom control with a possible life-shortening effect did not pose ethical dilemmas for a majority of their respondents (Moroccan men in Antwerp, Belgium), since they considered their life span to be determined by God.[48] However, their study was not conducted in a palliative care setting where people are directly confronted with such ethical dilemmas.

The possible life-shortening effect of pain and symptom control is a topic of discussion in ethical debates in general,[49] but is also discussed among Muslim religious scholars. At the center of these debates is the question whether it is similar to euthanasia which almost all Muslim religious scholars prohibit.[50] I will discuss two fatwas of leading *fatwa* councils that came to a different conclusion on this subject.

The Islamic Organization for Medical Sciences in Kuwait produces fatwas exclusively on issues of medical ethics. During a conference in 1999 about the rights of elderly people, the topic of euthanasia was discussed. Hassan Hathout (1924–2009), a physician and expert in the field of Islamic medical ethics, made a brief reference to pain and symptom management at the end of life that might have a life-shortening effect. According to him the intention of the physician plays a crucial role in its administration.[51] As a result, in the revised version of the *Islamic Code of Medical Ethics* (2004), pain and symptom management with a possible life-shortening effect was approved as long as death is not intended by the physician.[52]

Another leading *fatwa* council, the European Council for Fatwa and Research (ECFR) in contrast, expressed a different opinion. During a conference in Sweden in 2003, pain and symptom management with a possible life-shortening effect was prohibited just as euthanasia, even if death is not intended, but would be expected to result.[53]

Both the fatwas of the IOMS and the ECFR make no explicit mention of palliative sedation. However, both were issued before the guidelines of the Royal Dutch Medical Association (RDMA) and the European Association for Palliative Care (EAPC) regarding palliative sedation existed.

Van den Branden and Broeckaert[54] also found no reference to the term "palliative sedation" in their study about pain and symptom control in English Sunni e-fatwas. In some fatwas pain and symptom control with a possible life-shortening effect was considered a form of euthanasia and therefore forbidden. Others, however, held that it was allowed if the intention of the physician was to alleviate pain. Most English e-fatwas found no problem in using pain and symptom control and often referred to the principle of necessity (*darura*), allowing a patient to use such treatments and at the same time be in line with the Islamic normative-ethical framework.[55]

Thus, various fatwas exist on pain and symptom control, both in and beyond the Muslim world. Islamic religious opinions are diverse, and believers may form attitudes based on a particular situation, i.e. patients and their relatives may change their opinions in the process of medical decision-making.[56] However, certain views of patients and relatives that are religiously motivated may not correspond with the views or professional standards of medical professionals on "good" care. The struggle of physicians to deal with patients whose views on "good care" differ from theirs, is the topic of the next section.

Perspectives of Physicians

Some physicians in the cases described above felt the wish of their patient or their patient's relative to be in conflict with their professional standards. In Case I the physician wanted to administer intermittent palliative sedation but felt that this might be in conflict with the patient's religion and therefore consulted an imam. Although the imam actually agreed with the suggested intermittent palliative sedation, the physician still had mixed feelings because he found that the sedation should provide her rest but because of relatives praying around her, chatting and feeding her, palliative sedation would be a "senseless intervention."[57] Despite the divergent views regarding "good" care the medical team found that it helped them to accept their patient's "paradigm of religion," as they called it, and found that this attitude contributed to a patient-centered care.[58]

However, the situation becomes even more complicated when patients are mentally incompetent to decide for themselves and relatives decide issues of palliative treatment, as described in Case II. The patient was incapable of communicating and the relatives were divided over the use of morphine, causing physicians to face an even greater dilemma: should they administer morphine to the dying woman and thereby adhere to the principle of beneficence by alleviating her suffering, or should they respect the wishes of two relatives who objected to the administration of morphine for religious reasons?

After the death of this patient, her medical team presented the case to a professor of medical law, Aart Hendriks, in order to verify whether they acted correctly. Hendriks argued that it was unclear whether the eldest son, who fervently opposed the administration of morphine, was a true representative of his mother. Nothing indicated that he better represented his mother's wishes than the other siblings who disagreed with him. In such cases where the relatives are divided, Hendriks argued, physicians are not restricted by the objections of certain relatives, even if the objections are based on religious reasons. According to Hendriks, although freedom of religion is a fundamental right it does not include the right to prevent patients from receiving necessary medical treatment.[59]

In response to the events of Case II, Bert Keizer, a nursing home physician, wrote a column in the Dutch national newspaper *Trouw*, in which he stated that Islam offers little room for palliative care. Keizer found the collision of two irreconcilable versions of a "good deathbed" to be highly frustrating, and disadvantageous for all parties involved. He observed, "Physicians feel rude if they do not respect the – in their eyes – inhumane wishes of relatives, while relatives suffer from the – in their eyes – blasphemous course of events on the doorstep to eternity."[60] Keizer considered such wishes of relatives a threat to palliative care since they pose a challenge to medical efforts aimed at providing patients with a more comfortable death.[61]

The dilemmas the physicians encountered in the described cases were also found by de Graaff et al.[62] Some of the physicians in her study believed it was their responsibility to relieve their patient's suffering, while others tried to find solutions in between, by for example administering higher doses of sedatives during the night in order to give the patient rest, but less during the day to make contact between patient and relatives possible.[63]

Patients and relatives as well as physicians generally strive to act in the patient's best interest, but their opinions may differ as to what exactly the patient's best interest is. Van Dijk and Lokker[64] argue that physicians are usually not aware of their own culture. In Western countries, the modern vision of a "good death" is a death as free as possible from pain and suffering, while other cultures or even individuals within cultures may see it differently.[65] Such different visions regarding a "good death" need to be reconciled in order to provide "good" care.

In the cases described above third intermediary parties were involved in order to find a compromise: in Case I the physicians consulted an imam, in Case II the relatives tried to involve an imam, but his interference did not succeed, and in Case III a health care consultant, employed by the hospital was involved. Thus, when physicians, patients, and their relatives need to reconcile such different approaches to pain and suffering at the end of life, intermediaries may be consulted. Next, I will discuss the role of the intermediaries in more detail.

Perspectives of Intermediaries

Intermediary parties who act as advisors or mediators can be categorized as either informal or professional parties. Informal parties are not part of the medical establishment but may advise Muslim patients or their relatives about a treatment's religious permissibility, such as imams. Professional parties such as healthcare consultants and Islamic spiritual counselors, by contrast, are trained to deal with the complexities of medical treatments and the values and sensitivities of patients and their relatives. They are available in some healthcare institutions seeking to adapt to the growth of a culturally diverse population in the Netherlands. Such professional parties may guide Muslim patients and relatives from within Muslims' own normative framework, but without issuing a normative value judgement. I now turn to the role of such intermediaries.

Imams

Although imams are not healthcare professionals, they are regularly consulted by Muslims when complex medical ethical issues arise.[66] An essential element of an imam's daily work is to answer questions posed by believers, and in this way they fulfill the function of a religious counselor.[67]

Feeling that sedation at the end of life could be controversial due to the patient's religious background, the physicians in Case I sought a patient-centered solution from within religious circles. The imam they conferred with then discussed the issue with some of his colleagues before providing an opinion, indicating that medical ethical issues can be challenging for imams too, due to the complex nature of such problems. Along with religious knowledge, a certain level of medical knowledge is also necessary to respond to bioethical questions. After his own consultation with other colleagues, the imam returned to the team, and agreed with intermittent palliative sedation as long as it allowed her to perform her religious duties while also offering regular respite from her pain.

In Case II, however, mediation attempts by an imam did not succeed, although he had been approached by the relatives themselves.

While imams are *ad hoc* consulted by physicians and patients or relatives and are not formally trained to deal with such issues, professional parties who are trained to deal with these issues, such as health care consultants and Islamic spiritual counselors, are available in certain health care institutions only.

Healthcare Consultants

Healthcare consultants are intermediaries who, for over two decades, have been helping patients navigate the Dutch medical care system. Physicians frequently engage healthcare consultants with a similar cultural background as patients from other countries to bridge language gaps and cultural differences between physicians and patients, particularly in large institutions that serve large numbers of immigrants. Their task is twofold. First, they inform patients how the Dutch healthcare system works; second, they act as facilitators between physicians and patients and sometimes their relatives. Frequently they also provide physicians and medical staff with relevant cultural and religious background information.[68]

In Case III, a healthcare consultant was involved in the decision-making process for palliative sedation. She was familiar with Moroccan culture and had several conversations about the diagnosis and treatment with the patient while he was still able to communicate, but also with his relatives and the medical team. This consultant was aware that palliative sedation, as suggested by the physicians, would be acceptable neither to the patient nor his relatives. A creative solution was found using a local anesthetic that treated the patient's pain but allowed him to remain conscious enough to utter the *shahada* and to die with a clear mind.[69] This solution did justice to both the principle of beneficence and to the religious convictions of the patient and his relatives.

Islamic Spiritual Counselors

Other professional intermediaries who deserve attention, although not mentioned in the cases described above, are Islamic spiritual counselors who are trained to deal with the spiritual and religious dimensions of ethical issues in healthcare. According to Arslan Karagül, lecturer in Islamic spiritual counseling, counseling people in a crisis situation is at the heart of Islamic spiritual counseling, and cannot simply be done by local imams who are usually not able to bring together the complexities of medical treatments, the values of the Islamic tradition, the sensitivities of the family and the acute situation of a dying patient.[70]

Karagül wrote a response to Bert Keizer's above-cited column in *Trouw* arguing that Islam does provide room for palliative care. According to him, spiritual factors play an important role in healthcare settings, alongside mental, social, and emotional factors. He contends that little attention is paid to religion and spirituality in these settings, though it plays an important role in the experience of Muslim patients and relatives. It is Karagül's position that healthcare institutions should help guide relatives and prevent unnecessary suffering by providing them spiritual counseling. Thus the emphasis, he has noted, should not be put on the religiously correct view or answer but on a dialogue with patients and relatives about their experience of faith and how it may seem to contradict certain medical treatments. In this way, Karagül argued, "one can conscientiously acquiesce to the decisions of physicians."[71]

Despite the rapid growth of palliative care of which the spiritual dimension constitutes an important part,[72] the chairman of the Association of Spiritual Counselors in Healthcare Institutions indicated that spiritual counseling is under pressure due to budget cuts, merges of healthcare institutions, and changes in care legislation that shift care as much as possible from the hospital to the home. This might also affect the availability of Islamic spiritual counselors.[73]

Intermediaries can fulfill differing roles in the negotiation of end-of-life decisions. Imams can provide advice regarding the permissibility of certain treatments, while the health care consultants can bridge language gaps and cultural differences between physicians and patients and help in finding a compromising solution for the parties involved. Islamic spiritual counselors in contrast are more focused on the spiritual dimensions of caregiving. They have content knowledge of religion, but also on ethics and are trained to mediate between the professional norms of the medical staff and the values, sorrows and fears of Muslim families.[74]

In the preceding sections, I paid attention to the values Dutch Moroccans considered important at the end of life in the cases described, and how medical professionals sometimes struggle to do justice to the wishes of their patients and their patient's relatives as well as their professional standards, and how healthcare consultants or imams mediate between these sometimes-opposing views. In the final section, I discuss the current state of palliative care in Morocco.

Palliative Care in Morocco

It is as yet unclear if and to what extent patients and imams of Moroccan origin in the Netherlands relate to current medical practices in Morocco. As a relatively new area of specialization, palliative care in Morocco is still in development. For a long time the Moroccan Society of Management of Pain and Palliative Care (MSMPP) in Rabat remained the only medical center in the country providing palliative care.[75] However, pain management has attracted increasing interest and was endorsed as a national priority by Moroccan health authorities in 2003, resulting in Morocco's National Plan for Cancer Prevention and Control in 2010. An important focus of this project was to institutionalize and improve pain management as well as palliative care.[76]

In spite of these measures, problems encountered in relation to palliative care in Morocco continue, and they have a different character from those encountered by Moroccan immigrants in the Netherlands. Difficulties in Morocco are usually linked to the shortage and prohibitively high costs of such medical services, as well as the difficulties of access given the fact that palliative care is only available in major urban areas and not in the rural hinterlands where the majority of Moroccans live. Additionally, the use of opioids for pain control has long been limited in Morocco due to restrictive laws that have impeded the prescription of opioids. As recently as the early 1990s, only injectable morphine was used to treat acute pain, and it was available in only a small number of hospitals. In 1995 morphine tablets were introduced and made available in external pharmacies, but only a seven-day supply was allowed for outpatients. In 2013 the laws regarding opioids were amended, allowing morphine to be prescribed for up to 28 days to outpatients, though without a specified maximum dose. The reason behind these restrictive laws was an overriding anxiety about the risk of addiction and abuse, coined by Mati Nejmi, founder of the MSMPP "morphinofobia."[77] Though this fear of addiction is characteristic of many developing countries, it is less present in relation to terminally ill patients.[78]

Despite the new laws on opioid use, the costs of such treatments still form a major barrier to use in Morocco as only one third of the population has health insurance. Another barrier is the permission that physicians must seek from the Ministry of Health. According to Nejmi, many physicians are reluctant to apply for permission to prescribe these medications because of the long and complicated process involved.[79]

Scarce research is available on the cultural and religious barriers to the use of pain medication in Morocco. A study by McCarthy et al.[80] on managing children's cancer pain in Morocco identified no consistent cultural barriers to pain control. The physicians who participated in this study indicated that some Moroccans believe illness-related pain to be inevitable and suffering to be normal, but most physicians believed that pain should not be tolerated.[81] Although physicians mentioned that in the past people were reluctant to use morphine due to both costs and misconceptions, it was generally prescribed for terminally ill patients.[82] However, since this study is about pain management in general and not about palliative care in particular, no mention is made of issues such as potential high doses of opioids or sedatives that may accelerate death as well as the possible wish of some patients to be conscious enough to perform religious rituals.

Since palliative care is a relatively new area of specialization in Morocco, Dutch Moroccan patient's and relatives as well as the imams who are occasionally consulted cannot rely on the practices in their country of origin and find themselves pioneers in resolving such difficult end-of-life decisions.

Conclusion

Palliative care is a field in which cultural, religious, and family values converge. The cases discussed in this chapter illustrate how religious beliefs can influence the attitudes of Dutch Moroccan patients and relatives towards pain and symptom control at the end of life. Changing attitudes towards these issues impact populations with a migration background in Europe, and might in time reverberate back to their countries of origin. As this discussion of Dutch Moroccan patients, their relatives, and their physicians illustrates, religion can be an important factor in end-of-life decisions. Religious concerns can be mediated by a triangular process in which patients and their relatives, physicians overseeing treatment, and outside intermediaries work together to reconcile divergent opinions related to pain and symptom control.

The cases in this chapter illustrate the importance of adapting palliative care approaches to the needs of distinct groups of patients. This approach can be achieved by helping medical professionals learn more about the religious convictions not only of Muslim patients and their relatives, but also those of other religious patients who are faced with difficult end-of-life decisions. This will help medical professionals take a more open stance in discussions of religious concerns for the patient. It is also important that issues related to pain and symptom management and palliative sedation are discussed with patients, and relatives, before the need to make such a decision arises. Communication early in the process allows the physician to explain the various possibilities and allows the patient to clarify his or her wishes and preferences. In this way, the physician can become aware of the patient's preferences. Discussing end-of-life decisions in advance also enables the patient to think about the issues at hand, and if needed, to consult others for advice. In cases where patients, their relatives and physicians do not agree on a certain treatment, it is recommendable that physicians seek assistance from professional intermediaries who can discern the implications of acute medical dilemmas and at the same time understand the perspectives of physicians, patients, and relatives. Importantly, health care institutions need to be able to provide such trained intermediaries.

Endnotes

1 Clark, D. (2007). "From margins to centre: a review of the history of palliative care in cancer." *The Lancet Oncology*, pp. 430–438; World Health Organization (WHO) "Palliative care: fact sheet". Available at www.who.int/mediacentre/factsheets/fs402/en/ (accessed August 19, 2017).

2 Onwuteaka-Philipsen, B.D. et al. (2012) Trends in end-of-life practices before and after the enactment of euthanasia law in the Netherlands from 1990 to 2010: a repeated cross-sectional survey. *The Lancet*. Vol. 380, No. 9845, pp. 908–915.

3 Leenen, H.J.J. et al. (2014). *Handboek gezondheidsrecht [Handbook for Health Law]*. Den Haag: Boom Juridische uitgevers, p. 386–390.

4 Royal Dutch Medical Association (RDMA) (2009). *Guideline for Palliative Sedation*. Utrecht: KNMG, p. 5.

5 Buiting, H.M. et al. (December 2008). "A comparison of physicians' end-of-life decision making for non-Western migrants and Dutch natives in the Netherlands." *The European Journal of Public Health*. Vol. 18, No. 6, pp. 681–687.

6 Ibid, p. 686. Note that only 8.3% of the study population was Moroccan.

7 Centraal Bureau voor de Statistiek (November 2014). "CBS StatLine – Bevolking; generatie, geslacht, leeftijd en herkomstgroepering [CBS StatLine – Population, generation, gender, age and ethnic background]." http://statline.cbs.nl/StatWeb/publication/ (accessed November 12, 2014).

8 de Graaff, F.M. et al. (2010). "'Palliative care': a contradiction in terms? A qualitative study of cancer patients with a Turkish or Moroccan background, their relatives and care providers." *BMC Palliative Care*. Vol. 9, No. 1; Korfker, D.G. et al. (January 2014). "Infertility care in the Netherlands for Turkish and Moroccan migrants: the role of religion

in focus." Available at http://resolver.tudelft.nl/uuid:13de37f9-c6eb-4cfc-bc63-cdb339f5ddd8; Gitsels-van der Wal, J.T. et al. (March 2015). "A qualitative study on how Muslim women of Moroccan descent approach antenatal anomaly screening." *Midwifery.* Vol. 31, No. 3, pp. 43–49.

  9 Sachedina, A. (2012). *Islamic Biomedical Ethics: Principles and Application.* USA: Oxford University Press, pp. 170–171; Van den Branden, S. and B. Broeckaert (2010). "Necessary interventions: Muslim views on pain and symptom control in English Sunni E-Fatwas." *Ethical Perspectives.* Vol. 17, No. 4, pp. 626–651; Atighetchi, D. (Spring 2007). *Islamic Bioethics: Problems and Perspectives. International Library of Ethics, Law, and the New Medicine.* Vol. 31, pp. 285–290.

10 For examples of such studies, see de Graaff et al., "Palliative care"; Van den Branden, S. and B. Broeckaert (2008). "Medication and God at interplay: end-of-life decision-making in practicing male Moroccan migrants living in Antwerp, Flanders, Belgium." *Muslim Medical Ethics: From Theory to Practice.* Columbia, S.C: University of South Carolina Press, pp. 194–211.

11 Nejmi, M. and L. Hessissen (2014). "Moroccan experience." *Palliative Care to the Cancer Patient: The Middle East as a Model for Emerging Countries.* 1st Edition. S. Silbermann (ed.). Cancer Etiology, Diagnosis and Treatments. New York: Nova Science Publishers, pp. 141–154.

12 Leenen et al., Gevers and Legemaate, *Handbook,* p. 386.

13 Other (local) techniques for pain relief can be used, such as the techniques discussed by T. Picot and B. Hamid (January 2010). "Decision-making in the cancer pain setting: beyond the WHO ladder." *Techniques in Regional Anesthesia and Pain Management. Update in Cancer Pain Management.* Vol. 14, No. 1, pp. 21–23.

14 World Health Organization (WHO). "WHO | WHO's cancer pain ladder for adults." *WHO.* Available at www.who.int/cancer/palliative/painladder/en/ (accessed November 16, 2015); de Graeff, A., T.C. Besse, and R.J.A. Krol (2010). "Pijn: landelijke richtlijn, Versie: 2.0 [Pain: nation-wide guideline, Version: 2.0]." Integraal Kankercentrum Nederland [Integral Cancer Centre The Netherlands], p. 15.

15 Leenen, H.J.J. et al. (2014). *Handboek gezondheidsrecht [Handbook for Health Law].* Den Haag: Boom Juridische uitgevers, p. 386.

16 Boer, T.A. (2013). "Palliative sedation: an exploration from a Christian ethical point of view." *Looking Beneath the Surface: Medical Ethics from Islamic and Western Perspectives.* H.M. Vroom et al. (eds.). Amsterdam: Rodopi, pp. 227–341.

17 Since 2001 a question was included about palliative sedation in studies about death causes, see van der Heide, A., A. Brinkman-Stoppelenburg,

H. van Delden, and B. Onwuteaka-Philipsen (2012). _Sterfgevallenonderzoek 2010: Euthanasie en andere medische beslissingen rond het levenseinde [Death and disease studies 2010: Euthanasia and other medical end-of-life decisions]_, Den Haag: ZonMw, p. 28.

18 Royal Dutch Medical Association (RDMA) (2009). _Guideline for Palliative Sedation_. Utrecht: KNMG, pp. 5, 22, 40.

19 Leenen, Gevers and Legemaate, _Handbook_, p. 387.

20 RDMA, _Guideline for Palliative_.

21 Cherny, N.I., L. Radbruch, and The Board of the European Association for Palliative Care (October 2009). "European Association for Palliative Care (EAPC) recommended framework for the use of sedation in palliative care." _Palliative Medicine_. Vol. 23, No. 7, p. 582.

22 Leenen, H.J.J. et al. (2014). _Handboek gezondheidsrecht [Handbook for Health Law]_. Den Haag: Boom Juridische uitgevers, pp. 386–390.

23 RDMA, _Guideline for Palliative_, pp. 28–31.

24 Rietjens, J.C. et al. (April 2006). "Terminal sedation and euthanasia: a comparison of clinical practices." _Archives of Internal Medicine_. Vol. 166, No. 7, pp. 749–753.

25 Regarding pain and symptom management the question whether it hastens death is usually discussed, while in relation to palliative sedation additional issues were the subject of discussion such as the patient's loss of autonomy during sedation as well as his or her personhood. See for example Materstvedt, L.J. and G. Bosshard (June 2009). "Deep and continuous palliative sedation (terminal sedation): clinical-ethical and philosophical aspects." _The Lancet Oncology_. Vol. 10, No. 6, pp. 622–627; Sprung, C.L. et al. (January 2008). "Relieving suffering or intentionally hastening death: where do you draw the line?" _Critical Care Medicine_. Vol. 36, No. 1, pp. 8–13.

26 Hendriks, M.P. et al. (October 2012). "Palliative care for an Islamic patient: changing frameworks." _Journal of Palliative Medicine_. Vol. 15, No. 10, pp. 1053–1055.

27 van der Heide, A. et al. (May 2007). "End-of-life practices in the Netherlands under the Euthanasia Act." _New England Journal of Medicine_. Vol. 356, No. 19, pp. 1957–1965.

28 The authors refer to the general term "palliative sedation" but after contacting the author, I learned that he actually wanted to administer intermittent sedation. Continuous sedation would not be an option, because the patient's life expectancy was more than two weeks.

29 Hendriks et al., "Palliative care."

30 Kluge, G., E. Brewster, and S. Kuipers (2012). "Waardig sterven, godsdienstvrijheid en het recht van de oudste zoon [Dying with dignity,

religious freedom and the right of the eldest son]." *Medisch Contact.* Vol. 67. No 13, pp. 748–749.

31 In the published case the patient is defined only as a Muslim woman. Contact with the author confirmed the patient's Moroccan background.

32 Kluge, Brewster, and Kuipers, "Waardig sterven."

33 Choukat, A., B.C. Ter Meulen, and G. Widdershoven (2013). "Palliatieve sedatie voor moslims bezwaarlijk [Palliative sedation is inconvenient for Muslims]." *Medisch Contact.* Nos. 29–30, pp. 1550–1051.

34 Beauchamp, T.L. and J.F. Childress (2013). *Principles of Biomedical Ethics.* 7th Edition. New York: Oxford University Press, p. 202.

35 Choukat, Ter Meulen and Widdershoven, "Palliatieve sedatie."

36 de Graaff et al., "'Palliative care.'"

37 Ibid.

38 Ibid.

39 Gatrad, A.R. and A. Sheikh (November 2002). "Palliative care for Muslims and issues before death." *International Journal of Palliative Nursing.* Vol. 8, No. 11; C. Venhorst (2013). "Lived eschatology: Muslim views on life and death preliminary practices" *Changing European Death Ways.* E. Venbrux et al. (eds.). LIT Verlag Münster, p. 265.

40 Ibn Rushd, M.A. (1994). *The Distinguished Jurist's Primer.* I.A.K. Nyazee and M. Abdul-Rauf (eds.). *The Great Books of Islamic Civilization.* Vol. I. Doha, Qatar: Centre for Muslim Contribution to Civilization. Part I, p. 206.

41 Rispler-Chaim, V. (1931). *Disability in Islamic Law. International Library of Ethics, Law, and the New Medicine.* Vol. 32. Berlin: Springer Netherland, p. 27.

42 Atighetchi, *Islamic Bioethics*, p. 270.

43 Sachedina, A. (August 2005). "End-of life: the Islamic view." *The Lancet.* Vol. 366, No. 9487, pp. 774–779; Sachedina, *Islamic Biomedical Ethics.*

44 Plural form of *hadith,* a prophetic tradition. See for example *Sahih Bukhari.* Vol. 7, Book 70, No. 544–545. Available at www.sahih-bukhari.com.

45 Atighetchi, *Islamic Bioethics*, p. 268.

46 de Graaff, et al. "'Palliative care.'"

47 Van den Branden and Broeckaert, "Medication and God."

48 Ibid, p. 199.

49 See for example Sprung et al., "Relieving suffering"; Janssens, R., J.J.M. van Delden, and G.A.M. Widdershoven (November 2012). "Palliative sedation: not just normal medical practice. Ethical reflections on the Royal Dutch Medical Association's guideline on palliative sedation." *Journal of Medical Ethics.* Vol. 38, No. 11, pp. 664–668.

50 Ghaly, M. (2015). "Euthanasia." *Encyclopaedia of Islam, THREE*. K. Fleet et al. (eds.). Brill Online. Available at http://referenceworks.brillonline.com/ entries/encyclopaedia-of-islam-3/euthanasia-COM_26254.

51 Al-Rahman, A. et al. (October 1999). *Ru'ya islamiyya li-ba'd al-mushkilat at-tibbiyya al-mu'asira: thabt kamil li-a'mal al-nadwa al-fiqhiyya at-tib-biyya ath-thaniyata 'ashar (Huquq al-musinnin min manzur islami) [The Islamic vision on some contemporary medical problems: a full account of the proceedings of the twelfth symposium on medical jurisprudence (the rights of the elderly from an islamic point of view)]*. Part 2, p. 923.

52 Al-Rahman, A., A.A. al-'Awadi and A. Raja'i al-Jindī (2005). *The International Islamic Code for Medical and Health Ethics: December 11–14, 2004 29 Shawwal – 2 Zu AlKaida Cairo, Egypt*. Islam and Recent Medical Problems. Kuwait: Islamic Organization for Medical Sciences, p. 91.

53 European Council for Fatwa and Research (ECFR) (July 2003). Al-bayan al-khitami li-d-dawra al-hadiyata 'ashara li-l-majlis al-urubbi li-l-ifta' wa-l-buhuth al-mun'aqada fi maqarr ar-ribat al-islamiyya bi-l-markaz al-islami (stukhulm - as-suwayd), qarar 3/11 "qatl al-marhama" [Final Statement of the Eleventh Regular Session of the European Council for Fatwa and Research held at the Headquarters of the Islamic Association of Sweden, the Islamic Center Stockholm - Sweden, resolution 3/11 "Euthanasia"] Available at https://www.e-cfr.org/%D8%A7%D9%84%D8%A8%D9% 8A%D8%A7%D9%86-%D8%A7%D9%84%D8%AE%D8%AA%D8% A7%D9%85%D9%89-11-2/ (accessed September 26, 2017).

54 Van den Branden and Broeckaert, "Necessary interventions."

55 Ibid, pp. 644–645.

56 den Dikken, A. (2003). *Interculturele ethiek in de gezondheidszorg: morele uitwisseling via de spreekkamer [Intercultural ethics in health-care: moral exchange via the consulting room]*. Utrecht: Centrum voor Bio-ethiek en Gezondheidsrecht Universiteit Utrecht, pp. 72–75.

57 Hendriks et al., "Palliative care," p. 1054.

58 Ibid., p. 1055.

59 Kluge, Brewster, and Kuipers, "Waardig sterven."

60 Keizer, K. (April 7, 2012). "Islam biedt weinig ruimte voor palliatieve zorg [Islam offers little room for palliative care]." *Trouw*.

61 Ibid.

62 de Graaff et al., "Palliative care.'"

63 Ibid.

64 van Dijk, G. and I. Lokker (February 2011). "'Het is de wil van Allah' Bewuster omgaan met verschillende visies op lijden en sterven ['It is the Will of Allah' dealing conciously with various visions on suffering and death]." *Medisch Contact*. Vol. 66. No. 8, pp. 480–483.

65 Ibid, pp. 480–483.

66 den Dikken, *Interculturele ethiek*, pp. 76–77; Padela, A.I. et al. (June 2011). "The role of imams in American Muslim health: perspectives of Muslim community leaders in Southeast Michigan." *Journal of Religion and Health*. Vol. 50, No. 2, pp. 359–373.

67 Shadid, W.A. and P.S. van Koningsveld (2002). *Intercultural Relations and Religious Authorities: Muslims in the European Union* Leuven: Peeters Publishers, p. 151.

68 van Mechelen, P.M.F. and P. Nieuwenhuizen (2002). *De allochtone zorgconsulent: handboek voor invoering en professionalisering van de functie* [The immigrant health care consultant: Handbook for implementation and professionalization of the function]. M. Drewes (ed.). Utrecht: FORUM, pp. 18–20.

69 Choukat, Ter Meulen and Widdershoven, "Palliatieve sedatie."

70 Karagül, A. (2013). "Islamic care ethics: between law and conscience." *Looking beneath the Surface: Medical Ethics from Islamic and Western Perspectives*. Amsterdam: Rodopi, pp. 259–260.

71 Karagül, A. (April 16, 2012). "Islam biedt wél ruimte voor palliatieve zorg [Islam does provide room for palliative care]." *Trouw*.

72 WHO. "WHO definition of palliative care." Available at www.who.int/cancer/palliative/definition/en/ (accessed November 15, 2015).

73 (October 8, 2014). "Geestelijke verzorging in de knel [Spiritual care in trouble]." *Friesch Dagblad*. In April 2016, 19 Islamic spiritual counselors were registered at the Association of Spiritual Care, compared to 290 Roman Catholic, 405 Protestant, 113 Humanist, 7 Jewish and 1 Hindu spiritual counselors (numbers retrieved after contact with the Association of Spiritual Care).

74 Karagül, "Islamic care ethics," p. 261.

75 Wright, M. and D. Clark (2006). *Hospice and Palliative Care in Africa: A Review of Developments and Challenges*. Oxford University Press, pp. 301–313.

76 Nejmi and Hessissen, "Moroccan experience," p. 144.

77 Ibid, pp. 145, 149–150.

78 Cleary, J. et al. (2013). *Formulary Availability and Regulatory Barriers to Accessibility of Opioids for Cancer Pain in the Middle East: A Report from the Global Opioid Policy Initiative (GOPI)*. Available at http://annonc.oxfordjournals.org/content/24/suppl_11/xi51; McCarthy, P. et al. (March 2004). "Managing children's cancer pain in Morocco." *Journal of Nursing Scholarship*. Vol. 36, No. 1, pp. 11–15.

79 Nejmi and Hessissen, "Moroccan experience," p. 149.

80 McCarthy et al., "Managing children's."

81 Ibid, p. 14.

82 Ibid.

PART IV

What Is Law? Oral and Codified Law

11 | Kol B'Isha Erva

The Silencing of Jewish Women's Oral Traditions in Morocco

VANESSA PALOMA ELBAZ

Introduction

In Moroccan Jewish culture, women's sung oral traditions have greatly eroded.[1] Soon after Moroccan independence in 1956 and until the 1970s, large segments of the Moroccan Jewish population emigrated from Morocco, and the leadership vacuum that ensued was filled in part by rabbis coming to Morocco from outside of the country. These new rabbis brought different rabbinic interpretations of Jewish law, thus eliminating some of the particularities of Moroccan Jewish culture in situ. Among the most salient aspects of this culture has been the richness of the Judeo-Moroccan poetic and musical traditions, many of which were oral in nature in both the masculine and feminine spheres. At issue is the contemporary orthodox Jewish law that controls women's singing in mixed groups, a law extrapolated from the Talmudic dictum Kol B'Isha Erva (A woman's voice is akin to nakedness) and defined in its present form in early nineteenth-century Germany.

This chapter addresses Moroccan Jewish women's oral traditions in Morocco. In contrast with the large diasporic Moroccan Jewish communities in Israel, France and Canada, Moroccan Jewish traditions remain connected to their historical and societal sources in a different manner than those of communities in the Moroccan diaspora. The diasporic Judeo-Arabic and Judeo-Berber men's and women's oral traditions have been written about most recently by Joseph Chetrit[2] and the Judeo-Spanish traditions by Shoshana Weich-Shahak,[3] Oro Anahory Librowicz[4] and others.

This chapter concerns how changes in the attitudes of rabbis in Morocco toward Jewish women's public singing has had a direct impact on women's sung oral traditions by diminishing the presence of their voices in today's Moroccan Jewish culture in Morocco.

This change is most notable in Casablanca, where the largest remaining Moroccan Jewish community exists today. A sampling of all the Judeo-Berber, Judeo-Arab, and Judeo-Spanish communities of Morocco can be found in Casablanca.

Moroccan Jewish women have been using oral traditions for generations as a way to comment on topics at hand using statements that have the status of a communally approved (oral) text. As J. Chetrit says, "They give them semiotic power by connecting them with anonymous authoritative sources and relating them in a subtle way to the situation(s) evoked in the proverbial saying."[5] Songs, which are used as oral poetic texts, have the same function. Jewish Moroccan women's use of oral texts (songs and proverbs) are a way to counterbalance the transmission of Jewish beliefs which are passed as well through religious texts in Hebrew by Jewish men. Since women's oral traditions are in the particular Jewish vernacular language of their own community, women's transmission has an added function of transmitting cultural specificity and strengthening group identity. The eroding of these local traditions plays into the general trend of globalization of Jewish practice and erases particular identity markers that have functioned for generations, not only stripping the community of a sense of cultural pride in their millenary orality but minimizing the importance of women's contribution to the transmission of Jewish knowledge and beliefs.

This chapter is based on my ten years of fieldwork in Jewish communities around Morocco. Between 2005 and 2015, I conducted oral history interviews, participant observation, and reviews of academic and religious literature. The close to four hundred interviews of Moroccan Jewish men and women still living in Morocco covered a range of topics that includes music, gender issues, politics, identity, liturgy, Jewish-Muslim relations, and customs among others. A sampling of that corpus, which is the basis for *KHOYA: les archives sonores du Maroc juif*, a sound archive of Moroccan Judaism that I founded and direct, was used for this chapter.

I begin with an overview of Moroccan Jewish history describing the various populations that form such communities today, delineated along geographic and linguistic lines. Next, I introduce the manner in which Jewish law was formulated and organized, followed by an explanation of the different groups within Judaism and the place of Moroccan Jews within the larger Jewish body. The relationship between "local" Judaism, defined for the purposes of this paper as Judaism within Morocco, and global Judaism that is, general "mainstreamed" Orthodox practice with a main base in Israel's Rabbinate, as well as major centers of Judaism in New York, Montreal and Paris, is key to understanding current challenges to the oral sung traditions of Moroccan Jewish women. This is because the local-global dichotomy is at the heart of the struggle within Moroccan Jewish communities to define their allegiances and their extent of adherence to certain readings of Jewish law and global Jewish legal practice.

In the following section I focus on important Jewish women's singing traditions that existed before Moroccan independence as well as practices that remain and those that have been lost. I provide an explanation of the difference between Jewish religious law and practice and how the gap between the two impacts women's lives in Morocco. I also consider the interplay between the public and private dichotomy of life in Morocco, Jewish law, and the inherent fragility of orality. Finally, I draw from my fieldwork and personal participation to offer examples of occasions when women have continued to sing from the traditional repertoire of Moroccan Judaism in the early twenty-first century.

The History of Jews in Morocco

Jewish communities have existed in Morocco for at least two thousand years alongside the Amazigh (Berber), indigenous ethnic groups of North Africa. Jews were the first non-Amazigh community to arrive in Morocco. It is said that the first Jews came to Morocco after the destruction of the first Temple in 586 BCE, and a large second wave came in 70 CE after the Roman destruction of the second Temple in Jerusalem.

Some Amazigh tribes converted to Judaism after Jews arrived from the holy land. Similarly, Jews who had come from the holy land were influenced by their context, adapting to Amazigh way of life over centuries of life in the Atlas Mountains and the rural South. According to fourteenth century chronicles, when Idriss I, the first Arab ruler and the founder of Fez, arrived in the eighth century to conquer Morocco, he encountered Christian, Jewish, and pagan tribes.[6] Documents exist that confirm the Jewish presence in the imperial city of Fez soon after its founding. The southern city of

Marrakesh was slower to accept the Jewish presence within its walls. From the time of its founding in 1062 until the sixteenth century, Jews were not allowed to spend the night within the city walls. It was the Saadian Sultan Ahmed-Ed-Dahabi (1578–1603) who finally approved the construction of the *mellah*, the Jewish quarter of Marrakesh, near the Royal Palace.[7]

Until the late fifteenth century, Jews who lived in Morocco were all Judeo-Arabic or Judeo-Berber speakers and practiced local Moroccan rites. After the fall of Granada and the edict expelling Jews from Spain in 1492, massive migrations of Jews from Spain and soon, Portugal, poured into Morocco from the Iberian Peninsula. Having sought refuge from religious intolerance and forced conversions, the situation of these Jews paralleled that of the Andalusian Muslims who came to Morocco around the same time after the fall of Granada.

Jews coming from Iberia established Judeo-Spanish speaking communities in the northern cities of Tetuan, Tangier, Asilah, Ksar el Kebir, Larache, and Chefchaouen. Others integrated into existing communities throughout the country, from Fez to Taroudant, in the far south. The slow integration of the communities of the native *toshavim* (dwellers) and *megorashim* (expelled ones) created a rich dynamic and uniquely Moroccan Judaism known for its piety and its penetration into all social and economic levels of urban and rural Moroccan society.

At its height in the early twentieth century, the Jewish population in Morocco reached close to 350,000 people. Jews were active in all levels of society, from the ruling elite to petty peddlers and even beggars. Many cities had active Jewish quarters, which were social and cultural hubs of learning and traditions. In the Atlas Mountains, many Jews were traveling merchants. Jewish artisans fashioned jewelry, carpets, metalwork, leatherwork, and embroidery, among other Moroccan traditional crafts. The establishment of the state of Israel in 1948, the independence of Morocco in 1956, the various wars between the Arab states and Israel, and the rise of pan-Arabism in the 1960s and 1970s all contributed to massive Jewish emigration. Many Jews chose to leave in order to gain access to economic and educational opportunities in such countries as Canada, France, Spain, and Venezuela. The largest reduction in the population of Moroccan Jews occurred in the aftermath of the Six-Day War of 1967, when the population dropped to half its size in the space of four years.[8] Jews who emigrated feared the tensions reverberating throughout Morocco due to the war and Arab/Muslim-Jewish hostilities in the Middle East.

In 2016 less than two thousand Jews remain in Morocco. The Moroccan Jewish diaspora numbers close to two million; in Israel alone there are one million Jews of Moroccan background. According to official Moroccan statistics 140,000 Jewish tourists mostly of Moroccan origin from the United States, Canada, Israel, and other countries come to visit Morocco every year.[9] Serge Berdugo, the General Secretary of the Conseil de Communautés Israélites du Maroc, (Council of Jewish Communities in Morocco), has called the current community living in Morocco a *communauté matricielle*, a matrix community.[10] In other words, Jews from all over the globe come to Morocco to re-connect with their ancestral Judaism.[11]

Jewish Ethnic Groups

Jewish ethnic groups are divided according to geographical origins. People whose families came from Northern Europe are considered to be Ashkenazi Jews from the land of Ashkenaz, or Germany. Ashkenazim became a distinct community of Jews at the end of the first millennium. They spoke Yiddish, a version of German that incorporates Hebrew and Slavic words and grammar. Among Ashkenazi Jews there exist Hasidic and Mitnagdi approaches to Jewish life. Hasidic practice revolves around a charismatic spiritual leader (Rebbe) and tightly knit insular communities. Mitnagdim were opposed to the mystical brand of Judaism that Hasidic groups practiced starting in the late eighteenth century.

Chabad Lubavitch is a branch of Hasidism that originated in present-day Belarus and has been based in Brooklyn since 1940. They are the most active Jewish outreach group worldwide.[12] Chabad synagogues exist in far-flung corners of the globe. Their main imperative is to ensure that assimilated Jews add more ritual practice.

Sepharad means Spain in Hebrew. Sephardi Jews originated in the Iberian Peninsula before the Edict of Expulsion of 1492. They migrated in the fifteenth and sixteenth centuries and moved to Morocco, the Ottoman Empire (Turkey, the Balkans, Greece and others), Italy, Egypt, Syria, the Netherlands, and England among others.

Mizrahi Jews are Jews who lived in Muslim lands but were not Sephardi, such as the Jews of Iran, Iraq, Yemen, Libya, and Tunisia,

with some Syrians and Moroccans among others. *Mizrah* means
"East" in Hebrew. This appellation is primarily used in Israel to
nuance the traditional divide between Ashkenazim and Sepharadim.
Some Mizrahi Jews are also Sephardi (a Syrian Jew whose family came
from Turkey and was previously from Spain is Sephardi), but not all
Sephardim are Mizrahi.

Moroccan Jews are considered Mizrahi or Sephardi according to
their background. Those whose families came from Spain to Morocco
and still speak Moroccan Judeo-Spanish are considered to be pure
Sephardi. Those whose families were Amazigh and speak Judeo-Berber
and Judeo-Arabic are considered Mizrahi. Some whose families came
from Spain but assimilated into Arabic speaking Jewish populations
are Sephardi but might identify more with Arabic speaking Jews than
with those who speak Haketía, Moroccan-Judeo Spanish. One consequence of the globalization of Judaism is that particular local ways of
practicing Judaism are being erased in favor of a global Orthodoxy,
which is mostly defined by Ashkenazi, Eastern European standards.

Background to Jewish Law

Around 220 CE. in Babylon, Rabbi Samuel uttered a statement to the
effect that a woman's voice is akin to nakedness. This statement was
represented in the Talmud, the collection of rabbinical legal discussions
that codify Jewish law, as *Kol be'Isha erva*.[13] Since the Talmud is the
source material for all Jewish law, any statement found within its text
has been interpreted, codified and applied into the lives of Jewish
communities throughout the world.

The Talmud is divided into *Mishna* and *Gemara*. The *Mishna* is the
compendium from the Oral Torah written ca. 200 CE, a century after
the destruction of the second Temple in Jerusalem by the Romans. The
Gemara is the discussion around the original *Mishna* with commentary, digressions, and rabbinical discussions. It was written down
ca. 500 CE The word Talmud refers to the *Gemara* or both the
Mishna and *Gemara*. In general, the Talmud deals with two broad
categories: *halacha* or legal statements, and *aggada*, exegetical, homi-
letical, ethical, or historical statements.

The Talmud is often cryptic and difficult to understand. In the Middle
Ages various Rabbis wrote commentaries on the Talmud and wrote
books explaining laws used in daily Jewish life. Various seminal rabbis

wrote volumes that led to the final codification of Jewish law in the sixteenth century. Rabbi Yitzhak Alfasi (1013–1103) wrote a code of law based on the most important points in the Talmud called *Hilkhot haRif*. Maimonides, Moshe ben Maimon (1138–1204), wrote *Mishnei Torah*. Asher ben Yehiel (c. 1250–1328) wrote *Piskei HaRosh*, and his son Jacob ben Asher (c.1269–1343), wrote *Arba Turim*. These works eventually led to the *Shulhan Aruch*, by Rabbi Yosef Caro (1488–1575), who codified the definitive compendium of Jewish law used today.

Jewish Law and Women's Public Singing

Jewish law, called Halacha in Hebrew, delineates the manner in which a Jew should "walk" through life. In regard to Jewish women's singing, the strict application of Halacha in Morocco is as recently as the 1970s and 1980s. Although the Talmud states *kol be'isha erva*, Morocco has been an oral culture. For millennia, Jewish women in the Maghreb who live strictly according to Jewish laws and customs have been active in singing for communal celebrations and tragedies, and they have used song to educate new generations and to transmit information, often through encoded messages. Within families women have sung, and continue to sing publicly during Jewish holidays, weddings and circumcisions.

During the 1940s and 1950s, a choir of prepubescent boys and girls in Tangier regularly sang during the late afternoon Sabbath prayer (*minha*), according to reports from Sonia C., a member of Tangier's Jewish community. In the 1960s and 1970s, Tangier native Maurice Bengio directed a similar mixed gender choir for weddings and certain holidays at the Temple Beth El, a large synagogue established in 1949 by Algerian Jewish immigrants in Casablanca (see Figure 11.1).

Mr. Bengio's choir was cancelled abruptly, however, after Eastern European rabbinic emissaries from a Hasidic community in Brooklyn exerted pressure on the synagogue's leadership.[14]

These rabbis came to Morocco in the early 1960s, sent by their charismatic leader Rabbi Menahem Mendel Schneerson (the Lubavitcher Rebbe), and they influenced local Judaic practices at a time when the community of Moroccan Jews was facing massive emigration. At this time of cataclysmic change within the community, the Eastern European Hasidic interpretations of Jewish law added onerous restrictions on women's voices.

Figure 11.1 Maurice Bengio and his Choir at Temple Beth El in the 1960s, Casablanca.

The traditional flexibility of the Moroccan Jewish community with regard to the laws governing "*kol 'isha*" demonstrates that Moroccans followed a Mediterranean practice that understood and respected the centrality of feminine contributions within a strongly patriarchal system. The introduction of the stringent legal interpretation of "*kol 'isha*", however, has led to the erosion of millenary oral traditions among women, traditions that already had been impacted by modernity and emigration. Now, at the beginning of the twenty-first century, only a small fraction of these oral traditions remain alive among Jewish women in contemporary Morocco. Yet, Jewish women's voices have not been completely silenced.

Rabbinic Discussions on *Kol Isha*: Global and Local Interpretations

Global Interpretations

The rabbis of the Talmud (and those for centuries to come) discussed throughout the text if it is the woman's spoken or singing voice that is considered nakedness (*erva*).[15] In true Talmudic fashion, the opinions have covered a wide spectrum of thought, and there has been no consensus that establishes a clear decision. The most lenient states that a woman's voice is only prohibited while a man is praying the *keriat shema*, the statement of God's unity that requires a special state of concentration. The strictest ruling states that a man may not even speak to a woman that is not his wife or a close blood relative, because it crosses the boundaries of modesty between the sexes.

The insinuation that a woman's voice can be sexually stimulating, a nakedness of sorts, "*erva*" gave birth to strict laws around women's singing in mixed company.[16] Saul Berman, an Orthodox Rabbi and professor of Jewish law at Columbia University, has argued that the primary sources stressed a "purely functional concern,"[17] that is, that a woman's voice would distract a man from his prayers. However, certain important *poskim* (rabbis who make Jewish legal decisions) have not agreed with a strict reading of the Talmud. Rabbis from Ashkenazi, Sephardi, and Mizrahi interpreted traditions related to *kol'isha* in different ways.

Tenth-century Rabbi Hai Gaon of Iraq, for example, ruled that a man should not recite the *Shema*[18] when a woman is singing because *kol b'ishah ervah*, but when she is just talking normally it is permitted; and even if she is singing, if he can concentrate in his heart on his prayer so that he does not hear her or pay attention to her – it is permissible.[19] Interestingly, Hai Gaon allowed that a man could recite the *Shema* when a woman is singing if he is able to ignore her voice.

Rabbi Yitzhak Alfasi or "The Rif," was born in the eleventh century at Kala't ibn Ḥamad, and is still considered to be one of the most influential *poskim* in the Jewish world. He ignored Samuel's statement in both passages in the Babylonian Talmud, Berachot 24a and Kiddushin 70a–b. *Hilkhot Harif*, Rabbi Yitzhak's compendium (*Talmud Kattan*) codified Jewish law by abbreviating each *sugya*[20] (statements that are the building blocks of the Talmud) in the Talmud. In his code on *Kiddushin*,[21] the Talmudic tractate on wedding contracts, he quoted the dicta of Samuel quoted by Rabbi Yehudah but omitted the dictum *kol b'ishah ervah*. This omission indicates that he considered all four of the *Amoraic*[22] (codification from 500 CE) statements in *Berakhot*, the tractate containing Samuel's statement, to be Aggadah, not Halachah – in other words, commentary, not law.

The Rif's disregard for *kol 'isha* rulings points to a medieval Moroccan approach to women's voices as a normal and unproblematic part of life.

In the seventeenth century, the stringent approach to Jewish women's singing was first suggested as a possible interpretation by Rabbi Joshua Falk[23] in his *Perishah* to *Tur Even Haezer* 21, subparagraph 2, though he ultimately rejected it. The first to actually apply severe rules was Rabbi Moshe Sofer,[24] an influential Rabbi from Frankfurt, Germany. However, nineteenth-century Rabbi Hizkiyahu Medini (1832/4?–1904), from a Sephardic rabbinic dynasty and author of the *Sde Hemed*, ruled that men and women generally were permitted to sing together.

Contrary to rabbis in medieval Morocco, Spain and southern France, nineteenth-century Ashkenazi rabbis from Central and Eastern Europe ruled that men are forbidden to listen to women singing at all times. This ruling did not make its way to Jewish communities in urban and rural Morocco in the nineteenth and early twentieth centuries, as confirmed by historical sources who gave detailed descriptions of Jewish women's singing before mixed gender groups.[25]

Hatam Sofer's strict ruling was adopted by many later authorities, including Rabbi Ovadia Yosef (1920–2013), the Chief Sephardic Rabbi of Israel of Iraqi background. At the same time, however, in Ashkenazi Orthodox circles some tried to find "leniencies," such as allowing girls and boys to sing at the same time[26] or allowing men to listen to women who cannot be seen, such as on a record or on the radio. In 1998, I was given a ruling saying that listening to a woman's voice through a microphone is allowed because the voice is transformed as it passes through the microphone's system.[27]

Local Interpretations

In Morocco, the law of *kol isha* was traditionally applied in the context of public ritual within the synagogue, following the public-private duality that is intimately related to traditional gender divisions within the Jewish community. Jewish law expects and encourages men to lead in the public sphere while women have their freedom and leadership roles in the private sphere.

Rabbi Jacky S., who was born and raised in Morocco, told me that men should not listen to women's singing voices. At the same time, he specified that in Morocco there has always been the "*halachic*" part of Jewish life and the "folkloric" part of Jewish life. According to Rabbi S., in the folkloric aspects of life women routinely have sung at wedding celebrations, henna parties,[28] and other communal celebrations, that is, in primarily familial contexts. He argued that the real issue was whether a woman was singing in a "performative" setting where she would become the center of attention. Rabbi S., who studied Jewish law in England, follows the Ashkenazi ruling, and will not listen to the voice of a woman who is not his mother, wife, or daughter – whether in a public or private setting.

Minhag Hamakom and the Globalization of Rabbinic Laws

A Jewish traveler must adapt and follow the ruling of the community that he is in. This is, of course, assuming that the ruling is within the parameters of accepted law. This notion of local tradition is called *minhag hamakom*. Morocco has been a crossroads for Jewish travelers as far back as the sixteenth century.[29] However, the leadership vacuum brought about by the massive emigration of Moroccan Jews, and the corresponding diminishing of the religious and communal establishment, seems to have led to a religious climate in which foreign rabbis feel they have the right and the obligation to impose what they consider to be the only correct reading of the *halacha*.[30] Consequently, many Moroccan Jews have adopted traditions and rulings from outside of Morocco.

On the opposite side of this situation are young Jews of Moroccan ancestry who were born and raised outside of Morocco. A virtual Moroccan *halachic* community was founded in 2008 by two university students from Toronto, who were confronted by other young Moroccans about practices that are specifically Moroccan and inspired to start this project. They have a YouTube channel called *Darké Abotenou* (The Path of Our Ancestors) that sends weekly *halachic* rulings from Morocco, and has over 5,000 daily subscribers in both English and French.[31]

Back in Morocco however, Moroccan Jews continue to feel the intrusion of Jewish law from outside their own tradition. In the twentieth century, the emergence of a Jewish state meant that rabbinic rulings from Israel became a source of rabbinical legitimacy in the Jewish world. Even though no centralized leadership exists in Judaism, the chief Rabbis of Israel, as the spiritual and legal leaders of observant Jews in Israel, have become the *de facto* religious leaders of the Jewish world.

Historically though, Morocco has had a chief Rabbi, centralized for all Moroccan Jews and based in Casablanca. The chief rabbi at the time of this writing is Rabbi Aaron Monsonego, who has held the position since 1998. However, since 2012 he has resided outside Morocco because of his declining health. While he was in Morocco, he represented the highest authority for Moroccan Jewish rulings. Now that he is infirm and physically absent from Morocco, however, his legitimacy as Chief Rabbi is in question. Because the Jewish community in Morocco feels it would not be correct to strip him of his title as Chief Rabbi, the vacuum in religious leadership is being negotiated in various ways. One is the further internationalization of Moroccan Jewish traditions. Jews currently living in Casablanca have expressed concern that these increasing changes are altering the face of Moroccan Judaism.

Since the 1960 arrival in Casablanca of the Chabad Lubavitch emissary Rabbi Yehuda Leib Raskin,[32] many Moroccan Jews have become involved in the practice of Jewish law according to Hasidic custom. Some within the community, for example, have adopted the Hasidic approach to Jewish law, such as women who have begun to use a wig for their hair covering instead of the traditional Moroccan scarf.

Jewish visitors and visiting rabbis also have pushed Moroccan congregants to adopt rulings that are from other parts of the Jewish world. Some Moroccan synagogues have adopted new rulings, thinking they will be in line with the larger Jewish world, while others defend the practice of Moroccan Jewish customs:

Someone came here to tell me we had to change the way we did things regarding the lighting of the light of the synagogue by the non-Jewish guard. But we have always done it like this here and I don't want someone to come from Jerusalem and tell me how I have to run my synagogue in Casablanca. Because we live here and we have traditions here and we have a way that we have done our things here, and that our Rabbis and parents did things, following the *Halacha* in a way that is according to our ways.[33]

In the same way that some Moroccan rabbinic authorities feel they must guard the Moroccan ways transmitted to them by their elders, some women feel they must follow the traditional Moroccan Jewish laws surrounding kosher meat. Alegria B., who was raised in the 1940s in Ksar El Kebir, a small town in northwestern Morocco said in an interview in 2011:

They think they need to come to teach me how to make a chicken kosher?! The Rabbi's wife was teaching me how to kosherize a chicken, can you believe that? I don't need them to come and teach me the things that my mother and grandmother taught me before Lubavitch was even in Morocco. I have been doing those things since I was a child.[34]

In a conversation with Marcelle S., an observant Jew who has lived in Casablanca since the 1960s, I learned that before Lubavitch arrived in Morocco in the 1950s, there never had been an issue concerning women's voices. Marcelle S. is well versed in Jewish law and follows religious laws with commitment. She observed:

They came with the idea that they were here to educate our girls, to teach us how to be "good Jewish women" so to speak! As if our own mothers hadn't taught us well how to be good Jewish women … me, I don't ascribe to this business of women not singing, it was never like this before in Morocco.[35]

Ellen Koskoff, an anthropologist who has studied the Lubavitch movement says that their concern is to preserve the essential binary gender contrasts at the heart of Lubavitcher identity.[36] Moroccan Judaism long has functioned with a great degree of gender segregation, making the issue of women's singing at communal celebrations not a binding legal issue.

Jewish Women's Singing Practices before Moroccan Independence

Before Morocco's independence, women performed vernacular, secular, sacred and semi-sacred songs in gender-separate and gender-mixed groups. The variety of situations, languages, and musical genres represented in these performances reflects the universality of women's singing in Moroccan Jewish life, and its entertainment as well as ritual value (see Figure 11.2).

Examples of Judeo-Arabic Practices

During the *Tahdid* ceremony, which is still performed the entire week between a boy's birth and circumcision, men sing a series of liturgical

Figure 11.2 Celebrating the bride during the weeklong festivities in Tangier. After a drawing by Beauclerk during his voyage in 1826.

poems and mystical prayers – believed to protect the baby – while simultaneously tapping the corners of the room with a sword. Not all parts of this ritual have remained in the oral tradition. I have heard reports of women's participation in the singing, which is no longer in use today. Men and women would sing a humorous responsive improvisation in Judeo-Arabic, with the men inside the door and the women outside the door of the room where the baby slept. The women asked for the baby in song and both men and women sang off-color jokes. Both men and women tried to come up with the best lines and all would end in peals of laughter.[37]

Jauk Amram Elmaleh talked about his bar mitzvah party in the early 1950s in Casablanca (see Figure 11.3). His mother Zahra Mechaly who was a widow, wrote a song for him in Darija, the local Moroccan Arabic dialect. She stood in front of the guests and sang it to him while being accompanied by a saxophonist from the party's band.[38]

Examples of Judeo-Berber Practices

For centuries, Berber Jewish women would sing Ahidus[39] (Amazigh line dances and songs) during wedding and communal celebrations.

Figure 11.3 Zahra Mechaly, Jauk Amram Elmaleh's mother singing a song she wrote for the occasion at his bar mitzvah in Casablanca in 1957.

Interestingly, Muslim and Jewish Ahidus appear to be very similar, but further scholarship is still required to confirm nuanced differences and similarities. In the case of the Agzdour, a rhythmic mourning ritual involving a sing-song voice and feet tapping, Berber Jewish women would practice this ritual together with their Muslim neighbors as late as 1947.

In contrast, in one wedding ritual Berber women would sing for the bride call-and-response wedding songs. These "poetry duels" listed the blessings women wished the bride to have in her married life. Wishes for fertility, prosperity, happiness and *shalom bait* (family peace) would be among the main wishes bestowed by the older generation of women to the young bride. Some of these songs also instructed her on sexuality and the secrets of married relationships.[40]

Examples of Judeo-Spanish Practices

In the Moroccan town of Ksar el Kebir, until the 1940s, women would sing all night for a woman who had just given birth (*parida*), as well as for a baby boy the night before his circumcision. In addition, in the week preceding Passover, as women gathered and spent the entire night cooking Passover *Matza* (unleavened bread) for the community in the communal oven – which had been made kosher for Passover – they would sing songs until dawn.[41]

The traditional women's repertoire included songs of different genres: narrative poems for the bride with a repeating melodic phrase that spoke about faithfulness and unfaithfulness (Romances), *coplas*[42] for holidays such as Purim and Passover, *romances* about incest that served as lullabies, and *endechas* for the mourning period of Tisha Be'Av (the ninth of the Hebrew month of Av).[43]

The texts of these songs served as musical commentaries that women would sing when faced with different situations. Maurice H., originally from Tangier, shared his belief that the songs women sang served as means of expressing that which was unmentionable in normal conversation, "when they sang these songs they probably were saying what they felt they could not say in conversation. But they were themes that they felt they must address."[44]

Jewish Women's Singing Practices after Moroccan Independence

After Moroccan independence internal migration followed, displacing large groups of Jews towards the urban capital. These displacements from the community of origin were influential in the diminishing of certain oral traditions, because of the loss of the original communal context. Below, I present some anecdotes of remaining oral traditions sung by women in recent years in Morocco.

In February 2013 I attended a celebratory lunch for the circumcision of twin boys at Neve Chalom, one of the most observant synagogues in Casablanca. The mother's aunts, who currently live in Spain, were visiting for the birth. Their table of only women was positioned in the center of the room. In the middle of the lunch celebration, the women broke out singing the Romance (or Ballad) of Rahel Lastimoza while tapping the table in rhythm with their hands. In Moroccan Judeo-Spanish, its call-and-response Arabic refrain makes it one of the most participatory songs of the repertoire.

Just after the women sang, a table of men at the event immediately started to sing liturgical poems (*piyyutim*) in Hebrew. I understood their reaction in a broader context, as resulting from the almost complete elimination of traditional Moroccan women's singing in semi-sacred contexts. Thus, these younger men could not relate to this song as being appropriate in a context such as a Sabbath communal meal, that is, in a semi-sacred time and place.

During the late afternoon of a Yom Kippur in the fall of 2012, a woman whose husband was dying sang a *piyyut* (liturgical poem) from the women's section of the synagogue. Her voice rung out throughout the nave, and did not stop singing even after an ultra-Orthodox man visiting from Israel tried to silence her. She continued to sing until she had finished the text, and the ten to fifteen women in attendance came up to congratulate her afterwards.

In another instance, in March 2014, during the party for a bar mitzvah[45] celebration in Casablanca, the boy's maternal grandmother sang a Judeo-Arabic wedding song called *Ya Nass*. She sang it into the microphone in the synagogue's party hall after the luncheon that was served the morning after he wore *tefilin* (phylacteries) for the first time. As she sang, henna was put on his hands and on the hands of everyone present.

In February 2015, at David HaMelech, a large congregation in Casablanca's Ain Diab neighborhood, a celebration took place on the completion of a Sefer Torah, a scroll of the Torah. The completed scroll in its silver case was placed on a table in front of the rabbi, who was visiting from Jerusalem. After some deliberation, women sang in Judeo-Arabic to the rabbi. The main singer, a woman in her early fifties, explained this was a traditional song that she has always sung for this Tsaddik (Jewish saint).

The aunts singing at the communal Shabbat lunch and the soon-to-be widow singing from the women's gallery in the synagogue functioned as agents of resistance. When the aunts sang Rahel Lastimoza at the same time as the regular Shabbat liturgical poems (*piyyutim*) being sung by the men during the lunch at the synagogue, they inserted their understanding of what is accepted in Jewish law.

Moroccan Jewish Women's Voices in the Public Sphere

Moroccan Jews are culturally Moroccan, and the politics of gender in Moroccan Jewish circles is similar to that of Moroccan Muslims. Moroccan Jews are similarly segregated and gender-mixed group meetings outside of the family unit occur infrequently. At the same time, this traditional gender segregation permits women and men a certain independence of speech regarding the opposite sex. Groups of men invariably make jokes about women, and groups of women invariably disparage men, usually through song. One example is the wedding song exhorting the bride to prepare a turnip soup for the weak groom so that he may satisfy her sexual desire.

Mixed gender gatherings typically occur during Jewish life-cycle celebrations and communal holiday celebrations in Morocco. The public and private realms meet during such celebrations when women usually sing *los cantares antiguos*,[46] (the ancient songs) as they are called in Northern Morocco, or Ahidus (traditional Amazigh line dance and songs) and song duels in the Amazigh Jewish tradition. In these group gatherings men's musical contributions are usually limited to reciting the standard prayers for weddings or singing *piyyutim* (liturgical poetry) in Hebrew for the bride.

Although men lead the public ceremonies in the synagogue and the reading of the Torah from the lower level, many women privately participate in the balcony through prayer and song. This is not exclusive to the Jews of Northern Morocco, however, as Kay Kaufman Shelemay described in her book on Syrian Jewish prayer women "quietly singing along in their own, separate section of the synagogue or home."[47] Further, in spring 2008 in Tangier I saw learned women shout out corrections to the reader of the Torah from above when he made a mistake, and in October 2015 in Casablanca, I witnessed the men calling up to the women to ululate during the holiday celebrating the Torah (Simhat Torah). While the women ululated, they showered the men's section with candy.

Women's actual voices continue to be heard in the synagogue as punctuation with the *yuyus* ululating down from the women's gallery in celebration of a birth, bar mitzvah, marriage, or other moment of communal religious celebration. This ululation is the same as that of Moslem Moroccan women and also exists amongst other Mizrahi Jews. Since these *are* women's voices within the synagogue, the only explanation I can see for this ululation being sanctioned and requested in the celebration is because it is a high-pitched sung sound that is not derived from text, and therefore cannot be seen as a prayer or a song. Thus, the participation of women through ululation is simply locally recognized as a cultural exclamation of celebration.

Some Moroccan Jewish women sang publicly on stage in the 1940s. The most famous in the public sphere was Fez-native Zohra el Fassia, considered to be one of the great Judeo-Arabic popular song performers. Zohra sang at weddings and even at official communal gatherings. In Rabat at the beginning of the 1960s, during a gala evening for the Alliance Israelite Universelle schools, Zohra performed. Rabbis from Rabat, as well as Morocco's Great Rabbi, Shaul Ibn Danan, were in attendance for the gala, but left after the ceremonial portion – before Zohra began to sing.[48] This anecdote about Zohra's participation in the national gala dinner of the Jewish educational establishment of Morocco shows that by the 1960s, some Moroccan rabbis were making a public demonstration of not listening to a professional woman performer. However, the educational institution invited her to be the star of the evening because of her popularity.

Moroccan Jewish Women's Voices in the Private Sphere

Women's Judaism in Morocco is more visible in home-based or private practices and includes private silent repetitive ritual actions as well as music and song. Women's songs are dominant in the private realm of family, women-only groups, and communal life-cycle celebrations.

Jewish women are in charge of the ritual aspects in the home. Laws of family purity (*Taharat haMishpacha*) and appropriate food preparation and consumption (*Kashrut*) are completely entrusted to the woman. The woman is in charge of the purity (*tahara*) of the food that nourishes the body; and by following laws of family purity, the children she bears will either be considered more or less pure (*Tahor*). In Judaism, the creation of life and its sustenance exist within the feminine domain. The woman is the one who creates the physical container for spirituality.

The Inherent Fragility of Orality[49]

At all of the public communal life cycle celebrations of Moroccan Jews women's sung voices have traditionally been center stage. It is telling that the Haketía, Judeo-Arabic, and Judeo-Berber languages, with their deeply emotional forms of expression, are the languages linked to Moroccan Jewish women's cultural contributions. The changes brought about in the Protectorate period and by the Alliance Israélite Universelle schools were not only linguistic but also structural. Schools were transformative for gender roles and educational and economic opportunities for women. Young Jewish girls were educated in the Alliance schools, which ensured that they knew how to read, write, speak French, and learn a trade such as teaching or sewing. It is clear from my interviews that women who considered themselves educated learned more French and Spanish literature and fewer traditional songs and proverbs[50]. Julia B. from Asilah, a coastal town in Northwest Morocco, who worked in banking in Tangier for over thirty years, described the erosion of these oral traditions:[51]

I'm not talking about when things were progressing more and more and we started taking everything in a more modern manner. We'd say, that's not in fashion, that used to be sung in the olden days, my mother sang that, no, it's not in style anymore and so everything was being sung less and less, and all those songs of the Romancero[52] started to get lost. It was like that. [53]

This gradual shift away from the centrality of Moroccan Jewish traditional languages and oral sung repertory permitted women from Jewish Morocco to feel less bound to traditional gender roles. Gender roles had been drilled into young girls through songs highlighting their importance, but the language shift brought changes that led to an erosion of oral traditions (Figure 11.4). Many Jewish women in Morocco were confronted with opposing internalized views of what their contribution to their community and families could and should be. European, American, and Israeli models of women's emancipated roles provided enough inspiration to push many young Jewish women to leave for their studies and never return.

Today, most of the women who stayed in Morocco follow a predominantly patriarchal way of life. Husbands, fathers, or fathers-in-law play the traditional role of family patriarch regarding finances, decisions that affect the family publicly, and women's public activities. Women resist this patriarchal control through subterfuge rather than direct confrontation. And despite the erosion of women's songs, they are still celebrated as important cultural signposts.

Figure 11.4 Sultana Azeroual singing Judeo-Sahraoui women's songs, October 20, 2015, Casablanca.

Conclusion

In my research I have observed and/or recorded numerous instances of women singing Jewish songs with men present. The generally accepted communal interpretation forbidding women's voices is limited to the synagogue. Oral traditions of Moroccan Jewish women that have been passed down through generations by song have eroded over the last century, as women have replaced Judeo-Spanish, Judeo-Arabic, and Judeo-Berber languages with European languages.

Moroccan Judaism has historically recognized the power and centrality of women's contributions to the community. Dietary laws *(kashrut)*, preparation for Shabbat and kindling its lights and laws concerning sexual purity are the three realms of observance women control. These all center on the private sphere, the realm of women's power within the structure of Jewish communities.

Creating a musical group where women can gather to sing, learn, transmit, and share the songs of their mothers and grandmothers can nourish this latest generation's buried dreams of women's public participation by highlighting the centrality of their oral traditions to Jewish Moroccan history.

Endnotes

1 Various people were instrumental in the preparation of this article. I would like to extend my thanks to Paul Hamburg, David Hirsch, Chaim Seidler-Feller, Ron Duncan-Hart, Rabbi Moshe Cohen, Jayme Harpring, Doris Gray and Rachel Richman as well as to the discussions during the Gender and Women's Empowerment Workshop at Al Akhawayn University in March 2015.

2 Chetrit, J. (1986). "Stratégies discursives dans la langue des femmes judéo-arabophones du Maroc." *Massorot* II, pp. 41–66; (2003). *The Jewish Traditional Marriage: Interpretive and Documentary Chapters.* Haifa: University of Haifa; (2013). "Formation and diversity of Jewish languages and of Judeo-Arabic in North Africa I. Middle Arabic and its forms of hybridization." *Journal of Jewish Languages.* Vol. 1, No. 2, pp. 177–206.

3 Weich-Shahak, S. (1997). *Romancero sefardí de Marruecos.* Madrid: Alpuerto.

4 Anahory-Librowicz, O. (1980). *Florilegio de romances sefardíes de la diáspora (una colección malagueña).* Madrid: Catedra Seminario Menéndez Pidal.

5 Chetrit, J. "Formation and diversity," p. 95.

6 Zafrani, H. (1998). *Deux mille ans de vie juive au Maroc: histoire et culture, religion et magie.* Paris: Maisonneuve & Larose, p. 13.

7 Ibid.

8 These statistics are from the Joint Distribution Committee's internal numbers.

9 Available at http://lnt.ma/tourisme-religieux-le-retour-des-juifs-au-maroc/ (accessed June 23, 2016). "Toutefois, ce sont plus de 140 000 touristes juifs qui visitent annuellement le Royaume dont la majorité vient surtout d'Israël (à noter que ce sont plus de 900 000 Marocains de confession juive qui vivent en Israël), de la France, du Canada et des Etats-Unis d'Amérique."

10 Berdugo, S. (March 2010). "La communauté marocaine: communauté matricielle et diasporas." Speech given in Essaouira to open a colloquium on migrations in the Maghreb. Reprinted in *La bienvenue et l'adieu: Migrations au Maghreb XVe–XXe* (2012). Vol. 3, pp. 7–14.

11 Serge Berdugo gave a talk on this topic during the March 2010 conference in Essaouira on Jewish migrations from the Maghreb.

12 Heilman, S. (December 2005). "The Chabad Lubavitch movement: filling the Jewish vacuum worldwide." Jerusalem Center for Public Affairs.

13 Talmud. Berachot 24a and Kiddushin 70a–b.

14 Private interview with his widow Alegria B. January 2008.

15 In the Talmud and writings on the Talmud: Berachot 24a, Kiddushin 70a and Sotah 48a. R. Judah the Hasid in Sefer Hasidim Bologna sec. 313; Zarua (Laws of Keriat Shema sec 133); Maharal in the Gur Aryeh Bereshit 18.9; Rabad in Chidushei haRashba, Berachot 25a, R. Jacob ben Asher, Tur O.H. sec 560, Sde Chemed, Ma'arachet kuf klaf 42, in the name of Succat David, R. Yosef Karo Bet Yosef O.H. no. 75, Orach Haim Hagahot Maimoniot 75, Rav Hai Gaon Otzar HaGeonim, Berachot Sec 102, P. 30, quoted in Mordechai, Berachot sec 80, Rabbenu Hananel Otzar HaGeonim, Berachot, Perush R. Hananel 24a p. 24 quoted in Rabiah, Berachot sec 76, Ba'al HaTurim does not speak about the forbidden nature of a woman's voice during Shema (O.H. chp 75), Rambam says it's forbidden always except during Keriat Shema, Divrei Hefetz quotes Sde Hemed says hearing a woman sing a love song is the only forbidden voice – Ma'arechet Kuf, rule 42, The HIDA in Petach Einayim (Avida Zara 20a), Sde Hemet Ma'arachet Kol Sefer HaEshkol Hilchot tefila Sec 4.

16 Berman, S. (1980). "Kol Isha." *Rabbi Joseph H. Lookstein Memorial Volume.* L. Landman (ed.). New Jersey: Ktav Publishing House, pp. 54–55.

17 Ibid, p. 48. It is clear that the central concern with hearing a woman's voice is not in its intrinsic sensuousness, but the purely functional concern that it might distract a man from his concentration on prayer or study. It is certainly significant that the sole contexts in which the law of Kol 'Isha [woman's voice] is held applicable are ones which require some special degree of attentiveness, and in which distraction is of particular concern.

18 The quintessential Jewish prayer stating God as one: *Shema Israel, Ad-nai Elo-heinu, Ad-nai Ehad.*

19 Lewin, B.M. (1931). *Otzar ha-Geonim: Thesaurus of the Gaonic Responsa and Commentaries Following the Order of the Talmudic Tractates.* Jerusalem: The Hebrew University Press Association.

20 The building blocks of the Talmud, a proof-based elaboration of a Mishna.

21 Vilna Talmud version. Folio 30b.

22 Codifiers of the Babylonian Talmud, ca. 500 CE.

23 Poland, 1555–1614 CE.
24 Sofer, H. "Responsa." *Hoshen Mishpat*, No. 190.
25 Ortega, M.L. (1994). *Los Hebreos en Marruecos*. Málaga: Algazara. Re-edition from the original from Madrid, 1919; Picciotto, M.H. (1860). *Jews of Morocco, Report*. Tangier: Printed for the use of members of the committee only and not for circulation. Copy in Houghton Library, Harvard University; Fernández, A.P. (1905). *Españoles sin Patria y la Raza Sefardí*. Madrid: E. Teodoro; Watson, R.S. (1880). *A Visit to Wazan: The Sacred City of Morocco*. London: Macmillan.
26 Weinberg, Y.Y. (1999). *Shut Seridei Eish*. World Heritage Encyclopedia.
27 Private Conversation with Rabbi Yehoshua Levin-Landau at the Beth El Machon Roni women's Yeshiva in the Old City of Jerusalem, August 1998.
28 Henna is used in Jewish Morocco during life cycle celebrations on the eve of the ceremony to ward off the evil eye. The wedding henna party has become an elaborate festivity which includes a heavily adorned and symbolic bridal dress and songs evoking the couple's fertility and the bride's beauty.
29 García-Arenal, M. and G. Wiegers (2003). *A Man of Three Worlds: Samuel Pallache, A Moroccan Jew in Catholic and Protestant Europe*. Translated by M. Beagles. London: The Johns Hopkins University Press, p. 26.
30 Interviews and private conversations with David E., Rabbi S., Michel A. and Haim A.
31 Available at www.darkeabotenou.com (accessed October 15, 2015).
32 Available at http://judaism.stackexchange.com/questions/8373/what-is-the-typical-retirement-plan-for-a-chabad-lubavitch-shliach-emissary (accessed February 10, 2015).
33 Interview with RSJ. February 2015.
34 Creen que van a venir a enseñarme como kasherizar un pollo! La Rebisa estaba diciéndome cómo kasherizar un pollo, lo puedes creer? Yo no necesito que ellos vengan a enseñarme las cosas que mi madre y mi abuela me enseñaron antes de que Lubavitch estuviera en Marruecos. He estado haciendo esas cosas desde que era niña, y de pensar que ellos creen que necesitamos que vengan para enseñárnoslas. Interview with Alegria B. March 2013, Casablanca.
35 Interview with Marcelle S. February 19, 2015, Casablanca.
36 From the Lubavitcher point of view, then, *kol isha* and many other laws of Orthodox Judaism are socially agreed-upon rules for various forms of interaction between men and women that guard against their loss of sexual and physical control. In controlling women's voices, Lubavitchers (both men and women) believe that they are balancing out the shift of

power that might result in group disintegration if women were permitted true freedom, for in such a case the animal soul would dominate. Such laws are thus necessary to Lubavitcher life, for they preserve the essential binary contrasts that lie at the heart of Lubavitcher identity and form the underlying structure of Lubavitcher social relations. Koskoff, E. (1995). "Myriam sings her song: the self and the other in anthropological discourse." *Musicology and Difference: Gender and Sexuality in Music Scholarship*. R.A. Solid (ed.). Berkeley: University of California Press, pp. 149–163.

37 Interview with Jacob W. July 10, 2013, Casablanca.

38 Interview with Amram E. January 24, 2014, Casablanca.

39 Traditional dance and song which is practiced by Amazigh tribes in the Middle and High Atlas. Men and women standing side by side sing in Tamazight and punctuate the song with the *bendir*, a percussion instrument.

40 Interview with Marie B. November 2011.

41 Interviews with Alegria B. and Lili B. 2014.

42 Strophic songs, in many occasions they were paraliturgical songs.

43 Three week period which mourns the destruction of the first and second Temples of Jerusalem and many calamities which befell the Jewish people

44 Interview with Maurice H. July 15, 2012, Paris.

45 A Bar Mitzvah is a celebration to mark the change of status from boy to man when a boy turns 13.

46 The songs sung by "ancient" women. Interview with Sonia C. March 2008.

47 Shelemay, K.K. (1998). *Let Jasmine Rain Down: Song and Remembrance among Syrian Jews*. Chicago: University of Chicago Press, p. 4.

48 E-mail correspondence with Rabbi Moshe Cohen. February 17, 2015.

49 What kind of language can supply this need of transmission and still remain oral? The answer would seem to lie in *ritualized utterance*, a traditional language which somehow becomes formally repeatable like a ritual in which the words remain in a fixed order. Such language has to be memorized. There is no other way of guaranteeing its survival. Ritualization becomes the means of memorization. The memories are personal, belonging to every man, woman and child in the community, yet their content, the language preserved, is communal, something shared by the community as expressing its tradition and its historical identity. Havelock, E.A. (1986). *The Muse Learns to Write: Reflections on Orality and Literacy from Antiquity to the Present*. New Haven: Yale University Press, p. 70.

50 Interviews with Rogelia M. January 21, 2011, Tangier; Hilda Pinto. June 2008, Tangier; Simone Mellul. February 10, 2014, Paris; Marie Benhamou. January 20, 2015, Casablanca.

51 Interview with Julia B. April 7, 2008, Tangier.
52 Sephardi long narrative poem-songs in Judeo-Spanish.
53 "No te hablo de cuando ya mas tarde que fue progresando la cosa y
   fuimos tomándolo todo a lo mas moderno. Y decíamos ay no eso ya no
   es de moda, eso lo cantaban antiguamente, eso lo cantaba mi madre,
   no eso ya no es de moda y ya se empezó a cantar menos, todas
   esas canciones del romancero que se fueron perdiendo. Entonces pues
   era así."

12 Customary Law and Women's Rights among the Imazighen of the Middle Atlas and Southeast Morocco

MICHAEL PEYRON

Introduction

Women in the Moroccan Atlas have long labored under the writ of Customary Law, at the beck and call of their husbands and elder brothers, as hewers of wood and drawers of water. So it may seem strange to be discussing women's emancipation in relation to a traditionally minded population. However, as this chapter will show, there is progress with regards to greater gender equality for women in the Atlas Mountains.

Perceived in Morocco as an institution linked to a backwoods culture, *azerf* long had a strongly negative connotation among the more educated urban elite. With time, however, intelligent (*bel maɛqul*) attitudes took over, bearing in mind advances made elsewhere in respect to laws governing family relations. This chapter focuses on the extent to which the more malleable Customary Law of the Atlas Mountain region has affected gender-related matters over the past century up to the present day, and how it has been a harbinger of broader changes. In this chapter, an attempt will then be made to chart the progress of Amazigh women in being considered as equal partners by their men. The reader will no doubt agree that, overall, even if there is a long way to go before they achieve full parity, Amazigh women have made some recent major gains in terms of their emancipation, especially since King Mohamed VI's 2004 announcement of reforms to the *moudawana*, as Moroccan family law is called.

Contemporary researchers are fortunate in that written material on Amazigh culture, most of it in French, is readily available. Some is the result of Protectorate period (1912–1956) scholarship, and some of it is attributable to recent investigations by native speakers of Tamazight, as well as other researchers, including some from the United States, who have refocused on rural Morocco. The chapter is buttressed by my own fieldwork in the area of Amazigh oral tradition over the past forty years, an endeavor which involved learning Tamazight, the Middle Atlas variant of the Berber language.

Customary Law

Although the origins of this institution are shrouded in uncertainty, early references to Customary Law date back to Almohad times.[1] In the Middle Atlas, among the previously tent-dwelling Ayt Ndhir, Ayt Myill, or Ichqern tribes, it was known as *azerf* (also spelled *azref*, *izerf*, pl. *izerfan*) in Tamazight, while among the Izayyan, who were strongly Arabized after Moha ou Hammou had become a Makhzen (*caïd*), the term *lεurf/εurf* was used.[2] Further south another term appeared, *taεqqit* (pl. *taεqqidin*), especially in the Ayt Hadiddou, Ayt Morghad, and Ayt 'Atta tribal areas. Guennoun referred to Customary Law by a descriptive synonym, *abrid n lždud* (literally "path of the ancestors").[3] As for the Ayt Morghad, they were famous for their special court of appeal, the *ayt lheqq*, which used to meet under the aegis of the Irbiben clan at Tana. An institution highly respected for its impartiality, its rulings were unfailingly accepted by all and sundry.[4]

   Certain items of Customary Law have attracted scholars' attention, such as collective weddings (*timġriwin*). Long a well-respected custom among the Ayt Sukhman and Ayt Yafelman tribes, the most famous of these weddings still occurs in the autumn, a couple of months after a great gathering of the clans at the *agdud* of Sidi Hmad Oulmeghni, site of the tomb of this holy man in the High Atlas mountains.[5] Custom continues to govern various aspects of marriage, including repudiation (*uluf*), one rationale for which is captured in the Amazigh proverb *aryaz nna wr tri tmettut ammi wr yiwil!* (The man whose wife loves him not is little better than a bachelor!) All in all, with its flexibility and relative swiftness, *azerf* was remarkably well adapted to the former nomadic and self-governing lifestyle of Middle Atlas Imazighen.

Arabo-Amazigh Customary Law Documents

Until about the sixteenth century each group's *azerf* would be oral, and communities relied on the ability of elders sitting on the *džemaεt* (assembly of "greybeards") to faithfully memorize each item of the village code. In the seventeenth and eighteenth centuries, as Islam penetrated the High Atlas, Amazigh tribal leaders began to commit Customary Law to paper in order to obviate possible errors, omissions, favoritism, or fading memories. A brief perusal of these codes reveals several dispositions applying to women.

Local scholars of Amazigh origin have described similar documents, discovered elsewhere in Southeast Morocco during the postindependence period. Larbi Mezzine, for example, published a remarkable historical survey in which he translated the *taɛqqit* of the *qser* (castle) of Lgara in Tafilalt, together with other significant texts, including the *tayssa* (charter) of Asul, dating back to 1645. The last-named document is an invaluable item of reference as it lists all the major Amazigh groups gravitating within the orbit of the *dila' zawiya* at that time.[6] Another researcher, Mohammed el Manouar, has focused on the Dades Valley to the southeast, bringing to light more *izerfan* (Customary Law documents) couched in the same Arabo-Amazigh language.[7] Both scholars have pointed out that a thorough appreciation of these texts, with their strong earthy tang and important insights into the mechanisms of pre-Saharan societies, requires a sound knowledge of Classical Arabic, not to mention Moroccan Arabic and Tamazight.

Customary Law and Qur'anic Law

While conventional wisdom has highlighted a supposed incompatibility between *azerf* and *ššraɛ* (Qur'anic Law), in fact the two have mutually influenced each other for centuries, for example, in areas where the central government's hold was tenuous, or in periods of strife, such as during the sixteenth-century Portuguese invasion.[8] In fact, by 1908 another observer had noticed that among the Ayt 'Atta of Taouz, "a clause in their penal code allowed plaintiffs to resort to Qur'anic Law in the event of a simple law-suit."[9] To put this into perspective, even today Customary Law often complements Qur'anic Law, in certain cases being the only legal framework locally available.

In the Tounfit High Atlas some degree of co-existence between *ššraɛ* and *azerf/ɛurf* was still observable in the early 1980s. In fact, child marriage – one of the more conspicuous aspects of Customary Law – has survived in the area to the present day, and is seen locally as a sensible marital strategy. Several cases have been reported quite recently of early betrothal and actual marriage of girls barely past puberty among the Ayt 'Ameur of Anefgou,[10] a remote mountain clan where life goes on much as it has for centuries, with winter cold, in particular, causing great hardship. I will elaborate on early marriage later in the chapter.

That the two legal forms are complementary in nature there is little doubt. As Kherdi points out, "One can unhesitatingly affirm that the two do not constitute watertight compartments. There is no incompatibility between Qur'anic and Customary Law."[11] Other scholars make no mystery of the fact that, whereas for centuries Imazighen had recourse to *ššraɛ* for most cases, in penal and contractual matters they would generally fall back on *azerf*.[12] A far more recent illustration of the same idea was provided in 2012 by a member of the Ayt Merghad tribe named Bassou Ou-Yasser: "Customary Law was largely based on Qur'anic Law, thus were the two complementary" (*temtabaɛ tɛeqqit d ššraɛ, tsenned ġifs!*).[13]

Tribal Elders and the Application of Customary Law to Women

Prior to the protectorate period, Tamazight-speaking Middle-Atlas transhumant tribes were governed by *azerf*. In a situation reflecting a kind of *démocratie vécue*,[14] or democracy in everyday life, the decision-making process of each tribe or clan was enshrined in the *džemaɛt* who elected their sheikh (*amġar* in Tamazight) for a limited period, usually one year. As a penal and civil code, *azerf* contained a catalogue of offences of varying gravity. Once they had appointed the new *amġar* [...], he enforced Customary Law over the tribe (*adday gin midden amġar n tuya [...], lla yteqqen umġar xf teqbil azerf*).[15] Indeed, on consulting the Beni Mtir *azerf*, the observer is struck by the lengths Amazigh jurists went to make the punishment fit the crime.

A number of items from this and other *izerfan* relate to women. According to article 6 of the Ayt 'Atta of Boudenib *azerf*, "He who seduces a woman shall forfeit 100 *mithqal*-s (local currency unit). However, if she was willing, each one shall pay the fine.[16] From article 12 of the *taɛqqit* of *qṣer* of Lgara in Tafilalt:

He who enters a woman's house with the intention of seducing her, must, if caught by the sheikh, or if the husband or close relative swear under oath, pay 100 *mithqal*-s to the owner of each threshold (*ɛtba*) [before which he will have passed on his way to the house he has dishonored]. Half of the sum will accrue to the sheikh, the other half to the master of the [dishonored] house.[17]

The famous *taɛqqit* (Customary Law) of Ayt 'Atta is enshrined in writing at Ighrem Amazdar, in Jbel Saghro, and article 36 states:

A woman is attached to the soul (*rruḥ*) of the husband until she flees his house and goes to her agnates, that is to say her patrilineal kinsmen, until a month has elapsed. If her husband has not told her to return home to his house after a month, he must pay her a measure of wheat every day.[18]

In the above-mentioned Beni Mtir *azerf*, article 13 specifies: "He who rapes a virgin (*wenna ysxserr taɛrrimt*) is obliged by the sheikh to marry her, failing which he pays her family a sum (*lefra*) so that they are even. After that the girl returns to her family."[19] In this case, the rapist is expected to square things with the parents, if necessary marrying the victim. Here, parallels exist to recent cases in Morocco, where national judges have enforced this kind of ruling and caused quite an outcry, in 2014 leading to an amendment of article 475 in the Moroccan penal code that had allowed a rapist to escape punishment if he married his victim.

Customary Law Tribunals under the Protectorate

During the protectorate period, whereas areas under the jurisdiction of the legendary Berber leader Thami al-Glaoui were not covered by Customary Law,[20] 60 tribunals, and 6 appeals courts were established elsewhere, mainly in the Middle and Eastern High Atlas, and Tafilalt regions. Leading members of the *džemaɛt* sat in these courts, presided over by the resident French *Affaires Indigènes* officer, usually a *qebṭan* (captain) or *lfesyan* (lieutenant), as well as a secretary who could double as an interpreter. The purpose of the exercise was to mete out justice among Tamazight-speaking tribes in keeping with the spirit of Customary Law, yet with an admixture of Descartes-inspired logic. According to the French Protectorate authorities this system tallied with their avowed intent of respecting "Berber custom," since the leaders of dissident tribal groups (the Ayt 'Abdi, Ayt Hadiddou, and similar diehards) had insisted on retaining their *izerfan* when they surrendered to the French during the final phase of resistance in the Moroccan Atlas (1929–34).

In his survey of the Ayt Hadiddou, Kherdi publishes copies of relevant legal documents from courts in Agoudim (Ayt Yahya) and Itzer (Ayt Myill).[21] In these documents, under the heading *Justice Berbère*, are listed the details of each case, names of plaintiffs and defendants, and court rulings, all duly signed and stamped by the local Affaires Indigènes

Figure 12.1 A French officer presiding over Customary Law Tribunal, Ayt Hadiddou.
Weygand, 1954

officer who fulfilled a role similar to that of district commissioners in territories under British imperial rule. In his book, Aspinion provides a detailed description of the legal process applied in Izayyan country, with several concrete examples of court rulings.[22] Among the most complex of matters in the records of the Aguelmous Customary Tribunal is a case involving a local custom that enabled a woman to declare herself pregnant in her husband's absence. In one instance, for example, a woman named Fatma el Artouz gave birth to such a so-called "sleeping child" (*amžun,* in Middle Atlas Berber), resulting in a paternity suit involving several competing, would-be fathers. Ultimately, although he had in the meantime divorced Fatma, a certain Caïd Bouchta was declared the child's lawful father, and ended up having to pay alimony to his ex-wife for a limited period, plus midwife expenses.

How Custom and Gender Relations Work on the Ground

We now take a brief glance at the impressions I derived from my fieldwork in the region (1972–2005), so as to illustrate attitudes toward women, together with the social impact of marital status within the various tribal groups. As Hart put it in his survey of the Ayt 'Atta, "it is clear that the sex division of labor is basically unequal and women work considerably harder and longer than men."[23] This may have something to do with Qur'anic Law, which, according to Kasriel, "rather than favoring the woman, tends to increase her situation of bondage."[24] Yet, there are exceptions to this rule.

While the Imazighen of central Morocco compose an essentially male-dominated society, in some circumstances women may turn the tables on their husbands. Elderly ladies, for example, wield an unexpected amount of authority. I saw a typical example in the village of Assaka (Tounfit area), where I discovered one household run exclusively by the woman of the house, Zinbae, a formidable character who lorded it over her meek and mild spouse. I also recorded several instances in which young men in this area were ordered about in no uncertain manner by their elder sisters. Such relationships were especially the case in households where the paterfamilias was either absent (as a soldier or migrant worker in Europe) or incapacitated in some way (due to old age, invalidity, ill health, etc.), obliging the women to take matters into their own hands.

Among the Ayt Hadiddou, early marriage followed by divorce has long been seen by many young women as a worthwhile emancipation strategy.[25] In fact, the divorce rate has traditionally been exceptionally high in the area, especially in cases of early marriage with 12–15 year old girls. Moreover, divorce often is perceived locally as a type of "nubility rite"[26] that provides an opening for a promising remarriage of a more lasting nature. Incidentally, the area has also long been famous for its annual bridal fair, accounts of which date back to the 1930s.[27] On the other hand, among those privy to the "town-influenced value system,"[28] early marriage is perceived negatively, as it usually leads to divorce. Nevertheless, in the Eastern High Atlas, Ayt Hadiddou women of the Imilshil area have generally had a reputation for being good mothers. In common with neighboring tribes, there is no shame factor attached to divorce, though the bride's value on the marriage market declines marginally after she has lost her virginity.[29] Interestingly, few attempts appear to be made by the respective families to reconcile the estranged spouses. Their Ayt Yahya neighbours display similar social traits with regard to premature marriage followed by divorce.

COPIE DE L'ACTE DE MARIAGE D'UN PARENT DE L'AUTEUR

Région de Meknès   JUSTICE BERBERE
Cercle de *Midelt*
Affaires indigènes   Tribunal Coutumier des *Aït Ameur ou Hammi*
Bureau de *Tounfit*
Poste d'*Agoudime n'Aït*   extrait d'un acte de mariage
Yahia

                        inscrit sous le n° 172 du Registre des actes Divers

L'an mil neuf cent trente cinq et le vingt deux octobre
par devant les membres du Tribunal Coutumier des *Aït Ameur* ou *Hammi*

ont comparu :

Le nommé *Bassou ou Ali* des *Ihiouache*, Ksar d'*Anefgou*, d'une part

et le nommé *Moha ou Ali* originaire des *Aït Izdeg*, Ksar de *Bouzmella* (bureau des Affaires Indigènes
de Midelt), d'autre part.

Le premier comparant a requis de constater qu'il donne en mariage au second sa pupille *ITTO
MOUJANE des Aït Daoud d'Anefgou.*

Ce mariage a eu lieu conformément à la coutume des *Aït Ameur ou Hammi.*

Clauses spéciales : Si les torts viennent du côté du mari, la femme recevra son Sdaq soit : Cinquante
Francs (50 frs).

                                                         DONT ACTE

Vu Pour contrôle :   pour copie certifiée conforme
Le chef du Poste des A.I   *Agoudime n'Aït Yahia*, le 13 Novembre 1935
Agoudime n'Aït Yahia, le 13/11/35   Le Secrétaire du Tribunal Coutumier

Figure 12.2 Marriage certificate delivered in 1935 by Customary Law Tribunal
at Agoudim, Ayt Yahya area.
Kherdi archive

In this tribal grouping I have also observed instances of two interesting
social customs: fostering and second-wife (*tešna*) marriage. Fostering, a
noticeable phenomenon in and around Midelt, and especially practiced
after some cases of divorce, has been termed by one Western observer a
"safety net for the casualties of a discriminatory social system which tends
to work to the advantage of the men."[30] Near Tounfit, where sterility is
high,[31] the ability to foster a relative's child also is seen as a face-saving
solution, especially for childless parents, since failure to procreate carries
a dishonorable social connotation. The advantages of fostering, then, are
twofold: the childless couple is blessed with offspring, thereby enabling
them to achieve near normality in the eyes of the local society.

In this area, it also is not uncommon for husbands in the 40–50 age bracket to seek a second wife.[32] The first wife, who may have been overworked or unloved, occasionally contributes to finding a suitably amenable, youthful candidate, in which case the relations between the co-wives may be relatively trouble-free. Usually, however, the co-wife, or *tešna,* becomes a much-abused, second-rate spouse of the kind depicted in some of the folktales I have collected in my fieldwork.[33]

Brief Case Study: The Ayt 'Ameur of Anefgou (Eastern High Atlas)

During the winter of 2006–2007 intense media hype arose (even the Al-Jazeera TV network sent reporters) in the wake of the deaths of 28 infants and two mothers in the mountain-girt Anefgou region. It is most likely that these deaths were due to poorly treated cases of pneumonia and attendant complications, but certainly not because of winter cold, as claimed by the authorities. With the media spotlight on this remote village, however, it soon appeared that here was an anachronism: A neck of the woods in Morocco where child marriage and other *žahilīya*-inspired (pre-Islamic) practices still held sway. The outside world was discovering Anefgou, and many urban Moroccans, applying their "town-influenced value system" did not like what they saw. Nongovernmental organizations (NGOs) flocked to the place, and while officialdom (including King Mohamed VI) was quick to provide health care, blankets, and cell phones, together with the equipment and manpower to start building a road, many well-meaning voices denounced the region's wretched living conditions and the tribe's supposedly backward practices, such as child marriage. Locals, however, had always perceived early betrothals between young people as a *rite de passage,* or a form of insurance guaranteeing that a young woman would find a husband – particularly in a society where wedlock was very much the norm and failure to secure a spouse was unthinkable.

As my personal knowledge of Anefgou dates back to 1977, the public outcry left me indifferent. I had stopped in the village on several occasions, overnighting a couple of times. My impression had been that this was a traditional Berber hill community eking out a reasonably happy existence in a secluded nook of the Atlas, unsullied by close contact with the outside world. Far from appearing dissatisfied with their lot, the young women I met, some with babies strapped to their backs, had appeared cheerful and content with the way life was treating them.

Figure 12.3 Traditional home in Anefgou. "The Shangri-La effect had seemingly worn off."
May 2001, C. Mackenzie

Yet, when I went through this region in May 2001, there had been a noticeable air of despondency hanging over some young girls and an elderly grandmother. The Shangri-La effect had seemingly worn off. Perhaps, now that generator-operated TV sets were functioning in the village, *telfaza* (television) was bringing them direct views of the global village, and the Ayt 'Ameur, like many other Atlas Berber communities, were becoming increasingly aware that their seemingly idyllic existence was a poor excuse for being left out in the cold, literally and figuratively. Thus was born among them the sentiment of *hogra* (being subjected to contempt, neglect, or humiliation), along with their awareness of belonging to the Amazigh community of Morocco.

Not until May 2010 did I return to Anefgou, only to discover that it was now served by a tarred road. A hospital was being built courtesy of the

Mohammed V Foundation, and the place was no longer cut off, thanks to communication masts and cell phones. Also, local girls were being taught that for social and medical reasons they should not marry before they were 18 years old.[34] For all that, it was not clear whether all were heeding these messages, nor did they appear to have lost their innate cheerfulness.

Customary Law and Gender Relations in Poetry

Poetry of the *izlan* and *timawayin* genres that I collected upcountry from Midelt and Tounfit (1982–1993) contain but few references to the Customary Law of old. The following *izli* (couplet) reminds the village woodcutter that every day he must have his wits about him if he is to avoid the forest guard, a representative of the legal system ever on the lookout for timber-rustlers:

> *Matta lbrusi tyid-i, a wayd rix!* / Punishment sore did ye inflict upon me, my love!
> *ammiy imnaqqar bu ɛari d unezdam* ! 'Twas like when forester and woodcutter meet![35]

Similarly, the following two *timawayin* (strophes) contain allusions to Qur'anic law (*ššraɛ*): the first in a judicial context reminiscent of the present-day *moudawana,* with a hoped-for wedding jeopardized through the bride's mother apparently insisting on marriage under Qur'anic Law, whereas the bridegroom would prefer to 'appeal to the people' (i.e., be wed according to custom). The second concerns a suitor who, having come to pay court to his ladylove, is confronted outside the house by a watchdog and appeals to the animal's sense of justice (*tterx-aš ššraɛ* = lit. "I ask you for [justice as per] Qur'anic Law")!

> *A mmays n tenna rix, eg diyi lḥeqq, awra,* / Mother of my beloved, justice I do crave,
> *ger midden, ššraɛ ur i-yebḍi d usmun-inw!* / Let us appeal to the people, Koranic Law, from my beloved shall ne'er separate me!
> *Ay iydi tterx-aš ššraɛ, ad ur-ttaġ* / Watchdog, deal fairly with me, I beseech thee, bite me not!
> *ameddakul a ger d nedda wr idd ak"n našer* / Am come to see my beloved, not to steal from you![36]

And yet, to fully appreciate the extent to which Imazighen regret the passing of *azerf* as a non-complex, highly flexible law-enforcement institution, one

need only peruse contemporary verse from Southeast Morocco, especially
that of Ayt Merghad vintage. Just as they were among the last to knuckle
under to foreign invasion – the Zayd u-Hmad epic only came to a close in
1936 – since the events of Igoulmimen (Tizi n-Imnayn) in 1992, the tribe in
question has been unstinting in its demands for cultural recognition of its
"Berberdom" or *timuzġa*. This attitude is quite clear from the following
verse attributed to the famous bard Zayd ou 'Assou, alias *Lisiwr*:

> *Muḥal ad teḥyu dduyt s ti n tyirra,*/ Impossible to lead such a life,
> *irẓa leġla timizar yilli wmxilaf,*/ Cost of living high, in the land discord is
>   rife,
> *ku yiġrem iḥezza d axsar n tenbaḍin,*/ Each village respects not the rules,
> *zeggus rẓan imaziġn izerf ur illi!*/ Now is Customary Law truly no more![37]

Bewailing his fate, one of *Lisiwr*'s contemporaries, the troubadour, or
amdyaz, 'Assou Ikli composed this lament:

> *Ay aɛri nnun, ay aryaz lliġ amzwaru* / Happy he who in times of yore did
>   live,
> *nnay ḥaḍarn i ssiba, ilint tinbaḍin!* / Days when authority did with honor
>   rhyme!
> *dinnaġ ur illi qayd, ddun ggali,* / In those days no caïd, yet retribution
>   swift,
> *hat iwġent yan ulmu, ur da tesmduyant,* / Calmly on the pasture the herd
>   did feed,
> *illa lbaz ressan igdaḍ qqimn g^w asal,* / Gyrfalcon watched as small birds
>   the ground did hug,
> *dġi tɛayd tawušt, da tssara g ddunit!* / Today screech-owl is back, lords it
>   over the land![38]

In this instance the noble gyrfalcon stands for *azerf*, ever watchful in its
defense of Amazigh rights. However, the screech owl as a night-bird is
literally and figuratively associated with darkness and misfortune.

Yet another poet from Ayt Merghad, 'Ameur ou-Mahfoud, com-
plains about the appointment of female judges:

> *Wa raɛat leḥkam, ššraɛ ikkan yad zzman,* / Consider leadership, Koranic
>   Law of yore,
> *ur idd imki ayd asent akkan lanbya,* / A thing such as this did the Prophets
>   abhor,
> *ikka ġurġ lɛurf ass lli ayd nessexdam,* / We, in days of old, by Customary
>   Law did swear,

ur da tamẓent imġarn ula ayt lmeglis! / Ladies in politics or justice, nay, was ne'er their business![39]

A piece of modern, militant Amazigh verse from Southeast Morocco also makes mention of *izerfan*:

Seg yimgunen ar msemrir, seg tazarin ar tinġir, / From Imgounen to Msemrir, from Tazarine to Tinghir,
amaziġ ira ad yidir, adabu da t izizdir / Amazigh men aspire to live, unsympathetic authorities their rights deny.
izerfan llan nn g yir d, merruk da ittirir, / Customary law put on ice, Morocco drunkenly does sing.
*tiɛurrma tedda s uzir, da tnegg*ʷa am ubadir*, / Bespoiled youth, beneath wedding bread like burning embers glow,
tekkat ad innem ugadir ad taf, yan wass, ad tidir! / Try to make castle straight, one day ye shall live![40]

Thus, while feminist Amazigh militantism gains ground, likewise does the apparent antifeminism of diehard old-timers go more or less hand-in-glove with heightened social tensions in rural areas, as attempts to apply *moudawanna*–inspired philosophy challenge long-established conservative ideas concerning gender relations.

This is particularly the case in the Middle Atlas proper, especially along the Azrou–Mrirt–Khenifra axis, which has long been open to pro-feminist influences facilitated by the presence of automobiles, telephones, televisions, and cell phones. Inspired by the example of their town-based sisters, local women now feel empowered to stand up for their rights and refuse ill-treatment at the hands of their spouses, given that cases of wife-beating have not been uncommon.[41] Their feminism sits badly with socially conservative men raised by custom to consider women inferior creatures, and who perceive any hint of equality as a personal offense. Most of the criticism featured in the verse below is clearly aimed at diehard old-timers. Thus speaks a Middle Atlas bard from the Mrirt region:

1. *Šuf sebḫan llah ddunit may as-iwša rebbi*! / See what God has made of life!
2. *Ur tannaym yun n lexbar nsell-as lla iddur*? / Have you not heard the news?
3. *Kul yun ad iḥarb, hat ikšem ḥuquq lemra*, / Each one for himself must fight, women's rights are now imposed!
4. *Awd unna irra zzerb, issikl ifassen-ns.* / If you can't control your temper, get someone to tie your hands.

5. *Hudr, a bu nnefxa, tebda luqt lla k^{w}n tselka,* / Bow down, ye proud ones, the times they are a-changing!
6. *Sersat ul ddaw iduša-nš, ar iḥenna rebbi.* / Place your heart beneath your sandals, hold out till better days![42]

To drive the point home, here is an excerpt from the same corpus which, if anything, is even more explicit:

1. *Ad ur ttini lɛib a wenna ysawall,* / Refrain from blameful comments, ye who do speak,
2. *Hat mmu zabbur leḥsab-ns ag ttilin.* / Shall prevail the long-haired lady's opinion.
3. *Lliy as-ttušfan lḥuquq lla t ssamun,* / Now that you've granted her the right to participate,
4. *Taġul s waddur taġul lla tušawar.* / Honourable status she enjoys, her advice sought after.
5. *Tella y lbiru tya taneḥšamt ġifun,* / In offices shall be found, actually giving you orders,
6. *Uɛess i taddart ur as-ttameẓt awal.* / Even back home a word you can't get in edgeways!
7. *Mš tellef ad is-tebḍu anna ismuttur,* / If she gets a divorce, half of your estate she'll take.
8. *Iniy-as i bu tṣart xs arezzun gg^{w}awal,* / Tell the proud man on his speech to put a damper,
9. *Amma dɛen i ddelt amma ara s lmaḥal.* / To bow down or leave the house – he still has the choice![43]

In the Mrirt area events have moved apace. Conservative-minded men can see the writing on the wall, and it remains to be seen whether women's rights advocates will continue to make headway in achieving greater gender equality in the area, given the ongoing, Salafi-inspired Islamic revival affecting the whole of Morocco.

The Present Picture in the Eastern Moroccan Atlas

Over the past fifteen years, the everyday lives of women in the regions under discussion have changed noticeably. Recent interviews with young local women, especially of the Ayt Hadiddou tribe, reveal a certain willingness on their part to contemplate marriage with outsiders – a hitherto unheard-of phenomenon. Already in 2001, I observed near Imilshil a change in women's attitudes based on their readiness to discuss the problem of family planning and contraceptive

Figure 12.4 Ayt Hadiddou women listening to a lecture on birth control, near Imilshil.

May 2001, C. Mackenzie

pills. Likewise, the building of a girls' boarding house in Imilshil has proven to be a major step forward in guaranteeing that girls have access to basic education. The availability of relatively cheap butane gas cylinders for cooking is another factor that has eased the burden of women, in that it has reduced the necessity of daily foraging for wood.

For their part, NGOs operating in the area have done much to address the issue of women's rights. Upstream from Imilshil, the Akhiam Assocation in Agoudal has been particularly active. In April 2014 I attended a meeting in which a visiting NGO from Marrakesh – Jamila Hassoune's *Caravane du Livre* – lectured the local Akhiam women on empowerment, basic village democracy, and book reading as a key to self-education. Elsewhere, at Almis n Guigou, Timhadit in the Middle Atlas, also Tattiouin near Midelt and Tounfit among other places, in several instances NGOs have advised women on how to set up and manage carpet weaving co-operatives in order to create minimal cash flow, not to mention reduced dependence on their husbands. A bread-making co-operative also has been established in Midelt.

Even the local literary scene has recorded on-going developments. In *Hadhoum,* a first novel written in 2004, Midelt-based author Mohammed Mouhib depicts a local Moroccan woman who ventures into the male-dominated word of politics. More recently he penned *Le Monde de Aïcha Bassou,*[44] which graphically portrays the reluctance of Berber women to accept continuing subservience.[45] All of these underscore developments indicating that, despite some opposition from men, women are determined not to stand idly by now that the winds of social change are blowing.

Conclusion

A woman's lot in Amazigh-speaking areas of Morocco has long been an unenviable one, with a heavier workload than her spouse, to whom by dint of the law, whether *azerf* or *ššraɛ,* she plays second fiddle.[45] True, there have been some improvements. Since the workload between the sexes has become, in some cases, more evenly balanced; in many areas, girls now refuse marriage before the age of 18. However, the forces of change are up against a traditional mindset largely reluctant to part with time-approved practices. While Qur'anic Law reigns supreme in the country's courts,[46] a residual *ɛurf* presence is still observable in some areas. Even *fuqaha* (Muslim legal scholars) and other experts debating over the articles of the *moudawana* (Moroccan Family Code) have pointed to the need to incorporate some of the relevant dispositions of *izerfan.* Many believe that these *izerfan,* after all, reflect age-old wisdom and proven past practice, and are only minimally incompatible with Qur'anic Law. As such, in certain highly localized contexts and circumstances they will be taken into account and no doubt survive into the foreseeable future, whatever gains may be achieved by women seeking enhanced social status and rights.

Endnotes

1 Al-Baidaq (1928). *Documents inédits de l'histoire almohade.* Paris: Geuthner.
2 Aspinion, A. (1937). *Contribution à l'Etude du Droit Coutumier Berbère Marocain (Étude sur les Coutumes des Tribus Zayanes).* Casablanca:

A. Moynier. N.B. *azerf* (Tam.), or *εurf* (Ar.) = 'oral Customary Law, as opposed to written law'; Amazigh, pl. Imazighen = Berber / pl. Berbers.

3 Guennoun, S. (1938). *La Haute Moulouya*. Unpublished, p. 114.

4 Ou-Skounti, A. (2012). *Le sang et le sol: nomadisme et sédentarisation au Maroc*. Rabat: IRCAM, p. 84.

5 A large festive gathering on Asif Melloul sometimes inaccurately referred to as the *Imilshil* "moussem" in English. Cf. also F. Reyniers (1930). *Taougrat: Ou les Berbères racontés par eux-mêmes*. Paris: P. Geuthner, pp. 74–75; A. Kherdi (2012). *Les Aït Hdiddou: organisation sociale et droit coutumier*. Rabat: IRCAM, pp. 113–115.

6 Mezzine, L. (1987). *Le Tafilalt: contribution à l'histoire du Maroc aux XVIIᵉ et XVIIIᵉ siècles*. Rabat: Faculté des Lettres. The *Dila' zawiya* was a highly influential religious center in Central Morocco (1566–1667). Cf. M. Peyron, "Dila'", *Encylopédie Berbère*, XV/1995: 2340–2345.

7 El Manouar, M. (2004). *Le Sud-Est Marocain: réflexion sur l'occupation et l'organisation des espaces sociaux et politiques*. Mohamed El Manouar Publisher.

8 Kabli, M. et al. (2012). *Histoire du Maroc*. Rabat: IRRHM, p. 314.

9 Nehlil, L. (1915). "L'Azref des Tribus et Qsour berbères du Haut-Guir." *Archives marocaines*, pp. 86–93.

10 Anefgou, main village of the Ayt Ameur clan, is situated midway between Tounfit and Imilshil in the Eastern High Atlas. See H. Houdaifa (August 2010). "Anefgou, les filles se marient encore à 7 ans... Nouvelle Moudawana?" *La Vie Economique*.

11 Kherdi, *Les Aït Hdiddou*, p. 91.

12 Mezzine, *Le Tafilalt*.

13 Ou-Skounti, *Le sang*, p. 88.

14 Gellner, E. (1969). *Saints of the Atlas*. London: Weidenfeld & Nicolson, p. 29.

15 Cf. Laoust, E. (1939). "*Azref* des Beni Mtir" in *Cours de berbère marocain. Dialecte du Maroc central: Zemmour, Beni Mtir, Beni Mguild, Zayan, Ait Sgougou*. Paris: P. Geuthner, pp. 260–61. In this case the Middle Atlas Beni Mtir (or *ayt nḍir*) tribe. According to local custom, a handful of grass was placed in the turban of the newly-elected *amġar* to symbolize the short-lived nature of his stewardship; hence *amġar n tuya*.

16 Nehlil, "L'Azref," p. 87.

17 Mezzine, *Le Tafilalt*, p. 192.

18 Hart, D.M. (1981). "An Ayt 'Atta customary law (*izerf*) document." *Dadda 'Atta and his Forty Grandsons*. Wisbech: MENAS Press, p. 224.

19 Laoust, "*Azref* des Beni Mtir," pp. 260–261.

20 El-Qadery, M. *Azerf et le mythe de" la justice coutumière berbère."* Available at www.mondeberbere.com/droit/azerf.htm. During the Protectorate period Al-Glaoui was simultaneously Pasha of Marrakesh and

a feudal Atlas overlord. Cf. G. Maxwell, *Lords of the Atlas* (London: Longmans, 1966); also M. Peyron, G56, GLAOUI/GLAOUA, GLAWI/ IGLIWWA, *Encyclopédie Berbère*, Aix-en-P.: Édisud, XXI/1999: 3151–3160.

21 Kherdi, *Les Aït Hdiddou*, p.109.

22 Aspinion, A. (1937). *Contribution à l'Étude du Droit Coutumier Berbère Marocain (Étude sur les Coutumes des Tribus Zayanes)*. Casablanca: A. Moynier, pp. 233–238.

23 Hart, "An Ait 'Atta customary law document," p. 86.

24 Kasriel, M. (1989). *Libres femmes du Haut-Atlas? Dynamique d'une microsociété au Maroc*. Paris: L'Harmattan, p. 110.

25 *Ibid*, pp.138–141; Maher, V. (1974). *Women and Property in Morocco: Their Changing Relation to the Process of Social Stratification in the Middle Atlas*. CUP, p. 153.

26 Maher, *Women and Property*, p. 153.

27 Reyniers, *Taougrat*, pp. 74–75. Also known as *ssuq ɛam ayt ḥadiddu*, the Imilshil "moussem" has lost much of its authenticity, becoming first and foremost a tourist venue. Well-known to readers in the U.S.A. through Carla Hunt's article: "Berber brides' fair", *National Geographic*, January 1980.

28 Maher, *Women and Property*, p. 154.

29 Hart, *op. cit.*, p. 95.

30 Maher, *Women and Property*, p. 132. While staying at the house of a local dignitary in Anefgou in May 2010, I observed a case of fostering: that of an unhappy-looking 20-year old niece who, in exchange for board and lodging, was clearly filling the role of unpaid servant. A type of situation also referred to by Maher in pp. 40–41.

31 Fieldwork I conducted among the Ayt Yahya in the 1970s and 1980s revealed a number of cases where local husbands approached me inquiring whether I could recommend any remedy against impotency. Sterility also seemed to be the problem with some couples in the area. Concerning this problem see Chiapuris, J. [(1979), *The Ait Ayash of the High Moulouya Plain: Rural Social Organization in Morocco*, Michigan: Ann Arbor, p. 90], who confirms that, contrary to what had been earlier affirmed, there is little hard evidence to prove that crude contraceptive practices in the wake of the French-military-inspired brothel culture, with its attendant *ššixat*-style entertainers, are solely responsible for widespread sterility among local women.

32 Peyron, M. (1996/97). "La mujer tamazight del Marruecos central." *El Vigía de Tierra. Melilla: Revista de Publicaciones*. No. 2/3, pp. 140–141.

33 Peyron, M. (2003). *Women as Brave as Men: Berber Heroines of the Moroccan Middle Atlas*. Ifrane: AUI Press, pp. 44–45. Tale: "The boy with the missing finger."

34 According to Chuapuris, *The Ait Ayash*, p. 147, the ideal marrying age among Ayt Ayash girls appeared to be 16–17 years in the 1970s; at about the same time, between 13 and 15 according to Maher, *Women and Property*, p. 150. Interestingly, interviews conducted by my colleague Touriya X among young ladies at Zaouit Ahansal (Central High Atlas) in April 2015, revealed that women's social status had improved markedly, both in terms of workload and marital status. All were adamant that they would refuse to marry until they were 18 years of age.

35 Peyron, M. (1993). *Isaffen Ghbanin (Rivières profondes)*. Casablanca: Wallada, p. 108.

36 *Ibid*, p. 56.

37 Khettouch, H. (2004). "L'izerf dans la poésie de type *tamdyazt*." *Amazigh Days at Al Akhawayn University: Paving the Way for Tifinagh*. M. Peyron (ed). Ifrane: AUI Press, pp. 90–91.

38 *Ibid.*, pp. 92–93.

39 Ou-Skounti, *Le sang*, pp. 89–90.

40 Derouich/ Saghru Band. Song *"grat ifassen"*. Available at www.youtube.com/watch?v=AsEWJ4MAoIc (accessed 26 January 2017).

41 Interestingly though, in some cases, among the Ayt Hadiddou for example, wife-beating is perceived as a dishonorable practice. See Kasriel, *Libres femmes*, p. 151.

42 Azmi, F. (2015). "Etude sur la *tamdyazt*." *Mémoire de Master Langue & Culture Amazighe*. Rabat: Faculté des Lettres, p. 40.

43 *Ibid.*, p. 62.

44 Mouhib, M. (2014). *Le Monde de Aïcha Bassou*. Edilivre-Aparis.

45 This is evident from a perusal of my feminist-oriented, Middle Atlas folktales. See endnote 33. And yet, strangely enough, even that fund of traditionally-inspired material actually boasts a story – "Fatma and the ogress," pp. 7–20, that was visualized by certain American ladies as containing some glimmerings of "Women's Lib." So much so that they applied to me for permission to publish it in their journal!

46 Khettouch, "L'izerf dans *tamdyazt*." pp. 92–93.

13 Family Law Reform in Algeria

National Politics, Key Actors, and Transnational Factors

DÖRTHE ENGELCKE

Introduction

Whereas Tunisia and Morocco issued codified family laws immediately after independence in 1956 and 1957–58 respectively, a politically divided Algeria took 22 years to issue a family law. After achieving independence in 1962 – ending 132 years of French rule – the new government of Algeria undertook several attempts to codify the family law but none came to pass. One reason is that Algeria's war of independence, unlike those in Morocco and Tunisia, did not produce a united political leadership,[1] leaving the country with no political faction powerful enough to impose a family law right away.[2] The government gridlock endured until family law finally was codified in 1984,[3] but it was not until 2005 that Algeria enacted a family law reform.

Also known as personal status law, family law regulates marriage, divorce, custody, paternity, and inheritance rights. It is the only area of law that is still commonly perceived by ordinary citizens as well as policy-makers in the Middle East and North Africa (MENA) as Islamic law.[4] This chapter traces the trajectory of Algerian family law reform between 1984 and 2005 and explores why and how family law reform was carried out.

I argue that family law reform in Algeria in 2005 was not primarily the result of women's rights advocacy. The state did not consult the women's movement because the two entities had not established a successful model of cooperation – in part because the women's movement had been unwilling to compromise on a strictly secular stance and accept family law as Islamic law.[5] The family law reform of 2005 was part of a national reconciliation effort after the Algerian civil war of the 1990s that sought to address the injustices inflicted on different population groups including women. Transnational factors like the Moroccan family law reform of 2004 affected the timing, method, and content of the Algerian family law reforms.

Studies of family law reform point to the importance of *context* for the outcome of reform processes.[6] As Charrad argues, differences in family law codification in the post-independence Maghreb states of Algeria, Morocco, and Tunisia resulted from differences in the polity, that is, the political context.[7] Yet, the mechanics of how and why different contexts impacted family law reforms, warrants further investigation. To gain a more comprehensive understanding of Algerian family law reform, it is useful to look back over several decades. From the perspective of policy network theory, we must examine the context for policymaking, including decision-making processes, participants, and the influence of current policy outcomes on future policy processes.[8] According to policy network theory, context has three dimensions – transnational, national, and domain-specific. Transnational refers to influences that originate beyond the country's borders, national refers to state and administrative structures that shape how policy is made, and domain-specific refers to – in our case – factors specific to family law. These factors in turn influence who is allowed to participate in the process and how likely they are to shape the outcome of reform.[9]

Triangulating written and interview sources from state and non-state actors, this study makes a comparative, empirical contribution. To date, no comparison of the different Algerian family law reform processes has been conducted. It also provides a novel angle to the study of family law reform by applying policy network theory. As explained, scholars have emphasized the importance of contextual factors for family law reform. Policy network theory provides a fruitful way of framing and conceptualizing these factors in a systematic fashion. In particular, in addition to the more commonly considered national and domain-specific factors, it considers the impact of transnational factors on family law reform, which have not been sufficiently taken into consideration by existing scholarship.[10]

The following sections discuss the key contextual factors that have impacted on the processes and outcomes of family law reform. The first section focuses on the emergence of the women's movement in the 1980s and its positions towards family law around that time. It highlights the impact of the Algerian Civil War on the women's movement and family law reform in the 1990s. The second section discusses how national and domain-specific factors influenced the reform process itself. It analyzes the two-family law reform processes of 1996 and 2005, with particular attention to the national political arena; the key actors, their interrelationships and relative power positions; the role of the president; and opposition to the reform. The third and last section addresses the impact of transnational forces on Algerian family law, in particular the 2004 Moroccan family law reform.[11]

The Emergence and Positioning of the Algerian Women's Movement of the 1980s

As in other Middle East North African countries, family law reform has long occupied a central place in women's activism in Algeria. In fact, the very formation of the women's movement in Algeria was closely linked to the country's first codified family law in 1984.[12] Opposition to the 1984 law became the primary objective of these early women's rights activists,[13] with family law reform remaining the focus of the women's rights movement ever since.

Prior to the enactment of the 1984 family code, feminists at the University of Algiers had founded the Collectif Indépendant des Femmes (Independent Collective of Women) in February 1981. The association was established in response to rumors circulating in the media about a government study that was to form the basis for the reform of the family law.[14] On 28 September 1981, the Collectif Indépendant des Femmes drafted a petition for presentation before the parliament. The petition denounced the secrecy of the reform process and the lack of consultation with women's rights organizations.[15]

In 1982, the Algerian general assembly withdrew the draft family law, a move that the nascent women's movement interpreted as their success.[16] This achievement was short-lived, however. During the 1980s the socialist discourse of the post-independence era had increasingly been replaced by a religious discourse. Chadli Bendjedid, who had become president of Algeria in 1979, was representative of currents within the Front de Libération National (Algerian National Liberation Front, or FLN), Algeria's first post-independence ruling political party, and the military that were closer to the Islamist camp.[17] As a consequence, a socially conservative family code was adopted by parliament in 1984.

Thus, the family code of 1984 reflected a political shift away from the original socialist leanings of a newly independent Algeria and signified a concession to social conservatives.[18] For Algerian feminists, it "marked the year of the rupture between women and their government and women's radical questioning of the state's legitimacy."[19] The family code of 1984 was seen by feminists and other women's rights supporters as a dismissal of women's contributions to the Algerian War of Independence, when women fought alongside men and provided important logistical support for the war effort.[20]

Yet, the protests against the government's family law reform also highlighted the existing divisions within the feminist camp. One faction was against a possible cooperation with parliamentarians and in favor of a complete rejection of the draft law and the use of civil laws instead. The other faction was in favor of reforming the law and contributing to the process by making suggestions.[21] At the basis of this 1981 conflict was the question of what family law actually meant and whether or not family law should make references to Islamic law. While the *mujahidat* (women veterans of the Algerian War of Independence) and other non-organized women asked for the reform of the (Islamic) personal status law, the Collectif rejected the idea of a religiously based family law.[22] These divisions within the women's movement exposed its vulnerability and weakness at the time.[23]

The Women's Movement and the Algerian Civil War of the 1990s

Divisions within the Algerian women's movement were exacerbated by the political context of the 1990s, and more specifically, the Algerian Civil War, which interrupted activist networks and again raised questions about priorities and positioning.

In Algeria's first free and fair local and regional elections in June 1990, the Front Islamique du Salut, (Islamic Salvation Front, or FIS), an Islamist party that had begun to gain ground towards the end of the 1980s, won 55 percent of the communal council seats and almost 80 percent of the regional council seats. The FIS was thereby able to present itself as the sole viable alternative to the discredited regime and its FLN party. To prevent a similar victory in the national elections, the regime legalized new Islamist parties, arrested several FIS leaders, and issued a new electoral law intended to curb the influence of the FIS.

Despite these measures, the FIS went on to win 47 percent of the votes in the first round of national elections in December 1991, and most Algerians expected the organization to win more than two-thirds of the parliamentary seats in the round of elections to be held in January 1992. Senior military figures within the regime therefore intervened and cancelled the second round of elections, triggering the outbreak of the Algerian Civil War.[24]

Violent attacks that had begun in the late 1980s against Algerian women – particularly those living by themselves, attending university, or choosing not to wear the Muslim headscarf (hijab) – continued during the 1990s. Such attacks were often undertaken by FIS supporters and encouraged by the misogynist Islamist rhetoric articulated by the FIS.[25]

The Algerian Civil War accelerated the ideological divide within the women's movement by adding another position towards family law reform: l'optionalité (optionality). Some feminists adopted this position, which called for the principle of choice. L'optionalité would allow couples to choose the personal status law by which they wished to be governed in marriage, that is, a civil law or a religiously based personal status law. The position of women's groups on l'optionalité is best understood as an effect of the civil war. The political strength of Islamism, highlighted by the strong electoral showing of the FIS, made it appear even less likely to feminists that the government would opt for civil laws and abrogate the religiously based family code altogether – as this would trigger opposition from social conservatives in an already highly confrontational climate. The civil war, then, had an indirect but significant moderating effect, because it made some women's rights associations compromise on their secular stand.

The Oran-based Association Féministe pour l'Epanouissement de la Personne et l'Exercice de la Citoyenneté (Feminist Association for Individual Development and the Exercise of Citizenship, or AFEPEC) adopted the position of l'optionalité for strategic reasons in 1997. AFEPEC had been founded in 1989 and was a well-known organization within the Algerian women's movement that thought it unrealistic that the family code would be rescinded in favor of civil laws. As a senior member of AFEPEC admitted in an interview: "Optionalité was the last resort, but in reality we were in favor of civil laws."[26] (Interestingly, since then AFEPEC has remained faithful to its position.

On International Women's Day 2004, when family law reform was once more on the table, it issued a *communiqué* supporting *l'optionalité).*[27]

The theory of *l'optionalité* was introduced by Hocine Zahouane in an article that appeared in the Algerian periodical *Naqd* in 1992.[28] Zahouane was a prominent lawyer and intellectual who, in 1985, helped to found Algeria's first independent human rights organization, the Ligue Algérienne des Droits de l'Homme (Algerian League for Human Rights, or LADH). Zahouane contended that the 1984 family law was simply a translation of existing practices dominant at the time.[29] Thus, the law was actually an expression of the majority opinion. Zahouane stated that the women's movement was only able to mobilize a small minority in favor of civil laws. *L'optionalité,* according to Zahouane, was therefore a pragmatic solution that would even have helped women's groups achieve their overall goals in the long run, since it implied secularization by turning the question of family law into a private choice.[30]

Some members of AFEPEC critiqued the *l'optionalité* approach. In 1995, a group of women split from the AFEPEC and founded the Femmes Algériennes Revendiquant leurs Droits (Algerian Women Claiming their Rights, or FARD). A founder and president of the organization explained that FARD was against *l'optionalité* because it implied the creation of a dual legal system that would revive the legal inequalities the French colonial powers had put in place to divide Algerians. Algeria should therefore not go back to this system: "We already lived this during colonialism."[31]

Under French rule, Algerians were able to adopt French citizenship, but only if they renounced Islamic law, which many Algerian Muslims perceived as an attack on their national identity. Not until 1944 and 1946 were laws enacted that allowed Algerians to become French citizens without renouncing Islamic law.[32] As a consequence, a system was put in place that was similar to the concept of *l'optionalité* proposed by Hocine Zahouane in the 1990s. French law governed French citizens, and Algerians, who had become French citizens, could choose between French civil law, Islamic law, and customary law.[33] The renunciation of *l'optionalité* along with other colonial policies suggests that the colonial experience considerably shaped what Algerian women later saw as acceptable pathways towards post-independence family law reform.

The 1996 Reform Attempt

Since independence, the Algerian military had been a central player in national politics but had exercised its influence indirectly for the most part. This changed after a state of emergency was declared on 9 February 1992, after which the military assumed direct control of government. Senior military figures wanted to give a civilian face to the regime and to return to a more behind-the-scenes role.[34] It was therefore necessary to organize elections and restart the political process despite the ongoing Algerian Civil War. In addition, in 1996 the government of Prime Minister Ahmed Ouyahia – specifically the Secretariat of the State in charge of National Solidarity and the Family – undertook a serious attempt to reform the country's 1984 family law, though the reform did not materialize.

In April 1996, the Algerian Secretariat of State in charge of National Solidarity and the Family led by Rabéa Mechernène invited various political factions to participate in workshops on a variety of themes affecting women – including education, health, employment, and the prevention of violence. One workshop specifically addressed family law reform.[35] According to government records, around 70 organizations representing women from both urban and rural areas participated in the workshops.[36] Based on the resulting recommendations, a national plan of action was developed.

The 1996 attempt at family law reform had two remarkable aspects: the method of the reform attempt as well as the positioning of the women's movement. It was the first time that the state had adopted an inclusive approach that consulted the women's movement as well as various other political factions. Women's groups had not been consulted before the 1984 code was issued (nor consulted prior to the 2005 law, as will be discussed below). In 1996, however, all political stakeholders participated in the discussion about family law, including members of the women's movement, leftists, nationalists, and members of the Islamist Mouvement de la Société pour la Paix (Movement of Society for Peace, or MSP). As a prominent member of FARD described it, "It was the only meeting ever where all associations of all orientations were represented."[37]

It is likely that the Algerian Civil War of the 1990s made it necessary to run an inclusive process in order to avoid the further alienation and provocation of political actors. On the one hand, the government had to include the Islamist spectrum represented by the Islamist MSP as it could not risk protests by Islamists. On the other hand, the women's movement had become a symbol of resistance against the Islamist insurgency; they had organized several public protests against the increasing violence against women and the failure of the military government to effectively protect them.[38]

In addition to the inclusiveness of the consultation process, the 1996 reform attempt was remarkable because it was the first time the Algerian women's movement was willing to compromise on its secular position and make minimal reference to Islamic law. Instead of calling for the complete abrogation of the code and the adoption of civil laws, the different groups agreed to focus on the reform of the existing code. They proposed 22 unanimously supported amendments[39] that included propositions to abolish polygamy, the marriage guardianship for women, and a wife's obligation to be obedient to her husband, and eliminate the concept of the husband as the head of household.[40] It was the first time in Algerian history that family law reform was perceived as being shaped by grassroots advocacy and the product of negotiation.[41]

The Women's Movement and the 1996 Reform Attempt

During the 1990s, the rise of the Islamist FIS and the extreme levels of violence disproportionately targeting women had a moderating effect on the women's movement. As with the AFEPEC adoption of the doctrine of *l'optionalité*, the 1996 attempt demonstrated that the women's movement was willing to compromise on its secular stance, at least at first. Boutheïna Cheriet, the delegated Minister of the Family and Women's Condition between June 2002 and May 2003, explained:

It was interesting that during the discussions [in 1996] they could reach a point where they would say we have to take a minimum out of the shari'a on which we could all agree. This would have been very interesting all over the Muslim world if we had had women specialists of the shari'a who could undertake a positive if not a positivist reading of the shari'a like in Morocco. And the Moroccan specialists have done it and this is why for me this is the most successful process of personal status law reform in the Arab World. They have embraced a methodology that helps them to go forward.[42]

In the end, however, the proposed amendments were not adopted and the Assemblée Populaire Nationale, that is the Algerian parliament, never discussed the text. Some feminists claimed that the process broke down as negotiations began between the Islamists and the government over how to end the civil war. This breakdown led the government to retreat from its intention to reform the family law, as it was a thorny issue that could have led to further confrontation between the two parties.[43]

While the 1990s was a period of particular tension and ending the civil war was the paramount goal – at least partially explaining why family law reform was eventually abandoned – this account does not sufficiently explain why an issue like family law reform came to be tackled in the first place. In fact, the failure of the reform also was a sign of the persistent divisions within the women's movement.

Nadia Ait-Zaï, a professor of law and a prominent feminist, was a member of the workshop on family law, one of the government-sponsored workshops at the start of the 1996 reform process. She was responsible for submitting her group's report containing the 22 proposed amendments to Prime Minister Ouyahia at the time. Ait-Zaï blamed the women's movement for the failure of the reform effort. According to Ait-Zaï, the women's movement made a strategic mistake. The women's associations involved in the planning had accepted the amendments during the workshops, but shortly after the women's associations returned to their original position of calling for the abrogation of the code. Ait-Zaï stated:

The women's movement didn't handle the matter very well. I think we made a political and strategic error. The main difference between us and Moroccans is that Moroccans know how to sell their merchandise and we don't know how to sell ours. We could have had our first reform in 1997. But at that moment the associations made the work null and void. They destroyed our work, because they were in accordance with the draft law but then said: 'No, we no longer want the amendments. We want the abrogation of the code.' They lacked political strategy. They abandoned us halfway.[44]

Ait-Zaï had been in favor of accepting the amendments even though it meant including references to Islamic law. According to Ait-Zaï, associations that went back to their original position and called for the abrogation of the code included, among others, the Algerian Coalition of Democratic Women (RAFD), the Association for Independence and the Triumph of Women's Rights (AITDF), and the Association

Fatma n'Soumer. It is not entirely clear why the women's associations changed their minds at the last minute. It is likely that the civil war had a moderating effect on some of the organizations, such that they believed the adoption of a civil law was unrealistic and that gradual reform was, therefore, the way forward. However, at the last minute these associations' core commitment to a secular family law gained the upper hand and they decided to stick to their original position as a question of principle.

In this way, the process once more highlighted the divisions within the women's movement that had already become apparent in the early 1980s and demonstrated that the movement was unable to overcome these divisions. The political opening of 1989 that had ended the FLN's one-party rule in Algeria increased these divisions even further. After the issuing of the 1989 constitution, more than 60 political parties were formally legalized,[45] and many women's associations were established.[46] Many of the newly legalized political actors were against reform of the family law and instead called for its complete abrogation.[47] The wing of the women's movement that took this position therefore gained political backing.

The rejection of the 22 amendments was a blow to the women's movement, affecting intra-movement communication and cooperation. According to Boutheïna Cheriet, the former delegated Minister in charge of the Family and Women's Condition, "automatically, the women's movement was affected by this. Each of them went back to their quarters and closed the doors to each other."[48]

The fact that the women's movement was divided and could not agree on the parameters of reform, made it a less attractive partner for the state. In a climate where opposition from Islamists was an ongoing threat, the fact that the movement refused to agree to submit itself to the *orthodoxy* of the field – to accept family law as Islamic law – provided a real challenge to state-led reform.[49] Ultimately, the failure of reform was perceived as an implicit victory of Islamist actors, further damaging the relationship between the regime and women's groups.[50]

The Context for Algeria's 2005 Family Law Reform

The Political Context

As in the 1990s, Algerian family law reform in the 2000s happened at a time of great political uncertainty, and again, this instability affected how reform was carried out and how far it went. Abdelaziz Bouteflika's presidency was characterized by a precarious balancing act of different political actors. Atrocities committed by Islamist insurgents and state security forces during the Algerian Civil War of the 1990s had left tens, if not hundreds, of thousands dead. Not surprisingly, Bouteflika's presidential election campaign of 1999 placed peace, security, and national reconciliation at the center of his political program. Bringing the country back to normal was the key political objective of the Bouteflika presidency. This meant, at the very least, bringing down the level of violence and overcoming Algeria's international isolation.

Family law reform had been another of Bouteflika's electoral promises prior to the 2004 presidential elections. It was part of his overall reconciliation plan to address injustices of the past, and especially injustices inflicted on different groups of actors, particularly during the 1990s. Bouteflika declared that the 2005 law had to be perceived as an expression of renewed national solidarity, social cohesion, and collectively assumed responsibility.[51] Nevertheless, the fragile nature of the political balance in the country combined with the paramount need for national reconciliation and a reduction of hostilities after the civil war, meant that the president had to compromise on family law reform by giving in to Islamist opposition.

The Process of the 2005 Family Law Reform

As noted above, the attempt at family law reform that began in 2003 was less inclusive than the attempt undertaken in 1996. Overall, it seemed as if Algeria had returned to key practices of the 1980s when the first family code was developed: secrecy and the exclusion of key actors. Women's groups were not consulted or represented in the reform commission that was set up in 2003. The failure to produce a tangible result in 1996, together with the fact that the women's movement was not willing to compromise on the parameters of reform – it continued to call for the abrogation of the family code and the introduction of civil laws – partly explains this exclusion from this subsequent reform process.

In the 2000s, the same divisions within the women's movement that had emerged in the early 1980s persisted. Some women's groups were willing to accept reform while most called for complete abrogation of the code. On 8 March 2003, the year before the twentieth anniversary of the 1984 code, a new collective of women's groups from Algeria and France launched a campaign entitled Code de la Famille: vingt ans, barakat! (The family code: 20 years is enough!). Their accompanying petition called for the abrogation of the family code.[52]

On 26 October 2003 President Bouteflika put together a commission under the auspices of Taïeb Belaïz, the Minister of Justice. The commission had 52 members and was comprised of jurists, academics, sociologists, Islamists, and theologians, among others. It was presided over by Mohamed Zeghloul Boutarène, the president of the Supreme Court.[53] According to a professor of law and a reform commission member, the commission was dominated by Islamists. Secular parties such as the Rally for Culture and Democracy (RCD) and the Worker's Party (PT), which demanded the abrogation of the code on the basis of its unconstitutionality, were not represented. In fact, the exact number of participants and their names are unknown. He observed in an interview: "There was a list of participants, but even we did not receive it. It was all done secretly."[54] Neither were women's groups consulted or included in the process in any other way.[55]

Opposition to the Reform

Opposition to the draft reforms of the Algerian family law came from various sides: Islamist political parties, the FLN, and state religious institutions like the High Islamic Council (HIC). Even the Islamist MSP, a member organization of Bouteflika's governing coalition, opposed the draft law. At the same time, women's groups did not mobilize to defend the draft law. Thus, in the end, the Algerian family law was not debated in parliament but was issued as a presidential decree in order to avoid controversy.[56]

On 18 August 2004 the government of Prime Minister Ahmed Ouyahia adopted all the amendments proposed by the national commission for the revision of the family code, including the removal of the obligation of guardianship for adult women. Afterward, Islamic opposition increased and Islamists mobilized against the reform. The main reason for their opposition was the proposal to make the marriage guardian optional. The same day that the council of government adopted the law, the Islamist al-Islah party organized a parliamentary meeting to raise awareness in parliament of the alleged dangers posed by family law reform.[57] Abdellah Djaballah, the leader of al-Islah, criticized the MSP for supporting President Bouteflika and his reform agenda and called for the party to switch sides and to join the opposition against the reform.[58]

Remarkably, the Islamist MSP then joined al-Islah in its mobilization against the reform, distancing itself from the very governing coalition of which it was a part.[59] This move demonstrated that the MSP, which had done poorly in the 2002 elections, would not compromise on this issue in an effort to win some votes by taking a firm stand on family law. At the time, Bouguerra Soltani, head of the MSP declared, "The family code exceeds the alliance; the latter lasts five years, but the law is eternal."[60]

Opposition also came from the High Islamic Council (HIC), a state institution with two members on the reform commission. Sheikh Bouamrane, president of the HIC, echoed the criticisms articulated by the MSP and al-Islah and emphasized that the obligation of guardianship should remain in place. The commission countered the criticism by declaring that marriage without the guardian was in accordance with Islamic law.[61]

President Bouteflika played an ambiguous role in the process, leading opponents of the reform like the MSP to claim that family law was not a presidential project.[62] Bouteflika took a public stance on a few issues regarding family law, however. For example, he openly criticized the institution of guardianship during a speech on International Women's Day in 2004.[63] However, obligatory marriage guardianship for women was reintroduced in the final draft of the law. Bouteflika gave in to the opposition within the context of seeking support for his referendum on reconciliation scheduled for September 2005.[64] The women's movement perceived this as a betrayal by the president. Feminists saw the maintenance of the marriage guardian as "a humiliation of those who yesterday fought against colonialism and who had in the more recent past resisted terrorism."[65]

Transnational Factors in the 2005 Algerian Family Law Reform

In addition to the ratification of CEDAW in 1996, family law reform in neighbouring Morocco also presented a transnational influence on reform in Algeria. The Moroccan family law reform of 2004 affected the timing, method, framework and content of the Algerian family law reform.

The Timing of the Reform

The Moroccan Family Code was issued 3 February 2004. Just a little over a year later, Algeria issued its new family code on 27 February 2005. In Algeria, the president set up a commission to reform the Family Code on 26 October 2003 – only about two weeks after the Moroccan king had announced comprehensive family law reform during a speech to parliament on 10 October 2003.[66] The proximity of the Moroccan and Algerian reforms illustrates the influence of regional politics and indicates Algeria's fear of being isolated as the only country in the Maghreb that did not reform its family code.[67]

When Bouteflika issued the reformed code by presidential decree in 2005, he also issued amendments to the nationality law, allowing women married to foreigners to transfer their nationality to their children. This action was a surprise, as the issue was not something women's organizations had been lobbying for at the time. This particular reform likely exemplified intra-regional rivalries. Since Morocco had not reformed its nationality law at that time, Algeria was able to overtake Moroccans in this respect. As the President of SOS Femmes en Détresse confirmed, the Algerian nationality code reform "was a political coup, because we preceded the Moroccans."[68] The Moroccan king subsequently announced the reform of the Moroccan nationality law on 30 July 2005, a few months after the Algerian law was issued.

Historically, regional dynamics had been important. During the Algerian War of Independence in the 1950s, French authorities undertook two attempts to reform the personal status code. In this context two laws were issued. The ordinance of 1957 fixed the age of legal majority at 21 for men and women. Furthermore, the mother was declared the automatic legal guardian of her children after the death of the father.[69] A 1959 ordinance stipulated that marriage must be conducted in public and requires consent of the two parties. The legal marriage age was stipulated at 15 for women and 18 for men. Divorce was brought under tighter state control and needed to be granted by a judge. Theoretically, then, men could no longer divorce their wives outside the court.[70]

Apart from trying to undermine the anti-colonial struggle, the timing of the French reforms also was motivated by regional politics. Tunisia had issued a new family code in August 1956 right after its independence. A few days after the issuing of the Tunisian code, the

Moroccan king set up a legal reform commission to codify family law. This pressured the French colonial powers to follow suit. The legal changes that were proposed by the French in 1959 were closely modeled on the Tunisian family code of 1956.[71] As MacMaster put it, "France, whose position as a colonial power was under strong attack in the UN and before international opinion, could not be seen to be lagging behind its Muslim neighbors in the area of human rights."[72]

The Method and the Framework of Reform

More recently, the Moroccan 2004 case similarly influenced the parameters of the Algerian reform and what the Algerian government as well as Algerian feminists regarded as possible. The fact that the Moroccan reforms were couched in Islamic terms from the beginning of the process made it increasingly difficult to advocate for family law as civil law in Algeria. The civil law option thus became more and more unrealistic for its supporters. In response, the former Algerian Minister for Family Affairs, Boutheïna Cheriet, advocated for a rereading of Islamic sources. Cheriet stated that a rereading of shari'a that took into consideration the historical context in which it was elaborated, would help to reinstate Algerian women's rights, just as the Moroccan case had demonstrated.[73]

I was saying that we need a modernist reading of shari'a. I wasn't saying we must abrogate the code. You cannot say that we have to abrogate the code. It is too late. All you can do is what the Moroccans have done: to insist on a positive reading of the Qur'an.[74]

The practices of the Algerian reform commission also demonstrated that ijtihad (independent reasoning) was clearly the official method of reform. Mohamed Zeghloul Boutarène, president of the Supreme Court who presided over the reform commission, emphasized that all changes would be in accordance with Islamic law, and for this reason declared the inheritance and polygamy provisions of the code as "untouchable."[75] In a study of the family law amendments, Ghaouti Benmelha, a member of the reform commission, had laid out the approach of the reform during the work of the commission. The study stated that many provisions of the family law were the product of tradition and customs that had little to do with Islamic shari'a.[76]

As before, family law reform was portrayed as an effort to purify the law from non-Islamic influences.[77]

The couching of family law reform in Islamic terminologies and jurisprudence obviously was not a first. Even the reforms undertaken by the French colonial powers aimed "to formulate clearly and methodically the true principles of Islamic law."[78] Similarly, the report of the codification commission that developed the 1984 code stated that the sources of the law were the Qur'an, sunna, consensus (*ijma'*), deductive analogy (*qiyas*), *ijtihad*, the four Sunni schools, the individual opinions of scholars, and the personal status laws of Syria, Egypt, Morocco, and Tunisia.[79]

The Content of the Laws

The 2005 Algerian law adopted several provisions of the Moroccan 2004 law. In fact, numerous dispositions of the two laws are similar.[80] The most obvious example of attempted legal borrowing is the provision relating to the marriage guardian. The Algerian draft law proposed to adopt the Moroccan formula of the marriage guardianship, which stipulated that a woman who had reached the legal majority age can contract her own marriage or delegate this right to her father or a relative (Article 25, 2004 Moroccan family code). However, this suggestion was not adopted in the final law due to opposition. The obligation of the marriage guardian for women remained in place in the 2005 Algerian law (Article 11), stipulating that the woman conclude her marriage contract in the presence of her *wali*. Previously, it had been the *wali* who concluded the marriage contract. With the 2005 law the *wali* became a witness to the marriage contract but not the acting party.

Both the Algerian and Moroccan codes abolish the obedience obligation for women (see the obedience obligations in the previous law: Article 39, 1984 Algerian law; Article 36 of the 1957/58 Moroccan law). Both codes emphasize that marriage is based on consent (Algeria Article 4, Morocco Article 4). Both codes refrain from abolishing polygamy, but make polygamy subject to stronger judicial control (Article 40–44 Morocco) and (Article 8 Algeria). Both codes introduce the same marriage age for men and women. In Algeria the marriage age is stipulated at 19 for men and women (Article 7), in Morocco it is 18 (Article 19). Both codes also allow for exceptions if those are seen "as in the interest of the minor," thus underage marriage continues to be legal in both countries. Both codes introduce the possibility of a prenuptial agreement to regulate the assets acquired during marriage (Article 37 in Algeria, Article 49 in Morocco). A significant innovation of the Algerian law is that in the case of divorce the judge accords the guardianship to the party who has custody (Article 87), which means that mothers frequently assume the guardianship over their children. By contrast, in Morocco the father is the *wali* except if a court judgment says otherwise (Article 236). The close development of the two laws demonstrates their regional evolution and raises doubts about the recently constructed narrative of the 2004 Moroccan family law as an exceptional case.[81] The exceptionalism of Moroccan family law reform is further undermined when considering how the law is implemented. A decade after the reform, women's groups have become dismayed by the persistence of minor marriage, polygyny and marriage guardianship.[82]

Conclusion

This chapter offered an analysis of the transnational, national, and domain-specific contextual factors that shaped family law reform in Algeria between 1984 and 2005. The purpose of the analysis was to further understandings of the why and how Algerian family law reform was carried out. The women's movement in Algeria, though composed of different groups with various positions, never fully accepted the *heterodoxy* of family law in the region, that is, that family law is officially termed Islamic law. This was one of the reasons why in Algeria no strategic alliance between the Algerian women's movement and the state emerged and the state never (ostensibly) gave into women's groups' core policy demands. Since the Algerian women's rights movement was never successfully co-opted, it never moderated its position, that is, it never truly compromised on its secular positions.

The Algerian 2005 family law reform attempt abandoned the methodology of the 1996 attempt. Family law reform became less inclusive. As with the development of the 1984 code, the government did not consult the women's movement during the 2005 process. This was the case because the 1996 reform attempt had not been able to establish a successful model of cooperation between the women's movement and the government. Thus, the only time the Algerian government had adopted a grassroots approach to family law reform had failed – due mainly to the internal divisions in the women's movement and its failure to agree about whether to advocate for family law reform or complete abrogation of the law.

Structural factors like the 130-year French rule and the civil war had long-term effects on the positioning of actors. It was not by accident that the concept of *l'optionalité* – which implied giving Algerians the choice between civil and religious family laws – was adopted during the civil war by AFEPEC. The civil war had a moderating effect on some organizations like AFEPEC that were willing to compromise on their secular stand, because it led them to believe that the ongoing civil war made the abrogation of the family law and the issuing of a civil law even less likely. However, because colonial policies had divided the Algerian legal system along similar lines as the *l'optionalité* concept proposed, Algerian women's groups struggled to get behind this proposal.

Family law reform in Algeria happened at a time of domestic political uncertainty. In the lead up to the 2004 presidential elections, Bouteflika was struggling for his own political survival in a political field that was increasingly pluralistic.[83] Family law reform, therefore, represented a necessary compromise. Like at the time of independence, Algeria in the 2000s had no political force with absolute veto power and simply enforced a vision of family law against strong popular resistance.

The timing of the Algerian family law reform can be explained with reference to both regional and national contexts. On the national level, the need for reconciliation after the Algerian civil war made it necessary to cure, at least superficially, the ills of the past, and family law reform was part of that effort by providing some concessions to a group that had been the primary target of violent attacks during the 1990s: women. On the regional level, Algeria had become increasingly isolated from Tunisia, which had adopted a family code after independence in 1956 that outlawed polygamy and considerably enhanced women's legal rights, and from Morocco, which had issued a new family code in 2004 that was praised at home and abroad. The 2005 Algerian reform was a way to overcome the country's outlier status. Family law reform, therefore, is not always the result of women's rights advocacy – as is often assumed in literature.[84]

In the end, regional developments did not only impact the timing of family law reform in Algeria but the content and process of the 2005 reform. Both the Moroccan code of 2004 and the Algerian amendments of 2005 introduced similar changes, underlining the importance of regional legal developments. The portrayal of Morocco as an exceptional case is thus misguided. The prominence of the Moroccan case and the fact that it became one of the most well-known examples of *ijtihad* (independent reasoning) in the region helped to further undermine the concept of family law as civil law in Algeria.[85] This is not to say that it ever seemed likely after 1962 that Algeria would adopt a civil family code, but the Moroccan reform made it clear to some actors that this was indeed a lost cause. Prominent actors in Algeria began to claim that a civil family law was no longer possible and that the only possible path to reform was to follow what the Moroccans had done.

Endnotes

This article was written during a fellowship at the Lichtenberg-Kolleg, the Göttingen Institute of Advanced Study. The author would like to thank Irene Schneider, Sinem Adar, the volume's editors as well as the anonymous reviewers from Cambridge University Press for their comments and feedback. Many thanks also to the interviewees in Algeria for their time and help.

1 Quandt, W.B. (1969). *Revolution and Political Leadership: Algeria: 1954–1968*. Cambridge: M.I.T. Press, p. 10.

2 Charrad, M.M. (2001). *States and Women's Rights: The Making of Post-colonial Tunisia, Algeria, and Morocco*. Berkeley: University of California Press, p. 170.

3 Ibid, p. 183.

4 Ordinary citizens as well as policy-makers often consider family law to be Islamic law, an equation that can be seen as problematic. Ann Elizabeth Mayer for example shows that Morocco, Algeria and Tunisia share a common legal tradition of Maliki jurisprudence and French legal culture. See Mayer, A.E. (1995). "Reform of personal status laws in North Africa: a problem of Islamic or Mediterranean Laws?" *Middle East Journal*. Vol. 49, p. 433.

5 In this chapter, Algerian "women's movement" refers to organizations that have been engaged in legal reform and advocacy as opposed to charity work. The members of these groups conceptualize women's rights as human rights that are universal rather than culturally specific. In Algeria, Islamist women's rights activism has not been as organized and prominent as in neighboring Morocco.

6 Dennerlein, B. (1998). *Islamisches Recht und sozialer Wandel in Algerien: Zur Entwicklung des Personalstatuts seit 1962*. Islamkundliche Untersuchungen, Vol. 221. Berlin: K. Schwarz, p. 24. She also talks about "contexts." See p. 263.

7 Charrad, *States and Women's Rights*, p. 113.
8 Adam, S. and H. Kriesi (2007). "The network approach." *Theories of the Policy Process*. 2nd edition. P.A. Sabatier (ed.). Boulder: Westview Press, pp. 129–154.
9 Ibid, p. 148
10 But see Shaham, R. (1999). State, feminists, and Islamists: The debate over stipulations in marriage contracts in Egypt. *Bulletin of the School of Oriental and African Studies*. Vol. 62, No. 3, pp. 462–483; Sonneveld, N. (2012). *Khul' Divorce in Egypt: Public Debates, Judicial Practices, and Everyday Life*. Cairo: American University in Cairo Press.
11 To increase subject protection, most of the names of non-officials have been anonymized. Members of nonstate organizations are referred to in terms of their affiliation and position only.
12 Gray, D.H. (2009). "Women in Algeria today and the debate over family law." *Middle East Review of International Affairs*. Vol. 13, p. 52.
13 Dennerlein, *Islamisches Recht*, p. 98.
14 Ibid, p. 96.
15 Lazreg, M. (1994). *The Eloquence of Silence: Algerian Women in Question*. New York: Routledge, pp. 153–154.
16 Dennerlein, *Islamisches Recht*, p. 65.
17 Messaoudi, K. and E. Schemla (1998). *Unbowed: An Algerian Woman Confronts Islamic Fundamentalism*. Philadelphia: University of Pennsylvania Press, p. 48.
18 Lazreg, M. (1990). "Gender and politics in Algeria: unraveling the religious paradigm." *Signs*. Vol. 15, p. 777.
19 Lazreg, *The Eloquence of Silence*, p. 197.
20 Messaoudi and Schemla, *Unbowed*, p. 50.
21 Ibid, p. 49.
22 Dennerlein, *Islamisches Recht*, p. 97.
23 Smail Salhi, Z. (2011). "Algerian women as agents of change and social cohesion." *Women in the Middle East and North Africa: Agents of Change*. F. Sadiqi and M. Ennaji (eds.). New York: Routledge, p. 159.
24 Willis, M. J. (2012). *Politics and Power in the Maghreb: Algeria, Tunisia and Morocco from Independence to the Arab Spring*. Columbia University Press, pp. 170–171.
25 Lloyd, C. (2006). "From taboo to transnational political issue: violence against women in Algeria." *Women's Studies International Forum*. Vol. 29, p. 457–458.
26 Interview with senior member of AFEPEC. 13 September 2010.
27 AFEPEC (2005). *Theorie de l'Optionalité*.
28 Zahouane, H. (1992). "Théorie de l'optionnalité et statut matrimonial en Algérie." *NAQD* 2, pp. 65–70.

29 Interview with senior member of AFEPEC. 2010.
30 Ibid, p. 70.
31 Interview with Vice President of Femmes Algériennes Revendiquant Leurs Droits. 14 September 2010.
32 Borrmans, M. (1977). *Statut personnel et famille au Maghreb de 1940 à nos jours*. Paris: Mouton, p. 427.
33 The Kabyles are also referred to as Berbers. However, many local groups in Kabylia reject that label due to its etymological links to the term Barbarian. Amazigh is the singular of Imazighen which means "free man." Imazighen is the name of a tribe from southern Morocco. See Willis, *Politics and Power*, p. 209.
34 Willis, *Politics and Power*, p. 105.
35 Pruvost, L. (2002). *Femmes d'Algérie: Société, famille et citoyenneté*. Préface by Mohamed Charfi. Alger: Casbah éditions, p. 314.
36 Committee on the Elimination of Discrimination against Women (1999). Summary record of the 412th meeting. Chairperson: Ms Gonazalez. New York, p. 3. It is worth noting that a similar effort was undertaken in Morocco when in 1996 the government began formulating the Plan of Action for the Integration of Women into Development (PANAFID). For a detailed description of the content of the plan see L. Buskens (2003). "Recent debates on Family Law reform in Morocco: Islamic Law as politics in an emerging public sphere." *Islamic Law and Society*. Vol. 10, pp. 85–88.
37 Interview with Vice President of Femmes Algériennes Revendiquant Leurs Droits. 14 September 2010.
38 Moghadam, V.M. (2003). *Modernizing Women: Gender and Social Change in the Middle East*. Boulder: Lynne Rienner, p. 140.
39 Interview with B. Cheriet, former delegated Minister of the Family and the Female Condition. 24 September 2010. A delegated ministry is not a full ministry. It responds directly to the prime minister and does not have its own budget.
40 For an extensive list of the 22 amendments see Pruvost, *Femmes d'Algérie*, pp. 333–349.
41 Interview with N. Ait Zaï. 2010.
42 Interview with B. Cheriet. 24 September 2010.
43 Interview with former member of the feminist organization Raschda and member of the Rassemblement pour la culture et la démocratie (RCD). 14 September 2010.
44 Interview with Ait Zaï. 2010.
45 Zoubir, Y. H. and L. Ait-Hamadouce (2007). "The fate of political Islam in Algeria." *The Maghrib in the New Century*. B. Maddy-Weitzman and D. Zisenwine (eds.). University Press of Florida, p. 106.
46 Liverani, A. (2008). *Civil Society in Algeria: The Political Functions of Associational Life*. New York: Routledge. Vol. 8, p. 101.

47 Those parties included the Parti de Travailleur, the Worker's Party (PT) and the Rassemblement pour la Culture et la Démocratie, the Rally for Culture and Democracy (RCD).

48 Interview with B. Cheriet. 24 September 2010.

49 A *doxa* is a set of attitudes and beliefs that is seen as self-evident. A *doxa* becomes *orthodoxy* when it is no longer taken for granted and accepted unconsciously, but recognized as being at least in part arbitrarily constructed and in competition with other beliefs. P. Bourdieu (1977). *Outline of a Theory of Practice*. Translated by Richard Nice. Cambridge: Cambridge University Press, p. 164.

50 Bras, J.P. (2007). "La réforme du code de la famille au Maroc et en Algérie: quelles avancées pour la démocratie?" *Critique internationale*, p. 108.

51 S.H. and S.L (February 2005). "Le nouveau code de la famille adopté." *Liberté*.

52 Collectif 20 ans barakat pétition. Available at http://20ansbarakat.free .fr/petition.htm (accessed 23 February 2016).

53 Bras, "La réforme," p. 109.

54 Interview with professor of law and member of the family law commission. 21 September 2010.

55 Interview with Vice President of Femmes Algériennes Revendiquant Leurs Droits. 14 September 2010.

56 Interview with N. Ait Zai. 2010. According to Article 124 of the Algerian constitution, the president has the right to issue laws when parliament is not in session.

57 Beldjena, R. (September 2004). "Code de la famille." *EL Watan*.

58 H.M. (September 2004). "Les 16 commandements de Djaballah."

59 Oukaci, F. (September 2004). "Un conglomérat de la mouvance Islamiste." *L'Expression*.

60 Mammeri, A. (September 2004). "Le MSP menace de claquer la porte." *L'Expression*.

61 Mammeri, A. (December 2004). "Nous sommes pou-r la troisième voie." *L'Expression*.

62 Mammeri, "Le MSP menace."

63 Bouteflika, A. (March 2004). Speech at the occasion of International Women's Day, Algiers. Available at www.el-mouradia.dz/francais/dis cours/2004/03/D080304.htm (accessed 24 February 2016).

64 Bras, "La réforme." p. 120.

65 S.L. (February 2005). "Bouteflika a commis une grave concession." *Liberté*.

66 King Muhammad VI. (October 2003). Speech in Rabat at the occasion of the opening of the second legislative year of the seventh legislative period. Available at www.maroc.ma/fr/discours-royaux/discours-de-sm-le-roi-mohammed-vi-lors-de-louverture-de-la-2%C3%A8me-ann%C3%A9e-l %C3%A9gislative-de# (accessed 21 September 2014).

67 S.L. (July 2004). "Le rapport chez Belaïz jeudi." *Liberté.*
68 Interview with President of SOS Femmes en Détresse. 9 September 2010.
69 Dennerlein, *Islamisches Recht*, p. 43.
70 Ibid, pp. 43–44.
71 Borrmans, *Statut Personnel*, p. 493.
72 MacMaster, N. (2007). "The colonial 'emancipation' of Algerian women: the marriage law of 1959 and the failure of legislation on women's rights in the post-Independence era." *Stichproben. Wiener Zeitschrift für kritische Afrikastudien.* Vol. 7, p. 96.
73 S.R. (October 2003). "Boutheïna Cheriet: 'Je suis surprise…'"*Liberté.*
74 Interview with B. Cheriet. 24 September 2010.
75 S.L. (July 2004). "Des dispositions intouchables." *Liberté.*
76 Benmelha, G. (not dated). *Hawla Taʿdil Qanun al-ʿUsra [About the Amendment of the Family Law].* Personal copy of the author, p. 2
77 Lazreg, *The Eloquence of Silence*, p. 150.
78 Lazreg, "Gender and politics in Algeria," p. 761.
79 Dennerlein, *Islamisches Recht*, pp. 260–261.
80 For a relatively detailed comparison of the provisions of the Algerian and Moroccan code see Bras, "La réform," pp. 99–103.
81 For one account that portrays the reform as exceptional see Z. Mir-Hosseini (2007). "How the door of ijtihad was opened and closed: a comparative analysis of recent Family Law reform in Iran and Morocco." *Washington and Lee Law Review.* Vol. 64, pp. 1499–1511.
82 Engelcke, D. (2017) "Interpreting the 2004 Moroccan Family Law: Street-Level Bureaucrats, Women's Groups, and the Preservation of Multiple Normativities." Law & Social Inquiry.
83 Werenfels, I. (2007). *Managing Instability in Algeria: Elites and Political Change since 1995.* New York: Routledge, p. 157.
84 Charrad hints to that with respect to family law codification after independence when women's groups were non-existent. See Charrad, *States and Women's Rights*, p. 201.
85 To portray family law reform as an effort of *ijtihād* is of course not a new strategy to legitimize reforms, but had been used as a reform strategy in various MENA countries. For the debate over *ijtihād* in Egypt see Sonneveld, N. (2012). *Khulʿ Divorce in Egypt: Public Debates, Judicial Practices, and Everyday Life.* Cairo: The American University in Cairo Press, pp. 40–58. In Tunisia, president Bourguiba already justified the issuing of Tunisia's family code as a form of *ijtihād*. See Charrad, *States and Women's Rights*, p. 221. In an interview in 2011, Rached Ghannouchi, the president of the Tunisian Islamist Ennahda party, stressed that the Tunisian family code is in accordance with shariʿa. See Voorhoeve, M. (2015). "Women's rights in Tunisia and the democratic renegotiation of an authoritarian legacy." *New Middle Eastern Studies*, p. 5.

14 | The Case of Women's Unilateral Divorce Rights in Egypt

Revolution and Counterrevolution?

NADIA SONNEVELD

Introduction

In the year 2000, the Egyptian nation witnessed a revolution in family law when a new provision gave women the right to divorce their husbands unilaterally and at no-fault through a procedure called *khul'* (Art. 20 of law no. 1 of 2000). The inclusion of *khul'* in the new law was the result of a long and intensive campaign by women's rights' groups to secure final passage of the draft version of the legislation. At the time, this Egyptian family law reform was hailed as one of the most significant religion-based law reforms to occur in a Muslim-majority country. It was followed by other Arab states, most closely by Jordan in 2001, and, to differing degrees, by Algeria (2005), Palestine (2005, although a judge must assess the need for a *khul'* request), the United Arab Emirates (2005), and Qatar (2006).[1] It also inspired Moroccan women's rights organizations and four years later, in 2004, Morocco introduced even farther-reaching reforms in divorce law.[2]

While *khul'* was viewed as revolutionary, both by opponents and proponents, in and outside Egypt, studies in two distinct fields of scholarly inquiry have shown that the outcome of contentious social action, in this case legal reform, does not automatically lead to the intended impact. First, anthropological and sociological court studies on the implementation of *shari'a*-based family law in judicial practice and everyday life have shown that sometimes judges and other street-level bureaucrats do not implement the law according to the spirit of the legislator, oftentimes because the law contains open norms. This flexibility of judges takes various forms. For instance, the discretion of judges in the Ottoman period gave women litigants more opportunities for divorce than available under prevailing doctrines of the Hanafi school of Islamic jurisprudence, which will be addressed in more detail below.[3]

Second, political and sociological studies show that when the political status quo changes, through revolutionary regime change for example, this can have profound impact on extant women's rights.[4] Especially when former opponents of gender equality gain political power, women's gains may be reversed. After the 1979 Iranian Revolution, the new theocratic government replaced the progressive family laws of the ousted Shah Muhammad Reza Pahlavi (r. 1941–1979), replacing them with laws that severely restricted women's access to divorce and custody, for example. Similarly, after the forced departure of President Husni Mubarak in 2011, different groups in Egyptian society, organizations of divorced fathers in particular, were able to gain a prominent voice in the public debate on family law matters. One of their main aims was to amend the provision on *khul'* so that women would no longer be able to obtain a divorce *without* the consent of their husband.

In this chapter, I approach the issue of women's unilateral divorce rights in Egypt from both political-historical and empirical angles. First, through the lens of women's rights activism, I explain how the introduction of *khul'* in 2000 was the result of almost a century of family law reform during which new understandings of the principles of Islamic law (Qur'an and *sunna*) as well pressure from national and international organizations for the rights of women paved the way for the series of profound family law reforms in the 2000s. I then draw on empirical research to explore the actual implementation of *khul'* in the courts, and finally, give particular attention to the period between February 2011 and the ouster of President Muhammad Mursi in July 2013. After all, it was during this period that old and new opponents to the introduction of unilateral *khul'* divorce, such as Islamists and divorced fathers, gained a prominent political voice leading to a call for a counterrevolution of sorts in family law.

British Domination: The Liberation of the Nation and of Women

As early as 1883, a year after British domination in Egypt had begun in earnest, the British began a drastic transformation of the Egyptian legal system. Although the Ottomans had begun the selection and subsequent codification of Islamic law provisions and the inclusion of European law codes, it was under the British that this development intensified.

The new codification affected all fields of law, while substantively the new law codes were no longer based on the teachings of the dominant Hanafi school of law,[5] but on European law codes. Civil, commercial, criminal, and procedural law codes were adopted from French, German, and Italian models,[6] and a new system of appeal courts was introduced, taking away jurisdiction from the *shariʿa* courts. The field of Personal Status Law (hereafter, PSL) was an exception, however. It remained the only field of law where the teachings of the Hanafi school of law (as compiled by Qadri Basha in what is known until today as the Qadri Basha Compilation), continued to be applied in what was left of the *shariʿa*-court system.

It was during this turbulent period in Egyptian legal history that the voice of a Muslim judge, Qasim Amin, became the center of public attention, initially provoking an outcry of public protest and indignation from the Palace, religious leaders, journalists, and writers. Amin published two influential books[7] for which he gained credit as the father of Arab Feminism.[8] In his book *Tahrir Al-Marʾa* (The Liberation of Women), published in 1899, Amin directly addressed the intellectual strata of Egyptian society. He asked them to no longer close their eyes to the deplorable state of their country and the causes that underlay it. Amin contended that a clear relationship existed between the oppression of men by despotic rulers and the oppression of women inside the family by politically oppressed husbands. For Amin, the liberation of the nation from foreign oppression had to be linked to the liberation of women, since more rights for women would stabilize the Egyptian family, the cornerstone of the new nation.[9]

The most important issues related to family life, Amin argued, were marriage and divorce, and for this reason he proposed reforms in these fields alongside education for women. In doing so, he castigated the country's religious scholars for having failed to adjust Islamic law to the demands of modern times and proposed restrictions to limit husbands' abuse of their right to repudiation. Yet, even such restrictions he deemed inadequate, as he believed women also should have the right to end an unhappy marriage.[10] Since the dominant school of Islamic law in Egypt at that time was the Hanafi school, a woman only was allowed to divorce her husband in three cases – apostasy, impotence, and prolonged absence (i.e., if 90 years have elapsed since the date of his birth, which basically means that he will be dead).[11] Amin suggested instead a new marriage contract that could include substantive stipulations or the use of teachings from other schools of law that would give women more grounds for fault-based divorce, most notably the Maliki school of law.[12]

Despite the public controversy surrounding Amin's views and the attacks of the religious scholars of al-Azhar Mosque, journalists and others,[13] Amin was nevertheless supported by the grand Mufti of Egypt, Muhammad 'Abduh (1849–1905). In 1900, when the Minister of Justice was struggling with the plight of women who had no legal options for ending their marriages, Mufti Muhammad 'Abduh presented the Minister a list consisting of eleven recommendations that would make divorce easier for women. Like Amin, 'Abduh advocated the inclusion of the teachings of the Maliki school of law into Egyptian PSL.[14] Amin and 'Abduh's views triggered widespread debate on the status of women, moving it from a side issue to a major national concern.[15] More than two decades later nationalists and state legislators adopted their views, leading to a series of PSL reforms in the 1920s.[16] Significantly, women's rights activists, now appearing as a collective, participated in the discussions on reform of PSL for the first time.

A Century of Personal Status Law Reform

In 1920, Egypt's first codified PSL[17] was introduced, giving women more grounds for divorce. Reformers saw a husband's general failure to provide maintenance and, more specifically, to be absent for prolonged periods, as threats to the stability of the family. A woman also gained the option of ending a marital relationship if she learned that her husband had certain diseases of which she was unaware when establishing the marriage contract. The new law considered such relationships to be "unhealthy" not only from a medical point of view, but also a nationalist point of view: "unhealthy and diseased bodies were seen as unfit for the emerging Egyptian nation."[18] Although the substance of this first PSL was still *shari'a*-based, the government's choice to select provisions from the Maliki school of law introduced major innovations. For example, the 1920 law not only gave women additional grounds for divorce but also put restrictions of men's rights to *talaq* (repudiation) and required them to register the *talaq* with the *ma'dhun*, the registrar of marriages and divorces.

In addition to nationalists and state legislators, women's rights activists, especially those united in the Egyptian Feminist Union, played an active role in seeking to reform the PSL provisions. Their goal was to raise the position of women inside the family and thereby improve the Egyptian Muslim family itself.[19] In line with the proposals of Qasim Amin and Muhammad 'Abduh two decades earlier, they wanted to curtail husbands' unlimited right to repudiation and polygyny and expand women's grounds for divorce. However, their demands went even further. They proposed to abolish *bayt al-ta'a* (house of obedience),[20] extend maternal child custody,[21] and increase the minimum age for marriage.[22] Like Qasim Amin and Muhammad 'Abduh before them, the Egyptian Feminist Union presented its reforms within the framework of Islam, but their influence remained limited. They were successful only in, first, raising the minimum age for marriage to 16 for girls and 18 for boys,[23] and second, extending women's custody rights from seven to nine years for boys and from nine to eleven years for girls, when the interest of the child required it.[24] Law no. 25 of 1929 also gave women additional grounds for divorce on the basis of *darar* (harm) but it neither changed the *bayt al-ta'a* nor affected men's right to polygyny, the most important items of their reform agenda. Having failed to implement these reforms, the Egyptian Feminist Union concluded they could not change the law, and in the decade that followed they turned their attention to changing the performance of women's role in the family.[25]

Interestingly, the 1920 and 1929 PSLs did not codify *khul'*, which, at that time, existed as a consensual divorce, usually initiated by the wife, who would request her husband to divorce her in return for a waiver of her post-divorce financial entitlements, such as the deferred part of the dower and the *'idda* (i.e., period of three menstrual cycles) maintenance. This perhaps reflected the reformers' view that with the new laws, and women's additional grounds for divorce, there was no need to do so.[26] In fact, according to Kholoussy, "Because legislators failed to reference this type of divorce in their 1920 and 1929 national codification of personal status laws ... it nearly dropped out of practice over the course of the twentieth century."[27] Nevertheless, in a study of decisions by the Egyptian *shari 'a* courts between 1900 and 1955, Shaham noted that divorces by mutual agreement were very popular, while judicial divorce cases seemed to be rare.[28] Thus, despite the changes in the PSL that occurred in the 1920s, the consensual *khul'* type of divorce seemed to remain the norm in the *shari'a* courts.

Scholars Bernard-Maugiron and Dupret have noted that the "reformist momentum in the field of personal status was interrupted and relegated to the domain of questions of secondary importance when the Arab Republic of Egypt was declared in 1952."[29] Although the government of Gamal Abdel Nasser abolished the *shari'a* courts and transferred the jurisdiction over PSL affairs to the civil courts in 1955,[30] it is true that in terms of substance the PSL provisions remained unchanged. It was only under President Anwar al-Sadat that substantive reform of the PSL later was addressed. Thus, by the mid-twentieth century, Qasim Amin's early efforts to improve the lot of his country by enhancing women's access to education and changing the PSL provisions on marriage and divorce had stalled. Although women's access to education and entry into the workforce were facilitated greatly under Nasser, within the domain of the family and the institution of marriage, a woman still could not leave the house without the permission of her husband. Even worse, until 1967, the *bayt al-ta'a* provision gave a husband the right to summon the police to help return his disobedient wife to the marital home. In 1975, this discrepancy between the disparate rights of women in the public and private domains was forcefully addressed in the iconic Egyptian film *Uridu Hallan* (I Want a Solution).

Uridu Hallan (I Want a Solution)

Duriya visits the Minister of Justice. She tells him the following story: A woman approaches the Prophet Muhammad telling him that she hates living with her husband although she thinks of him as a good and religious man. The Prophet asks her if she is willing to give him back the mahr *[dower], which he gave to her upon marriage. She agrees and, after she returns it to her husband, the Prophet divorces her from him.*

Uridu Hallan tells the story of a professional middle-aged upper-class woman, Duriya, who, after being married for more than 20 years, wishes to divorce her abusive, alcoholic, and unfaithful husband. Since he refuses to grant his wife a divorce, Duriya is forced to file for a judicial divorce in which she must convince the judge of her legal grounds.[31] As her case drags on (judicial divorce cases were notorious for taking as long as five, sometimes even ten years),[32] she sets out to find a solution and learn more about women's rights in Islam. Imbued with her newly gained religious knowledge, she approaches the Minister of Justice in order to tell him that Egyptian women have a *shari'a*-based right to a divorce without the consent of the husband through a procedure called *khul'*. Although he is impressed by her knowledge of Islamic law, the Minister of Justice does not implement *khul'*, although he does abolish the *bayt al-ta'a* ordinance. In the end, after four years of legal battle, Duriya learns from the judge that he is not willing to grant her a divorce.

Uridu Hallan was released in 1975, during a turbulent period in Egyptian history. The country's devastating defeat in the 1967 Six Day War had left it in bewilderment. Wondering what had gone wrong, Egyptian Muslims and Christians alike concluded that the defeat represented God's punishment to a people who had gone astray, a conclusion that led many to embrace religion in a more serious way. After President Gamal Abdel Nasser (Jamal 'Abd al-Nasr) died in 1970, his successor Anwar al-Sadat moved to eliminate leftist opposition in the country by setting free the many Islamists who Nasser had imprisoned. Then, to ally with the Islamists, he changed the Egyptian constitution such that "the principles of the *shari'a*" became one of the main sources of legislation in 1970 and *the* main source in 1981. At the same time, he opened up the Egyptian economy to the outside world through a policy called *infitah* (open door).

It was during this period that Egypt became a major recipient of foreign donor funds, in return for which Sadat was obligated to respond to the demands of international development agencies. He consequently implemented major PSL reforms[33] and signed international treaties like the Convention on the Elimination of all Forms of Discrimination Against Women (CEDAW, 1980). This increased foreign influence on domestic policies gave Egyptian women's rights activists and organizations more leeway to demand additional reforms in the country's PSL, and it was during this period that they started looking for a "solution," as the film title suggests, that would address the plight of women in unwanted marriages. A group of women lawyers and activists who called themselves The Group of Seven first tried to introduce a marriage contract that would contain substantive stipulations for divorce, such as the right to automatic divorce in the case a husband married a second wife. In 1995, after the project failed to overcome heavy societal resistance, The Group of Seven turned its attention to amending the procedural PSL of 1931.[34]

A Decade of Family Law in Revolution

Both in the 1920s and the 1990s, the PSL reform committees consisted of religious leaders and prominent figures from the Ministry of Justice. Yet, while the demands of the Egyptian Feminist Union were only incorporated to a limited extent in the 1920s, in the 1990s women's rights activism was more significant. The Group of Seven actively sought the cooperation of the Ministry of Justice and the religious establishment within al-Azhar. Backed by international organizations for the rights of women, the Egyptian government could not easily dismiss The Group of Seven, although it would take 15 years before their demands were translated into legislation.

On January 26, 2000, the Egyptian People's Assembly passed a new procedural law on personal status called the Reorganization of Certain Terms and Procedures of Litigation in Personal Status Matters. Three days later, ex-president Husni Mubarak promulgated the law in the Official Gazette as Law no. 1 of 2000. The new law aimed at speeding up litigation in matters pertaining to personal status disputes like divorce by compressing the 600 clauses of the old procedural law into 79. Interestingly, the new procedural law contained a few substantive clauses, such as the legalization of divorces from informal (*'urfi*) marriages and women's right to divorce without the consent of the husband and without the need to prove legal grounds in front of a judge through a procedure called *khul'*.

This provision on *khul'* sparked heated controversies throughout Egyptian society – among citizens, religious scholars, and even within the (otherwise docile) People's Assembly. Both those with and without religious training claimed that the teachings of the four schools of Islamic jurisprudence defined *khul'* as a divorce requiring the consent of the husband. Since the new provision framed *khul'* as both a consensual and unilateral divorce right, opponents argued that it violated the principles of the *shari'a*.[35] They also claimed that women were irrational beings who would use *khul'* for frivolous reasons, thereby putting into jeopardy the stability of their families and the futures of their young children. Whereas in the early twentieth century, reformers had castigated husbands for the high Egyptian divorce rate,[36] this time around women were seen as potentially causing the divorce rate to skyrocket.[37] The heated debates notwithstanding, the High Constitutional Court (hereafter, HCC) declared in December

2002 that *khul'* was in line with Article 2 of the Constitution (i.e., the principles of *shari'a* are the main source of legislation) since the Prophet himself had approved of *khul'* as a unilateral divorce. Many other PSL reforms followed in what might be called a decade of family law in revolution.

Just a few months after its introduction, law no. 1 of 2000 was amended in May 2000, leading to the re-inclusion of the article on the imprisonment of nonproviding husbands for a period not exceeding 30 days.[38] The marriage contract was changed in August 2000. In the same way as advocated by Qasim Amin at the turn of the twentieth century and The Group of Seven almost a century later, the law finally allowed women to make substantive stipulations in their marriage contracts – a common practice during the Ottoman period. Later that year, in November 2000, women were given the right to travel without the consent of the husband, a right that initially had not survived fierce resistance to it in the People's Assembly in January 2000. In 2004, Egyptian women were given the right to pass on their nationality to their children and a new Family Court system was introduced. The new system was aimed at safeguarding the stability of the Egyptian Muslim family in two ways: by providing mediation in cases involving marital disputes and by treating all related PSL lawsuits in one court in front of one judge.

In 2005, the maternal custody period was extended considerably. Where previously boys and girls from divorced parents could stay with their mother until the ages of nine and twelve, respectively, Article 1 of law no. 4 of 2005 gave both boys and girls the option of staying with their mother until the age of 15, after which they could choose to live with their father or remain with their mother until boys reached the age of *rushd* (sound mind) or girls married. Finally, in 2008 the Child Law was amended so that in cases of divorce *wilaya al-ta'limiyya* (educational guardianship) would move to the custody holder. To the knowledge of this author, Egypt, together with Algeria and Tunisia, holds a unique position in this regard. Not even the relatively liberal Moroccan family code of 2004 allows mothers to assume educational guardianship unless the father is deceased or absent, or the judge deems the father unfit to exercise this right.[39] In fact, compared to the difficult conditions faced by wives during the epoch represented in *Uridu Hallan* (I Want a Solution),[40] the reform movement of the 2000s provided many legal "solutions" for women who wanted to divorce their husbands and were willing and able to shoulder the financial responsibilities of bringing up their children and maintaining their household on their own.

Both in and outside Egypt, the changes were viewed as revolutionary, and they inspired family law reform throughout the Arab-speaking world, from Morocco and Algeria to Jordan and Palestine, and to Qatar and the United Arab Emirates. Nevertheless, a growing body of literature dealing with the implementation of *shari'a*-based family laws in the courts and everyday life shows that what might look as revolutionary change, sometimes constitutes more of a symbolic legislation to the outside world (see also Bordat and Kouzzi, this volume). For Egypt, Shaham notes that a wave of family reform proposals is awakened inside Egypt whenever a United Nations World Conference on Women is seen on the horizon.[41] Hence, in the next section, I deal with the implementation of *khul'* in practice to see whether this legal reform was really revolutionary or merely constituted a nonchange.

Egyptian Women Go to Court

The women of the Egyptian Feminist Union (EFU) of the 1920s were driven by a direct and personal desire to improve their position within the family. They had suffered personally from the effects of polygyny, underage marriage and the impossibility to divorce as well as husband's right to unconditionally pronounce the repudiation. For example, EFU founder and upper class member Huda al-Sha'rawi (1879–1947) married her legal guardian, the son of her father's sister when she was 13.[42] In the 1990s, however, the extent to which women's rights advocates were motivated by personal interest was not entirely clear. Some saw women's right to travel without the consent of their husband as a way for upper-class women to circumvent the legal prohibition on leaving the house without the consent of the husband. At the same time, the traveling alone provision benefitted women of the lower- and lower-middle classes who wished to work in the countries of the Gulf.[43] Similarly, with regard to *khul'*, it is questionable that The Group of Seven had in mind only the interests of upper class women since women from these strata of society are unlikely to approach the court for a solution of their private marital problems. The high-profile paternity case of fashion designer Hind al-Hinnawi (2004–2005) against actor Ahmad al-Fishawi Shanawi shows how uncommon and controversial it is for members of the Egyptian upper-class to expose to public scrutiny one's private affairs.[44] Nevertheless, opponents accused women's rights advocates of primarily having personal interest in PSL reform and used both written media and film to make it clear that they considered the reform to be a rich women's law.[45]

However, my fieldwork in 2004 and 2005 revealed that mainly lower and lower-middle class Egyptian women use family courts and that in the majority of the cases their main problem was nonmaintenance by the husband. Halima, whose story is told below, was one such woman.

Women Providers: The Case of Halima

At the time of her *khul'* court case, Halima was a 44 year-old mother of two who had been married for 20 years.[46] Her husband had become addicted to drugs even before they married and over the years his addiction had deeply affected the financial situation of their family. When Halima first met her husband she did not know he was addicted to drugs, but she soon found out, as he would severely beat her when under the influence of drugs. His behavior had compelled Halima to ask repeatedly for a divorce, but each time her mother prevented her from doing so, arguing that divorce carried a very negative meaning in Egyptian society. Her mother told Halima that people would gossip about her status and say that she was to blame for the divorce.

Eventually, however, Halima's husband dropped their first-born child on the floor while intoxicated. The child died soon after from head injuries, and Halima again asked her husband for a divorce. He accepted and pronounced the repudiation. Severely traumatized by the death of her baby, Halima sought psychological treatment for an extended period and was determined never to see her husband again. When her ex-husband asked for her hand again, however, Halima's mother pressured her into accepting his offer. The second marriage produced two other children, but did not stop his drug addiction and concomitant beatings. As soon as her mother died, Halima was determined to divorce her husband again.

This time, however, Halima's husband was not willing to give her a divorce and she was left with no other choice but to file for divorce in court. Although she had legal grounds for a fault-based divorce, which would entitle her to all her financial rights, in order to protect the interests of her son and daughter, Halima chose not to disclose in court her reasons for seeking dissolution of her marriage. She changed her lawsuit to a divorce through *khul'*, which enabled her to simply tell the judge, "*ana karha*" ("I am hating") rather than disclose her reasons for divorce.

As required by law, the judge sought to reconcile Halima and her husband (who was not present) but Halima was determined not to return to him this time and, according to her lawyer, the reconciliation session only lasted a few minutes. Since the law requires couples with children to go through another attempt at reconciliation, two shayks from al-Azhar also unsuccessfully attempted to persuade Halima to return to her husband. As the last court session started, her case was six months underway. That particular session was an important one as her husband finally appeared in court, creating a real possibility that he would appeal the mandated return of the prompt dower. Such an appeal would lead to another delay of Halima's case. In many cases, husbands do not accept the return of the registered prompt dower and judges are likely to respond in one of two ways: (1) conclude that the dispute over the dower should be transferred to a civil court so as not to prolong the *khul'* case, or (2) settle the dispute before continuing with the *khul'* case, thus delaying the case considerably.[47] Fortunately, In Halima's case, her husband accepted the return of one Egyptian pound (the prompt dower registered in their marriage contract), and Halima's case was concluded smoothly.

After her divorce, Halima and her two children left the marital home. Over the years, she had become used to her ex-husband scarcely being able to provide for his family and had found a job and even was able to save some money. She was able to rent a flat and maintain her household herself.

Halima's case is representative in that it shows that for a legal reform to have the intended impact it must meet the approval of the general public at the grassroots level. In Halima's case, it was only in the absence of fierce opposition of her mother, who had died, that Halima found the strength to finally divorce her addicted husband. In many cases, wives like Halima opted for *khul'*. This was not because they did not have legal grounds such as absence, nonprovision of maintenance, or abuse that would have made them eligible for a fault-based divorce in which they could have kept all their financial rights, such as the deferred part of the dower and the *'idda* maintenance. Rather, they saw *khul'* as a way to gain a speedy and hence, less costly, divorce, or, as in the case of Halima, preferred to not disclose in public the private and intimate details of their marital struggles. In many *khul'* cases women were shouldering the household expenses and the costs for raising their children alone, long before going to court. In such cases, it makes little sense to invest the time, money, and energy required for a fault-based divorce case – especially given that it might result in a positive ruling, but with legal effects that are impossible to execute.

Though opponents of *khul'* had called it a rich women's law, in the years following its implementation, *khul'* revealed a widespread and previously hidden phenomenon, namely, the prevalence among lower and lower-middle classes of households where women were the main providers.[48] Although constituting approximately 18–30 percent of urban Egyptian families, these households where women bear the main economic responsibility were an "officially unrecognized phenomenon in Egypt."[49] I found it ironic that most of the judges I interviewed argued that women in *khul'* cases should return to their husbands a compensation greater than the amount stipulated as the prompt dower in the marriage contract.[50] Some judges even ordered women to pay back the deferred dower, an amount they never had received. This freedom of judges to interpret the dower as they deemed fit was a consequence of the legislature having defined the provision on *khul'* in ambiguous terms.[51] Nevertheless, over the course of years, it seems that unilateral *khul'* has become the default divorce for women, in which they return the prompt dower as registered in the marriage contract, as the case of Halima demonstrates. The introduction of unilateral no-fault divorce gave women across the class spectrum stronger tools to bargain the terms of the marital relationship, and, if they failed to do so, divorce in a speedy and relatively inexpensive way.

Yet, while the implementation of unilateral *khul'* divorce in judicial practice seemed achieved, sudden changes in the political status quo can be disruptive to extant women's rights and sometimes even undo the gains made. In the next section, I assess the impact of the Egyptian Revolution of January 25, 2011 on women's right to unilateral no-fault divorce through *khul'*. I specifically focus on the period in which the previously forbidden political movement of the Muslim Brotherhood rose to power (February 2011–July 2013). It was during this period that the most fervent opponents of the provision on *khul'* gained a much more prominent voice in the political debate.

A Counterrevolution in Personal Status Law?

Immediately after ex-president Husni Mubarak was ousted from power in February 2011, the PSL provisions issued during the 2000s came under heavy attack. In particular, various organizations for the rights of divorced fathers succeeded in garnering much public attention for their cause: amending the PSL reforms of the 2000s, particularly the provisions on *khul'*, age of maternal custody, and visitation rights after divorce. They felt these provisions went against the principles of *shari'a* and had caused havoc in their families.[52] They were even supported by the President of the Cairo-based Family Appeal Court, judge 'Abdallah al-Baja, who approached the Prime Minister of the transitional movement with a draft proposal to abolish *khul'* in April 2011, when Egypt was officially ruled by the armed forces.[53]

Almost a year later, when Egypt's first post-revolutionary parliament, dominated by Islamists, had just been installed, an independent MP and deputy head of the Legislative Committee of the parliament, Muhammad al-'Umda, submitted a law proposal to abolish the provision on *khul'*. In a memorandum accompanying the proposal, al-'Umda said *khul'* had been granted to women at the behest of the National Council for Women, which is widely regarded as the vehicle for former first lady Suzanne Mubarak to promote her favorite causes. Al-'Umda said *khul'* was an offense to Islamic law and an attempt to Westernize Egypt.[54] However, his proposal was swiftly rejected in April 2012 by the parliament's Committee of Proposals and Complaints in April 2012,[55] shortly before the High Constitutional Court dissolved the parliament in June 2012.

Al-Azhar's Academy for Islamic Research also rejected, in May 2012, the demand of al-'Umda to abolish the provision on *khul'*. The Academy argued that *khul'* is a right guaranteed to women by Islamic *shari'a* in the same way that repudiation is permissible for men.[56] Given that al-Azhar had played a decisive role in the implementation of *khul'* (2000) and the provisions on custody (2005), it is not completely surprising that it upheld its original positions as these provisions being in line with the principles of the *shari'a*.[57]

The danger of women losing their right to *khul'* had not disappeared yet. November 30, 2012, a new Egyptian Constitution was approved by the Islamists who dominated the Constitutional Assembly. The new constitution immediately provoked an outcry of protests and heated debates. Opponents claimed that the Assembly, which had prepared the draft, was almost exclusively composed of Islamists and therefore did not adequately represent the Egyptian population. While this is not the place to explore the intricacies of the debate surrounding the new constitution, for the purpose of this chapter, two features are especially important. Not only did the new constitution consider the family to be the basic unit of society (Article 10) and speak of women as persons existing purely within the framework of the family (Article 10), for the first time in Egyptian history it also said that the state shall provide aid and assistance to divorced and widowed women as well as *women providers (al-mara' al-mu'ila)* (Article 10, italics mine).[58]

Here the Islamist government seemed to acknowledge that in a significant number of Egyptian households, such as that of Halima, not men but women constituted the main breadwinners and, hence, were de facto heads of households. At the same time, the constitution equated the "principles of the *shari'a*" with Sunni jurisprudence (Article 219). The inclusion of Article 219 provoked much controversy in the Egyptian public debate with many expressing a fear that this provision would pave the way for a conservative reading of the sources and teachings of Islamic religion.[59] These concerns applied all the more so to the domain of PSL, which was, by and large, the only field of law where the principles of the *shari'a* still applied.

Article 219 assigned an important place to the teachings of the four Sunni schools of law, all of which stress that the consent of the husband is a prerequisite for a *khul'* request to be valid.[60] In contrast, the *sunna* of the Prophet – used by the HCC to justify in 2002 the constitutionality of *khul'* as a unilateral divorce – stresses the unilateral character of a *khul'* divorce.[61] Thus, Article 219 paved the way for amending *khul'* from a unilateral to a consensual divorce. Perhaps the declaration of Egypt's leading religious institute, al-Azhar, that *khul'* was in line with the teachings of *shari'a* a few months earlier, can explain why no further attempts were undertaken to abolish *khul'* as a unilateral divorce through legal constitutional channels. With the overthrow of president Muhammad Mursi in July 2013 the constitution was abolished. In the new constitution of 2014, Article 219 is replaced by a preamble, which states that the principles of *shari'a* should be interpreted according to the body of relevant HCC rulings, instead of the teachings of the four schools of Islamic jurisprudence. Most of the court's past rulings were progressive from the human development perspective discussed in the introduction.[62] Perhaps it is no coincidence that barely two months after the constitution was passed through popular referendum in January 2014, the HCC issued a landmark ruling in a long-pending case of educational guardianship after divorce. According to the court, educational guardianship should go to the parent with custody, which is usually the mother.[63]

Conclusion

In this chapter, I traced the role of women's rights activists and organizations in the development of Egyptian *shari'a*-based Personal Status Law from the early twentieth to the early twenty-first century. In addition, I analyzed the implementation of these legal reforms in judicial practice, and assessed the impact of the Egyptian Revolution of January 25, 2011 on extant PSL.

In the 2000s, during a decade of revolution in PSL, advocates for the rights of women together with high officials within the Ministry of Justice and religious scholars within al-Azhar were instrumental in providing a solution of sorts for the plight of Egyptian women in unwanted marriages. The most controversial reform concerned a provision giving women the right to divorce without the consent of the husband and without the need to prove grounds in court. This divorce procedure, called *khul'*, was criticized harshly for being a law for rich women only and for allowing women to divorce for frivolous reasons (thereby destroying the stability of their families).

My fieldwork made clear that many judges shared these ideas, despite the fact that many women in *khul'* cases come from families where the husband, regardless of the reason, has not shouldered his marital duty of providing maintenance to his wife and children, and where women have had to manage on their own the financial and emotional affairs of the household and the upbringing of their children. Such households, however, were a previously unrecognized phenomenon in Egypt. Nevertheless, while a significant number of judges might not personally believe in *khul'*, it seems that over the course of the years a judicial consensus has emerged that has stopped judges from requiring women to return to their husbands an amount of dower that exceeds the amount registered in the marriage contract.

After the Egyptian Revolution of January 2011, *khul'* and other PSL reforms issued during Husni Mubarak's presidency became an instant target of much controversy, and were even popularly denigrated as the "Suzanne Mubarak Laws." Inside parliament, draft proposals were submitted to abolish these provisions, and the first post-revolutionary constitution of December 2012, although exceptional for acknowledging, for the first time in Egyptian history, the existence of households in which women are the main providers, equated "the principles of the *shari'a*" with Sunni jurisprudence. Since under Sunni jurisprudence, women cannot divorce without the consent of the husband, there was a real possibility that legal channels would be used to change *khul'* from a unilateral to a consensual divorce, and, hence, undo a century of women's rights activism. Major external changes – the forceful removal of ex-president Muhammad Morsi from power in July 2013 and the introduction of a new constitution in 2014 – have put a stop to this process, at least temporarily.

Endnotes

1 Welchman, L. (2007). *Women and Muslim Family Laws in Arab States: A Comparative Overview of Textual Developments and Advocacy.* Amsterdam: Amsterdam University Press, pp. 116–119.

2 Sonneveld, N. (Forthcoming). *Men and Women's Unilateral Divorce Rights in Egypt and Morocco: Differences in Popularity, Interpretation and Context.*

3 See for example Tucker, J.E. (1999). *In the House of the Law: Gender and Islamic Law in Ottoman Syria and Palestine.* Cairo: American University in Cairo Press.

4 See for example Molyneux, M. (1985). "Mobilization without emancipation? Women's interests, the State, and revolution in Nicaragua." *Feminist Studies.* Vol. 11, No. 2, pp. 227–254. However, in other geographical areas, such as East Central Europe and Latin America, "divorce and family law has been the least controversial area." Waylen, G. (2007). *Engendering Transitions: Women's Mobilization, Institutions, and Gender Outcomes.* Oxford: Oxford University Press, p. 164.

5 There are four schools of Sunni law jurisprudence. They are: the Hanafi, Maliki, Shafi'i, and Hanbali schools of Islamic jurisprudence. The Hanafi school was established by Imam Abu Hanifa (700–767 CE) in Kuffa, Iraq. It is the first and largest school. The Ottoman Empire greatly facilitated its

expansion. The Hanafi school is prevalent in central Asia, Afghanistan, South Egypt, Syria, Lebanon and Iraq. Second is the Maliki school, founded by Imam Malik Ibn Anas (710–795 CE) in Medina, Saudi Arabia. The Maliki school spread over North and West Africa. Third is the Shafi'i school, founded by Imam Muhammad al-Shafi'i (767–820 CE) in Medina where he was a student of Imam Malik. The Shafi'i school prevails in central and north Egypt, Palestine, Jordan, Indonesia, and Malaysia. Finally, the Hanbali school was founded by Imam Ahmad Ibn Hanbal (780–855 CE) in Baghdad, Iraq. It is the most traditional school and is favored by the Wahhabi movement, which was established in the eighteenth century in Saudi Arabia. In both Saudi Arabia and the United Arab Emirates the teachings of the Hanbali school represent the main source of legislation.

6 Berger, M. and N. Sonneveld (2010). "Sharia and National Law in Egypt." *Sharia Incorporated: A Comparative Overview of the Legal Systems of Twelve Muslim Countries in Past and Present*. J.M. Otto (ed.). Amsterdam: Amsterdam University Press, p. 54.

7 They were: (1899). *Tahrir al-Mar'a* [The Liberation of Women] and (1900). *Al-Mar'a al-Jadida* [The New Woman].

8 See, for example, Badran, M. (1996). *Feminists, Islam, and Nation: Gender and the Making of Modern Egypt*. Cairo: American University in Cairo Press.

9 Amin, Q. (1972). *Tahrir al-Mar'a*. Beirut: Al-Mu'assasa al-'Arabiyya li-l-Dirasat wa-l-Nashr.

10 Ibid.

11 In British India, the strict Hanafi rules concerning women's right to initiate divorce led many women to use apostasy as a legal device in order to rid themselves of unwanted marriages. See Masud, M.K. (1996). "Apostasy and Judicial Separation in British India." *Islamic Legal Interpretation: Muftis and Their Fatwas*. M.K. Masud, B. Messick and D.S. Powers (eds.). Cambridge: Harvard University Press, pp. 193–203.

12 Amin, *Tahrir al-Mar'a*.

13 See for example Al-Muqaddam, A.M.I. (2006). '*Awda al-Hijab: Mu'arka al-Hijab wa-l-Sufur*. Cairo: Dar Tiba li-l-Nashr wa-l-Tawzi', pp. 31–40.

14 Amin, *Tahrir al-Mar'a*.

15 Peterson, S.S. (2000). *The Liberation of Women and The New Women: Two Documents in the History of Egyptian Feminism*. Cairo: American University in Cairo Press.

16 Kholoussy, H. (2005). "The nationalization of marriage in monarchical Egypt." In *Re-Envisioning Egypt, 1919–1952*. A. Goldschmidt, A.J. Johnson and B.A. Salmoni (eds.). Cairo: American University in Cairo Press, p. 325.

17 Law no. 25 of 1920.

18 Kholoussy, "Nationalization of Marriage," p. 326.

19 Badran, *Feminists, Islam, Nation*, p. 135.

20 Under *bayt al-ta'a* (house of obedience), a husband has the legal right to use police force to return a wife who has left the marital home without his consent.

21 In line with the teachings of the Maliki school of law, the EFU suggested that girls stay with their mother until marriage and boys until they reach puberty. See, Badran, *Feminists, Islam, Nation*, p. 133.

22 Ibid, pp. 126–133.

23 Decree law 56 of 1923.

24 Law no. 25 of 1929.

25 Badran, *Feminists, Islam, Nation*, p. 135.

26 Zulficar, M. (2008). "The Islamic marriage contract in Egypt." *The Islamic Marriage Contract: Case Studies in Islamic Family Law*. A. Quraishi and F.E. Vogel (eds.). Cambridge: Harvard University Press, pp. 235, 238.

27 Kholoussy, H. (2010). *For Better, For Worse: The Marriage Crisis That Made Modern Egypt*. Stanford: Stanford University Press, p. 93.

28 Only a small number (approximately 70 cases) out of the thousands that Shaham studied concerned fault-based divorce cases. R. Shaham (1997). *Family and the Courts in Modern Egypt, A Study Based on Decisions by the Shari'a Courts, 1900–1955*. Leiden: Brill, p. 119.

29 Bernard-Maugiron, N. and B. Dupret (2002). "From Jihan to Susanne: twenty years of personal status law in Egypt." *Recht van de Islam-RIMO*. Vol. 19, p. 2.

30 Law no. 462 of 1955.

31 As provided in PSL no. 25 of 1929.

32 See for more, Tosson, N. (1999). *Women in Personal Status Courts: A Field Study*. Cairo: Arab Alliance for Women.

33 PSL no. 44 of 1979. In 1985, the HCC declared this law unconstitutional on procedural grounds saying that it had been implemented in a period of parliamentary recess while there was no urgent need to do so.

34 Decree no. 87 of 1931.

35 By defining *khul'* as both a consensual and a unilateral divorce option open to women, the legislature retained the Qur'anic provision of 2:229 as well as the Habiba *hadith*, each one treating *khul'* as a separate divorce structure. While the Qur'an clearly describes *khul'* as a consensual divorce (the husband must approve the ransom his wife offers him in return for the divorce), the *hadith* (see endnote 61) clearly treats it as a divorce to which the consent of the husband is irrelevant. O. Arabi (2001). "The Dawning of the Third Millennium on *Shari'a*: Egypt's Law

No. 1 of 2000, or Women May Divorce at Will." In *Studies in Modern Islamic Law and Jurisprudence*. O. Arabi (ed.). The Hague: Kluwer Law International, pp. 69–188.

36 It was still 50 percent at the beginning of the 1930s. Fargues, P. (2003). "Terminating marriage." *The New Arab Family*. N.S. Hopkins (ed.). Cairo: American University in Cairo Press, p. 258.

37 See for an extensive analysis of the debate surrounding *khul'*, Sonneveld, N. (2012). *Khul' Divorce in Egypt: Public Debates, Judicial Practices, and Everyday Life*. Cairo: American University in Cairo Press, chs. 2 and 3.

38 Article 76 of law no. 91 of 2000. See Bernard-Maugiron, N. (2004). "Quelques développements récents dans le Droit du statut personnel en Égypte." *Revue internationale de droit comparé*. Vol. 2, p. 376.

39 Art. 231 of Mudawwana al-Usra 2004.

40 While *Uridu Hallan* features and criticizes the Nasser era, a period in which little was done to bring the PSL in accordance with the demands of modern times, it was released under Sadat, in 1975, and simultaneously provides a critique of this period.

41 Shaham, R. (1999). "State, feminists and Islamists: the debate over stipulations in marriage contracts in Egypt." *Bulletin of the School of Oriental and African Studies*. Vol. 62, No. 3, p. 481.

42 Badran, *Feminists, Islam, Nation*.

43 Sonneveld, *Khul' Divorce Egypt*, pp. 153–154.

44 Hind al-Hinnawi became pregnant from an informal (*'urfi*) marriage to famous Egyptian actor Ahmad al-Fishawi Shanawi. When the alleged father denied the relationship and the pregnancy, Hind al-Hinnawi filed a paternity dispute court case. What is of interest here is that although many of the public sympathized with al-Hinnawi, many also condemned her for not having kept her case private. See *Al-Ahram Weekly*, December 29, 2005–January 4, 2006.

45 Sonneveld, *Khul' Divorce Egypt*, chs. 2 and 3.

46 I interviewed her lawyer in Cairo on April 1, 2004.

47 See also Al-Sharmani, M. (2009). "Egyptian family courts: a pathway of women's empowerment?" *Hawwa*. Vol. 7, p. 102.

48 In a study on Egyptian households, Bibars employs the term female-headed households. They include all households where women bear "the main economic responsibility for the management and maintenance of the household." Bibars, I. (2001). *Victims and Heroines: Women, Welfare and the Egyptian State*. London: Zed Books, p. 47. These households are composed of deserted wives, widows, divorcees, spinsters, women who are married to men without regular work, and similar situations. Bibars, *Victims and Heroines*, p. 58.

49 Ibid, p. 58.

50 The prompt dower is the amount the husband pays to the wife upon marriage. The deferred dower is the amount he pays later during the marriage or upon divorce or death.

51 See for more, Sonneveld, N. (2010). "Khul' divorce in Egypt: how family courts are providing a 'dialogue' between husband and wife." *The Anthropology of the Middle East*. Vol. 5, No. 2, pp. 100–120. See also, Al-Sharmani, "Egyptian Family Courts," p. 102.

52 For a fuller discussion, see Sonneveld, N. and M. Lindbekk (2015). "A revolution in Muslim Family Law? Egypt's pre- and post-revolutionary period (2011–2013) compared." *New Middle Eastern Studies*. Vol. 5. Available at www.brismes.ac.uk/nmes/archives/1409.

53 Gómez-Rivas, C. (2011). "Women, Shari'a, and personal status law reform in Egypt after the revolution." *Middle East Institute*. Available at www.mei.edu/content/women-shari%E2%80%98-and-personal-status-law-reform-egypt-after-revolution (accessed January 11, 2017).

54 See for example Abu Zayd, M. (March 2012). "Mashru' qanun li-ilgha' al-khul' [A draft law to abolish khul']." *Al-Shuruq*. Available at http://shorouknews.com/news/view.aspx?cdate=17032012&id=b98eeade-39d4-4db7-b010-62dbbcaa80f4 (accessed July 5, 2013).

55 See for example Gharib, M. (April 2012). "Al-Iqtirahat wa-l-Shakawi" tur-fud mashru'i ilgha' al-khul' wa tarshah madhduji al-jinsiyya li-l barlaman [The Committee of Proposals and Complaints refuses to cancel the draft to abolish khul' and they propose dual nationality to Parliament]." *Al-Masry Al-Yawm*. Available at www.almasryalyoum.com/node/759121 (accessed July 5, 2013); El-Hennawy, N. (April 2012). "Parliament rejects proposal to cancel women's right to divorce." *Egypt Independent*. Available at www.egyptindependent.com/news/parliament-rejects-proposal-cancel-womens-right-divorce (accessed July 5, 2013).

56 See for example *Al-Yawm Al-Saba'*. May 22, 2012.

57 Sonneveld and Lindbekk, "A revolution in Muslim."

58 The provision on women providers was retained in Article 11 of the constitution of 2014.

59 Earlier, in 1993, the judges of the HCC had defined "the principles of the *shari'a*" as those rulings whose origin and interpretation are definitive, with no binding reference to the orthodox interpretation of the four Sunni schools of law.

60 See, for example, Zantout, M. (2006). "Khul': between past and present." *Islamic Law and Law of the Muslim World*. Paper 08–14. New York: New York Law School. Available at https://papers.ssrn.com/sol3/papers.cfm?abstract_id=1094367.

61 Here the *sunna* of the Prophet refers to the so-called Habiba *hadith*. The version presented below shows the most common wording of the *hadith*, and it also is the one employed by the Egyptian HCC in an effort to

justify the introduction of a unilateral form of *khul'* in Egypt. Al-Bukhari reported: "The wife of Thabit b. Qays b. Shammas [Habiba] came to the Messenger, peace be upon him, and said: 'O Messenger of God, I do not hate Thabit neither because of his faith nor his nature, except that I fear unbelief.' The Messenger of God, peace be upon him, said: 'Will you give back his orchard?' She said 'Yes' and she gave it back to him and he [the Prophet] ordered him and so he [Thabit] separated her."

62 See for a fuller discussion, Arabi, O. (2002). "Beyond power: neo-Shafi'-ism or the Islamic constructive metaphor in Egypt's high constitutional court policy." *Arab Law Quarterly*. Vol. 4, pp. 323–354.

63 See (March 2016). "Al-dusturiyya al-'ulya" taqdi bi-haqq al-hadin fi-l-wilaya al-ta'limiyya 'ala al-tifl [The High Constitutional Court rules that the custody holder has the right to educational guardianship of the child]." *Al-Mogaz*. Available at http://almogaz.com:8181/news/politics/2016/03/05/2203403 (accessed March 8, 2016). For more details on the background of the case, see Sonneveld and Lindbekk, "A revolution in Muslim."

15 | Emerging Norms
Writing Gender in the Post-Revolution Tunisian State

ZOE PETKANAS

Introduction

The 2011 Tunisian election of the National Constituent Assembly (NCA) and the resulting 2014 Constitution represent the first attempt at redefining Tunisian citizenship in the postauthoritarian democratic transition. The successful passage of an inclusive and democratic constitution stands out amongst other countries that deposed a leader in 2011 in the region. In fact, in October 2015, the Norwegian Nobel Committee awarded the Nobel Peace Prize to the Tunisian National Dialogue Quartet for its role in brokering an agreement between "Islamists and secularists" following a breakdown of the political process after two assassinations of high-level opposition leaders in 2013. Essentially, the Quartet is credited with saving Tunisian democracy when the country was "on the brink of civil war."[1] The Quartet played an important role at a pivotal moment in Tunisia's democratic transition. However, the elevation of the Quartet as the savior of Tunisian democracy obscures the two and a half years of arduous daily negotiation, compromise, and cooperation by elected deputies.

In this chapter, I examine the process by which elected women deputies of the NCA worked to remake women's citizenship in the constitutional drafting process, and also analyze how existing power structures in Tunisia can mediate the implementation and practice of the Constitution. In doing so, I draw on interviews with major political actors conducted in April 2012 and September 2013 to May 2014 in order to explore the historical role of gender in the Tunisian state and the ways this gender dynamic has endured or been ruptured by the women drafting the new Constitution.[2] This chapter, then, pairs the analysis of the construction of the female citizen in the new Constitution with a detailed and novel articulation of the role that women across the political spectrum played in the constitutional writing of gender. This close reading of the constitutional process complicates the discursive notion of Tunisian politics as defined by a binary between Islamism and secularism, and reveals a political landscape that is both fluid and nuanced when viewed through a gendered lens.

Female Subject-Making in Tunisian History

Defining a citizen has been the task of the state, through its legislation, courts, practices, and its limitations.[3] But the process of constructing a citizen is not just a legal one. It employs subjectification, more specifically,[4] "cultural process[es] of subjectification," referring to the process by which human beings, as subjects, are constituted.[5] The term subject, in this context, refers to the Foucauldian "modes of objectification that transform human beings into subjects."[6] According to Foucault, various forms of power in a society facilitate this transformation:

[The] form of power that applies itself to immediate everyday life categorizes the individual, marks him by his own individuality, attaches him to his own identity, imposes a law of truth on him that he must recognize and others have to recognize in him. It is a form of power that makes individuals subjects. There are two meanings of the word "subject:" subject to someone else by control and dependence, and tied to his own identity by a conscience or self-knowledge. Both meanings suggest a form of power that subjugates and makes subject to.[7]

Ultimately, then, the definition of citizenship and access to it are mediated through cultural and historical lenses. In other words, although the state constructs the parameters of citizenship, individuals entering that structure are culturally and historically constituted as subjects. Historically in Tunisia, the state has used the tools at its disposal to constitute a certain political subject out of Tunisian women that suited the particular needs of the State. Further, given that citizenship is mediated through existing structures of power, gaps exist between the law and implementation of the law.

Throughout modern political history, the Tunisian government has relied on legislation as the primary tool of state consolidation, utilizing it to engineer the country to fit the social and political goals of its leader.[8] The State's relationship with women was situated within a larger framework of state feminism, a postcolonial phenomenon typical of the Arab world. State feminism, popularized by Mervat Hatem, "involves policies directed from (and formulated at) the state leadership level, which aimed at mobilising or channelling women's (re)productive capabilities and co-opting them into support for the state."[9] This postcolonial state feminism was not intended to fully renegotiate patriarchy; instead it tapped into unused capacities of large swaths of the population.[10] Rather than emancipating women, it increased women's dependence on the state for their rights and opportunities, in turn, decreasing the chance that they would rely on alternative structures of power.

Tunisia's first president Habib Bourguiba, for example, brought about significant family law reforms in the 1956 Code of Personal Status (known by its French acronym, CSP), serving as the lynchpin of Bourguiba's vision for the new state. The CSP laid a legal foundation that profoundly changed the relationship between women, the family unit, and the state. It shifted the object of the law from the family to the individual, by abolishing polygyny, repudiation, and matrimonial guardianship, which put these issues in the hands of individuals rather than the family governed by a patriarch.[11] Bourguiba also created a civil court system for the arbitration of family law, which had previously been subject to religious courts or considered to be internal family matters, giving women equal rights in respect to the marriage contract and divorce proceedings.[12] Preempting the development of an autonomous women's movement, Bourguiba created the National Union of Tunisian Women (UNFT) in 1956.[13] Although ostensibly a nonstate actor, UNFT was actually an arm of the state, tasked with socializing women to their new roles as tools of secularization and modernization and to control the development of female political activity.[14] With the rise of the Islamic Tendency Movement (MTI, now Ennahdha) in the 1970s, Bourguiba positioned Islamism as antithetical to the promotion of women's rights, as a way to pit potential forces of opposition against each other. Through the decades-long conflation of women's rights, in particular the CSP, and State secularism, Bourguiba was able to manufacture a binary between Islamism and women's rights. Although Bourguiba did expand women's individual rights, these policies were centered on the needs of the modern state. They incorporated Tunisian women into the State apparatus on the State's terms, consolidating its power, while simultaneously

neutralizing potential centers of opposition, such as kinship communities and the Islamic establishment.[15]

When Zine al-Abidine Ben Ali came to power in 1987, he continued
to utilize women as a State tool and as a balancing force against
Islamism. Ben Ali's dynamic authoritarianism relied on the creation of
highly managed spaces for nominal opposition. This allowed for the
emergence of a semiautonomous women's movement in the form of The
Tunisian Association of Democratic Women (ATFD) and the Tunisian
Women's Association for Development Research (AFTURD), whose
secularist discourse did not fundamentally challenge the secular modernist agenda embedded within Bouguiba and Ben Ali's state feminism.
Ben Ali also instituted state-party gender quotas, projecting a strong
commitment to women's rights and using the guise of democracy
to strengthen his pluralist, democratic image abroad. These quotas
allowed Ben Ali to operate under the guise of democratic reform without
actually altering the patterns of participation. Ben Ali deployed secular
women as symbols of democracy, positioning them as "broader state-
building and regime-consolidating tool(s) and part of a larger project to
reinforce patriarchal structures"[16] in a "patriarchal bargain."[17] Intensifying Bourguiba's antagonistic binary between Islamism and women's
rights, Ben Ali justified his violent repression of Islamists by positioning
himself as "the defender of a progressive, secular republic under threat
from religious chauvinism" and by extension the legacy of women's
rights in Tunisia.[18]

Thus, between 1956 and 2010, the Tunisian state employed this
process to construct a certain kind of political subject out of Tunisian
women, one that embodied an identity that suited the political needs
of the State. Bourguiba's modernization program, and in particular
the CSP, began the process by engineering a singular public image of
the "modern" Tunisian woman, defined in large part by secularism.
Access to citizenship and civil rights depended on a woman's con-
formity with this image. Those who did not conform were excluded
and marginalized – namely Islamist women. Nonetheless, Bourguiba's
reforms informed the construction of a public role for women under
Ben Ali, who continued the process of subject-making under the guise
of democratic pluralism. The result of these processes was a manufac-
tured dominant and singular image of Tunisian womanhood, portrayed as secular and "emancipated," ultimately serving the interests
of the state.

Scholarship on Women's Rights in Tunisia

Prior to the 2011 uprisings, most of the scholarship on Tunisian women reflected the broader political dynamics within the country and produced a unified narrative. As such, it was situated within a discourse framed by secular legal victories for women initiated by the state.[19] Within this literature, prominent scholars have employed different approaches to analyze the evolving relationship between the Tunisian state and its female citizens, such as, gendered citizenship,[20] equality,[21] state manipulation of civil society actors within a broader context of authoritarian state-building,[22] and women's groups as non-state actors.[23] There are major gaps in this literature, however, as Islamist women are rendered virtually invisible. The literature thoroughly examines the processes of subject-making for secular women, through a rigorous charting of secular women and their relationship with the state, as well as the development of a semi-autonomous secular feminist discourse and movement. There is no comparable account of the subjectification of Islamist women, who were marginalized by state feminism and unrepresented by organizations like ATFD and AFTURD.

The emergence and prominence of Islamist women in contemporary politics and their role in writing gender into the constitution suggests a rich, yet unwritten, history of political organization, participation, and an Islamic feminism. In tandem with the political pluralization since the 2011 uprisings, scholars have begun to address this gap in the literature, and it is to this emerging literature that this chapter contributes.[24]

Tunisian Women and the Familial Unit

The family unit and its relationship with the state is a construction of power to which women historically have been subject and which objectifies them as a particular subject within a particular discourse. Historically, one of the characterizing social structures of Tunisia has been the kinship community. Within these communities, individuals are embedded within larger kin relations, and within these relations individuals construct connective or relational notions of personhood, as opposed to individual or contractual ones. Such individuals rely on relational rights, such that, a person's sense of rights flows out of relationships that he or she has. It is by being invested in relationships that one comes to have rights. As a basis for citizenship practices, relational rights further require that citizens embed themselves in family and other subnational communities such as religious sects, ethnic, and tribal groups to gain access to the rights and privileges of citizenship. [25]

However, the family unit, as the base unit of society, is not a gender-neutral institution, but rather, a masculinized one. When the family is seen as the subject, its masculinization occurs through the perpetuation of familial patriarchy. In other words,

it suggests that the masculine legal subject is privileged on the basis of his status as patriarch. The head of a patriarchal family, legally constituted as the basic unit of the political community, would accrue rights and responsibilities concomitant with that legal status. [26]

Intersecting this construct of the masculine legal subject, is the positioning of women within *shari'a*, a legal system originally constructed to reconcile the inequality of pre-Islamic tribal communities, but which ultimately codified legal patriarchy. For everyone, citizenship is differentiated by a constellation of socio-political or economic signifiers such as class, race, ethnicity, language or geography. For women, however, mediating patriarchal structures adds a gendered dimension to the signifiers that differentiate citizenship. As such their rights are refracted through gendered, as well as socio-political and economic, lenses.[27]

Gender and the Post–Ben Ali Political Discourse

Immediately following Ben Ali's fall in 2011, the issue of women's rights came to the forefront of public discourse. The revolution ushered in unprecedented political pluralism. More than 100 new political parties formed and Ennahdha reemerged in force. Ennahdha's newly legalized presence in the public sphere reanimated the historical antagonism between secular women's groups and Ennahdha, and secular women's discourse increasingly centered on fear of losing past achievements, like the CSP. On January 29, 2011, ATFD and AFTURD, along with the Tunisian League of Human Rights, organized a major demonstration in Tunis to support the safe-guarding of women's rights, organized in response to Ennahdha's founder and former leader Rached Ghannouchi's return from twenty-two years of exile.[28]

In exile, Ghannouchi had attempted to rehabilitate the perception of Ennahdha as hostile to women's rights, writing a book titled *Women's Place between the Quran and the Muslim's Reality*. He offered "alternate interpretations, both old and new, to Qur'anic verses that have long been misinterpreted and misused against women."[29] Upon its re-emergence in 2011, Ennahdha's official rhetoric on women's rights was progressive and moderate. On November 2011, Ghannouchi affirmed his party's commitment to maintaining the CSP and women's rights.[30] However, critics accused Ennahdha of employing a "double discourse," essentially paying lip service to progressivism publicly, in particular to women's rights, while saving conservative rhetoric for more radical audiences.[31]

As the October 2011 election to elect the NCA approached, women's rights came to be situated in a broader confrontational narrative between Islamists and secularists. Gender became the platform from which to cement a binary of two broad political categories. Within this context, the simplified perception of a party as pro-women's rights or anti-women's rights enabled individuals to make a broad distinction between "secularists" and "Islamists" or "progressive" and "regressive." These dichotomies limited and overshadowed the nuances of the political landscape, derived in part from the anti-Islamist propaganda from Bourguiba and Ben Ali.[32]

Gender and the 2011 Election

In May 2011, the High Commission for the Realization of Revolutionary Goals, Political Reforms, and Democratic Transition, which acted as the source of public authority before the elections, passed a gender parity provision as part of the interim electoral code.[33] The High Commission determined that the elections would follow a closed list proportional representation system. Parties submitted lists of ranked candidates for each district. The proportion of votes a party received in a given district would determine how many candidates from that list, starting from the top, would become deputies.[34] The gender parity law required these lists to be evenly split between men and women and for the genders to be alternating, known as vertical parity, otherwise the list would be invalidated.[35]

Women fared moderately well in the election, originally taking 58 out of 217 seats in the NCA, about 27 percent, 40 of whom were from Ennahdha. Between 2011 and 2014, the number of women deputies increased to 68, or 31 percent.[36] Vacancies, such as appointments of (mostly male) deputies to ministries, allowed candidates further down the list (often women) to ascend to the NCA. These were impressive numbers, relative to the small proportion of women's political representation across the globe. However, a substantial disparity remained between the number of women candidates and the number of resulting women deputies. The High Commission did not specify the gender breakdown of the heads of lists, known as horizontal parity. Women headed only 7 percent of lists, although they comprised roughly 50 percent of candidates. In 93 percent of cases, a party would have to win more than one seat per district to send a woman to the NCA.[37] Ennahdha was able to win more than one seat in thirty out of thirty-three districts, a feat accomplished by only one other party in two districts, and three parties and one independent list in one district. Consequently, the voting structure amplified the heavy male bias at the heads of lists, resulting from the lack of horizontal parity, into the NCA.

Gender and the Constitutional Drafting Process

The 2012 Draft of the Constitution

The NCA released the first draft of the Constitution in August 2012, representing the first time that Tunisian citizens could measure public statements by deputies and party members against concrete results in the Constitution. In examining the process of (re)creating the Tunisian woman citizen, it is necessary to look at the way gender featured in the specific discursive landscape of the evolving constitutional language.

Gender and equality were relatively prominent in the first draft. The first draft of the preamble, released April 24, 2012, affirmed gender neutral "equality in rights and duties between individuals," echoing the 1959 constitution.[38] Due largely to Lobna Jribi, vice-president of the Commission of the Preamble, Fundamental Principles and Constitutional Revision,[39] that language had shifted by August, affirming equality between citizens, using "\muwaāṭinaāt\" and "\muwaāṭiniīn\," the female and male plurals of citizens.[40] This language represented a distinct change from the 1959 Constitution, which simply guaranteed "equality among citizens in terms of rights and duties" in the preamble and stated that "all citizens have the same rights and obligations. All are equal before the law."[41] By explicitly guaranteeing equality between men and women in the 2012 draft Constitution, the NCA was acknowledging the potential for de facto gender discrimination despite Tunisia's long constitutional history of de jure equality. Article 1.6[42] and 2.22[43] affirmed equality using only the male plural "citizens" or "\muwaāṭinuūn\," echoed the language of the 1959 Constitution, creating inconsistency with the way that the Constitution explicitly tied gender to equality.

Article 1.10 stated that "the state shall protect the rights of women as well as protect family structures and maintain the coherence thereof," eliding women's rights and the rights of the family.[44] This article seemed to affirm collective rights, which contained potential challenges to Article 1.7's affirmation of individual rights.[45] Furthermore, women's rights and the rights of the family can conflict with one another. Historically, situating women's rights within the collective rights of the family has mediated women's access to individual rights, as the rights of the (masculinized) collective superseded her own. It was also unclear how these articles, and the conflict between collective and individual rights, would interact with the CSP, and its codification of individual rights at the expense of the extended family, or Article 2.21, which affirmed the stability of the family but "in an environment of equality between the spouses."[46]

Complementarity and Article 2.28

Article 2.28 on Women's Rights further complicated this tension, which proved to be the most controversial provision on women. Written by the Commission on Rights and Liberties, Article 2.28 was passed with twelve votes and is most commonly translated as:

The State shall guarantee the protection of the rights of women and shall support the gains thereof as true partners to men in the building of the nation and as having a role complementary thereto within the family.

The State shall guarantee the provision of equal opportunities between men and women in the bearing of various responsibilities.

The State shall guarantee the elimination of all forms of violence against women.[47]

The word "complementary" in the section above was translated from the Arabic word \yatakaāmalu\ to describe the roles of men and women in the family.[48] In a proposed version of Article 2.28, which garnered eight votes in the Commission but was ultimately rejected, the notion of complementarity is notably absent. It read: "The state guarantees the rights of women and their achievements in all fields. It is forbidden to enact laws that may harm them in any way whatsoever."[49]

The version of Article 2.28 in the draft Constitution immediately ignited a firestorm of criticism and protest both within and outside the Assembly, even before the draft was officially released. Selma Mabrouk, member of the Commission on Rights and Liberties who was elected from a list of the ruling coalition's *Ettakatol* party but had defected to secular-leftist *Al Massar* in 2012, revealed the text of Article 2.28 on Facebook on August 2, 2012, in a viral post titled "A bad day at the Committee on Rights and Liberties."[50] Hasna Mersit, another member of the Commission who was elected on a *Congrès pour la République* (CPR) list but left the party to become an independent soon after the election, described her reaction to the inclusion of \yatakaāmalu\:

When we voted in the commission on women, it didn't have equality or parity or anything! I left the commission right away and went straight to *Mosaique FM* to get civil society to take charge of this issue, because now we are in a dangerous situation. I said, "Your gains are in danger and we have to save women's gains!"[51]

The reaction of civil society was swift and fierce. Women's organizations immediately released statements denouncing the draft. Hinda Ben Rejeb, a member of ATFD, stated that the draft Constitution in general "doesn't respond to the aspirations and expectations of the Tunisian people and particularly Tunisian women," claiming it as part of an ideology "that Tunisian society and Tunisian women refuse."[52] A joint statement by human rights groups and the General Tunisian Workers Union (UGTT), the country's largest syndicate, condemned Article 2.28 as a threat to the achievements of women, creating "a patriarchal system that gives all power to men and denies women their rights ... and [will] deny women their full citizenship and independence."[53] Civil society organizations, including women's groups, UGTT, and human rights organizations scheduled a protest for 13 August 2012, the anniversary of the CSP. Estimates of attendance ranged from between 5,000 to 30,000.[54]

Defenders of the language in Article 2.28 of the draft Constitution mainly blamed the discontent on mistranslation, misinterpretation, and decontextualization. Monica Marks, at the time a doctoral student at Oxford University, wrote in August in *Foreign Affairs* that the first clause of Article 2.28 was more accurately translated as, "the state guarantees the protection of women and supports their achievements, considering them as men's true partners in building the nation, and their (men's and women's) roles *fulfil one another* within the family" (emphasis added).[55] Marks argued that fears over setbacks to women's rights were overblown. She maintained that the controversial language in Article 2.28 defined women and men in relational terms in a manner consistent with historical conceptions of family relations in Tunisia and Islamism, and therefore departed from the "liberal, individualistic template of Western human rights norms."[56]

Amel Azzouz, a Nahdhawia deputy and member of the Shura Council or the internal executive council of the Ennahdha party, participated in a February 2014 panel discussion with Rached Ghannouchi at the Carnegie Endowment in Washington DC. There, she asserted that \yatakaāmalu\ can be translated as "complementary" but that the true meaning of the word differs from its French and English translations. She interpreted the clause in this way, "[\yatakaāmalu\] is trying to put an end to men's selfishness. There are public spheres and private spheres, and what you wanted is to bring men back to the private spheres and get women out to the public sphere."[57] Azzouz had articulated this point in an interview with the author on January 24, 2014:

We have aspired for sort of men returning back to the private and women (to the public) ... and so that women can really act in the public sphere ... if men continue to resign from the private sphere, women will never be active and will never act suitably in the public life. This is how we understood \yatakaāmalu\.[58]

Farida Labidi, another Nahdhawia deputy on the Commission on Rights and Liberties and member of the Shura Council, voted for the draft language in Article 2.28, but also became one of the biggest proponents of electoral gender parity. She took a slightly different approach to the meaning of \yatakaāmalu\, asserting that critics intentionally removed \yatakaāmalu\ from its larger context by ignoring Article 2.22, which affirmed equality between all citizens.[59]

In an interview with Mehrezia Labidi in 2014, the Vice-President of
the NCA and arguably the most powerful woman in Tunisian politics
at the time, also weighed in on the word \yatakaāmalu\. She agreed
with Farida Labidi that the word was being misconstrued, however,
she also observed:

I find this sentence really nonsense in the article related to women['s rights]
and I was amongst those who said "sorry, but this sentence may have a sense
and a meaning in Article 21, the article speaking about family, but if you put
it in the article about women's rights, then it adds nothing. It is just literature
and what kind of legal or traditional impact might it have? It might even be
dangerous. So a judge might interpret this sentence as 'ok, men and women's
roles are complementary in the family, so women get the children and raise
them, educate them, and men work.'"[60]

Mehrezia Labidi also noted that Rached Ghannouchi and Ali
Larayedh, two of the principle leaders of Ennahdha, agreed with her
in the Shura Council, indicating the existence of internal disagreements
in the Ennahdha party, despite its propensity for voting as a bloc.

The interesting aspect of the debate around Article 2.28 and the
meaning of \yatakaāmalu\ is that both sides seemed to be articulating a
similar vision for the role of women in public and in private – that of
full participation of women (and men) in both public and private
spheres and comprehensive access to citizenship, social and economic
rights. The rift arose from the articulation of these rights in different
discursive frameworks, one steeped in relational rights with an Islamic
connotation and the other in liberal, individualistic rights that echoed
international language on human rights.

The problems associated with the use of \yatakaāmalu\ in Article
2.28, an article specifically pertaining to women's rights, are best
understood by placing the word in a historical context. Mehrezia
Labidi's objection captures these nuances. Because patriarchal structures still exist in Tunisia, the confluence of several factors – the
specific placement of \yatakaāmalu\ in an article on women's rights,
the sociocultural and historical context of Tunisian politics and society, and the discretionary room inherent in the process of defining
and enacting citizenship – all provide an opening for the erosion of
the vision for the role of women in Tunisian society and politics
shared by both the supporters and opponents of this specific iteration
of Article 2.28.

The Role of Le Groupe des Femmes

By the time the final Constitution was approved on January 26, 2014, most of the clauses that related to gender had gone through marked changes over a series of four drafts in August 2012, December 2012, April 2013, and June 2013. These changes were largely due to the formation of Le Groupe des Femmes, a parliamentary women's group within the NCA that was formed to "fight for the rights of women" in late 2012.[61] This project was spearheaded by Lobna Jribi, who was also a member of the important Consensus Committee, in consort with Mehrezia Labidi.

Jribi had immediately recognized that because women represented less than a third of the NCA they would be unable to adequately defend women's rights. As she later observed, "we realized that we few women were a bit scattered and we realized that we had to create a synergy among us, within the Assembly."[62] As Jribi described it, the objective of Le Groupe des Femmes was to "work on lobbying to adopt the articles of the constitution concerning male-female equality and concerning parity."[63] Group membership was flexible and could include up to 30 of the then 61 female deputies serving in the NCA. It was an exemplar of multi-partisanship, including members from "the extreme left-wing to the extreme right-wing. And all of them were sensitive when we were talking about the issue of working women, rural women, abused women, etc. It is not sectarian. This is a female cause. And this has been very important."[64] Other scholars have written about the failure of female deputies in the NCA to create a formal women's caucus in 2012 due to a lack of consensus.[65] Due to polarization in the public discourse and lack of definitive consensus within the NCA, Jribi said Le Groupe des Femmes avoided formalizing as a bloc:

We didn't want to talk about this (formalizing the group) at an early stage because we knew that it would demotivate the formal structuring of this group ... we didn't want to make public statements to the media saying that I am behind this and that I want to write this ... we want this group to be all the groups. We want there to be no political reclamation because it would weaken the project. Each woman has to feel that this is her group and that she has created it and is behind it.[66]

The most immediate issue for Le Groupe was ensuring that the Constitution explicitly referenced gender when guaranteeing equality. It was due to their commitment to this issue that the constitutional language on gender significantly evolved between 2012 and 2014.

Gender and the 2014 Constitution of the Tunisian Republic

Since the first draft in 2012, the preamble of the Constitution had remained consistent in referencing gender in terms of equality. In the final Constitution, Articles 21 and 40 also explicitly referenced male and female citizens in establishing equal rights and duties;[67] individual as well as collective rights;[68] and the right to adequate working conditions and to a fair wage.[69] The final Constitution still identified the family as "the basic structure of society"[70] and guaranteed to protect it, but it no longer conflated women's rights and family rights in the same provision. Compared to previous drafts, the final Constitution significantly improved upon language and organization of ideas related to gender by separating women's rights and family rights while at the same time affirming individual rights with an explicit reference to gender. In this way, the 2014 Constitution acknowledges and protects women's rights outside the construct of the family – so as to avoid mitigating women's access to citizenship, economic, and social rights – and validates the full participation of women in the public sphere.

In fact, in the final Constitution of the Tunisian Republic, women's rights merit their own provision, that is, Article 46, the most pivotal for women. The full text of the article in English reads:

The State shall commit to protecting women's achieved rights and seek to support and develop them.

The State shall guarantee equal opportunities between men and women in the bearing of all the various responsibilities in all fields.

The State shall seek to achieve equal representation for women and men in elected councils.

The State shall take all the necessary measures to eliminate violence against women.[71]

Unlike the preamble, which had remained relatively consistent in terms of gender since 2012, Article 46 addressed broad goals and underwent substantial changes throughout the drafting process. It is important to understand the nuances of the evolution of the rights and protections guaranteed within Article 46, since they have the largest potential to impact Tunisian women and demonstrate the process of redefinition involved in citizenship construction. Comparing and contrasting the succession of Article 46 drafts requires an unpacking of each clause, due both to the article's breadth and the nonlinear process by which it was developed.

Clause One: The State shall commit to protecting women's achieved rights and seek to support and develop them.

The language of this clause in the final Constitution explicitly protects women's past gains while simultaneously pledging to "support and develop them" in the future, and represents an important change from previous drafts. Although the second (December 2012), third (April 2013), and fourth (June 2013) drafts protected existing women's rights, they did not explicitly reference the development of future rights. The framing within the drafts situated the state as reactive to challenges to the coveted gains of Tunisian women without signaling a commitment to being proactive. The wording in the final Constitution is meaningful in that it acknowledges existing inequalities for women, despite the declared equality between citizens enshrined in the 1959 Constitution.

Clause Two: The State shall guarantee equal opportunities between men and women in the bearing of all the various responsibilities in all fields.

In this clause, the evolution of the word \yatakaāmalu\ is evident. After the public outcry and opposition to the inclusion of \yatakaāmalu\ in the first draft, the Commission on Rights and Liberties omitted that specific word in all further drafts. However, the second, third, and fourth drafts contained the controversial subtext of \yatakaāmalu\ in the phrasing on equal opportunities. The prefinal drafts of this clause all referred, with only minor differences, to a guarantee that the State "shall ensure equal opportunities for men and women in carrying different responsibilities." In each of these drafts, "responsibilities" was qualified by "\mukhtalifi\", as in "\mukhtalifi al-mas'uūliyyaāti\", translated as "different responsibilities." The final version also employed "\mukhtalifi al-mas'uūliyyaāti\," but the clause also included the phrase "\fī jamiī'a al-majaālaāti\" or "in various fields". Taken as a whole, the clause is translated as "The State shall guarantee equal opportunities between women and men in the bearing of all the various responsibilities in all fields"[72] or "The State guarantees equality of opportunity between women and men to have access to all the levels of responsibilities in all domains."[73] The subtle linguistic changes helped to remedy the potential contradictions produced by earlier draft language that had simultaneously protected equal opportunities between women and men while implying that they have different roles and responsibilities to carry out by virtue of their gender. The final version is clearer and also avoided controversy like that associated with the critical interpretation of \yatakaāmalu\.

Nevertheless, the issue of complementarity continues to surface in the discourse of secular activists and opposition party members, echoing broader regional tensions between feminisms that are anchored in different discourses, who reference it as indicative of Ennahdha's actual stance on women's rights. This discourse perpetuates and strengthens the narrative that a binary exists between pro- and anti-women's rights groups in Tunisian politics, when clearly the situation is more nuanced. Nahdhawiat deputies and other Islamist stakeholders similarly point to such public complaints as evidence of opposition members and secularists' desire to undermine Ennahdha for political gains. This too enhanced the confrontationalist narrative of Islamists vs. secularists, the perpetuation of which obscures points of similarity and undermines democratic consensus.

Clause Four:[74] *The State shall take the necessary measures to eliminate violence against women.*

This clause emerged in the second draft of the constitution and remained virtually unchanged until the final version. The inclusion in the final Constitution of State protection from gendered violence is important, as it goes beyond any previous legislation. Nearly half of all Tunisian women have experienced violence and experts estimate that one in five women will experience domestic violence at least once in their lives.[75] However, the constitutional provision itself is far from sufficient to address gendered violence. Marital rape is not legally recognized and, until July 2017, loopholes allowed rapists to avoid punishment by marrying their victim.[76] Furthermore, existing laws matter on a practical level insofar as they can be enforced. Because violence in the home, like many other issues that impact the daily lives of women, is widely seen as a private issue and enforcement is compromised by the belief that it is inappropriate to intervene within the home. Although the inclusion of this provision in the Constitution does not immediately address the lack of legal recourse of victims of gendered violence or the gap between law and application, it does constitutionally codify the State's commitment to ending gendered violence. This clause set the groundwork for a landmark bill to eliminate violence against women passed in July 2017.[77]

Clause Three: The State shall seek to achieve equal representation for women and men in elected councils.

What sets this clause apart from the others is that it does not appear in any of the four previous drafts of the Constitution, despite being arguably the most consequential. It only came to debate at the General Assembly on January 6, 2014, mere weeks before the final approval of the Constitution on January 26. With the other Articles, it is possible to chart the progression of language and concept through various iterations in the drafting process, providing insight into the fluidity of certain ideas and values within the NCA. For this clause on gender parity, however, this process remained internal until 2014.

Le Groupe des Femmes had not been able to come to a quick consensus regarding electoral gender parity, but their years in the NCA had caused some of women deputies to shift their views on obligatory parity. Although, Jribi would become one of the strongest advocates for constitutionalized gender parity, she had not always been the strongest proponent of "positive discrimination."[78] Working in the private sector as an entrepreneur, she had always believed that, "a woman, by her skills and her knowledge doesn't need positive discrimination" and that "parity is something that should not be offered by men ... this is how I acted before." Her attitude changed after she entered politics, however, when she "discovered a very masculine environment and it's really, I would say, impossible for women to have a really equal chance with a man if there is not this "*coup de pouce*" [boost]. Equality is not something yet in the culture."[79] Similarly, Farida Labidi experienced a change of opinion. As a member of the High Commission, she gave a speech opposing gender parity within the 2011 interim electoral law. In the speech, she objected to the concept because she believed that women are qualified enough and

do not require legal intervention to prove themselves. By 2014, however, Farida Labidi was one of the strongest proponents of constitu-
tionalizing gender parity after seeing the obstacles that qualified
women faced in the political sphere.[80]

The December 2012 vote in the NCA on the formation of Instance
Supérieure Indépendante pour les Elections, ISIE, also served as a
turning point for some of the members of Le Groupe des Femmes.
An amendment to Article 6 required ISIE's elected committee to
employ gender parity in seat allocation. According to Jribi, most of
the women in the group assumed that ISIE's role as the regulatory body
on electoral parity guaranteed passage of the amendment. However,
the debate was contentious and because of significant disagreement the
final vote was delayed until the last possible day.

This event was deeply unsettling to some members of Le Groupe des
Femmes and impacted future strategy, as Jribi described:

When we founded ISIE was precisely when I really felt concerned and
realized that parity absolutely had to be included in the Constitution. I had
thought, for example, that vertical parity had already been acquired. For me,
it was self-evident that the composition [of ISIE] should be egalitarian.
The least we could have done was to make the candidacy egalitarian. And
when we discussed this, it was not evident and people even rejected this!
What does this mean? It means that even though we were all elected
according to egalitarian lists, and we thought that this was already acquired,
when we got to the first ... jurisdiction from this assembly-there had been a
step back or at least a risk.[81]

Jribi's description captures what several of the most prominent deputies in Le Groupe des Femmes articulated during my interviews. They
described this vote as the moment when the need to constitutionalize
gains already conceived of as won, crystallized. In light of this disappointment, Hasna Mersit described that ensuring that equality clauses
included both \muwaāṭinaāt\ and \muwaāṭiniīn\ had to become the first
priority, before trying to implement gender parity.[82]

The July assassination of prominent opposition figure, Mohamed
Brahmi, fomented a political crisis that brought to a halt the ongoing
constitutional project. The National Dialogue, mediated by the Quartet, resulted in a road map for finalizing the Constitution and appointing a new government, allowing the NCA to re-start its work. The
deadline for submitting any amendments before the final vote was

December 30, 2013. During this time, members of Le Groupe des Femmes wrote an amended version of Article 45 (now Article 46) that included electoral gender parity and circulated a petition with the new language, garnering 78 of the 120 signatures required for an amendment to make it onto the floor. A counter-petition was circulated and until the last minute it was unclear whether the amendment would be included. Due to the collective efforts of the members of Le Groupe des Femmes, and their male allies, however, gender parity made it onto the floor of the General Assembly just in time.

The debate took place on January 8 and 9 and was particularly contentious. Lobna Jribi spoke in favor of the amendment, based on the idea that "a constitutional obligation on the State to ensure equal representation was vital for protecting women's rights and participation."[83] Monia Ibrahim, a Nahdhawia deputy, spoke against it by asserting that this amendment clashed with other articles that ensured equality between men and women.[84] The NCA broke for private discussions amongst the parliamentary blocs. Eventually, after a tense vote, the amendment passed with 127 votes in favor, 43 votes against, 24 abstentions, and 23 absences. The gallery and the yes-voters erupted into cheers, singing the Tunisian national anthem. Like the debate on \yatakaāmalu\, the main arguments for and against existed within the same democratic framework and articulated a similar vision for the state, albeit through different means.

The final wording of the amendment is significant, as it went farther than the 2011 electoral decree by extending the obligation for parity to all elected councils, including all locally elected bodies. This achievement, Mehrezia Labidi noted, was the most revolutionary aspect of the Constitution in terms of women's rights, as it is in rural areas and at the local level that women face the biggest obstacles to political power.[85]

Conclusion

The election of 2011 and the following two-year process of crafting a new Constitution of the Tunisian Republic, allowed for the emergence of a political plurality, and with it a new net of norms and discourses. A universalized language of democracy has come to define the discursive landscape of politics in Tunisia, and this shift has coincided with renewed processes of subjectification by Tunisian women, as

articulated by powerful female political personalities across ideological perspectives. As they moved from object to subject of the
State, Islamist and secular women enacted and defined the new female
political subject and made clear that a commonality exists in their
respective visions. Their work together undermines the notion that a
binary between Islamism and secularism defines the landscape of
gender politics.

The coordinated efforts of women members of the NCA, and the
resulting writing of gender in the language of the final Constitution,
resulted from the recognition that patriarchy had to be explicitly
challenged. In doing so, the women of the NCA implicitly addressed
the structures mediating women's access to citizenship throughout the
various axes of their identity and positionality. In many cases, the
understandings of the women who shaped the 2014 Constitution
developed in response to the kinds of obstacles that women in the
public bodies continued to face, despite having achieved positions of
political power. In fact, the actions of Tunisian women deputies who
worked together across political positions revealed the fluidity and
multiplicity of their subjectivities as gendered identity took precedence
over political identity in this case.

The process of defining citizenship and subjectivity goes beyond the
Constitution of Tunisia – a document enshrining the values and norms
that are intended to shape the new Tunisian state. The Constitution
articulates the foundational ideas of a new vision of Tunisia, but the
accompanying legal and political processes of implementation and
enforcement will determine how these ideas are realized and provide
opportunities to reify or subvert existing power structures. As individuals entering this new framework bring with them subjectivities
defined by multiple and interrelated historical, cultural, economic,
and social constellations of power, they will find inherent discretionary
space within which to shape Tunisia's future.

Endnotes

1 The Norwegian Nobel Committee (October 2015). "Press Release: The
  Nobel Peace Prize for 2015."
2 The terms "Islamist" and "secularist," which are often used in a binary,
  do not adequately capture the complexities and fluidity of Tunisian political affiliation and identity. They are used here as analytical terms and not
  as ontological categories. For the purposes of this paper, I use Islamist to

mean one either self-identifies as an Islamist or whose politics are grounded in Islam as a source.

3 Joseph, S. (2000). "Gendering citizenship in the Middle East." *Gender and Citizenship in the Middle East.* S. Joseph (ed.). London: Syracuse University Press, p. 9.

4 Foucault, M. (1984). *The History of Sexuality Vol. 1: An Introduction.* New York: Random House.

5 Ong, A. (1996). "Cultural citizenship as subject-making." *Current Anthropology.* Vol. 37, No. 5, p. 737.

6 Faubion, J. (ed.) (2001). *Power: The Essential Works of Foucault, 1954–1984, Vol. 3.* New York: The New Press, p. 326.

7 Ibid., p. 331.

8 Brand, L. (1998). *Women, the State, and Political Liberalization: Middle East and North African Experiences,* Columbia University Press, p. 178.

9 Charrad, M. (1998). "Cultural diversity within Islam: veils and laws in Tunisia." *Women in Muslim Societies: Cultural Diversity within Islam.* H. Bodman and N. Tohidi (eds.). Boulder: Lynne Reinner Publisher Inc., p. 70.

10 Hatem, M.F. (1992), "Economic and political liberation and the demise of State feminism." *International Journal of Middle East Studies.* Vol. 24, No. 2, p. 232.

11 Charrad, M. (2000). "Becoming a citizen: lineage versus individual in Tunisia and Morocco." *Gender and Citizenship in the Middle East.* S. Joseph (ed.). London: Syracuse University Press, p. 80.

12 Voorhoeve, M. (2014). *Gender and Divorce Law in North Africa: Sharia, Custom, and the Personal Status Code in Tunisia.* London: I.B. Tauris, p. 32.

13 Brand, *Women, the State, and Political Liberalization,* p. 181.

14 Ibid.

15 Charrad, "Becoming a citizen," p. 80.

16 Goulding, K. (2009). "Unjustifiable means to unjustifiable ends: delegitimizing parliamentary gender quotas in Tunisia." *Al-Raida.* Issue 126–127, p.76.

17 Kandiyoti, D. (1988). "Bargaining with patriarchy." *Gender and Society.* Vol. 2, No.3, pp. 274–290.

18 Perkins, K. (2004). *A History of Modern Tunisia.* Cambridge: Cambridge University Press, p. 190.

19 See Charrad, "Cultural diversity within Islam"; "Becoming a citizen" (1997). "Policy shifts: State, Islam, and gender in Tunisia, 1930s–1990s." *Social Politics.* Vol. 4; (2001). "State and gender in the Maghrib." *Women and power in the Middle East.* S. Joseph and S. Slymovics (eds.). Philadelphia: University of Pennsylvania Press; (2001a). *States and*

Women's Rights: The Making of Postcolonial Tunisia, Algeria, and Morocco. Berkeley: University of California Press; (2007). "Tunisia at the forefront of the Arab World: two waves of gender legislation." *Washington & Lee Law Review*. No. 64; Brand, *Women, the State, and Political Liberalization*; Kandiyoti, D. (2000). "Foreword." *Gender and Citizenship in the Middle East*. S. Joseph (ed.). Syracuse: Syracuse University Press; Grami, A. (2008). "Gender equality in Tunisia." *British Journal of Middle Eastern Studies*. Vol. 35, No. 3; Chekir, H. (1996). "Women, the law, and the family in Tunisia." *Gender and Development*. Vol. 4, No. 2; Marzouki, I. (1993). *Le movement des femmes en Tunisie au XXème siècle, feminism et politique*. Paris: Maisonneuve and Larose; Labidi, L. (2007). "The nature of transnational alliances in women's associations in the Maghreb: the case of AFTURD and ATFD." *Journal of Middle East Women's Studies*. Vol. 3, No. 1; Gilman, S. (2007). "Feminist organizing in Tunisia." *From Patriarchy to Empowerment: Women's Participation, Movements, and Rights in the Middle East, North Africa, and South Asia*. V. Moghadam (ed.). Syracuse: Syracuse University Press; Arfaoui, K. (2007). "The development of the feminist movement in Tunisia 1920–2000s." *International Journal of the Humanities*, p. 4.

20 Charrad, "Cultural diversity within Islam"; "Becoming a citizen"; "State and gender"; "Tunisia at the forefront."

21 Chekir, "Women, the law"; Grami, "Gender equality."

22 See: Brand, *Women, the State, and Political Liberalization*; Charrad, "Policy shifts."

23 Marzouki, *Le movement des femmes*; Labidi, "The nature of transnational alliances;" Gilman, "Feminist organizing in Tunisia;" Arfaoui, "The development of the feminist movement."

24 Gray, D.H. (2013). *Beyond Feminism and Islamism: Gender and Equality in North Africa*. London: I.B. Tauris; Voorhoeve, M. (2015). "Women's rights in Tunisia and the democratic renegotiation of an authoritarian legacy." *New Middle Eastern Studies*. Vol. 5; Gray, D.H. (2012). "Tunisia after the Uprising: Islamist and secular quests for women's rights." *Mediterranean Politics*. Vol. 17, No. 3.

25 Joseph, "Gendering citizenship," pp. 24–25.

26 Ibid., p. 22.

27 Ibid., pp. 10–11.

28 Asfour, L. (June 2011). "A revolution of equals." *Granta 115: The F Word.*

29 Bughaighis, W. (2014). "Prospects for women in the new Libya." *Arab Spring and Arab Women: Challenges and Opportunities*. M.S. Olimat (ed.). New York: Routledge, p. 120.

30 Al-Ghannouchi, R. and E. Abrams (November 2011). "Tunisia's challenge: a conversation with Rachid al-Ghannouchi." Council on Foreign Relations.
31 Hamid, S. (February 2015). "Tunisia field report: the Islamist balancing act." Brookings Center for Middle East Policy.
32 Voorhoeve, "Women's Rights in Tunisia," p. 3.
33 Decree Law No. 35 on Election of the National Constituent Assembly.
34 Pickard, D. "Challenges to legitimate governance in post-revolution Tunisia." *The Journal of North African Studies.* Vol. 26, No. 4, p. 641.
35 From the ISIE website. Available at www.isie.tn.
36 Tchaïcha, J.D. and K. Arfaoui (2017). *The Tunisian Women's Rights Movement: From Nascent Activism to Influential Power-broking.* Abingdon: Routledge, pp. 141–144.
37 Labidi, L. (2014). "Electoral practices of Tunisian women in the context of a democratic transition." The Wilson Center, p. 1.
38 First Formula of the Preface of the Draft Project of the Constitution of the Tunisian Republic (Arabic). April 24, 2012, p. 3.
39 Interview with Lobna Jribi. March 7, 2014.
40 Draft Constitution of the Republic of Tunisia (Arabic). August 14, 2012, p. 3.
41 The Constitution of Tunisia. June 1, 1959.
42 Draft Constitution of the Republic of Tunisia (Arabic). August 14, 2012, p. 4.
43 Ibid., p. 9.
44 Draft Constitution of the Republic of Tunisia. August 14, 2012. Nonofficial English translation prepared by International IDEA, p. 10.
45 Ibid.
46 Ibid., p. 15.
47 Draft Constitution of the Republic of Tunisia (International IDEA, English). August 14, 2012, p. 16.
48 Draft Constitution of the Republic of Tunisia (Arabic). August 14, 2012, p. 10.
49 (December 2014). "La femme tunisienne condamnée par Ennahda à devenir la complémentaire de l'homme." *Tunis Tribune.*
50 Mabrouk, S. (2012). "A bad day at the Committee on Rights and Liberties." Facebook.com.
51 Interview with Hasna Mersit. March 12, 2014.
52 As quoted by C. Bouazzaoui (October 2012). "In the constitution: Tunisian women torn between 'complementarity' and 'equality.'" *Our Catharsis: Blog de Chaïmae Bouazzaoui.*
53 McNeil, S.T. (August 2012). "Wording on women sparks protest in Tunisia." *Al Jazeera.*

54 Ibid.
55 Marks, M. (August 2012). "'Complementary' status for Tunisian women." *The Middle East Channel: Foreign Policy.*
56 Ibid.
57 (February 2014). "Rached Ghannouchi on Tunisia's Democratic Transition." Carnegie Endowment for International Peace Event Transcript, p. 14.
58 Interview with Amel Azzouz. January 24, 2014.
59 Interview with Farida Labidi. March 17, 2014.
60 Interview with Mehrezia Labidi. March 13, 2014.
61 Interview with Lobna Jribi. March 7, 2014.
62 Interview with Lobna Jribi. March 13, 2014.
63 Ibid.
64 Ibid.
65 See: Perez, D. "Becoming a Decision-maker in the Assembly of Postrevolutionary Tunisia." *Middle East Law and Governance.* Vol. 8, No. 2–3. de Silva de Alwis, R., A. Mnsari, and E. Ward. "Women and the Making of the Tunisian Constitution." *Berkeley Journal of International Law.* Vol. 35, No. 1.
66 Ibid.
67 The Constitution of the Tunisian Republic. January 26, 2014. Non-official English translation prepared by The Jasmine Foundation, pp. 10, 13–14.
68 Ibid., p. 10.
69 Ibid., p. 14.
70 Ibid., p. 6.
71 Ibid, p. 15.
72 Ibid.
73 Draft Constitution of the Republic of Tunisia (International IDEA, English). August 14, 2012, p. 10.
74 Clause Three will follow Clause Four due to the extended nature of the discussion and analysis of Clause Three.
75 (2010). "Enquête Nationale sur la violence à l'Egard des Femmes en Tunisie." *Office National de la Famille et de la Population de Tunisie.*
76 (December 2015). "Tunisia – Stop punishing survivors." *Amnesty International.*
77 (2017). "Tunisia: Landmark Step to Shield Women from Violence." *Human Rights Watch.*
78 Interview with Lobna Jribi. March 7, 2014.
79 Ibid.
80 Interview with Farida Labidi. March 17, 2014.

81 Interview with Lobna Jribi. March 7, 2014.
82 Interview with Hasna Mersit. March 12, 2014.
83 (January 2014). "Summary of day 7: historic parity rule adopted amid heated debate and celebration." *The Jasmine Foundation.*
84 Interview with Monia Ibrahim. March 15, 2014.
85 Interview Mehrezia Labidi. March 13, 2014.

Bibliography

Abou-Bakr, O. (Winter–Spring 2001). "Islamic feminism: what's in a name?" *Middle East Women's Studies Review*. Vol. 15, No. 4, pp. 1–2.

Abu-Lughod, L. (1989). *Veiled Sentiments: Honor and Poetry in a Bedouin Society*. Berkeley: University of California Press.

(February 2009). "Dialects of women's empowerment: the international circuitry of the Arab Human Development Report 2005." *International Journal of Middle East Studies*. Vol. 41, No. 1, pp. 93–103.

Adam, S. and H. Kriesi (2007). "The network approach." *Theories of the Policy Process*. 2nd edition. A. Sabatier (ed.). Boulder: Westview Press, pp. 129–154.

Afshar, H. (1996). *Women and Politics in the Third World*. New York: Taylor & Francis.

Ahmed, L. (1982). "Feminism and feminist movements in the Middle East, a preliminary exploration: Turkey, Egypt, Algeria, People's Democratic Republic of Yemen." *Women's Studies International Forum*. Special Issue: Women and Islam. Vol. 5, No. 2, pp. 153–168.

(1992). *Women and Gender in Islam: Historical Roots of a Modern Debate*. New Haven, CT: Yale University Press.

Aït Hamza, M. (2002). *Mobilité Socio-Spatiale et Développement Local au Sud de l'Atlas Marocain (Dadès-Todgha)*. Passau: LIS Verlag.

Ajmi, S. (November 2011). "Ennahdha discourse: the sixth Caliphate or a misunderstanding?" *Tunisia Live*. Available at www.tunisia-live.net/2011/11/16/ennahdha-flipflopping-the-sixth-caliphate-a-misunderstanding/.

Al-Ali, N. (2000). *Secularism, Gender and the State in the Middle East: The Egyptian Women's Movement*. Cambridge: Cambridge University Press.

Al-Ghannouchi, R. and Abrams, E. (November 2011). "Tunisia's challenge: a conversation with Rachid al-Ghannouchi." *Council on Foreign Relations*. Available at www.cfr.org/tunisia/tunisias-challenge-conversation-rachid-al- ghannouchi/p26660.

Ali, K. (2006). *Sexual Ethics and Islam: Feminist Reflections on Qur'an, Hadith and Jursiprudence*. London: Oneworld Publications.

Althusser, L. (1976). "Ideology and ideological state apparatuses." *Essays on Ideology*. London: Verso Books.

Amahan, A. (1998). *Mutations Sociales dans le Haut Atlas: Les Ghoujdama*. Paris: MSH/Rabat.

An-Na'im, A.A. (2008). *Islam and the Secular State: Negotiating the Future of Shari'a*. Cambridge: Harvard University Press.

Anderson, L. (1986). *The State and Social Transformation in Tunisia and Libya, 1830–1980*. Princeton: Princeton University Press.

(1991). "Political pacts, liberalism, and democracy: the Tunisian National Pact of 1988." *Government and Opposition*. Vol. 26, No. 2, pp. 245–260.

Arfaoui, K. (2007). "The development of the feminist movement in Tunisia 1920–2000s." *International Journal of the Humanities*. Vol. 4, pp. 53–59.

Atighetchi, D. (2007). *Islamic Bioethics: Problems and Perspectives*. International Library of Ethics, Law, and the New Medicine. Vol. 31, Dordrecht: Springer.

Badawi, J. (1995). *Gender Equality in Islam: Basic Principles*. Plainfield: American Trust Publications.

Badran, M. (2001). "Understanding Islam, Islamism, and Islamic feminism." *Journal of Women's History*. Vol. 13, No. 1, pp. 47–52.

(2007). *Feminism beyond East and West: New Gender Talk and Practice in Global Islam*. New Delhi: Global Media Publishers.

Bakhtiar, L. (1996). *Encyclopedia of Islamic Law: A Compendium of the Major Schools*. Chicago: ABC International Group, Inc.

Barlas, A. (March 2003). "The antimonies of 'feminism' and 'Islam': the limits of a Marxist analysis." *Middle Eastern Women's Study Review*. Vol. 18, No. 1–2.

Baylocq, S. (2005). *Review of Politics of Piety: The Islamic Revival and the Feminist Subject*, by Mahmood Saba. Princeton: Princeton University Press.

Beauclerk, C. (1828). *A Journey to Morocco in 1826*. London: Poole and Edwards.

Bekkaoui, K. and Larémont, R.R. (2011). "Moroccan youth go Sufi." *Journal of the Middle East and Africa*. Vol. 2, pp. 31–46.

Beldjena, R. (September 2004). "Code de la famille." *EL Watan*. Available at www.elwatan.com/archives/liste.php.

Bendahan, B. (1930). *Mazaltob*. Paris: Editions du Tambourin.

Berman, S. (1980). "Kol Isha." *Rabbi Joseph H. Lookstein Memorial Volume*. L. Landman (ed.). New Jersey: Ktav Publishing House, pp. 45–66.

Bernard, H.R. (2002). *Research Methods in Anthropology: Qualitative and Quantitative Approaches*. Lanham: Altamira.

Bidwell, R. (1973). *Morocco under Colonial Rule: French Administration of Tribal Areas 1912–1956*. London: F. Cass.

Binzel, C. and Carvalho, J.P. (2013). "Education, social mobility, and religious movements: a theory of the Islamic Revival in Egypt." Working Paper. *The Economic Journal*.

Boer, T.A. (2013). "Palliative sedation: an exploration from a Christian ethical point of view." *Looking Beneath the Surface: Medical Ethics from Islamic and Western Perspectives*. H.M. Vroom et al. (eds.). Amsterdam: Rodopi, pp. 227–341.

Borrmans, M. (1977). *Statut personnel et famille au Maghreb de 1940 à nos jours*. Paris: Mouton.

Bouazzaoui, C. (October 12, 2012). "In the constitution: Tunisian women torn between 'Complementarity' and 'Equality.'" *Our Catharsis: Blog de Chaïmae Bouazzaoui*. Available at https://ourcatharsis.wordpress.com/2012/10/29/in-the-constitution-tunisian-women-torn-between-complementarity-and-equality/.

Bourdieu, P. (1990). *Language and Symbolic Power*. Cambridge: Harvard University Press.

Bracke, S. (2003). "Author(iz)ing agency - feminist scholars making sense of women's involvement in religious 'fundamentalist' movements." *European Journal Of Womens Studies*. Vol. 10, No. 3, pp. 335–346.

Brand, L. (1998). *Women, the State, and Political Liberalization: Middle East and North African Experiences*. New York: Columbia University Press.

Branden, S. and Broeckaert, B. (2008). "Medication and God at interplay: end-of-life decision-making in practicing male Moroccan migrants living in Antwerp, Flanders, Belgium." *Muslim Medical Ethics: From Theory to Practice*. Columbia: University of South Carolina Press, pp. 194–211.

(2010). "Necessary interventions: Muslim views on pain and symptom control in English Sunni e-fatwas." *Ethical Perspectives*. Vol. 17, No. 4, pp. 626–651.

Bras, J.P. (2007). "La réforme du code de la famille au Maroc et en Algérie: quelles avancées pour la démocratie?" *Critique Internationale*, Vol. 4, No. 37, pp. 93–125.

Browne, I. and Misra, J. (2003). "The intersection of gender and race in the labor market." *Annual Review of Sociology*. Vol. 29, pp. 487–488.

Bruce, J. (1989). "Homes Divided." *World Development*. Vol. 17, No. 7, pp. 979–991.

Bughaighis, W. (2014). "Prospects for women in the new Libya." *Arab Spring and Arab Women: Challenges and Opportunities*. M.S. Olimat (ed.). Oxford: Routledge, pp. 106–120.

Buiting, H.M. et al. (December 2008). "A comparison of physicians' end-of-life decision making for non-Western migrants and Dutch natives in the Netherlands." *The European Journal of Public Health.* Vol. 18, No. 6, pp. 681–687.

Buskens, L. (2003). "Recent debates on family law reform in Morocco: Islamic Law as politics in an emerging public sphere." *Islamic Law and Society.* Vol. 10, pp. 70–131.

Cavatorta, F. (2006). "Civil society, Islamism and democratisation: the case of Morocco." *Journal of Modern African Studies.* Vol. 44, No. 2, pp. 203–222.

(2007). "Neither participation nor revolution - the strategy of the Moroccan Jamiat al-Adl wal-Ihsan." *Mediterranean Politics.* Vol. 12, No. 3, pp. 381–397.

Cavatorta, F. and Dalmasso, E. (2010). "Reforming the family code in Tunisia and Morocco - the struggle between religion, globalisation and democracy." *Totalitarian Movements and Political Religions.* Vol. 11, No. 2, pp. 213–228.

Carvalho, J.P. (2013). "Veiling." *The Quarterly Journal of Economics.* Vol. 128, No. 1, pp. 337–370.

Chaara, I. (2015). "Women as decision-makers within households: does religiosity matter? Evidence from Morocco." Working Paper.

Collyer, M. (September 2007). "In between places: trans-Saharan transit migrants in Morocco and the fragmented journey to Europe." *Antipode.* Vol. 39, No. 4, pp. 668–690.

Cherny, N.I., Radbruch, L. and The Board of the European Association for Palliative Care (October 2009). "European Association for Palliative Care (EAPC) recommended framework for the use of sedation in palliative care." *Palliative Medicine.* Vol. 23, No. 7, pp. 581–593.

Chetrit, J. (2003). *The Jewish Traditional Marriage: Interpretive and Documentary Chapters, Miqqedem uMiyyam VIII (Hebrew).* Haifa: University of Haifa.

(2013). "Textual orality and knowledge of illiterate women: the textual performance of Jewish women in Morocco." *Women and Knowledge in the Mediterranean.* Fatima Sadiqi (ed.). Oxon: Routledge, pp. 89–107

Cherney, B.R. (Fall 1985). "Kol Isha" *The Journal of Halacha and Contemporary Society.* Vol. 10, pp. 57–75.

Cohen, J.R. (1990). "Musical bridges: the contrafact tradition in Judeo-Spanish songs." *Cultural Marginality in the Western Mediterranean.* F. Gerson and A. Perceval (eds.). Toronto: New Aurora Editions, pp. 120–127.

(1993). "Women and Judeo-Spanish music." *Bridges.* Vol. 3, No. 2, pp. 113–119.

Charrad, M. (1997). "Policy shifts: state, Islam, and gender in Tunisia, 1930s–1990s." *Social Politics*. Vol. 4, pp. 284–319.

(1998). "Cultural diversity within Islam: veils and laws in Tunisia." *Women in Muslim Societies: Diversity within Unity*. H. Bodman and N. Tohidi (eds.). London: Lynne Rienner Publishers, pp. 63–79.

(2000). "Becoming a citizen: lineage versus individual in Tunisia and Morocco." *Gender and Citizenship in the Middle East*. S. Joseph (ed.). London: Syracuse University Press, pp. 70–87.

(2001). *States and Women's Rights: The Making of Postcolonial Tunisia, Algeria, and Morocco*. Berkeley: University of California Press.

(2001). "State and gender in the Maghrib." *Women and power in the Middle East*. S. Joseph and S. Slymovics (eds.). Philadelphia: University of Pennsylvania Press, pp. 61–71.

Chekir, H. (1996). "Women, the law, and the family in Tunisia." *Gender and Development*. Vol. 4, No. 2, pp. 43–46.

Chiapuris, J. (1979). *The Ait Ayash of the High Moulouya Plain: Rural social organization in Morocco*. Michigan: Ann Arbor.

Crenshaw, K. (1991). "Mapping the margins: intersectionality, identity politics, and violence against women of color." *Stanford Law Review*. Vol. 42, No. 6, pp. 1241–1300.

Dalmasso, E. (2008). "Family Code in Morocco. State feminism or democracy." Unpublished.

De Graaff, F.M. et al. (2010). "'Palliative Care': a contradiction in terms? A qualitative study of cancer patients with a Turkish or Moroccan background, their relatives and care providers." *BMC Palliative Care*. Vol. 9, No. 1, pp. 1–14.

De Haas, H. (March 2014). "Morocco: setting the stage for becoming a migration transition country?" *Migration Policy Institute*. Available at www.migrationpolicy.org/article/morocco-setting-stage-becoming-migration-transition-country

De Haas, H. and Vezzoli, S. (June 2013). "Migration and development on the South-North frontier: a comparison of the Mexico-US and Morocco-EU Cases." *Journal of Ethnic and Migration Studies*. Vol. 39, No. 7, pp. 1041–1065.

De Nesry, C. (1956). *Le Juif de Tanger et le Maroc*. Tanger: Editions Internationales.

Dessing, N.M. (2001). *Rituals of Birth, Circumcision, Marriage, and Death among Muslims in the Netherlands*. Leuven: Peeters.

Deshen, S. (1989). *The Mellah Society: Jewish Community Life in Sherifian Morocco*. Chicago: University of Chicago Press.

Díaz-Mas, P. (1992). *Sephardim: The Jews from Spain*. Chicago: University of Chicago Press.

Døving, C.A. (September 2014). "Position and self-understanding of Sunni Muslim Imams in Norway." *Journal of Muslims in Europe*. Vol. 3, No. 2, pp. 209–233.

Duflo, E. (2003). "Grandmothers and granddaughters: old-age pensions and intra-household allocation in South Africa." *The World Bank Economic Review*. Vol. 17, No. 1, pp. 1–25.

(2012). "Women empowerment and economic development." *Journal of Economic Literature*. Vol. 50, No. 4, pp. 1051–1079.

Elharras, M. and Serhane, F. (2006). *L'application du Code de la Famille: Acquis et Défis*. L'association marocaine de lutte contre la violence à l'égard des femmes, UNIFEM and PNUD.

Elmadmad, K. (July 1991). "An Arab convention on forced migration: desirability and possibilities." *International Journal of Refugee Law*. Oxford Journals Vol. 3, No. 3, pp. 461–481.

Engelcke, D. (2017). "Interpreting the 2004 Moroccan Family Law: Street-Level Bureaucrats, Women's Groups, and the Preservation of Multiple Normativities." Law & Social Inquiry.

Esack, F. (1999). *On Being a Muslim: Finding a Religious Path in the World Today*. Oxford: Oneworld Publications.

Esposito, J.L. (2003). *The Oxford Dictionary of Islam*. New York: Oxford University Press.

Fernea, E. (1998). *In Search of Islamic Feminism*. New York: Doubleday.

Foa, E., and Foa, U. (1980). "Resource theory: interpersonal behavior as exchange." *Social Exchange: Advances in Theory and Research*. K. Gergen, M. Greenberg, and R. Willis (eds.). New York: Plenum Press, pp. 74–97.

Forum (2012). *Moslims in Nederland 2012*. Utrecht: FORUM Instituut voor Multiculturele Vraagstukken.

Foucault, M. (1990). *The History of Sexuality Vol. 1: An Introduction*. New York: Pantheon.

Freedman, J. (2007). *Gendering the International Asylum and Refugee Debate*. New York: Palgrave Macmillan.

Garzón, J.I. (2008). *Los judíos hispano-marroquíes (1492–1973)*. Madrid: Hebraica Ediciones.

Gatrad, A. R. and Sheikh, A. (November 2002). "Palliative care for Muslims and issues before death." *International Journal of Palliative Nursing*. Vol. 8, No. 11, pp. 526–531.

Geertz, C. (1968). *Observer l'islam: changements religieux au Maroc et en Indonésie*. Paris: Editions la découverte.

Gennep, A. V. (1960). *The Rites of Passage*. Chicago: University of Chicago Press.

Gera, G. (2007). "Reflections on the aftermath of civil strife: Algeria 2006." *The Maghrib in the New Century*. B. Maddy-Weitzman and D. Zisenwine (eds.). Gainesville: University Press of Florida, pp. 75–103.

Gilman, S. (2007). "Feminist organizing in Tunisia." *From Patriarchy to Empowerment: Women's Participation, Movements, and Rights in the Middle East, North Africa, and South Asia*. V. Moghadam (ed.). Syracuse, pp. 97–119.

Gitsels-van der Wal, J.T. et al. (March 2015). "A qualitative study on how Muslim women of Moroccan descent approach antenatal anomaly screening." *Midwifery*. Vol. 31, No. 3, pp. 43–49.

Goeury, D. (2014). "La visite royale comme réponse au stress territorial: les conséquences des manifestations rurales dans le Haut Atlas central et oriental marocain." *L'Espace Politique*. Vol. 24, pp. 2–16.

Goulding, K. (2009). "Unjustifiable means to unjustifiable ends: delegitimizing parliamentary gender quotas in Tunisia." *Al-Raida*, pp. 71–78. Available at http://inhouse.lau.edu.lb/iwsaw/raida126-127/EN/p001-105.pdf.

Grami, A. (2008). "Gender equality in Tunisia." *British Journal of Middle Eastern Studies*. Vol. 35, No. 3, pp. 349–361.

Gray, D.H. (2014). "The many paths to gender equality in Morocco." *Oxford Islamic Studies Online*.

Gray, D.H. (2009). "Women in Algeria today and the debate over family law." *Middle East Review of International Affairs*. Vol. 13, pp. 45–56.

(2012). "Tunisia after the uprising: Islamist and secular quests for women's rights." *Mediterranean Politics*. Vol. 17, No. 3, pp. 285–302.

(2013). *Beyond Feminism and Islamism: Gender and Equality in North Africa*. London: I.B. Tauris.

Haenni, P. (2005). *L'Islam de marché: L'autre révolution conservatrice*. Paris: Seuil.

Hale, S. (1997). *Gender Politics in Sudan: Islamism, Socialism, and the State*. Boulder: Westview Press.

Hamdy, S. (August 2008). Review of *Politics of Piety: The Islamic Revival and the Feminist Subject*, by Saba Mahmood. *American Ethnologist*. Vol. 35, No. 3, pp. 3063–3067.

Hamed, E. (November 2013). "Egypt's 'Muslim Sisterhood' moves from social work to politics." *Al-Monitor*. Available at www.al-monitor.com/pulse/originals/2013/11/egypt-muslim-sisterhood-social-work-politics.html#.

Hamid, S. (February 2015). "Tunisia field report: the Islamist balancing act." *Brookings Center for Middle East Policy*. Available at www.brookings.edu/blogs/markaz/posts/2015/02/12-tunisia-islamists-ennahda-hamid.

Hamri, B. (2011). *La poésie amazighe de l'Atlas central marocain: approche plurielle*. Rabat: IRCAM.

Handa, S. (2002). "Raising primary school enrolment in developing countries: the relative importance of supply and demand." *Journal of Development Economics*. Vol. 69, pp. 103–128.

Harris, A.P. (1990). "Race and essentialism in feminist legal theory." *Stanford Law Review*. Vol. 42, No. 3, pp. 581–616.

Hart, D.M. (1981). "An Ayt 'Atta Customary law (*izerf*) document." *Dadda 'Atta and His Forty Grandsons*. Wisbech: MENAS Press, pp. 219–227.

Hart, R.D. (2016). *Sephardic Jews: History, Religion and People*. Santa Fe: Gaon Books.

Hashemi, S.M. and Schuler, S.R. (1993). "Defining and studying empowerment of women: a research note from Bangladesh." *JSI Working Paper* 3. Boston: JSI Research and Training Institute.

Hatem, M.F. (2006). "'In the eye of the storm: Islamic societies and Muslim women in globalized discourses.'" *Comparative Studies of South Asia, Africa and the Middle East*. Vol. 26, No. 1, pp. 22–35.

Hathaway, J. (1984). "The evolution of refugee status in international law: 1920–1950." *International and Comparative Law Quarterly*. London. Vol. 33, pp. 348–380.

Hausmann, R., Tyson, L.D. and Zahidi, S. (2009). *The Global Gender Gap report*. World Economic Forum.

(2012). *The Global Gender Gap report*. World Economic Forum.

Havelock, E.A. (1986). *The Muse Learns to Write: Reflections on Orality and Literacy from Antiquity to the Present*. New Haven: Yale University Press.

Hendriks, M.P. et al. (October 2012). "Palliative care for an Islamic patient: changing frameworks." *Journal of Palliative Medicine*. Vol. 15, No. 10, pp. 1053–1055.

Hidayatullah, A.A. (2014). *Feminist Edges of the Qur'an*. New York: Oxford University Press.

Hoffman, K. (2010). "Berber law by French means: customary courts in the Moroccan hinterland." *Comparative Studies in Society and History*. Vol. 52, No. 4, pp. 851–880.

Høigilt, J. (2011). *Islamist Rhetoric: Language and Culture in Contemporary Egypt*. Routledge.

Houdaifa, H. (August 2010). "Anefgou, les filles se marient encore à 7 ans … Nouvelle Moudawana?" *La Vie Economique*.

Huisman, J. and Smits, J. (2009). "Effects of household- and district-level factors on primary school enrolment in 30 developing countries." *World Development*. Vol. 37, No. 1, pp. 179–193.

Ibn, R. (1994). *The Distinguished Jurist's Primer*. Translated by I.A.K. Nyazee. South Street: Garnet Publishing.

Inglehart, R. and Norris, P. (2003). *Rising Tide: Gender Equality and Cultural Change around the World.* New York: Cambridge University Press.

International Foundation for Electoral Systems (January 2011). "Elections in Egypt: Analysis of the 2011 Parliamentary Electoral System." Available at www.ifes.org/publications/analysis-egypts-2011-parliamentary-elect oral-system.

Iqtidar, H. (2011). *Secularizing Islamists? Jama'at-E-Islami and Jama'at-Ud-Da'wa in Urban Pakistan.* University Press Scholarship Online. Chicago: University of Chicago Press.

Jacobs, A. and McKanders, K. (May 2012). "The Moroccan Arab spring: protecting migrant's rights in theory and practice." *Rights in Exile.*

Janssens, R. et al. (November 2012). "Palliative sedation: not just normal medical practice. Ethical reflections on the Royal Dutch Medical Association's Guideline on Palliative Sedation." *Journal of Medical Ethics.* Vol. 38, No. 11, pp. 664–668.

Jaziri, A. al- (2009). *Islamic Jurisprudence According to the Four Sunni Schools.* Volume 1. Modes of Islamic Worship. Translated by N. Roberts. Canada: Fons Vitae.

Johnson, K. (1995). "Public benefits and immigration: the intersection of immigration status, ethnicity, gender and class." *UCLA Law Review.* Vol. 42, No. 6, pp. 1509–1576.

Johnson, M. (2000). "The view from the *Wuro*: a guide to child rearing for fulani parents." *A World of Babies: Imagined Childcare Guides for Seven Societies.* J. DeLoache and A. Gottlieb (eds.). Cambridge: Cambridge University Press.

Jonker, G. (1996). "The knife's edge: Muslim burial in the diaspora. *Mortality.* Vol. 1, pp. 27–43.

Joseph, S. (1996). "Gender and citizenship in Middle Eastern states." *Middle East Report.* Vol. 198, pp. 4–10. Available at www.jstor.org/stable/3012867.

(2000). "Gendering citizenship in the Middle East." *Gender and Citizenship in the Middle East.* S. Joseph (ed.). Syracuse, pp. 3–30.

Kabeer, N. (1999). "The conditions and consequences of choice: reflections on the measurement of women's empowerment." *UNRISD Discussion Paper.* No. 108.

(1999). "Resources, agency, achievements: reflections on the measurement of women's empowerment." *Development and Change.* Vol. 30, pp. 435–464.

Kadrouch-Outmany, K. (2014). "Islamic burials in the Netherlands and Belgium: legal, religious and social aspects." Dissertation. Leiden: University of Leiden.

(2015). "Religion in the cemetery: Islamic burial plots in the Netherlands." *Contemporary Islam. Dynamics of Muslim Life*. Vol. 10, pp. 87–105.

Kandil, H. (2014). *Inside the Brotherhood*. 1st edition. Malden: Polity Press.

Kandiyoti, D. (1988). "Bargaining with patriarchy." *Gender and Society*. Vol. 2, No. 3, pp. 274–290.

(1991). *Women, Islam, and the State*. Philadelphia, PA: Temple University Press.

(1996). *Gendering the Middle East: Emerging Perspectives*. New York: I.B. Tauris.

(2000). "Foreword." *Gender and Citizenship in the Middle East*. S. Joseph (ed.). Syracuse: Syracuse University Press, pp. xiii–xvi.

Karagül, A. (2013). "Islamic care ethics: between law and conscience." *Looking Beneath the Surface: Medical Ethics from Islamic and Western Perspectives*. Amsterdam: Rodopi, pp. 243–263.

Karam, A.M. (1998). *Women, Islamism, and the State – Contemporary Femininisms in Egypt*. New York: Palgrave McMillan.

Keddie, N.R. (2012). *Women in the Middle East: Past and Present*. Princeton: Princeton University Press.

Kepel, G. (1985). *The Prophet and Pharaoh: Muslim Extremism in Egypt*. London: Al Saqi Books.

Korfker, D.G. et al. (January 2014). "Infertility care in the Netherlands for Turkish and Moroccan migrants: the role of religion in focus." University of Amsterdam, UvA-DARE, Digital Academic Depository. pp. 1–13.

Koskoff, E. (1995). "Myriam sings her song: the self and the other in anthropological discourse." *Musicology and Difference: Gender and Sexuality in Music Scholarship*. R. A. Solid (ed.). Berkeley: University of California Press, pp. 149–163.

Labidi, L. (2007). "The nature of transnational alliances in women's associations in the Maghreb: the case of AFTURD and ATFD." *Journal of Middle East Women's Studies*. Vol. 3, No. 1, pp. 6–34.

Lacroix, S. (June 2012). "Sheikhs and politicians: inside the new Egyptian Salafism." Brookings Doha Center Publications. Available at www .brookings.edu/research/papers/2012/06/07-egyptian-salafism-lacroix.

Lazreg, M. (1990). "Gender and politics in Algeria: unraveling the religious paradigm." *Signs*. Vol. 15, pp. 755–780.

(1994). *The Eloquence of Silence: Algerian Women in Question*. New York: Routledge.

Le Glay, M. (1930). *Les Sentiers de la Guerre et de l'Amour: récits marocains*. Paris: Berger-Levrault.

Lehrer E.L. (2004). "Religion as a determinant of economic and demographic behavior in the United States." *Population and Development Review*. Vol. 30, No. 4, pp. 707–726.

Levy, S. (2011). *Parlers arabes des Juifs du Maroc: Histoire, sociolinguistique et géographie dialectale.* Zaragoza: Instituto de Estudios Islámicos y del Oriente Próximo.

Librowicz, O.A. (1980). *Florilegio de romances sefardíes de la diáspora (Una colección malagueña).* Madrid: C.S.M.P.

Liverani, A. (2008). *Civil Society in Algeria: The Political Functions of Associational Life.* London: Routledge.

Lloyd, C. (2006). "From taboo to transnational political issue: violence against women in Algeria." *Women's Studies International Forum.* Vol. 29, pp. 453–462.

Maddy-Weitzman, B. and Zisenwine, D. (eds.) (2007). *The Maghrib in the New Century.* Gainesville: University Press of Florida.

Mahmood, S. (2004). *Politics of Piety: The Islamic Revival and the Feminist Subject.* Princeton, NJ: Princeton University Press.

Malhotra, A., Schuler, S.R. and Boender, C. (2002). "Measuring women's empowerment as a variable in international development." Background paper prepared for the World Bank workshop on Poverty and Gender: New Perspectives. Gender and Development Group, World Bank, Washington, DC.

Marks, M. (August 2012). "'Complementary' status for Tunisian women." *The Middle East Channel: Foreign Policy.* Available at http://mideastafrica.foreignpolicy.com/posts/2012/08/20/complementary_status_for_tunisian_women.

Marzouki, I. (2003). *Le movement des femmes en Tunisie au XXème siècle, feminism et politique* [The women's movement in Tunisia in the 20th century]. Tunis.

Materstvedt, L.J. and Bosshard, G. (June 2009). "Deep and continuous palliative sedation (terminal sedation): Clinical-ethical and philosophical aspects." *The Lancet Oncology.* Vol. 10, No. 6, pp. 622–627.

Mayer, A.E. (1995). "Reform of personal status laws in North Africa: a problem of Islamic or Mediterranean laws?" *Middle East Journal.* Vol. 49, pp. 432–446.

McCarthy, P. et al. (March 2004). "Managing children's cancer pain in Morocco." *Journal of Nursing Scholarship.* Vol. 36, No. 1, pp. 11–15.

McKanders, K. (2010). "The unspoken voices of indigenous women in immigration raids." *Journal of Gender, Race and Justice.* Vol. 14, No. 1, pp. 1–40.

McNeil, S. (August 2012). "Wording on women sparks protest in Tunisia." *Al Jazeera.* Available at www.aljazeera.com/indepth/features/2012/08/201281981854620325.html.

Mernissi, F. (2011). *Beyond the Veil: Male-Female Dynamics in Muslim Society.* London: Saqi Books.

Merriam, S.B. (2009). *Qualitative Research: A Guide to Design and Implementation*. San Francisco: Jossey-Bass.

Messaoudi, K. and Schemla, E. (1998). *Unbowed: An Algerian Woman Confronts Islamic Fundamentalism*. Philadelphia: University of Pennsylvania Press.

Mezgueldi, Z. (1997) "El papel de la Madre en la formación del imaginario." *La Mujer en la Otra Orilla*. A. Belarbi and F. Mernissi (eds.). Barcelona: Ediciones Flor del Viento.

Mir-Hosseini, Z. (2000). *Islam and Gender: The Religious Debate in Contemporary Iran*. London: I.B. Tauris.

  (2007). "How the door of Ijtihad was opened and closed: a comparative analysis of recent family law reform in Iran and Morocco." *Washington and Lee Law Review*. Vol. 64, pp. 1499–1511.

Moghadam, V.M. (2001). "Organizing women: the new women's movement in Algeria." *Cultural Dynamics*. Vol. 13, pp. 131–154.

  (Summer 2002). "Islamic feminism and its discontents: toward a resolution of the debate." *Signs*. Vol. 27, No. 4, pp. 1135–1171.

  (2003). *Modernizing Women: Gender and Social Change in the Middle East*. Boulder: Lynne Rienner.

Mohanty, C.T. (October 1988). "Under Western eyes: feminist scholarship and colonial discourses." *Feminist Review*. No. 30, pp. 61–88.

Mojab, S. (November 2001). "Theorizing the politics of Islamic feminism." *Feminist Review*. Vol. 69, No. 1, pp. 124–146.

Moll, Y. (2010). "Islamic televangelism: religion, media and visuality in contemporary Egypt." *Arab Media & Society*. Vol. 10, pp. 1–27.

Moors, A. (2003). "Introduction: public debates on family law reform participants, positions, and styles of argumentation in the 1990s." *Islamic Law and Society*. Vol. 10, pp. 1–11.

Mosk, C. (2013) *Nationalism and Economic Development in Modern Eurasia*. New York: Routledge.

Mouhib, M. (2014). *Le monde de Aïcha Bassou: une idylle berbère*. Edilivre.

Muhammed A.M. (1950). *The Religion of Islam: A Comprehensive Discussion of the Sources, Principles and Practices of Islam*. Lahore: The Ahmadiyyah Anjuman Ishaat Islam.

Myersson, E. (2014). "Islamic rule and the empowerment of the poor and pious." *Econometrica*. Vol. 82, No. 1, pp. 229–269.

Naciri, R. (1998). "The women's movement and political discourse in Morocco." Occasional Paper 8. United Nations Research Institute for Social Development.

Nejmi, M. and Hessissen, L. (2014). "Moroccan experience." *In Palliative Care to the Cancer Patient. The Middle East as a Model for Emerging Countries*. 1st edition. S. Silbermann (ed.), pp. 141–154. Cancer Etiology, Diagnosis and Treatments. New York: Nova Science Publishers.

Nielsen, J. et al. (2011). *Yearbook of Muslims in Europe*. Boston: Brill.

Ong, A. (1996). "Cultural citizenship as subject-making." *Current Anthropology*. Vol. 37, No. 5, pp. 737–762.

Padela, A.I. et al. (June 2011). "The role of Imams in American Muslim health: perspectives of Muslim community leaders in Southeast Michigan." *Journal of Religion and Health*. Vol. 50, No. 2, pp. 359–373.

Pearsall, J. (July 2003). "Misogyny." *The Concise Oxford English Dictionary*. Oxford: Oxford University Press.

Perkins, K. (2004). *A History of Modern Tunisia*. Cambridge: Cambridge University Press.

Peyron, M. (2007). "Women in water management and water-related issues in the Atlas Mountains in Morocco." *Women in Water Management*. El Kasmi, A. (ed.). Ifrane: AUI Press.

Philips, A. (2005). *Funeral Rites in Islam*. 2nd edition. Riyadh: International Islamic Publishing House.

Pickard, D. (2011). "Challenges to legitimate governance in post-revolution Tunisia." *The Journal of North African Studies*. Vol. 26, No. 4, pp. 637–652.

Picot, T. and Hamid, B. (January 2010). "Decision-making in the cancer pain setting: beyond the WHO ladder." *Techniques in Regional Anesthesia and Pain Management*. Update in Cancer Pain Management. Vol. 14, No. 1, pp. 19–24.

Platteau, J.P. (forthcoming). *Religion, Politics, and Development. Is Islam a Special Problem?*

Pruzan-Jorgensen, J.E. (2010). "The Islamist movement in Morocco: main actors and regime responses." Danish Institute for International Studies (DIIS) Report.

Pulido Fernández, A. (1905). *Españoles sin Patria y la Raza Sefardí*. Madrid: E. Teodoro.

Quandt, W.B. (1969). *Revolution and Political Leadership: Algeria: 1954–1968*. Cambridge: M.I.T. Press.

Quisumbing, A.R. (ed.) (2003). *Household Decisions, Gender and Development: A Synthesis of Recent Research*. Washington D.C.: Ifpri.

Ramírez, A. (2006). "Other feminisms? Muslim associations and women's participation in Morocco." *Etnográfica*. Vol. 10, No. 1, pp. 107–119.

Riera, J. (December 2006). "Migrants and refugees: why draw a distinction?" *United Nations Chronicle*, pp. 31–32.

Rietjens J.C. et al. (April 2006). "Terminal sedation and euthanasia: a comparison of clinical practices." *Archives of Internal Medicine*. Vol. 166, No. 7, pp. 749–753.

Rispler-Chaim, V. (2007). *Disability in Islamic Law*. International Library of Ethics, Law, and the New Medicine. Vol. 32. Springer Netherlands.

Royal Dutch Medical Association (RDMA) (2009). *Guideline for Palliative Sedation*. Utrecht: KNMG.

Sabiq, A.S. (1991). *Fiqh us-Sunnah. Funerals and Dhikr*. Translated by M.S. Dabas and Zarabozo, J.M. Indianapolis: American Trust Publications.

Sachedina, A. (August 2005). "End-of-life: the Islamic view." *The Lancet*. Vol. 366, No. 9487, pp. 774–779.

(2012). *Islamic Biomedical Ethics: Principles and Application*. New York: Oxford University Press.

Sadiqi, F. (2014). *Moroccan Feminist Discourses*. New York: Palgrave Macmillan.

Salime, Z. (2012). *Between Feminism and Islam: Human Rights and Sharia Law in Morocco*. Minneapolis, MN: University of Minnesota Press.

Sengers, E. and Sunier, T. (2010). *Religious Newcomers and the Nation State. Political Culture and Organized Religion in France and the Netherlands*. Delft: Eburon Academic Publishers.

Shaham, R. (1999). State, feminists, and Islamists: The debate over stipulations in marriage contracts in Egypt. *Bulletin of the School of Oriental and African Studies*. Vol. 62, No. 3, pp. 462–483.

Shadid, W.A. and van Koningsveld, P.S. (2002). *Intercultural Relations and Religious Authorities: Muslims in the European Union*. Dudley: Peeters Publishers.

(2002a). *Religious Freedom and the Neutrality of the State: The Position of Islam in the European Union*. Leuven: Peeters.

Shank, G.D. (2002). *Qualitative Research: A Personal Skills Approach*. Upper Saddle River, NJ: Merril Prentice Hall.

Shelemay, K.K. (1998). *Let Jasmine Rain Down: Song and Remembrance among Syrian Jews*. Chicago: University of Chicago Press.

Shirayanagi, K. (November 2011). "*Ennahda* spokeswoman Souad Abderrahim: single mothers are a disgrace to Tunisia." *Tunisia Live*.

Smail Salhi, Z. (2011). "Algerian women as agents of change and social cohesion." *Women in the Middle East and North Africa: Agents of Change*. F. Sadiqi and M. Ennaji (eds.). New York: Routledge, pp. 149–172.

Sonneveld, N. (2012). *Khulʿ Divorce in Egypt: Public Debates, Judicial Practices, and Everyday Life*. Cairo: The American University in Cairo Press.

Spivak, G.C. (1995). "*Can the Subaltern Speak?*" London: Routledge.

(2010). "Féminisme et déconstruction." *Tumultes*. No. 1.

Sprung, C.L. et al. (January 2008). "Relieving suffering or intentionally hastening death: where do you draw the line?" *Critical Care Medicine*. Vol. 36, No. 1, pp. 8–13.

Stroomer, H. and Peyron, M. (2003). *Catalogue des archives berbère du "Fonds Arsène Roux."* Köln: Rüdiger Köppe Verlag.

Surdon, G. (1935). *Institution et coutumes berbères du Maghreb.* Tanger: Editions Internationales, pp. 204–211.

Taifi, M. (1991). *Dictionnaire Tamazight-Français (Parlers du Maroc central).* Paris: L'Harmattan-Awal.

Taitz, E. (1986). "Kol Ishah – the voice of woman: where was it heard in medieval Europe?" *Conservative Judaism.* Vol. 38, No. 3, pp. 46–61.

Thomas, P.N. and Lee, P. (2012). *Global and Local Televangelism.* Palgrave Macmillan.

Toth, J. (November 2003). "Islamism in Southern Egypt: a case study of a radical religious movement." *International Journal of Middle East Studies.* Vol. 35, No. 4, pp. 547–72.

Tremlett, G. (January 2004). "Morocco boosts women's rights." *The Guardian.*

Turino, T. (2008). *Music as Social Life: The Politics of Participation.* Chicago: University of Chicago Press.

Turner, V. (2002). "Liminality and Communitas." *A Reader in the Anthropology of Religion.* M. Lambek (ed.). Oxford: Blackwell Publishing, pp. 358–374.

Van der Heide, A. et al. (May 2007). "End-of-life practices in the Netherlands under the Euthanasia Act." *New England Journal of Medicine.* Vol. 356, No. 19, pp. 1957–1965.

Venhorst, C. (2013). "Lived eschatology: Muslim views on life and death preliminary practices." *Changing European Death Ways.* E. Venbrux et al. (eds.). Münster, Germany: LIT Verlag Münster.

Verratti, I. (2014). "Une lecture de la poétique amazighe: des *timdyazin* à la chanson engagée dans le Sud-Est marocain." Unpublished.

Voorhoeve, M. (2014). *Gender and Divorce Law in North Africa: Sharia, Custom, and the Personal Status Code in Tunisia.* London: I.B. Tauris.

(2015). "Women's rights in Tunisia and the democratic renegotiation of an authoritarian legacy." *New Middle Eastern Studies.* Vol. 5, pp. 1–16.

Waltz, S. (1986). "Islamist appeal in Tunisia." *Middle East Journal.* Vol. 40, No. 4, pp. 651–670.

Watson, R.S. (1880). *A Visit to Wazan: The Sacred City of Morocco.* London: Macmillan.

Weich-Shahak, S. (1997). *Romancero Sefardí de Marruecos.* Madrid: Alpuerto.

Werenfels, I. (2007). *Managing Instability in Algeria: Elites and Political Change since 1995.* New York: Routledge.

Weygand, J. (1954). *Goumier de l'Atlas.* Paris: Flammarion.

Willis, M.J. (2012). *Politics and Power in the Maghreb: Algeria, Tunisia and Morocco from Independence to the Arab Spring.* New York: Columbia University Press.

Wright, M. and Clark, D. (2006). *Hospice and Palliative Care in Africa: A Review of Developments and Challenges.* Oxford: Oxford University Press.

Zafrani, H. (1998). *Deux mille ans de vie juive au Maroc: histoire et culture, religion et magie.* Paris: Maisonneuve & Larose.

Zerhouni, S. (2004). "Morocco: reconciling continuity and change." *Arab Elites: Negotiating the Politics of Change.* V. Perthes (ed.). Boulder: Lynne Rienner Publishers, pp. 61–87.

Zoubir, Y.H. and Ait-Hamadouce, L. (2007). 'The fate of political Islam in Algeria." *The Maghrib in the New Century.* B. Maddy-Weitzman and D. Zisenwine (eds.). Gainesville, FL: University Press of Florida, pp. 103–132.

Index

'Abduh, Muhammad, 334–5
Aalimate project, 156
agency, 3, 5, 7, 9–10, 14, 154, 160–1,
    169, 180, 183, 233
Agzdour, 277
Ahidus, 277, 280
al-'Adl, 145, 149–62, See Jama'a
    al 'Adl wa-l Ihsan; Justice and
    Spirituality Movement
al-Nour, 166–7, 170–2, 174–6, 181–2
Al Qaradawi, Yusuf, 219
al-Azhar, 334, 338, 342, 344–6
Alexandria, 4, 166–7, 170–2,
    174–7, 181
Algerian Civil War, 308–9, 311–12,
    314, 318, 325
Aqertit, Kenza, 45
Ashkenazi Jews, 267
Ashkenazim, 267–8
Atlas Mountains
    Jibal 'atlas, 15, 92, 100–2, 108,
    265–6, 289
Azzouz, Amel, 363

ballad (Berber)
    mawwāl, 299
bargaining power, 144, 148
Bejing Conference on Women 1995,
    120
Ben Ali, Zine al-Abidine, 16, 35, 91,
    356, 358–9
Boff, Leonardo, 121, 139
Bourguiba, Habib, 16, 330, 355–6, 359
Bouteflika, Abdelaziz, 318–21, 325
Brahmi, Mohamed, 370
burials, 216–17, 228

Câmara, Hélder, 139
Cantares de los antiguos
    gina' li l'qadim, 280

Casablanca, 57, 60, 146, 150,
    203, 233, 264, 269–70, 274–80,
    283
Centre d'écoute
    listening center
    hotline, 48, 50
Chabad Lubavitch, 267, 269,
    274–5
Code of Personal Status,
    see moudawana al 'usra,
    family law
    namus al 'usra, 45–6, 83–4, 108,
    355
Collective Land
    'ard al jam'iyy, 69–79, 86
colonialism, 313, 320
    isti'mār, 132
Commission on Rights and Liberties,
    361–3, 367
commodification of land, 70
complementarity, 153, 361–2, 368
Congrès pour la République
    Congress for the Republic
    CPR, 362
Consensus Committee, 365
Constitution of the Tunisian Republic
    (2014), 366, 371
counterrevolution, 331–2, 344
customary law, 82–3, 86,
    289–93, 296, 299–300,
    304

Da'wa Salafiyya. See Salafi call to
    religion
darija, 101, 276, See Moroccan
    Dialect
divorce, 331–47
divorced fathers, 332, 344
domestic violence shelters, 46–7, 51,
    55, 58–9, 64

Ech-Chenna, Aïcha, 57, 60
Edict of Expulsion, 267
educational decisions
    household decision-making, 144–5,
        148–9, 159–60, 162
Egyptian Feminist Union, 334–5, 338,
    340
Egyptian Revolution, 91, 167, 170,
    182, 343, 346–7
El Hajjami, Aïcha, 123
endechas, 278
enlightenment, 154, 157
Ennahda, 16, 25, 30, 119
Ettakatol, 362
European Council for Fatwa and
    Research (ECFR)
    majlis 'urubbiyy li fatwa wa baht,
        219, 246
euthanasia, 240, 245–6

family law, 8, 69, 289, 308–11,
    313–14, 316–17, 319–20, 322,
    324–6, 331–2, 338–40
family law reform, 309–14, 316–17,
    320, 323, 331–2, 340, 355
    'islah namus al 'usra, 108, 174,
        325
family law reform, Algeria, 15, 308–10,
    315–20, 324–5
family purity, 281
    taharat al 'usra, 281
fatwa, 137, 219, 244–6
    Islamic legal pronouncement, 79
Foucault, Michel, 354
funeral prayer, 217–18, 221–2, 224,
    226–9
funeral procession, 1, 215–16, 218,
    221–2, 228, 232

Gemara, 268
gender equality, 10, 13, 45, 55, 65,
    83–4, 87, 96, 99, 119, 122–4,
    129, 131–3, 135, 139, 153, 289,
    302, 332
gender justice, 122, 133, 153, 155
gender parity, xvi, 119, 359, 363,
    369–70
General Tunisian Labor Union, 362
Ghannouchi, Rached, 358–9,
    363–4

GIERFI
    International Research Group on
        Women in Islam, 126
Guardianship
    quiwamah, 127, 129, 151, 315, 319–
        20, 323–4, 339, 346, 355

Haketia, 268, 282
Halacha, 268–9, 271, 273–4
Hanafi school of law, 333
Hasidic, 267, 269, 274
Hasidim, 285
headscarf, 9, 25, 102, 129–30, 312
healthcare consultant
    ra'iyy sihiyy, 242, 248–51
hermeneutics, 125, 127, 132–3, 136
High Commission for the Realisation of
    Revolutionary Goals, Political
    Reforms, and Democratic
    Transition, 359, 369
High Constitutional Court (HCC), 338,
    344
hijab, 25, 101–2, 129–30, 179–80, 227
horizontal parity, 360
human rights
    huqquq al 'insan, 8, 10, 13, 21–2,
        26–8, 31–5, 39, 51, 69, 75, 120,
        135, 189, 194, 206, 313, 322,
        362–4

Ibrahim, Monia, 371
ijtihad, 119, 132
imam, 241, 243, 247–51, 253
implementation, xvi, 28, 30–1, 38, 69,
    79, 81, 83, 86, 192, 195, 204,
    206, 331–2, 340, 343–4, 346,
    353–4, 372
Independent Electoral Commission
    (ISIE), 370
independent reasoning, 119, 322, 326
inheritance, 70, 79–80, 82–3, 130–1,
    308, 322, See 'irt
Islamic law, 8, 11, 69–70, 79–80, 119,
    308, 311, 313, 315–17, 320,
    322–4, 332–3, 337, 344
Islamic legal pronouncement, 79
Islamic Organization for Medical
    Sciences
    munazzama 'islāmiyya li 'ūlum
        tibbiya, 245

Islamic Tendency Movement, 355
Islamism, 167, 169, 176, 312, 354–6, 363

Jamaa Al Adl wal Ihsane, 145, 151
Jewish law
    namus al yahudiyy, 11, 263–5, 268–9, 271–5, 279
Jewish Women's Voices
    aswat nisa' yahudiyy, 270, 280–1
Jribi, Lobna, 360, 365, 369–70
Judeo-Arabic
    yahudiyy- 'arabiyy, 263, 266, 268, 275, 279, 281–3
Judeo-Berber
    yahudiyy-'amazigiyy, 263, 266, 268, 276, 282–3
Judeo-Spanish
    yahudiyy-'isbaniyy, 263, 266, 268, 278–9, 283
Justice and Charity Movement. *See* Al Adl, Jamaa Al Adl wal Ihsane

khalifah, 135
KHOYA
    les archives sonores du Maroc juif, 264
khul', 331–2, 335, 337–8, 340–7
King Mohammed VI, 126, 194–5
kinship community, 357
Kol be'Isha erva, 268–9
kol isha, 270, 272

Labidi, Farida, 363, 369–70
Labidi, Mehrezia, 364–5
Lamrabet, Asma, 122–3, 125–32, 135–9
land rights
    huqquq al ard, 69, 71–2, 74, 76, 81, 86–7
Larayedh, Ali, 363
Le Groupe des Femmes, Tunisia, 365, 369–71
liberation theology, 121, 125, 138
liminal period, 221
listening center, 48, 50
liturgical poems, 276, 279

Ma'ruf, 128
Mabrouk, Selma, 362

maqasid, 123, 128
marriage age
    'amr a zawaj, 321, 323
megorashim
    yahud min chib jazirati 'ibiriyy, 266
mellah
    hara yahudiyy
        Jewish district in Morocco, 266
Mernissi, Fatema, 1, 16, 120, 123–6, 128, 135, 139
Mersit, Hasna, 362, 370
migration, xvi–xvii, 1–2, 10–11, 13, 187, 190–5, 197, 203, 205–6, 216, 218, 228, 232–3, 237, 253, 266, 278
Ministry of Solidarity, Women, Family and Social Development, 55
Mishna
    abbaniyy 'asl li namus yahudiyy, 268
Mizrahi Jews, 267, 280
Moroccan Constitution 2011, 28, 80
Moroccan dialect, 276
Moroccan Family Code, 304, 321, 323, 339
Moroccan independence, 263, 265, 275, 278
Moroccan penal code, 54, 293
Moroccan Society of Management of Pain and Palliative Care (MSMPP), 251–2
Morocco's National Plan for Cancer Prevention and Control, 252
Morphine, 239, 241, 247, 252–3
Moudawana al 'usra, 46, 83–4, 108, 289, 299, 301, 304
Moudjahidat, 311
Mubarak, Hosni, 91, 171, 332, 338, 344, 347
Mursi, Muhammad, 173–4, 332, 345
Musawah, 127, 130–1
Muslim Brotherhood, 166–7, 169–70, 172, 178, 182, 343

National Constituent Assembly (NCA), 353, 359
National Institution of Solidarity with Women in Distress (INSAF), 53
National Union of Tunisian Women, 355

Optionalité, 312–13, 315, 325
oral traditions, 263, 270, 278, 282–3

pain and suffering, 239, 243–4, 246,
    248
palliative sedation, 237–40, 242–6,
    249–50, 253
Personal Status Code
    qanun wad' saksiyy, 8, 15, 29, 45,
        131, 135, 321
Personal Status Law, 308, 311–12, 315,
    323, 333–5, 344, 346
piety, 130, 168–9, 183, 266
PJD (Party of Justice and Development)
    hizb al 'adl wa numuww, 24, 30,
        145, 151, 154–5
Polyani, Karl, 53
prayer, 127, 136, 147, 175–6, 226–7,
    229, 231, 241, 243, 269, 271,
    276, 280–1
privatization of land, 70

Quasim, Amin, 333, 335–6, 339
qiwamah, 128–9

Rabita Mohammadia des Oulémas du
    Maroc, 123, 126
religious denomination, 217,
    220, 229
religious movements, 145, 147,
    149–50, 154, 159–61, 165,
    380
repudiation, 290, 333–4, 340–1, 344,
    355
rites of passage, 218
ritual shrouding, 217–18, 221–6,
    228–9
ritual washing, 217–18, 221–6, 228–9

Salafi
    salafism, 3–4, 13, 35, 166, 168, 170,
        172–4, 176–83
Salafi call to religion, 166
Sandberg, Eve, 45
secularism, 354–6
Sephardic Jews, 272
Shabbat, 279, 283
Sharabi, Hisham, 46

sharia
    namus al 'islamiyy, 322
Shulhan Aruch, 269
Sisters for Eternity, 153, 157–9, 161
socioprofessional training, 50–1, 58
spiritual counselor, 248–51
state feminism, 355–7

talaq, 334
Talmud, 263, 268–9, 271
taqwa, 138
tawhid, 133–4, 136, 151
Temple Beth El, 269–70
Temple in Jerusalem, 265, 268
The Group of Seven, 337–40
toshavim, 266
Tsaddikim, 279
Tunisian Association of Democratic
    Women (ATFD), 356–8, 362
Tunisian League of Human Rights, 358
Tunisian National Dialogue Quartet,
    353
Tunisian Personal Status Code
    tūnisiyy qānūn waḍ' šakṣiyy, 29
Tunisian Women's Association for
    Development Research
    (AFTURD), 356–8

UGTT, 362
UNFT, 355
Unilateral divorce, 331–2, 338–9, 345
Union de l'Action Féminine (UAF), 45
'urf, 72, 87, 290–1, 300, 304, 338
Uridu Hallan (I Want a Solution), 336,
    339

vertical parity, 359, 370

Wadud, Amina, 120, 123, 127–8, 130,
    132–9
wilayah, 127, 129
women section (of Al Adl), 145,
    149–53, 155–62
women's movement in Algeria, 310,
    324
Woolcock, Michael, 53

Yassine, Fouzia, 54